THE PERSISTENCE OF EMPIRE

THIS BOOK WAS THE WINNER OF THE
JAMESTOWN PRIZE FOR 1993.

The Persistence of EMPIRE

BRITISH POLITICAL CULTURE IN THE AGE
OF THE AMERICAN REVOLUTION

Eliga H. Gould

Published for the Omohundro Institute of

Early American History and Culture, Williamsburg, Virginia,

by the University of North Carolina Press,

Chapel Hill and London

The Omohundro Institute of Early American History and Culture is
sponsored jointly by the College of William and Mary and the Colonial
Williamsburg Foundation. On November 15, 1996, the Institute adopted the
present name in honor of a bequest from Malvern H. Omohundro, Jr.

© 2000 The University of North Carolina Press
All rights reserved
Designed by April Leidig-Higgins
Set in Caslon type by Keystone Typesetting, Inc.
Manufactured in the United States of America

Library of Congress Cataloging-in-Publication Data
Gould, Eliga H.
The persistence of empire : British political culture in the age
of the American Revolution / Eliga H. Gould.
p.   cm.
Includes bibliographical references and index.
ISBN 0-8078-2529-8 (cloth : alk. paper)
1. Great Britain—Politics and government—1760–1789.   2. United
States—History—Revolution, 1775–1783.   3. Great Britain—Colonies—
History—18th century.   I. Omohundro Institute of Early American
History & Culture.   II. Title.
DA510.G68   2000
941.07′3—dc21   99-34607
CIP

The paper in this book meets the guidelines for permanence and
durability of the Committee on Production Guidelines for Book Longevity
of the Council on Library Resources.

04 03 02 01 00   5 4 3 2 1

For my parents, and for Nicky,
with all my love

PREFACE

To the generation that came of age during the Vietnam War, the United States' disastrous intervention in Southeast Asia offered a model for understanding Britain's otherwise inexplicable response to the American Revolution. According to this interpretation, an arrogant government, emboldened by past triumphs and convinced of its own moral superiority, embraced reckless policies that enjoyed little domestic support. It was, of course, a timely argument, but it was also one with deep roots in the scholarship of the twentieth century. During the interwar period, historians mindful of the "special relationship" between Britain and the United States often depicted Parliament's attempts at colonial taxation as a series of unintended blunders, none of which reflected the wishes of ordinary Britons. Such ideas gained added force at the end of the Second World War, as the Labour Party's electoral victory and the coming of decolonization encouraged scholars to emphasize popular hostility and indifference to Britain's overseas empire. In each instance, the result was an interpretation of the American Revolution based on a perceived dichotomy between an aristocratic, unrepresentative, and self-absorbed government, and a wider public for whom Parliament's actions were blatantly unjust.

In recent years, however, historians have been reminded of what we probably should have recognized from the start, namely that no government could project the kind of sustained external power that Britain did during the American Revolution without a measure of popular acquiescence at home. Inspired in part by the jingoism of the Falkland's War, scholars working in the history of eighteenth-century Britain have begun rethinking a number of cherished assumptions. This book is one product of that reassessment. Without discounting those men and women who identified with the colonists' plight, I am primarily concerned with the arguments that made the actions of George III and his ministers seem acceptable to the metropolitan public. This rationale was not chiefly that of an ancien régime or a hidebound, aristocratic establishment—though it certainly had elements of both—but of a political culture where the government had to maintain at least the appearance of popular approval. Despite the colonists' radically different view of the matter, this book is thus the story of a people whose own sense of modernity and what it meant to be free played a central, albeit ironic, role in the making of the American Republic.

Without the generous assistance of numerous friends and colleagues, I could not have written this book. Foremost among these are J. G. A. Pocock and Jack P. Greene. As readers will discover, I am indebted to John Pocock for my understanding of British political thought and the way ideas shape the contexts within which people think and act. To Jack Greene, I owe my appreciation of the complexities of Britain's constitutional development, both at home and in America. I am also grateful to Nicholas Phillipson, with whom I spent a delightful year studying the Scottish Enlightenment at the University of Edinburgh. Finally, I must thank John R. Gillis and Lawrence Stone, neither of whom allowed his awareness of the vagaries of the academic job market to inhibit the enthusiasm of an undergraduate who aspired to write and teach history. Insofar as I have succeeded, it is in no small measure because of the generous example and continuing friendship of such gifted teachers.

On a more tangible level, I wish to thank the many people and institutions that provided me with the necessary financial and scholarly support to complete this project. The editorial staff at the Omohundro Institute of Early American History and Culture is famous for the scrupulous care with which they shepherd manuscripts to completion; I greatly appreciate the efforts of Fredrika J. Teute, James Horn, Gil Kelly, and, especially, Kathryn Burdette, whose meticulous copyediting has been wondrous to behold. While researching the book, I benefited from the expertise of numerous librarians, in particular those at the Huntington Library in San Marino, California, and the British Library (then at Great Russell Street), who cheerfully fulfilled what must have seemed like an unreasonably large number of requests for pamphlets and manuscripts. The Johns Hopkins University and the University of New Hampshire both provided me with crucial financial support; I am likewise thankful for the generous assistance I received from the Fulbright-Hays Foundation, the National Endowment for the Humanities, the William Andrews Clark Library at UCLA, the Charles Warren Center at Harvard University, and the Huntington Library, in the last instance with special thanks to Martin Ridge.

Over the last decade, I have accumulated an even larger number of debts to colleagues on both sides of the Atlantic. Among the people who generously gave of their time by discussing problems and posing questions are Fred Anderson, Bernard Bailyn, Daniel Baugh, John Brewer, J. H. Burns, Jonathan Clark, Linda Colley, Joanna Innes, Mark Kishlansky, Thomas Laqueur, Paul Langford, P. J. Marshall, John Morrill, John Robertson, Nicholas Rogers, and Laurel Ulrich. Daniel Baugh also read the entire manuscript, and Bernard Bailyn, John Robertson, and P. J. Marshall each read parts. The initial inspiration for this book came from the seminars that John Pocock organized in the history of British political thought at the Folger Library in Washington. I have since been fortunate to participate in similar ventures at the Institute of Historical Research in London, the Massachusetts Historical Society, and Harvard University, both as a member of the International Seminar in Atlantic History and as a fellow at the Charles Warren Center. Bernard Bailyn, Susan Hunt, and the other Warren Center fellows, Steven Beherndt, Rosalind Beiler, David Hancock, Willem Klooster, and Mark Peterson, were especially encouraging during the book's final revisions. In addition, I have benefited immeasurably from sharing work and discussing ideas with David Armitage, Christopher Brown, Philip Harling, Lawrence Klein, Paul Landau, Patricia Lin, Elizabeth Mancke, Ian McBride, Paul Monod, Andrew O'Shaughnessy, Jeffrey Ravel, Stuart Semmel, Dror Wahrman, Joseph Ward, and Kathleen Wilson. I also thank Margot Finn, Fred Leventhal, Maura O'Connor, and Christopher Waters for their constant encouragement and support. Closer to home, both the Dean of Liberal Arts, Marilyn Hoskin, and my colleagues in the History Department at the University of New Hampshire have been invariably supportive. I am especially grateful to Jeffry Diefendorf and William Harris, for their assistance as department chairs; to Jeffrey Bolster, Charles Clark, Ellen Fitzpatrick, Jan Golinski, Lucy Salyer, and Cynthia Van Zandt, for their timely thoughts and suggestions; to David Frankfurter, for dragging me off to climb Mount Washington; and, again, to Charles Clark, for serving (gratis) as my personal grammar consultant.

My final thanks go to those people for whom it is most difficult to make an adequate acknowledgment. I have known Jebtha Palmer for more than half my life; road trips, Scrabble, and a camaraderie born of misspelled first names cannot begin to describe what our friendship has meant to me. Over the last fifteen years, Kurt Nagel, with whom I roomed in Baltimore and London, has likewise been a wonderful friend and intellectual companion. I would also like to thank Dave Brown and Mary Brunton, who continue to make London feel like a second home, and my English in-laws, Florence Tallerman and John and Ruth Keeble, whose gracious hospitality has always made me feel the same way in Suffolk. Sabrina Klein has been a dear friend throughout, as have Thomas Goebel and Ronald Yanosky.

My deepest thanks of all are for my family. My wife's parents, Hilary and Carmelo Gullace, have supported me in ways that most people would reserve for their own children. My brother, Warren Gould, who was both flatmate and roommate during the first of my two years in London, has participated in the ups and downs of this book as if it were his own. I owe more than I can possibly express to my parents, Glen Hibbard and Mildred Nisbet Gould, two gifted teachers in their own right who nurtured in every conceivable way my interest in history. I credit my mother with imparting her love of writing and a sense of ancestral time reaching back to the Reformation, and it was my father, through his own field of music theory and history, who first introduced me to the joys of historical analysis. Last of all, in a category by themselves, are two people. Charlie Gould arrived just in time to save me from superficial analogies between parenthood and completing a book. Becoming a father is one of the two best things I have ever done. The other was marrying Nicoletta Gullace, my closest colleague, dearest friend, and partner for life.

CONTENTS

MAPS AND ILLUSTRATIONS

INTRODUCTION

William Cobbett never forgot the fascination that the American Revolution held for his native village of Farnham in Surrey. Though only a boy when the fighting began, the future champion of England's poor remembered the war as a captivating drama, seizing the attention of his family and their neighbors as few external events ever had. As Cobbett recalled, this was partly out of sympathy for the Americans, especially among people like his father, a humble farmer for whom the principle of no taxation without representation embodied truths essential for freedom everywhere. But Cobbett was equally clear that such sentiments were far from universal. For many of Farnham's inhabitants, the cause of liberty and justice lay not on the side of the Americans but on that of the British king and Parliament, and it was the ministry of Lord North that deserved the support of men and women on both sides of the Atlantic. "It is well known," wrote Cobbett, "that the people were, as to numbers, nearly equally divided in their opinions, concerning that war." Indeed, as he reflected on the passionate debates that the Revolution stirred in the England of his youth, Cobbett had to concede that the better arguments belonged to the government's supporters—including his father's principal antagonist, "a shrewd and sensible old Scotchman" who gardened for a local nobleman and who, whenever the discussion turned to the war in America, proved to be his father's "superior in political knowledge."[1]

For anyone with even a passing knowledge of Georgian politics, Cobbett's observation about the degree of support for the government is hardly surprising. Although Britain's eighteenth-century rulers were notorious for regarding the common people with disdain, it was also well known that neither the king's ministers nor Parliament could afford to ignore their wishes indefinitely, especially when they were engaged in an

---

1. [William Cobbett], *The Life and Adventures of Peter Porcupine* (1927; Philadelphia, 1796), 22. There is, of course, no such thing as a completely impartial observation. During his time in Philadelphia, when Cobbett wrote the passage quoted here, he was a staunch anti-Jacobin and opponent of Thomas Jefferson's Democratic Republicans. Despite Cobbett's polemical purpose in making such claims, even avowed friends of America admitted that support in Britain for the Revolutionary cause was not nearly as broad as they might have wished.

undertaking as massive and expensive as the War of American Independence. To a surprising degree, though, the question of why so many people accepted the government's ill-fated policies is one that few historians have treated as a subject worthy of study in its own right.[2] There are books on British military and diplomatic strategy, books on the formation of colonial policy at Whitehall and in Parliament, and books—enough to fill a small library—on the people who, like Cobbett's father, found themselves in broad sympathy with their "fellow subjects" on the far shores of the Atlantic. Despite this interest in the British dimensions of the American Revolution, we have much to learn about the public support that helped make the Revolutionary war the longest colonial conflict in modern British history. On what ought to be one of the period's central questions, it is as though there were still some truth in the words of Sir John Seeley, the great nineteenth-century historian of the British Empire, who jested that, insofar as the British gave the Revolution any thought at all, it was to discount it as an embarrassing episode, "which we have tacitly agreed to mention as seldom as we can."[3]

2. On British colonial, military, and diplomatic policy, see Lawrence Henry Gipson, *The British Empire before the American Revolution*, 15 vols. (New York, 1939–1970); Jack M. Sosin, *Whitehall and the Wilderness: The Middle West in British Colonial Policy, 1760–1775* (Lincoln, Nebr., 1961); Piers Mackesy, *The War for America, 1775–1783* (London, 1964); John Shy, *Toward Lexington: The Role of the British Army in the Coming of the American Revolution* (Princeton, 1965); John L. Bullion, *A Great and Necessary Measure: George Grenville and the Genesis of the Stamp Act, 1763–1765* (Columbia, Mo., 1982); Jonathan R. Dull, *A Diplomatic History of the American Revolution* (New Haven, Conn., 1985); H. M. Scott, *British Foreign Policy in the Age of the American Revolution* (Oxford, 1990). The literature on the Americans' British sympathizers is even larger, but see Ian R. Christie, *Wilkes, Wyvill, and Reform: The Parliamentary Reform Movement in British Politics, 1760–1785* (London, 1962), chap. 3; Colin Bonwick, *English Radicals and the American Revolution* (Chapel Hill, N.C., 1977); John Sainsbury, *Disaffected Patriots: London Supporters of Revolutionary America, 1769–1782* (Montreal, 1987); James E. Bradley, *Religion, Revolution, and English Radicalism: Nonconformity in Eighteenth-Century Politics and Society* (Cambridge, 1990); Peter N. Miller, *Defining the Common Good: Empire, Religion, and Philosophy in Eighteenth-Century Britain* (Cambridge, 1994), esp. chap. 4; Kathleen Wilson, *The Sense of the People: Politics, Culture, and Imperialism in England, 1715–1785* (Cambridge, 1995), esp. 237–283.

3. J. R. Seeley, *The Expansion of England: Two Courses of Lectures* (1883; Boston, 1900), 26. On the need for further investigation of British loyalism among the general public during the Revolution, see Linda Colley, "The Politics of Eighteenth-Century British History," *Journal of British Studies*, XXV (1986), 375–376; T. H. Breen, "Ideology and Nationalism on the Eve of the American Revolution: Revisions *Once More* in Need of Revising," *Journal of American History*, LXXXIV, no. 1 (1997), 13–39. Colley's path-breaking work has been indispensable in opening up British patriotism as a

With this tendency in mind, I have set out to examine the public rationale that, despite its eventual repudiation, made the North American policies of George III and his ministers appear both necessary and justifiable. As we shall see, this rationale was chiefly the result of a burgeoning desire for imperial self-sufficiency. The pursuit of empire held a tremendous appeal for the metropolitan public throughout the eighteenth century. Although this interest waxed and waned according to the vagaries of popular opinion, almost every foreign initiative between the Glorious Revolution of 1689 and the battle of Waterloo had something to do with protecting the nation's imperial standing, usually from the competing interests of Catholic France.[4] If empire represented a persistent theme in Georgian politics, however, the isolationism implicit in the British understanding of the term became increasingly pronounced in the decades just before the American Revolution. Although the colonists obviously saw things differently, the proponents of both the Stamp Act (1765) and the Townshend Revenue Act (1767) claimed that strengthening the government's administrative powers in North America would reverse decades of neglect by ministers who cared more for maintaining the balance of power in Europe than they did the welfare of Britain's prodigious maritime empire. At the same time, people assumed that, because the Americans formed integral parts of a greater British nation, they could be taxed in the same manner as the inhabitants of

---

subject for scholarly inquiry; see Colley, *Britons: Forging the Nation, 1707–1837* (New Haven, Conn., 1992). In response to the trends noted here, historians have begun to broaden their perspective to include the wider public; see James E. Bradley, *Popular Politics and the American Revolution in England: Petitions, the Crown, and Public Opinion* (Macon, Ga., 1986); J. C. D. Clark, *The Language of Liberty, 1660–1832: Political Discourse and Social Dynamics in the Anglo-American World* (Cambridge, 1994); Stephen Conway, *The War of American Independence, 1775–1783* (London, 1995), esp. chaps. 1, 2, 8. There is, of course, a substantial literature on the strength of the government's support within Parliament, much of it following arguments first advanced by Sir Lewis Namier in *England in the Age of the American Revolution,* 2d ed. (New York, 1961).

4. Colley, *Britons;* Wilson, *The Sense of the People;* John Brewer, *The Sinews of Power: War, Money and the English State, 1688–1783* (New York, 1989); C. A. Bayly, *Imperial Meridian: The First British Empire and the World, 1780–1830* (New York, 1989); Paul Langford, *A Polite and Commercial People: England, 1727–1783* (Oxford, 1989), esp. 621–636; Daniel Baugh, "Maritime Strength and Atlantic Commerce: The Uses of 'a Grand Marine Empire,'" in Lawrence Stone, ed., *An Imperial State at War: Britain from 1689 to 1815* (New York, 1994), 185–223; P. J. Marshall, "A Nation Defined by Empire, 1755–1776," in Alexander Grant and Keith J. Stringer, eds., *Uniting the Kingdom? The Making of British History* (London, 1995), 208–222; David Armitage, *The Ideological Origins of the British Empire* (Cambridge, forthcoming).

England, Scotland, and Wales. Indeed, most Britons accepted the project of colonial taxation in the mistaken belief that the government possessed the military and political resources necessary to defend Parliament's imperial sovereignty without placing undue burdens on ordinary men and women at home.[5]

Because these assumptions proved so wrong-headed, the British quickly forgot how widespread they had once been. But to understand what the American Revolution meant to people on both sides of the Atlantic, we must grasp a paradox. On one hand, we need to bear in mind the enlarged, often unrealistic, expectations that characterized British opinion about the empire beyond their shores; on the other, we have to account for a system of political obligation that turned patriotism itself into a kind of collective act of theater, replete with symbolic meaning but with few deeper consequences, at least for its most vocal partisans. The result was explosive: the remote and limited nature of Britain's wars left the shapers of metropolitan opinion free to respond in the most bellicose manner to any external threat or provocation, no matter how exaggerated the danger or how great the costs, without suffering unduly from the error of their ways. As one of the Americans' British sympathizers admitted in 1783, there was a time when the government's determination to force the colonists to pay parliamentary taxes was "popular." Without understanding why, we cannot hope to comprehend either Britain's own response to the problems of empire or the reasons that eventually per-

5. To American historians, Parliament's attempt to tax the colonists has often been taken as a sign that the British government was treating them "differently from ordinary men and women who happened to live in England" (Breen, "Ideology and Nationalism on the Eve of the American Revolution," *Journal of American History,* LXXXIV, 33). However, the metropolitan proponents of Parliamentary taxation understood the issue in exactly the opposite way, that is, as a vehicle for incorporating people who enjoyed the full rights of British subjects into the national system of revenue as it existed in Britain. In a sense, the American Revolution had its origins in a failed attempt to complete the integration of a Greater British nation. See Eliga H. Gould, "A Virtual Nation: Greater Britain and the Imperial Legacy of the American Revolution," *American Historical Review,* CIV, no. 2 (April, 1999). For the collision between metropolitan and colonial conceptions of British rights and obligations, see Bernard Bailyn, *The Ideological Origins of the American Revolution* (Cambridge, Mass., 1967); Jack P. Greene, *Peripheries and Center: Constitutional Development in the Extended Polities of the British Empire and the United States, 1607–1788* (Athens, Ga., 1986); J. G. A. Pocock, "Empire, State and Confederation: The War of American Independence as a Crisis in Multiple Monarchy," in John Robertson, ed., *A Union for Empire: Political Thought and the British Union of 1707* (Cambridge, 1995), 318–348.

FIGURE I
Apothecaries, Taylors, Etc. Conquering France and Spain. *1779. In this satire
on a London coffeehouse, the martial spirit of the British people is at its most
conspicuous among those with the least direct military experience.*
© *The British Museum*

suaded the American colonists that declaring independence was the only
possible solution to the resulting crisis.[6]

Because this is primarily a study of political consciousness, the bulk of
its evidence comes from nearly a thousand political pamphlets, most of
which were published somewhere in Britain between the early 1740s and
the end of the Revolution. As readers versed in the history of printing
and publication will be aware, there are definite advantages to looking at
this sort of material. With prices that ranged from a few pennies to a

6. [Andrew Kippis], *Considerations on the Provisional Treaty with America, and the
Preliminary Articles of Peace with France and Spain* (London, 1783), 9. The current work
on British patriotism has tended to emphasize the breadth of support for Britain's
foreign adventures, but for some salutary reminders about the underlying resentment
over the costs such wars generated at home, see E. P. Thompson, "The Making of a
Ruling Class," *Dissent*, XL (1993), 377–382; Nicholas Rogers, *Crowds, Culture, and
Politics in Georgian Britain* (Oxford, 1998), chaps. 2–5.

AN ENGLISHMANS DELIGHT OR NEWS OF ALL SORTS.

NOON GAZETT

Morning Herald.
Morning Chronicle.
Morning Post.
Gazetteer.
St James Evening
London Evening
Lloyds Evening
Public Ledger
Sunday Cronicle

All Englishmen delight in News
In London there's enough to chuse
Of morning papers near a Ream
Fill'd with every kind of theme
At Noon there's such a duced Clatter
Strangers must wonder what's the matter
And E'en that day the Lord hath blest
Is now no more a day of rest

Forth from the Press the Papers fly
Each greedy reader to supply
Of battles fought, and numbers slain,
Of Towns besieg'd, and prisoners ta'en.
Engagements both by Sea and Land
Eccho from Aldgate to the Strand
Hail! happy land, sure none's so blest
With News to comfort every breast.

Published as the Act directs 30. Dec.r 1780 by W. Richardson N.o 68 high Holborn.

FIGURE 2

An Englishmans Delight; or, News of All Sorts. *1780. During the later
eighteenth century, observers attributed the expansion of the British press partly
to widespread interest in the American Revolution.* © *The British Museum*

shilling or two, pamphlets were inexpensive and readily available to readers of all ranks and both sexes. They also tended to circulate widely, with the more popular often running through numerous subsequent imprints, some with the consent of their authors, others in editions pirated by interlopers scattered throughout the English-speaking world. Boosting this reach even further, excerpts from particularly successful ventures were typically reprinted either in periodical journals like the London-based *Literary Magazine* or in one or more of the metropolitan and provincial newspapers whose number expanded at such an astonishing rate during the period covered by this book. Indeed, there is no better indication of the genre's popularity than the tendency of taverns and coffeehouses to maintain collections of whichever titles their patrons seemed most likely to want to read and discuss. "For my part," remarked Anglican archdeacon of Carlisle William Paley during the early 1780s, "I know not whether I could make choice of any [entertainment] in which I could find greater pleasure than what I receive from expecting, hearing and relating public news."[7]

For all their strengths as primary documents, of course, pamphlets tend to privilege controversy over consensus and to give special weight to the perspectives of what contemporaries referred to as the "middling sort." For this reason, the book also draws on a variety of other sources, including newspaper and journal articles, speeches delivered in Parliament, satiric prints and cartoons, popular memoirs, political petitions, and even such apparently nonpolitical documents as published drill manuals and the private descriptions of riots and other public disturbances. Wherever possible, I have used this material to leaven my

7. William Paley, *The Principles of Moral and Political Philosophy* (1785), in *The Works of William Paley D.D.* (Philadelphia, [1857]), 121. There is an enormous literature on the popularity of pamphlets and newspapers on both sides of the Atlantic, but see G. A. Cranfield, *The Development of the Provincial Newspaper, 1700–1760* (Oxford, 1962); John Brewer, *Party Ideology and Popular Politics at the Accession of George III* (Cambridge, 1976), 148–150; John Money, *Experience and Identity: Birmingham and the West Midlands, 1760–1800* (Manchester, 1977), esp. chaps. 3–6; Bernard Bailyn and John B. Hench, eds., *The Press and the American Revolution* (Worcester, Mass., 1980); Ian K. Steele, *The English Atlantic, 1675–1740: An Exploration of Communication and Community* (Oxford, 1986), 132–167; Jeremy Black, *The English Press in the Eighteenth Century* (Philadelphia, 1987); Charles E. Clark, *The Public Prints: The Newspaper in Anglo-American Culture, 1665–1740* (Oxford, 1994); David W. Conroy, *In Public Houses: Drink and the Revolution of Authority in Colonial Massachusetts* (Chapel Hill, N.C., 1995), 158, 177–179, 233–236.

FIGURE 3
The British Empire in 1775. *Drawn by Richard Stinely*

analysis with insights from social history and the history of popular politics. In addition, following the lead of J. G. A. Pocock, I have assumed that we cannot possibly comprehend the full meaning of the concepts employed in the press without some appreciation of the various ways in which people used them to explain events like the American

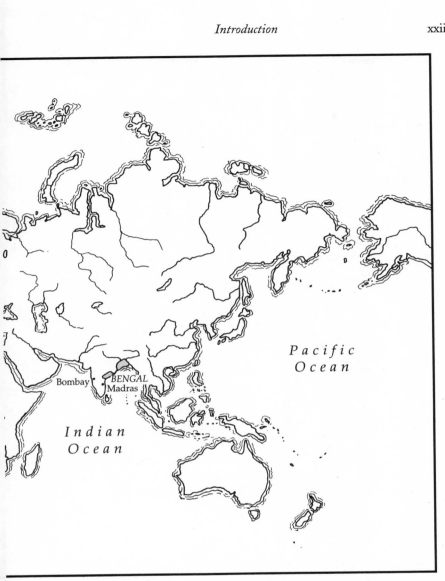

Revolution. After all, one of the more conspicuous ironies in the controversy over colonial taxation was that people on both sides of the Atlantic
used the same political vocabulary and were in general agreement about
the necessary conditions for civil liberty and constitutional government.
Before deciding what the claims of the pamphlet literature meant in

either Britain or America, we have to know something of the social and political contexts within which they were expressed and received.[8]

Although wider contexts clearly matter, however, the language found in pamphlets and newspapers could also generate its own "reality" independent from the actual experiences of either its authors or readers. As is evident from the repeated occasions when the British misjudged the situation in the colonies, this sort of representational autonomy tended to be especially pronounced when the subject involved people or places too distant for most readers to acquire direct knowledge for themselves. Because of the passive character of British patriotism, though, even domestic questions like how far the metropolitan public supported the government's policies in North America were susceptible to imaginative reconstruction by the men and women that wrote pamphlets and edited newspapers. Indeed, as Benedict Anderson has written, the nation as an "imagined community" took its rise from just these sorts of deliberations in the periodical press. Although the denizens of Grub Street hardly enjoyed the same authority as the aristocrats and landed gentlemen who controlled affairs at court and in Parliament, they helped determine the answers to crucial questions like who did and did not belong to the British nation, what membership in that nation ought to entail in terms of political rights and responsibilities, and the extent to which the British could expect their fellow subjects to abide by these national obligations in places as distant as British North America. If we are to understand the complex ways in which the American colonists fit into the emerging sense of nation in Georgian Britain—and if we wish to know why this greater British identity briefly seemed to take on a life of its own—the question of what was being said in the public discourse of the period is a good place to start.[9]

8. See, for example, J. G. A. Pocock, "Introduction: The State of the Art," in his *Virtue, Commerce, and History: Essays on Political Thought and History, Chiefly in the Eighteenth Century* (Cambridge, 1985), 1–34.

9. Benedict Anderson, *Imagined Communities: Reflections on the Origin and Spread of Nationalism* (1983; New York, 1991), 22–36, 37–46. In thinking about the way language (and the press) shapes its own reality, I have been especially influenced by Pocock's methodology (see "The State of the Art," in *Virtue, Commerce and History*, 1–32), and by Pierre Bourdieu, *Language and Symbolic Power*, ed. John B. Thompson and trans. Gino Raymond and Matthew Adamson (Cambridge, Mass., 1991). For works where the language of the popular press is treated in a manner similar to that used here, see Brewer, *Party Ideology and Popular Politics*, 33–35; Gareth Stedman Jones, *Languages of Class: Studies in English Working Class History, 1832–1982* (Cambridge, 1983), esp. chap. 3 ("Rethinking Chartism"); Dror Wahrman, *Imagining the Middle Class: The Political Representation of Class in Britain, c. 1780–1840* (Cambridge, 1995).

THE PERSISTENCE OF EMPIRE

1

An Empire of Liberty

WHIG IDENTITY IN THE REIGN
OF GEORGE II

On June 27, 1743, an allied army of British, Hanoverian, and Austrian troops under the personal command of George II, king of Great Britain but acting in his capacity as a prince-elector of the Holy Roman Empire, achieved a decisive, if fortuitous, victory over a numerically superior French force near the village of Dettingen in western Germany. Thanks to partisan divisions within the royal entourage, the allies failed during the ensuing months to capitalize on their spectacular triumph, turning what had initially appeared as an unexpected boon for Britain's beleaguered war effort into yet another missed opportunity. Nonetheless, the battle of Dettingen marked a watershed of sorts. From a German perspective, it represented a turning point in the War of the Austrian Succession (1740–1748), forcing Louis XV to withdraw his armies across the Rhine and ending the threat posed by France's ally Charles Albert of Bavaria to the integrity of the Austrian Habsburg dominions. Closer to home, the king's victory guaranteed that France would not intervene in the war that Britain had been waging with Spain since 1739 over shipping rights in the Caribbean. But most important of all, the battle of Dettingen cast in relief the growing bellicosity that had characterized Britain's relations with France for nearly a decade. By the spring of 1744, the détente of the preceding quarter-century was over, and the two

FIGURE 4
George II at Dettingen. *By John Wootton. 1754.*
Courtesy of the Director, National Army Museum, London

ancient rivals were once again openly at war, locked in a global struggle
that would continue with only brief pauses for the next forty years.[1]

It is a commonplace among British historians that the War of the
Austrian Succession and the Seven Years' War (1756–1763) were fundamentally contests for trade and empire, with the substantial commitments that Britain made to campaigns in western Germany and the Low
Countries playing a role subordinate to far more important objectives in
North America, the Caribbean, and India. As with any generalization,
this one contains an element of truth central to understanding the evolution of British strategy over the course of the two wars, as well as the
terms on which the government finally agreed to make peace in 1763. But
it tends to obscure the fact that Britain engaged in both conflicts as a
European power with legitimate interests to protect on the Continent.
Nothing illustrates this fact more vividly than the British response to the
battle of Dettingen. Although George II took the field as the elector of

1. For a general survey of the War of the Austrian Succession, see Walter L. Dorn,
Competition for Empire, 1740–1763 (New York, 1940), 122–177; M. S. Anderson, *The
War of the Austrian Succession, 1740–1748* (London, 1995).

Hanover, no one denied that he was also acting as the king of Great Britain. Indeed, from the standpoint of the king's Court Whig apologists, the battle's true significance lay in the memories it revived of the great European campaigns of William III and the duke of Marlborough, of battles like Blenheim (1704), Ramillies (1706), and Oudenarde (1708), where British arms successfully thwarted Louis XIV's ambitions to establish a "universal monarchy" and reaffirmed Britain's historic commitment to maintaining the balance of power in Europe. When British Whigs proclaimed theirs to be an empire of liberty, they were certainly conjuring up images of personal freedom, commercial prosperity, and constitutional government. With few exceptions, though, they were also glorying in the way Britain's prodigious overseas trade and global possessions enabled them to play such a central role in European affairs, and most assumed that the benevolent nature of their government's activities on the Continent undergirded the freedom enjoyed by people throughout the English-speaking Atlantic.[2]

I. MAINTAINING THE BALANCE OF POWER

As the British were well aware, this perception of their place in Europe owed little to international sympathies or pan-European patriotism. In commenting on matters of foreign policy, British observers frequently noted the irrelevance of the Christian concept of charity, and any minister who took too great an interest in the affairs of Europe ran the risk of appearing to ask the British people "to love certain Neighbours of ours, not only as well, but better than ourselves." Even people who accepted Britain's international obligations without question were inclined to see

2. George II's own sense of the significance of his presence at Dettingen is evident from his decision to wear the same tunic, sash, and "Ramillies" tricorn that he had worn as a young man with Marlborough at Oudenarde; see Uriel Dann, *Hanover and Great Britain, 1740–1760: Diplomacy and Survival* (Leicester, 1991), 53. For contemporary British policies and attitudes toward Europe, see Richard Pares, "American versus Continental Warfare, 1739–63," *English Historical Review*, LI (1936), 429–465; Jeremy Black, *British Foreign Policy in the Age of Walpole* (Edinburgh, 1985); H. M. Scott, "'The True Principles of the Revolution': The Duke of Newcastle and the Idea of the Old System," in Jeremy Black, ed., *Knights Errant and True Englishmen: British Foreign Policy, 1600–1800* (Edinburgh, 1989), 55–91; John Robertson, "Universal Monarchy and the Liberties of Europe: David Hume's Critique of an English Whig Doctrine," in Nicholas Phillipson and Quentin Skinner, eds., *Political Discourse in Early Modern Britain* (Cambridge, 1993), 356–368; Steven Pincus, "The English Debate over Universal Monarchy," in John Robertson, ed., *A Union for Empire: Political Thought and the British Union of 1707* (Cambridge, 1995), 37–62.

their European neighbors as less free, less prosperous, and far less enlightened. In the words of a Whig assize sermon from the 1730s, the
British were the "chosen People of God," latter-day Israelites whom
Providence had separated from the "rest of Mankind" by making their
"Country of all others the most Productive of the Comforts and De-
lights of Life" and giving them a government based on a "System of wise
human Laws" more perfect than "any European State can boast of." It is
no wonder that Britons often had to contend with a reputation for
extreme chauvinism, frequently from those with whom they were supposed to be allied. "Why this general Contempt of Foreigners?" wondered a Hanoverian officer shortly after the battle of Dettingen. "They
plume themselves not only upon their being *free* themselves, but being
the Assertors and Bulwarks of Liberty all over Europe; and [yet] they
vilify most of the Nations on the Continent . . . for being Slaves, as they
call us."[3]

If the British felt little affection for their neighbors across the Channel, however, few were willing to deny that they belonged to a European
nation with an important role to play in Continental affairs. Indeed, it
was generally assumed that Britain's own welfare ultimately depended
on preserving Europe's structure as a consortium of independent states,
one whose members were bound together, not by conquest or the domi-
nation of any single power, but by the mutually beneficial ties of commerce and freely negotiated treaties. Because people tended to regard
this balance of power as a thing of extraordinary fragility, most Whigs
also believed that Europe's vulnerability to the territorial ambitions of
a would-be "universal monarchy" like France left Britain no choice but
to take an active role in the conflicts that seemed to erupt so frequently
on the Continent. Horace Walpole's internationalist sympathies might
have been somewhat unusual, but few people would have found anything remarkable in his commitment to "that exalted Kind of patriotism
that considers the Liberties of Europe as inseparably interwoven with
the interest of Great-Britain; that makes the Common Cause its own,
and knows no Distinction of Parties, but the Friends to the Balance of
Power, and the Partizans of France."[4]

3. *German Politicks; or, The Modern System Examined and Refuted* . . . (London, 1744),
4; James Bate, Rector of St. Paul's, Deptford, *An Assize Sermon Preach'd at Maidstone in
Kent on the 13th of March 1733–4 before the Lord Chief Baron Reynolds* . . . (London, 1734),
12; *Popular Prejudice concerning Partiality to the Interests of Hanover, to the Subjects of
That Electorate, and Particularly to the Hanoverian Troops in British Pay* . . . (London,
1743), 12–13.
4. [Horace Walpole], *A Second and Third Letter to the Whigs* . . . (London, 1748), 44.

This commitment to Europe was partly a legacy of the Protestant Reformation and the long shadow cast by the religious wars of the sixteenth and seventeenth centuries. Although the hatred spawned by Europe's confessional schism was beginning to subside, the threat of a Catholic resurgence continued to exert an enormous influence over how the British public viewed its rivalry with France and Spain. During national emergencies, for example, the British frequently reminded themselves of what the novelist and Whig pamphleteer Henry Fielding called the evil "Genius of Popery" and the tendency of Catholic rulers to "break thro' all Restraints," no matter how long established or clearly stated. As far as most Britons were concerned, the most terrifying manifestation of this "papist" threat involved France's intermittent support for the exiled heirs of James VII and II, the Stuart king whose Catholicism had prompted Parliament to offer the throne to William and Mary during the Glorious Revolution of 1689. In 1708, 1715, and 1745, the Jacobite adherents of the Stuart cause staged serious rebellions in northern England and the Scottish Highlands, on the last occasion marching with French assistance as far as the English town of Derby, 120 miles from London, before being forced to retreat into Scotland. Elsewhere in the British Isles, Jacobites generally opted for more subtle forms of treason, like satiric poetry, ambiguous gestures, and carefully worded correspondence, but these hardly made the prospect of a Stuart restoration any less alarming. "Is there a Briton so mean," wrote the West Indian planter Samuel Martin of Antigua during the last great Jacobite rebellion in 1745, "as to bend his neck to the yoke of France, upon the nonsensical supposition of a divine right in the Pretender?" London's Anglican clergy spoke for men and women throughout the British world when they insisted on the same occasion that there was apparently no limit to "the restless spirit of Popery, which never neglects the least prospect of enlarging it's borders," nor to "the pleasure which arbitrary powers naturally take, in destroying the liberties of a free nation."[5]

Britain's vulnerability in the face of this threat was enough to con-

---

5. Henry Fielding, *A Serious Address to the People of Great Britain* . . . (1745), in W. B. Coley, ed., *Henry Fielding: The True Patriot and Related Writings* (Middletown, Conn., 1987), 25; [Samuel Martin], *A Plan for Establishing and Disciplining a National Militia in Great Britain, Ireland, and in all the British Dominions of America*, 2d ed. (London, 1745), 4; Clergy of London, Address to the Throne (1745), P.R.O., S.P. 36/79/80–81. For anti-Catholicism and British involvement in the wars against France, see Linda Colley, *Britons: Forging the Nation, 1707–1837* (New Haven, Conn., 1992), 18–43; Colin Haydon, *Anti-Catholicism in Eighteenth-Century England, c. 1714–80: A Political and Social Study* (Manchester, 1993), 23–28.

vince many people of the need for allies on the Continent. Even when they looked beyond their own borders, the British could—and did—list many more examples of the pernicious tendencies of Catholicism. These ranged from lurid, but apocryphal, accounts of Jesuits who encouraged North American Indians to eat the flesh of English settlers, to better-documented transgressions like Louis XIV's savage persecution of his Protestant subjects starting in 1685 and the equally harsh treatment that forced thousands to flee the German territories of Emperor Charles VI during the 1720s and 1730s. Indeed, eighteenth-century Britain contained a substantial number of people who had experienced such persecution directly. Following the revocation of religious toleration in France, for example, approximately 100,000 Huguenots found a safe haven in England and the outlying regions of the British Atlantic. Over the next few decades, the English-speaking colonies in North America received comparable numbers from Germany, many of them refugees from Charles VI's attempt to curtail the rights of religious minorities within the Holy Roman Empire. As an indication of the scale of this influx, historians have estimated that, as late as the Seven Years' War, approximately a tenth of the British army's active officer corps consisted of émigrés from France, Switzerland, and Germany, and North American ports like Philadelphia and New York were as notable for the waves of European immigrants who disembarked on their docks as they were for the polyglot diversity of their own inhabitants. Virginia's Samuel Davies was invoking an idiom common to Protestants throughout Europe when he reminded a regiment of provincial militia that Britain had a long history of defying the "Ignorance, Superstition, Idolatry, Tyranny over Conscience, Massacre, Fire and Sword and all the Mischiefs beyond Expression, with which Popery is pregnant."[6]

All this goes a long way toward explaining why George II's triumph at Dettingen struck such a resonant chord with the British public. In pulpits throughout the English-speaking world, Anglicans and Dissenters

6. Jesuits: Peter Williamson, *French and Indian Cruelty; Exemplified in the Life and Various Vicissitudes of Fortune, of Peter Williamson, a Disbanded Soldier*, 2d ed. (York, 1758), 16; Huguenots: Bernard Bailyn and Philip D. Morgan, "Introduction," in Bailyn and Morgan, eds., *Strangers within the Realm: Cultural Margins of the First British Empire* (Chapel Hill, N.C., 1991), 16; Samuel Davies, *Religion and Patriotism the Constituents of a Good Soldier* . . . (1755; London, 1756), 19–20. See also A. G. Roeber, " 'The Origin of Whatever Is Not English among Us': The Dutch-speaking and the German-speaking Peoples of Colonial British America," in Bailyn and Morgan, eds., *Strangers within the Realm*, 239; John Brewer, *The Sinews of Power: War, Money, and the English State, 1688–1783* (New York, 1989), 56.

alike hailed the battle as a great victory in the tradition of Queen Elizabeth, William of Orange, and Gustavus Adolphus. There was just one
hitch. Although hard to square with their apocalyptic view of international Catholicism, the British struggle to protect their liberties from
France and Spain repeatedly led them to form alliances with some of
Europe's principal Catholic powers. As an indication of this apparent
irony, the army that George commanded during the summer of 1743
included a sizable contingent of soldiers supplied by Maria Theresa, the
devoutly Catholic queen of Hungary and heir to the Habsburg dominions in Austria and central Europe.[7] Indeed, one of Britain's principal
goals during the War of the Austrian Succession was to keep control of
the Holy Roman Empire in the hands of the same ruling family who
drove so many Protestants into exile during the 1730s. To complicate
matters further, the gravest threat to the Habsburgs' standing in Germany came, not from Catholic France, but from Frederick II of Prussia,
George II's Protestant nephew whose cynical annexation of the Austrian
province of Silesia in 1740 set in motion the train of events that brought
the armies of Britain and France to blows outside the village of Dettingen three years later. Although British Protestants certainly had reason to rejoice in the glorious victory that resulted, there was no denying
that the oldest and most prestigious Catholic dynasty in Europe had
benefited as well.[8]

Just how much this ironic conjunction did to temper the British public's stated hatred for Catholicism is hard to say. However, for anyone
who gave the matter much thought, it was abundantly clear that Protes-
tantism represented only one factor in determining Britain's relations
with the neighboring states of Europe. For this reason, Whig theorists
often preferred to depict maintaining the balance of power as a worthy
end in itself. Indeed, in the decades following the Peace of Utrecht (1713),

7. Because of her sex, Maria Theresa was constitutionally barred from the throne of
the Holy Roman Empire; therefore, contemporaries referred to her by her principal
title as queen of Hungary.

8. On the incompatibility of the Austrian alliance with Britain's Protestant identity,
see *A Letter from a Member of the Last Parliament, to a New Member of the Present,
concerning the Conduct of the War with Spain* (London, 1742), 45–59; see also Henry
Fielding's remarks in *Serious Address*, in which he affirmed the general wisdom of
Britain's support for the Habsburg claim to the throne of the Holy Roman Empire while nonetheless expressing misgivings over the repeated occasions when Maria
Theresa's father, Emperor Charles VI, had violated the rights of Protestants both
within the Habsburg dominions and among the other states of the German Empire
(Coley, ed., *Henry Fielding: The True Patriot*, 25).

FIGURE 5

Northern and Western Europe, 1740. *Drawn by Richard Stinely*

which ended the final war against Louis XIV, it became something of a Whig truism that the permanence of Europe's political and religious divisions actually encouraged a kind of moral unity by giving its various rulers and peoples—Catholic as well as Protestant—a vested interest in conducting relations with each other on the basis of mutually beneficial agreements and shared standards of international law. At the very least, this meant a growing respect for the customary "rules of war" in sensitive areas like the exchange of prisoners, the treatment of civilians, and the negotiation of treaties. But many thinkers claimed to see evidence of the new spirit in a more general willingness to temper the use of force with considerations of expediency, to abandon extensive conquests and the intoxicating quest for "universal monarchy" in favor of more limited objectives, and to recognize that even "natural enemies" like Britain and France shared a common humanity. "Even foreign wars abate of their cruelty," wrote the Scottish essayist David Hume of the prevailing trend in European politics during the early 1750s, "and after the field of battle, where honour and interest steel men against compassion as well as fear, the combatants divest themselves of the brute, and resume the man."[9]

Although this way of thinking was not confined to Britain, the emphasis that thinkers like Hume placed on the European balance of power had a profound effect on how the British thought about their activities on the Continent. For example, Whig writers frequently attributed Britain's role as the "arbiter of Europe" to its character as a limited monarchy where the constitution required the king and his ministers to govern with Parliament's approval. Because most Britons assumed that their system of government distinguished them from every other people in Europe, Protestant as well as Catholic, this way of thinking did not encourage them to feel much affection for allies like Austria or Hanover. But as the British had learned from the long, costly wars against Louis XIV, safeguarding their "matchless constitution" from Jacobitism and the threat of French universal monarchy had often required them to make common cause with the other "independent" states of Europe, even when those states did not share the full extent of their commitment to civil and religious liberty. In the words of Corbyn Morris, the English pamphleteer whose influential *Letter from a By-Stander* (1741) played a significant role in shaping British attitudes toward the War of the Austrian Succession, the last hundred years had witnessed the growth of "prodigious military Establishments in every Kingdom and Province of Europe"; Britain's only hope for constitutional security in such a hostile environment was to maintain a standing army at home and assist its allies on the Continent. "Great as the Power of France may be," concurred Lord John Perceval, history had shown that the British were no less formidable—but only when they pooled their resources with the other independent states of Europe. "When *Britain* is free," remarked an anonymous pamphleteer in 1742, "the Liberties of *Europe* are safe." It

9. David Hume, "Of Refinement in the Arts and Sciences," in Hume, *Essays: Moral, Political, and Literary*, ed. Eugene F. Miller (Indianapolis, 1985), 274. See also Thomas [Barton], bishop of Norwich, *A Sermon Preach'd before the House of Lords in the Abbey-Church of Westminster, on Wednesday, January 9, 1739* . . . (London, 1739), 9: "For it is not to be imagined, that the great and righteous Governor of the World, who provides so well for the Peace and Welfare of private Communities, by pointing out the Method of Civil Government, should leave the great Community of the World, so much more his proper Inspection and Care, to blind Accidents and Chance."

hardly needed to be added that Britain benefited in equal measure from the same relationship.[10]

According to most observers, Britain's commitment to the balance of power also came from its character as a commercial nation whose people regarded their neighbors in western Europe, not as potential subjects to be governed from London, but as trading partners whose economic well-being was inextricably linked with their own. As was evident from the popularity of imperial anthems like Thomas Arne's *Rule Britannia,* the British took an intense pride in the fact that they possessed a great maritime empire with outposts and settlements in every quarter of the globe. Because the prosperity of this global community depended on the ability of British merchants to trade freely with ports from the Baltic to the Mediterranean, however, Whig writers also assumed that Britain had a strong interest in preserving what one pamphleteer called "that happy Distribution of Power, which renders Europe the most potent, and at the same time the most civilized Quarter of the Globe." Indeed, the British were quite sure that the purely commercial nature of their ties to Europe had brought them far greater wealth and influence than the sorts of costly conquests that had periodically tempted ambitious rulers like France's Louis XIV and Philip II of Spain. "Let who will spend their Strength and Wealth upon the Continent for Ambition or Power" was how an observer expressed the point during the mid-1750s; Britain's only interest in the affairs of Europe was to act as "the Sovereign of Merchandize."[11]

Not surprisingly, perhaps, this view of the benefits of protecting Britain's trade with Europe enjoyed broad public support during the first half of the eighteenth century—and not just within the metropolitan con-

---

10. [Corbyn Morris], *A Letter from a By-Stander to a Member of Parliament: Wherein Is Examined What Necessity There Is for the Maintenance of a Large Regular Land-Force in This Island . . . ,* 2d ed. (London, 1742), 6, 21–24; [John, Lord Perceval], *Faction Detected, by the Evidence of Facts . . . ,* 2d ed. (London, 1743), 81; *An Important Secret Come to Light . . .* (London, 1742), 15.

11. *Observations on the Conduct of Great-Britain, in Respect to Foreign Affairs . . . ,* 2d ed. (London, 1743), 7; *A Constituent's Answer to the Reflexions of a Member of Parliament upon the Present State of Affairs at Home and Abroad . . .* (London, [1755]), 21; *The Conduct of the Government with regard to Peace and War, Stated* (London, 1748), 5. For contemporary assumptions about the benefits of maritime empire, see Robertson, "Universal Monarchy and the Liberties of Europe," in Phillipson and Skinner, eds., *Political Discourse,* 368–373; Istvan Hont, "Free Trade and the Economic Limits to National Politics: Neo-Machiavellian Political Economy Reconsidered," in John Dunn, ed., *The Economic Limits to Modern Politics* (Cambridge, 1990), 41–120.

fines of England, Scotland, and Wales, but among the inhabitants of Britain's outlying plantations, colonies, and factories as well, many of whom reaped enormous benefits from the increasing tempo of overseas commerce. Indeed, during the first half of the eighteenth century, some of the most forceful Whig paeans to Britain's "dominion of the deep" were penned by Americans like South Carolina's Charles Woodmason, William Smith of Pennsylvania, and Boston's unofficial poet laureate, Mather Byles. As skeptics occasionally noted, the expanding trade that was the object of these tributes exacted high costs in the form of tightly regulated markets, prohibitive tariffs, and predatory abuses like the Atlantic slave trade. There were likewise people, particularly among the government's Tory and Patriot Whig opponents, who wondered whether military expeditions like the one George II commanded at Dettingen really did help ensure British access to markets on the Continent. When it came to adding up the countervailing advantages, however, most Whigs agreed that commerce not only reinforced the benevolent character of Britain's domestic government but also provided yet another reason for taking an active role in European diplomacy.[12]

In addition to these constitutional and economic arguments, Whigs occasionally claimed that forming alliances with Catholic powers like Portugal, Savoy, and Austria had the potential to weaken the universalistic claims of the Roman Church—and as such to reduce the Catholic threat to Britain's own religious institutions. In explaining themselves on this score, Whig writers often noted that their problem with the Church of Rome had less to do with local practices in Catholic countries like

12. See, for example, Charles Woodmason, "Indico" (1758), in Hennig Cohen, ed., "A Colonial Poem on Indigo Culture," *Agricultural History*, XXX (1956), 42–43; William Smith, *Discourses on Several Public Occasions . . .* (London, 1759); [Mather Byles], "A Poem on the Death of King George I, and Accession of King George II," *New-England Weekly Journal* (Sept. 4, 1727). The American response to the expansion of British trade is the subject of David S. Shields, *Oracles of Empire: Poetry, Politics, and Commerce in British America, 1690–1750* (Chicago, 1990), esp. chap. 2. That the British gave so little thought to the contradictions inherent in a free people practicing slavery is certainly disturbing, but it is hardly surprising, given the ability of white colonists to do the same thing; see esp. Edmund S. Morgan, *American Slavery, American Freedom: The Ordeal of Colonial Virginia* (New York, 1975). There was also black slavery in England, although it was chiefly confined to larger ports and cities and did not involve nearly the same numbers as in the colonies; see Philip D. Morgan, "British Encounters with Africans and African-Americans, circa 1600–1780," in Bernard Bailyn and Philip D. Morgan, eds., *Strangers within the Realm: Cultural Margins of the First British Empire* (Chapel Hill, N.C., 1991), 157–219; Gretchen Holbrook Gerzina, *Black London: Life before Emancipation* (New Brunswick, N.J., 1995).

Austria or France than with what Benjamin Colman of Boston's Brattle Street Church called "the Romish imposture" of claiming sovereignty over all of Christendom. Although there were good reasons to oppose any monarch who used Catholicism to challenge the Protestant succession in Britain or the rights and privileges of Britain's various churches and denominations, the British actually stood to benefit from joining forces with Catholic rulers who shared their vision of Europe as a community of independent states, each of which respected the religious rights and liberties of its neighbors. As an indication of such views, publicists like Henry Fielding occasionally expressed the hope that Britain's support for Austria would persuade Maria Theresa to relax her father's assault on the rights of Protestants living in places like Bohemia and Hungary. During the Anglo-French entente that followed the death of Louis XIV in 1715, the archbishop of Canterbury, William Wake, even opened a brief correspondence with two Jansenists at the Sorbonne about the possibility of forming a union between the Anglican and Gallican Churches, the main stipulation being that France reduce the pope's role to one of purely symbolic importance. In the end, of course, neither Fielding's wishes nor Wake's proposals came to anything, but they indicate the sorts of Protestant objectives that the British hoped to realize by joining forces with some of Europe's principal Catholic rulers.[13]

At no point during the eighteenth century did the British take the stability of this political, commerical, and religious balance of power for granted—not when it involved long-standing allies like the Austrian Habsburgs, and certainly not when it came to dealings with natural enemies like France and Spain. In fact, for all the period's buoyant optimism, Europe's recurring cycles of warfare provided a depressing reminder that relations between states remained subject to nothing more exacting than a voluntary, culturally determined willingness to abide by the dictates of "God, and the law of nature," as Glasgow University's Francis Hutchinson observed in his influential *System of Moral Philosophy* (1737). If the European balance of power remained fragile, however, the British were nonetheless convinced that it was both their pecu-

13. Benjamin Colman, *Government the Pillar of the Earth: A Sermon Preached at the Lecture in Boston, before His Excellency Jonathan Belcher, Esq.* . . . (1730), in Ellis Sandoz, ed., *Political Sermons of the American Founding Era, 1730–1805* (Indianapolis, 1991), 20; Fielding, *Serious Address*, in Coley, ed., *Henry Fielding: The True Patriot*, 25–26; Norman Sykes, *Old Priest and New Presbyter: Episcopacy and Presbyterianism since the Reformation, with Especial Relation to the Churches of England and Scotland* (Cambridge, 1957), 196–207.

liar interest and solemn obligation to see to its preservation. In other countries, rulers might still entertain hopes of unlimited conquest and boundless empire. Given the opportunity, governments elsewhere might even succumb to temptation and act on such fantasies, as Whig polemicists were sure Louis XV and his chief minister Cardinal Fleury were doing during the early 1740s. Of the Continent's principal powers, only Britain seemed immune to such dreadful ambitions—and only its people could be trusted to hold the line against those who were not. As Israel Mauduit wrote in 1761:

> I never read the history of the two grand alliances, which were formed by King William against the growing power of France, without feeling the warmest sentiments of gratitude to that great deliverer of Europe. Never did King of England appear with greater dignity, than he did in that great Congress, held at the Hague in the year 1691; when the Emperor and Empire, the Kings of Spain, Sweden, and Denmark, by their several ambassadors, the Electors of Germany by their particular ministers, and several of them in their own persons, with at least fifty of the greatest Princes of Germany, all attended to hear him plead the cause of Europe; and all joined in one common league and declaration against France.[14]

There were thus compelling reasons for Britain to maintain its ties to the Continent, some based on the legacy of the Reformation, others on more recent thinking about the balance of power. But whichever rationale people used, the Whig commitment to the liberties of Europe explains a lot about why the government continued to field armies and subsidize allies on the Continent even as Britain's primary objectives shifted to North America and India during the later 1740s. To be sure, the advocates of such policies had to concede that waging war in Europe was not always popular and that there were critics who wondered why Britain should have anything at all to do with the Continent. "Imperial, independant, self-sufficient, separated by nature from all the rest of the world," wrote one in 1746; "why should we busy ourselves with the affairs of other nations, and by interposing in their quarrels make ourselves parties in matters, which very little, if at all, concern us?" But as the author of the popular *Plain Reasoner* observed the year after George II's victory at Dettingen, defensive alliances and treaties remained "the Out-

14. Francis Hutchinson, *A System of Moral Philosophy, in Three Books* . . . , 2 vols. (London, 1755), I, 283; [Israel Mauduit], *Considerations on the Present German War*, 5th ed. (London, 1761), 11.

works and Redoubts of Kingdoms" even for a great maritime nation like Britain. No matter how confident some might be "that *England* can stand upon her own Bottom, without Regard to Alliances with any other Power on Earth," the last sixty years had shown that the religious, political, and economic fate of both Britain and its empire were intimately bound up with that of every independent state in Europe, and that no minister with the British people's real welfare at heart dared forget that by "contributing to defend *Flanders* and *Germany*, we are only defending ourselves at a Distance."[15]

II. A MATCHLESS CONSTITUTION

When the British spoke of defending themselves at a distance, of course, they were not just talking about the need to protect their foreign interests on the Continent. More often than not, they also meant Britain's ability to play a decisive role in Europe while placing as few burdens as possible on ordinary men and women at home. As their political opponents never tired of pointing out, the Whigs derived considerable domestic power from their military activities in Europe, power that was at least as broad in some areas—notably taxation—as that of absolute monarchies like France. By the standards of contemporary Europe, however, the British enjoyed a remarkable degree of civil liberty. Not only were they largely free from the sorts of extraordinary requisitions and demands that were all too often the benchmark of military power and diplomatic influence on the Continent, but the pressures of war also made little difference in their ability to enjoy benefits like religious liberty, constitutional government, and the rule of law. Furthermore, the government's success at waging war in Europe ensured that the armed confrontations that seemed necessary to protect Britain's domestic liberties took place on foreign soil and were partly, if not entirely, fought by the armies of other nations. In short, whatever else they thought of the Whigs' interventions in Europe—and there were certainly people who had serious reservations—ordinary men and women clearly benefited from the fact that they generated so few domestic burdens and hardships.

Eighteenth-century Britons hardly needed to be reminded that they owed much of this freedom from intrusive government to the same

15. *The Important Question Discussed; or, A Serious and Impartial Enquiry into the True Interest of England, with Respect to the Continent* (London, 1746), 2–3; *The Plain Reasoner: Wherein the Present State of Affairs Are Set in a New, but Very Obvious Light* (London, 1745), 11–12.

constitutional limitations that made it impossible for the king and his ministers to wage war on the Continent without the consent of Parliament. Although the monarchy still enjoyed considerable powers, no ruler could ignore the control that the House of Commons had acquired over the royal finances during the Glorious Revolution; nor were Britain's Hanoverian kings likely to forget the stipulations in the Bill of Rights (1689) and the Act of Settlement (1701) that limited the crown's formal prerogative and effectively replaced the divine right kingship of the seventeenth century with a monarchy based on the sanction of legislative statute. Indeed, the British took considerable comfort from the knowledge that their own rights and privileges did not depend on the king's personal benevolence or the influence of a particular minister or faction, but on the unshakable foundation of Parliament's unlimited authority. "I desire," wrote the Whig historian Samuel Squire during the 1740s, "to be informed of any one Stretch of Power, one Act of Violence, one Invasion of civil or religious Liberty, one unparliamentary Suspension of Law, or Interruption of Justice, since the Accession of his present Majesty to the Throne." "Were any of the most judicious of the last Century to become Spectators of the present Times," concurred the bishop of Saint Asaph, Isaac Maddox, in 1739, "what Satisfaction would they receive from the Form of Government that now subsists, how earnestly would they recommend a thankful Acquiescence?"[16]

As critics occasionally noted, the sheer breadth of Parliament's sovereignty carried its own potential for arbitrary government—a potential that would become only too apparent during the crisis over colonial taxation during the 1760s and 1770s. Nonetheless, one of the main effects of Westminster's growing powers was to force the crown's abandonment

16. [Samuel Squire], *A Letter to a Tory Friend: Upon the Present Critical Situation of Our Affairs* ... (London, 1746), 16; Isaac [Maddox], *A Sermon Preach'd before the House of Lords in the Abbey-Church of Westminster, on Monday, June 11, 1739* ... (London, 1739), 15. There is presently some disagreement among English historians whether the Revolution Settlement altered the relationship between king and Parliament or it simply reasserted the settlement established at the Restoration in 1660. For the latter view, see J. C. D. Clark, *English Society, 1688–1832: Ideology, Social Structure and Political Practice during the Ancien Regime* (Cambridge, 1985), 119–141; Clark, *Revolution and Rebellion: State and Society in England in the Seventeenth and Eighteenth Centuries* (Cambridge, 1986), 68–91. The argument here is closer to the qualified emphasis on change in Lois G. Schwoerer, *The Declaration of Rights, 1689* (Baltimore, 1981); John Morrill, "The Sensible Revolution, 1688," in Morrill, *The English Revolutions of the Seventeenth Century* (London, 1993); Robert Beddard, "The Unexpected Whig Revolution of 1688," in Beddard, ed., *The Revolutions of 1688* (New York, 1996), 11–101.

of the intrusive, centralizing initiatives that had characterized the Stuart monarchy for much of the seventeenth century. In matters of colonial administration, for example, the Whig ministries of both George I and George II generally opted for what Edmund Burke would later call a policy of "salutary neglect," in effect permitting much of the crown's imperial authority to devolve onto provincial assemblies and great trading concerns like the East India and Royal African Companies. In a similar manner, the Revolution Settlement placed definite limits on how far and in what ways the government could meddle in local affairs in England, Scotland, and Wales. Indeed, the notoriously corrupt character of Georgian politics owed a good deal to the fact that the king's ministers now had to purchase through venality the loyalty that they no longer possessed the authority to compel by law. In towns and counties controlled by the "king's friends," local notables invariably expected to have their support solicited through lavish entertainment, charitable donations, and other expensive gestures. Likewise, Whig ministers often had little choice but to respect the autonomy of hostile boroughs and corporations, even when—as was true of Oxford University into the early 1760s—such bodies remained firmly in the hands of the ruling family's Tory and Jacobite foes. The royal chaplain, Richard Terrick, did not exaggerate by as much as we might think when he boasted in 1745 that the Hanoverian regime possessed "all the Power which is necessary to make his People happy, but none to make them Slaves and miserable."[17]

Although checking the power of the crown represented a considerable accomplishment, the beneficial effects of these limitations did not end with the actions of the king's ministers, but extended to the manners and mores that governed behavior in the wider political nation. As the British were well aware, the same commitment to liberty that made their constitution the envy of the world also left them unusually susceptible to what Edward Wortley Montagu called "civil dissentions"—not just among the quarter of the male population whose wealth and status

17. Richard Terrick, *A Sermon Preach'd before the Rt. Honble. the Lord Mayor, the Aldermen, and Liveries of the Several Companies, of the City of London . . .* (London, 1745), 8. The classic account of the relationship between the Whigs' commitment to political liberty and their equally strong penchant for venality is J. H. Plumb, *The Growth of Political Stability in England, 1675–1725* (London, 1967); for the devolutionary tendencies of Whig government on Britain's periphery, see James A. Henretta, *"Salutary Neglect": Colonial Administration under the Duke of Newcastle* (Princeton, N.J., 1972); Alexander Murdoch, *"The People Above": Politics and Administration in Mid-Eighteenth-Century Scotland* (Edinburgh, 1980); J. C. Beckett, *The Making of Modern Ireland, 1603–1923* (1966; London, 1981).

entitled them to vote for members of Parliament but also among the much larger group (more than a few of them women) who felt free to participate in coffeehouse debates, write political pamphlets, join associations, and circulate petitions. As we might expect, commentators occasionally voiced misgivings on this score; however, many also thought that the government's willingness to tolerate the political activities of all but the most seditious Jacobites encouraged the British people to observe the same tolerance in their dealings with each other. As David Hume explained during the political crisis that finally drove the Court Whigs' long-serving prime minister, Sir Robert Walpole, from office in 1742, the very scope of the people's rights and privileges meant that it was in the interest of all Britons, including the ministry's Tory and Patriot Whig opponents, "not to contend, as if they were fighting *pro aris et focis*," but to conduct themselves in a manner that left ample room for negotiation and compromise. In his influential treatise on the party divisions of the 1740s, Lord John Perceval even conceded that political dissidents who confined their activities to "legal Ways alone" and who were willing "quietly [to] sit down under their Disappointment" might "in time produce good laws, and good Effects." Neither Hume nor Lord Perceval expected the Whigs and Tories to settle all their differences or to achieve complete political harmony. In an age of liberty and moderation, however, there was no reason why even the most unyielding of the government's critics might not fulfill their duties as loyal members of the body politic.[18]

Indeed, the increasingly moderate character of British politics played a crucial role in enabling the government to cultivate at least the appearance, if not always the reality, of national unity amid the renewed warfare of the 1740s and 1750s. Although politics in expanding towns like Bristol and Norwich frequently remained contested, the overall impression—especially in England—was of increasing stability, where neither the ministry's supporters nor their opponents needed to worry about the

18. E[dward] W[ortley] Montagu, *Reflections on the Rise and Fall of the Antient Republicks: Adapted to the Present State of Great Britain* (London, 1759), 4; David Hume, "That Politics May Be Reduced to a Science" (1741), in Hume, *Essays*, ed. Miller, 31; [Perceval], *Faction Detected*, 76. The role of women in eighteenth-century British politics is the subject of a small but expanding literature; see, for example, Colley, *Britons*, chap. 6; G. J. Barker-Benfield, *The Culture of Sensibility: Sex and Society in Eighteenth-Century Britain* (Chicago, 1992), esp. chap. 5; Elaine Chalus, "'That Epidemical Madness': Women and Electoral Politics in the Late Eighteenth Century," in Hannah Barker and Elaine Chalus, eds., *Gender in Eigtheenth-Century England: Roles, Representations, and Responsibilities* (London, 1997), 151–178.

danger of Jacobite unrest, let alone outright civil war. Significantly, during the Jacobite Rebellion of 1745, more than a few Tories found it possible to set aside their objections to nearly thirty years of Whig rule and to participate in the loyal associations that formed on behalf of the Hanoverian succession in towns and counties across England. Likewise, the gradual subsiding of party antagonism produced a growing number of proposals for "patriotic" administrations where people of all political persuasions would unite in the common cause of service to king and country. "It was reserved for our Times," wrote the anonymous author of *Power and Patriotism* in 1746, "to see that the greatest Struggles for Power may be carried on, without any of those Violences, and without producing any of those Mischiefs, which deform our antient Chronicles, and which are not absolutely effaced in the Stories of later Times." As Hume put the issue a decade later: "The transition from a moderate opposition against an establishment, to an entire acquiescence in it, is easy and insensible." "Moderation," Hume concluded, "is of advantage to every establishment."[19]

For most men and women, of course, the form of toleration that mattered most had less to do with the legitimacy of political dissent than it did with the broad liberty that the Hanoverian regime extended to all but Catholics and Deists in matters of religious belief. Notwithstanding the changes wrought by the Glorious Revolution, Hanoverian Britain was still a "confessional state," one where the Church of England enjoyed substantial advantages both over nonconformists in England and Wales and over the members of provincial denominations like the Presbyterian Church of Scotland and New England's Congregational Standing Order. Within these limits, however, the Whigs who managed ecclesiastical politics under George II never tired of congratulating themselves on the religious liberty that their regime secured for Protestants throughout Britain's empire. Although the Tories, with their High Church sympathies, remained ambivalent about the proliferation of Dissenting chapels and meeting houses, Whig clerics regularly praised the enlightened wisdom that the church had shown when it accepted measures like the

19. *Power and Patriotism: A Poetical Epistle, Humbly Inscribed to the Right Honourable H. P. Esq.* . . . (London, 1746), 6–7; Hume, "Of the Coalition of Parties" (1759), in Hume, *Essays*, ed. Miller, 500. For the continuation of party divisions in many localities, see esp. Linda Colley, *In Defiance of Oligarchy: The Tory Party, 1714–60* (Cambridge, 1982), chaps. 9, 10; Nicholas Rogers, *Whigs and Cities: Popular Politics in the Age of Walpole and Pitt* (Oxford, 1989), 286–299. However, note the gradual subsiding of party conflict in Rogers, *Whigs and Cities,* 339–343, and Norma Landau, *The Justices of the Peace, 1679–1760* (Berkeley, Calif., 1984), 109–145.

Toleration Act of 1689 and those portions of the Anglo-Scottish Treaty of Union (1707) that preserved the Presbyterian structure of the Church of Scotland. Indeed, Anglicans liked to note that in this respect the differences between the Church of England and that of Rome could not be more pronounced. Bishop Isaac Maddox was making a common observation when he remarked on the anniversary of George II's accession in 1739:

> It is but Justice now to admit, that tho' supported by the Evidence of Reason, Scripture, and Antiquity, and with the Superiority of a legal Establishment, such is the Christian Temper, the amiable Candour and Condescension of the Church of *England,* she abhors all the Methods of Violence, and all the Influence of Persecution: With other gross Absurdities of Popery, [our church] most cordially rejects that cruel Spirit, which spreads Devastation and Misery upon Earth, and calls down Fire from Heaven; in *Meekness instructing those that oppose,* she endeavours their Conviction, pities their Mistakes, but desires not to awaken any Terrors of the Secular Arm.[20]

This was obviously a partisan perspective, one more likely to appeal to Anglican communicants than to those men and women—perhaps half a million in England and Wales—whose Dissenting convictions relegated them to the status of second-class citizens. Nonetheless, the fact that all Protestants were free to worship as they chose helped neutralize the great religious differences that had kept the three British kingdoms in civil turmoil during the seventeenth century. Although Dissenters still balked at their subordinate situation, observers like the English historian of Puritanism Daniel Neal noted how religious toleration promoted "loyal and dutiful behavior" among all men and women, regardless of their convictions. Indeed, the sheer variety of Britain's sects and denominations appeared to encourage people to behave as though it were of no concern what their friends or neighbors believed. "Go into the London Stock Exchange," remarked the French philosopher Voltaire of his time in England during the 1720s,

20. [Maddox], *Sermon before House of Lords, June 11, 1739,* 16. For Whig ecclesiastical policy during the eighteenth century, see Carl Bridenbaugh, *Mitre and Sceptre: Transatlantic Faiths, Ideas, Personalities, and Politics, 1689–1775* (New York, 1962), chaps. 2–4; G. V. Bennett, *The Tory Crisis in Church and State, 1688–1730: The Career of Francis Atterbury, Bishop of Rochester* (Oxford, 1975), 10–16, 20–22, 307–309; J. C. D. Clark, *The Language of Liberty, 1660–1832: Political Discourse and Social Dynamics in the Anglo-American World* (Cambridge, 1994).

and you will see representatives from all nations gathered together
for the utility of men. Here Jew, Mohammedan, and Christian deal
with each other as though they were all of the same faith, and only
apply the word infidel to people who go bankrupt. Here the Presbyterian trusts the Anabaptist and the Anglican accepts a promise
from the Quaker. On leaving these peaceful and free assemblies
some go to the Synagogue and others for a drink, this one goes to be
baptized in a great bath in the name of Father, Son and Holy
Ghost, that one has his son's foreskin cut and has some Hebrew
words he does not understand mumbled over the child, others go to
their church and await the inspiration of God with their hats on,
and everyone is happy.[21]

This commitment to religious toleration obviously dovetailed with
the cosmopolitan character of the Whig regime's activities in Europe.
Of equal importance, however, was the way such attitudes helped con-
solidate an emerging sense of belonging to a single British nation among
the peoples of the English-speaking Atlantic. Although the theological
differences that structured the politics of England, Scotland, Ireland,
and America retained much of their force, Whig religious policy nonetheless encouraged the development of a common nationality based, not
on confessional loyalties, but on allegiance to the civil authority of king
and Parliament. Significantly, in each of the various naturalization laws
passed during the first half of the eighteenth century, Parliament omitted the Tory language obliging foreign-born Protestants to take communion in the Church of England. Likewise, the annual indemnity acts
that the government approved from 1727 onward conferred on Dissenters
most of the political rights enjoyed by Anglicans. Despite the Whigs'
light hand in most matters of colonial administration, moreover, the
ministers of both George I and George II showed little hesitation in
pressuring legislatures and assemblies in places as scattered as Ireland,
New England, and the West Indies to adopt toleration acts of their own.
As George Whitefield reminded his listeners during a sermon preached
in Philadelphia: "We breathe indeed in a free air; as free (if not freer)
both as to temporals and spirituals, as any nation under heaven."[22]

21. Daniel Neal, *The History of the Puritans or Protestant Non-Conformists*, I (1732),
quoted in Bridenbaugh, *Mitre and Sceptre*, 49; Voltaire, *Letters on England* (1733), trans.
and ed. Leonard Tancock (New York, 1980), 41.

22. George Whitefield, *Britain's Mercies, and Britain's Duties; Represented in a Sermon
Preach'd at the New-Building in Philadelphia, on Sunday August 24, 1746 . . .*, in Sandoz,
ed., *Political Sermons*, 125. On naturalization, see James H. Kettner, *The Development of*

Indeed, despite the British people's well-known antipopery, such attitudes even extended—at least in theory—to Catholics living in Britain and its outlying dependencies. As was evident from the activities of missionary groups like the Society for the Propagation of the Gospel and the Society for Promoting Christian Knowledge, the British remained deeply committed to evangelizing "non-believers" within their own borders—including, wherever possible, those who adhered to the teachings of Rome. Increasingly, though, they also recognized that Britain's commitment to the balance of power carried a corresponding obligation to accord Catholics at least the trappings of religious freedom. Following Spain's cession of the Mediterranean island of Minorca at the Peace of Utrecht, for example, Britain permitted the pope to appoint a Catholic vicar apostolic with full powers of episcopalian consecration, but without territorial jurisdiction. During the 1710s and 1720s, the East India Company arrived at similar arrangements for Bombay and the Malabar Coast, many of whose inhabitants had converted to Catholicism under Portuguese rule. Even in metropolitan Britain, where anti-Catholic riots were a recurring problem throughout the century, Whigs like Henry Fielding took care to point out that Catholics were entitled to the equal protection of the law "while they remain in Peace and Submission to the Government." As the future archbishop of Canterbury Thomas Herring put the issue in a sermon before the London-based Society for Promoting English Protestant Working Schools in Ireland:

> My Business, if I will follow the Precepts and Example of my Saviour, is to do Good to all: And it matters not to me, if I can promote their Happiness, whether they be Acquaintance or Stranger, Countrymen or Foreigners, Friends or Enemies, of contrary Persuasions, or of bad Practices; whether they be of the Eastern, or the Western Church; whether they dwell in the North, or in the South.

American Citizenship, 1608–1870 (Chapel Hill, N.C., 1978), chap. 4; Sykes, *Old Priest and New Presbyter*, 148; Roeber, "'The Origin of Whatever Is Not English among Us,'" in Bailyn and Morgan, eds., *Strangers within the Realm*, 225. For the Irish Toleration Act (1719), passed despite bitter Tory opposition, see J. L. McCracken, "The Ecclesiastical Structure, 1714–1760," in T. W. Moody and W. E. Vaughan, eds., *Eighteenth-Century Ireland, 1691–1800* (Oxford, 1986), 101, vol. IV of *A New History of Ireland*; the often acrimonious implementation of religious toleration in British North America is treated in Bridenbaugh, *Mitre and Sceptre*, 65, 123, 131–132; Patricia U. Bonomi, *Under the Cope of Heaven: Religion, Society, and Politics in Colonial America* (Oxford, 1986), 156, 166, 182–183.

Let their Differences be what they will, if they are Men, they are for
that Reason objects of my Care and Compassion.[23]

Taken together, these civil and religious safeguards seemed to provide
the British people with an unusual degree of individual freedom from
interference by the state, the church, or others—what modern political
philosophers would call "negative liberty."[24] Although this image was
hard to reconcile with intrusive measures like the laws against plebeian
poaching and the growing number of crimes that carried capital penalties, contemporary observers were repeatedly struck by the Whigs' reluctance to compel the popular observation of "positive" political duties
like holding office, attending worship service, and serving in the armed
forces of the crown. As a Whig cleric put matters in 1734, the British
could be grateful that their government required nothing more of them
than to "keep and do those Statutes and Ordinances to which the Greatness of our State is owing." Horace Walpole made much the same claim,
insisting that the British lived under a "Constitution most admirably
calculated for the Ease and Freedom of the Subject."[25] Although this in
no way detracted from the British people's well-known sense of public
duty, their Whig rulers ultimately expected relatively little in the way of
compulsory obligations, but instead were content to leave them free to
pursue activities that contributed only indirectly to the public good.
George II's Britain might have been a nation of patriots, but it was also a

23. "Memorandum on the Appointment of a Vicar-General Apostolic to Govern
Roman Catholics in Minorca" (n.d.), in Cambridge University Library, Cholmondley
(Houghton) MSS, paper 31; Stephen Neill, *A History of Christianity in India, 1707–1858*
(Cambridge, 1985), 436–437; Fielding, *The True Patriot and the History of Our Own
Times . . .* , no. 2 (1745), in Coley, ed., *Henry Fielding: The True Patriot,* 124; Thomas
Herring, *A Sermon Preached before the Society Corresponding with the Incorporated Society
in Dublin . . .* (1740/41), in *Seven Sermons on Public Occasions, by the Most Reverend Dr.
Thomas Herring, Late Lord Archbishop of Canterbury . . .* (London, 1763), 143–145.

24. For the modern concept of negative liberty, see esp. Sir Isaiah Berlin, *Two Concepts
of Liberty* (Oxford, 1958), reprinted in Berlin, *Four Essays on Liberty* (Oxford, 1969). For
the Anglo-American commitment to negative liberty in the eighteenth century, see J. G.
A. Pocock, *The Machiavellian Moment: Florentine Political Thought and the Atlantic
Republican Tradition* (Princeton, N.J., 1975), chaps. 13, 14; Gordon S. Wood, *The Creation of the American Republic, 1776–1787* (Chapel Hill, N.C., 1969), esp. chap. 15.

25. Bate, *An Assize Sermon,* 12; [Walpole], *Second and Third Letter to the Whigs,* 41.
The argument here owes a great deal to J. G. A. Pocock's perceptive essay "The
Significance of 1688: Some Reflections on Whig History," in Beddard, ed., *Revolutions
of 1688,* 271–292, and to the revealing remarks of the great Marxist historian E. P.
Thompson about the Whig commitment to the rule of law in *Whigs and Hunters: The
Origin of the Black Act* (New York, 1975), 258–269.

nation where people were generally free to attend to all sorts of other matters, if—and when—they so desired.

By itself, the extent of this liberty represented a significant departure from the practices of other states in Europe. But as far as many Whigs were concerned, what distinguished Britain even more was the government's ability to provide military protection for these rights and privileges while demanding almost nothing of most men and women in the way of active service—or rather, nothing beyond paying the taxes necessary to maintain a professional army and navy. For those who did wish to serve their king and country, of course, military duty was certainly an option. Indeed, although historians disagree over whether the proportion of "national soldiers" on the British establishment was comparable to the figures for states like France and Prussia, the number that did serve in either the army or the navy was considerable. Despite the navy's use of compulsory impressment, however, recruiting for both forces depended heavily on volunteers; furthermore, most of the actual fighting in Britain's wars took place at sea or on foreign soil. As a result, it was perfectly acceptable for ordinary Britons to confine their involvement in military matters to sedentary activities like signing petitions, reading accounts of battles and campaigns in the press, and supporting the king's troops in coffeehouse debates and public discussions. "The patriot who lays down his life" for the good of his country, wrote Glasgow professor of moral philosophy Adam Smith in 1759, "excites not only our entire approbation, but our highest wonder and admiration." As Smith explained, however, this sense of admiration came, not from a sense of shared suffering, but from a keen awareness of "how difficult it is to make" such a sacrifice "and how few people are capable of making it." In other words, the British "nation" represented an imagined community in the fullest sense of the word—an entity that inspired an increasingly strong allegiance among people throughout the English-speaking world but that asked remarkably little of them in return.[26]

26. Adam Smith, *The Theory of Moral Sentiments* (1759), ed. D. D. Raphael and A. L. Macfie, vol. I of *The Glasgow Edition of the Works and Correspondence of Adam Smith* (Indianapolis, 1982), 228. For evidence suggesting that the number of British "nationals" in the king's forces was unusually low by eighteenth-century standards, see André Corvisier, *Armies and Societies in Europe, 1494–1789*, trans. Abigail T. Siddall (Bloomington, Ind., 1979), 112–114. By contrast, John Brewer suggests that the British figures on this score were probably comparable to those of Europe's other major powers; for Brewer, the main distinguishing feature between Britain and the rest of Europe consists in its relative security from invasion. See *Sinews of Power*, 41–42, 46–48. For the voluntary character of most military service—including the navy—see

Nothing illustrated the voluntary basis of the British state's military capacity more clearly than the public response to the Jacobite Rebellion of 1745. As the king's ministers were well aware, the national emergency triggered by Charles Stuart's initial victories in Scotland and northern England left the government no choice but to undertake a range of extraordinary measures, including raising the militia in England, issuing proclamations calling on the justices of the peace to disarm Catholics and suspected Jacobites, and—most controversially of all—encouraging the county gentry to participate in armed associations along the lines of the famous gathering that Archbishop Thomas Herring organized at York in October 1745. On several occasions, local magistrates even permitted the regime's plebeian supporters to undertake such initiatives without waiting for approval from Westminster, and, during the critical months between the middle of September and early December, the government considered offers of military assistance from such well-known dissidents as the Cornish tinners, the Spitalfields weavers, smugglers on the Sussex coast, and the colliers from the Forest of Dean. As the earl of Hardwicke wrote to his son Philip Yorke, it was necessary at such a crucial juncture for everyone to assist the civil magistrates "in any act of zeal for the government, [including] addresses, associations, subscriptions, etc., for those are not acts of office, but voluntary acts of duty and loyalty, which any subject may perform."[27]

Even at the height of the crisis, though, there was a curious disjunction between the rhetoric of Hanoverian loyalism and what the people who made such professions were actually willing to undertake. For all the talk about the need for personal sacrifice and popular involvement,

---

Sinews of Power, 49–51; N. A. M. Rodger, The Wooden World: An Anatomy of the Georgian Navy (London, 1986), chap. 5. Nicholas Rogers, Crowds, Culture, and Politics in Georgian Britain (Oxford, 1998), chap. 3, has challenged Rodger's contention about service in the navy; however, he also concedes the growing "accountability of the impress service" as the century progressed (89).

27. At the height of the crisis, for example, Lord Poulett wrote the duke of Newcastle that he was permitting associations of men to arm and drill without formal commissions, activities that, in times of peace, he would have directed the local justices of the peace to prohibit under the terms of the Riot Act; see letter dated Nov. 18, 1745, P.R.O., S.P. 36/74/ii/24. Cornish tinners: John Harris to Newcastle, Dec. 17, 1745, P.R.O., S.P. 36/77/i/169; Spitalfields weavers: Alderman Wm. Baker to Newcastle, Sept. 7, 1745, P.R.O., S.P. 36/67/ii/30–32; Sussex smugglers: letter from Nicholl, Sept. 12, 1745, P.R.O., S.P. 36/67/ii/77–78; Richmond to Newcastle, Sept. 15, 1745, BL Add. MSS, 181–182; colliers of Dean: earl of Berkeley to Newcastle, Sept. 26, 1745, P.R.O., S.P. 36/69/ii/1–2; Hardwicke to Yorke, Oct. 8, 1745, BL Add. MSS, 35,351, 90.

the general public demonstrated a pronounced willingness to leave responsibility for its suppression in the hands of the regular army and the legally commissioned officers of the crown. This certainly helps explain why so few counties responded to the crisis by raising the militia upon which England's defense had historically rested. According to some correspondents, the militia laws were too "prodigiously inconsistent and ineffectual" to be implemented; according to others, such levies placed a particularly "heavy burden on the lesser sort and [were] only light to those who could best bear any burden." And in the few places where the magistrates did succeed in mustering the necessary men, the results were predictably disappointing, giving rise to frequent requests for regular soldiers. For whatever reason, most English Whigs chose to express their loyalty either by pledging funds to support the public credit or by raising subscriptions to pay volunteers to fight in their place.[28]

Furthermore, those who did participate in independent companies and associations did so in the full knowledge that their efforts were largely symbolic. In Yorkshire's East Riding, for example, the county magistrates reported little difficulty in raising men for several companies, but many of the recruits were "farmers sons or servants" who refused to march beyond the limits of their own shire. The same thing occurred in Cornwall, where the lord lieutenant observed that the people "all profess great readiness to defend their country, but they mean their county." Elsewhere, the main effect of forming local associations seems to have been to create fresh opportunities for opposing factions to continue long-standing feuds, as happened when the members of two rival (and equally loyal) companies nearly came to blows while celebrating the

28. Sir George Oxenden to Newcastle, Dec. 29, 1745, P.R.O., S.P. 36/78/ii/53–56; Lord Edgecumbe to Newcastle, Oct. 18, 1745, P.R.O., S.P. 36/72/i/3. For the range of possible responses to the rebellion, see Newcastle to Lord Edgecumbe, Oct. 10, 1745, P.R.O., S.P. 71/i/35–37; for subscriptions on behalf of the public credit, see speech of James Bradshaw at the Crown Tavern, London, in "An Estimate of the Charge, for One Month, of One Thousand Men, to Be Raised for His Majesty's Service, and to Be Employed Any Where within Ten Miles of London," Oct. 11, 1745, P.R.O., S.P. 36/72/iii/134–135. See also Lord Hardwicke's letter to his son Philip Yorke, Sept. 21, 1745, BL Add. MSS 35,351, 82, on the merits of offering to help fund temporary regiments: "I advise you to offer to subscribe generously, and to be one of the first, and, if there is any occasion for immediate payments, draw upon me for the money. . . . I am not sanguine enough to expect a vast deal of military service from these commissions, but however they will raise a spirit and zeal for the government, and convince foreign powers that this part of the kingdom is not in that abominable way in which Scotland has appeared."

FIGURE 6

Briton's Association against the Pope's Bulls. *1745. The horrors allegedly
perpetrated by the Jacobites in Scotland are contrasted with the lethargy shown by
the figures on the right, representing the independent companies raised in
Yorkshire and other English counties. One soldier refuses to "go out of the parish";
another will travel no farther than "five miles to fight." Observer at the far right:
"I wish they'd go to Dinner."* © *The British Museum*

King's Birthday at Exeter. After witnessing such a dispute at Chichester,
one writer observed that his fellow townsmen seemed bent on waging "a
civil war within a civil war." Lord Derby, whose own county of Lancashire was unusual for its large number of Catholics and Jacobites, was
nonetheless giving voice to a common sense of exasperation when he
"heartily" wished that all the subscriptions in England "be paid into the
Exchequer, to raise troops in the manner his Majesty should judge most
proper."[29]

 Perhaps that was why so many people exercised their right to do
nothing at all. "I have been labouring to stir up the phlegm of the people
of this place, and to excite them to express some kind of zeal and spirit

29. Lord Irwin to Newcastle, Dec. 27, 1745, P.R.O., S.P. 36/78/ii/12–13; Lord Edge-
cumbe to Newcastle, Nov. 19, 1745, P.R.O., S.P. 36/74/i/52; *The Disbanded Volunteers'
Appeal to Their Fellow-Citizens* . . . (Exeter, 1746), preface, 4–20; Page to Newcastle,
Dec. 18, 1745, P.R.O., S.P. 36/77/ii/74–75; Lord Derby to Newcastle, Oct. 13, 1745,
P.R.O., S.P. 36/71/ii/33–34.

upon this occasion," reported the Anglican dean of Raphoe, Anthony Thompson, in a particularly telling letter from Stratford-upon-Avon at the height of the crisis. Thompson was sure that there was no "disaffection amongst them to his Majesty's person or government." However, the people in his own corner of England refused to heed his appeal:

> I have endeavoured to awaken them with the notion of their religion, their laws, their liberties and properties being at stake; at which they yawn, and ask if they do not pay soldiers to fight for them. Yes. But suppose there [*sic*] soldiers to be necessarily employed elsewhere, or that they may not be sufficient to stop the rebels, so soon as might be wished. Why then, they say, the rebels are a great way off, and it will be time enough to think of that two months hence. Talk to them about associations, they are afraid that would be attended with an extraordinary expence. Ask about the militia, they have no Deputy Lieutenant nor officers to command them. In case a posse comitatus should be called, what arms have they? Why truly none that they know of.

In an attempt to organize some sort of local defense, Thompson did manage to persuade the town's leaders "to have ten muskets cleaned, which have hung in their Guild Hall untouched ever since the Preston Rebellion [in 1715]." But even this had little effect, and the magistrates soon changed their minds, "for fear of frighting the people." "In a word," Thompson concluded, "I believe nothing is capable of moving them at present without . . . the actual appearance of an enemy amongst them."[30]

It is always tempting to write political history from the standpoint of the most enthusiastic partisans, to concentrate on those men and women actively involved in shaping the course of events and for whom the ideals of one side or the other represent matters of deep personal conviction. Perhaps the most striking feature of British politics in the reign of George II, however, is the extent to which the Hanoverian regime declined to make such demands of its subjects. As Hume remarked in his 1748 essay debunking the notion of an original contract, political obligation for the inhabitants of a complex, variegated nation like Britain had less to do with formal allegiance to particular measures or forms of government than it did with the subtler but more enduring ties of economic and political self-interest. In fact, for many observers, the key to British patriotism lay in the way "the interest and necessities of soci-

30. Letter from Anthony Thompson, Sept. 28, 1745, P.R.O., S.P. 36/69/iii/10–11.

ety"—as Hume termed them—prompted ordinary men and women to create a vast, self-regulating network of social and economic interaction which, though beyond the purview of either the church or the state, nonetheless encouraged the virtues necessary to sustain civil society. In place of the sort of intrusive, and generally ineffective, supervision characteristic of absolutist and enthusiastic regimes alike, the British could thus rely on the competitive dynamics of commerce and polite society to teach them the virtues of obedience, self-mastery, and restraint. This is certainly how Hume saw the progress of refinement among the members of a prosperous society like Britain:

> They flock into cities; love to receive and communicate knowledge; to shew their wit or their breeding; their taste in conversation or living, in clothes or furniture. Curiosity allures the wise; vanity the foolish; and pleasure both. Particular clubs and societies are everywhere formed: Both sexes meet in an easy and sociable manner: and the tempers of men, as well as their behaviour, refine apace. . . . Thus *industry, knowledge*, and *humanity*, are linked together by an indissoluble chain, and are found, from experience as well as reason, to be peculiar to the more polished, and, what are commonly denominated, the more luxurious ages.[31]

There is an almost utopian feel to passages like this, one that belies the violent, coercive underside that we know was also characteristic of the early Hanoverian state.[32] Indeed, at the very moment when Hume was writing the passage quoted above, the northern and western half of his native Scotland lay under brutal military occupation—a casualty of the British Parliament's determination to eradicate the last vestiges of the semifeudal, clan-based society that had made the Highlands such fertile

31. Hume, "Of the Original Contract," "Of Refinement in the Arts," both in Hume, *Essays*, ed. Miller, 271, 486. This is what contemporary moral philosophers generally understood as *doux commerce;* see Albert O. Hirschman, *The Passions and the Interests: Political Arguments for Capitalism before Its Triumph* (Princeton, N.J., 1977), 58–63. See also Duncan Forbes, *Hume's Philosophical Politics* (Cambridge, 1975), chap. 5; Lawrence E. Klein, *Shaftesbury and the Culture of Politeness: Moral Discourse and Cultural Politics in Early Eighteenth-Century England* (Cambridge, 1994).

32. For the historiographical confrontation between these two perspectives in England, compare the critical analysis of Whiggery and commercialization in E. P. Thompson's *Whigs and Hunters* and *Customs in Common: Studies in Traditional Popular Culture* (New York, 1991) with the almost celebratory tone of Neil McKendrick, John Brewer, and J. H. Plumb, *The Birth of a Consumer Society: The Commercialization of Eighteenth-Century England* (Bloomington, Ind., 1982).

ground for Jacobite intrigue and rebellion. Although the Whigs' dominance could exact extraordinary costs, however, those who defended such policies nonetheless insisted that their ultimate goal was to make every part of Britain and its empire safe for liberty and prosperity. As an indication of the prevalence of such views, the members of the Committee for Forfeited Estates in Scotland expressed confidence that, for all the pain and suffering that had attended their efforts, reconstructing Highland society "would . . . soon diffuse a spirit of trade and Industry, as well as promote Agriculture through all this extensive country." Even the members of Ireland's Protestant ascendancy professed to believe in such values—and not just for themselves but for the island's predominantly Catholic peasantry as well. Although the Irish earl of Orrery was speaking of his native country, his words could have been used by improvers in practically any region of the British Atlantic at midcentury: "I have known this kingdom fifteen years. More improvements than I have visibly observed of all kinds could not have been effected in that space of time. Duels are at an end. Politeness is making some progress. Literature is close behind her. Industry must follow. As Popery decreases, cleanliness and honesty will find place."[33]

Though undeniably smug and naive—especially when they involved places like Ireland or the Scottish Highlands—such rosy estimates of the potential of ordinary men and women for self-mastery and enlightenment were nonetheless significant. Indeed, the Whigs' convictions on this matter go a long way toward explaining why the ministers of the first two Hanoverian monarchs preferred to keep their authority so relatively circumscribed within the metropolitan confines of England, the Scottish Lowlands, and most of Wales, as well as among the settler societies of British America. Although anyone who mounted a serious challange to

---

33. *A Selection of Scottish Forfeited Estates Papers, 1715, 1745 . . .* , ed. A. H. Millar, Scottish History Society (Edinburgh, 1909), 62; Lord Orrery to Birch, May 26, 1747, in Countess of Cork and Orrery, eds., *Orrery Papers*, I (London, 1903), 320–321, as quoted in S. J. Connolly, *Religion, Law, and Power: The Making of Protestant Ireland, 1660–1760* (Oxford, 1992), 73. For the prevalence of such views among Whigs in Ireland and Scotland, see Connolly, *Religion, Law, and Power*, chap. 2; Jacqueline Hill, "Ireland without Union: Molyneux and His Legacy," in Robertson, ed., *Union for Empire*, 273–277; T. C. Smout, *A History of the Scottish People, 1560–1830* (1969; London, 1985), chap. 14; Bruce Lenman, *Integration, Enlightenment, and Industrialization: Scotland 1746–1832* (Toronto, 1981); for the cult of improvement in the American colonies, see esp. Jack P. Greene, *Pursuits of Happiness: The Social Development of Early Modern British Colonies and the Formation of American Culture* (Chapel Hill, N.C., 1988), chap. 8.

Hanoverian rule could expect a harsh response, it is no accident that the reign of George II coincided with the remarkable success of new literary genres like the novel, with its clear preference for the innate virtues of humble heroes like Samuel Richardson's Pamela and Fielding's Tom Jones and its open hostility to the unchecked intrusions of tyranny and enthusiasm. Nor is it surprising that the middle decades of the eighteenth century witnessed a growing determination on the part of Scottish literati like David Hume and Adam Smith to turn the insights of moderate Whiggery into a systematic philosophy that located the roots of law, morality, and political obligation in the daily interactions of civil society and the commercial marketplace. Thanks in no small measure to Britain's success at waging war in Europe, the civil and religious liberties of ordinary people were secure. The convictions that now mattered most were social rather than political, and the virtues upon which this matchless constitution ultimately depended were moderate, tolerant, and civilized.[34]

III. THE LIBERTIES OF BRITAIN AND EUROPE

Taken together, the international and domestic facets of Whig rule provided the Hanoverian regime with an identity that was at once firmly grounded in the "national" interests of England and its British periphery while also being deeply enmeshed in the cosmopolitan affairs of the neighboring states of western Europe. There was no question that the domestic took priority in the conduct of government and the formation of policy. In the eyes of George II's Whig apologists, however, the internal and external dimensions of Britain's identity were better seen as two halves that comprised a whole. Foreign trade stimulated domestic prosperity, tolerance at home reinforced moderation abroad, and the efforts of the king's ministers on behalf of the liberties of Europe represented a natural extension of the sacred regard in which they held the rights of his subjects in Britain. As we have seen, Voltaire was sure that liberty and commerce combined to make Britain a truly international country, whose borders contained "representatives from all nations gathered to-

34. Paul Langford, *A Polite and Commercial People: England, 1727–1783* (Oxford, 1989), 95–96, 127–128; Pocock, *The Machiavellian Moment*, 497–505; Forbes, *Hume's Philosophical Politics*, chaps. 5, 6; Nicholas Phillipson, "Adam Smith as Civic Moralist," in Istvan Hont and Michael Ignatieff, eds., *Wealth and Virtue: The Shaping of Political Economy in the Scottish Enlightenment* (Cambridge, 1983), 179–202.

gether for the utility of men." It was certainly a flattering image, at once nationally based and internationally minded, cosmopolitan without being anything less than patriotic. But it was also one that British Whigs liked to think conformed to the reality that they and the generation before them had done so much to bring about.[35]

No doubt this is why so many commentators regarded George II's victory at Dettingen as the finest hour of his reign. Notwithstanding the reports of royal favoritism toward Hanoverian officers serving in the allied army, the king's personal courage remained a prominent feature of court panegyric for the rest of his life. Indeed, for the Hanoverian regime's Whig partisans, the battle supplied the occasion for theatrical displays and celebrations of regal charisma of a kind that Britain's German ruling family had generally failed to achieve. The best known of these today is probably George Frederick Handel's majestic *Dettingen Te Deum*, but images of heroic kingship pervaded celebratory pieces ranging from Lord Perceval's widely read pamphlet *Faction Detected* to popular ballads of the kind that sold for a penny or two on city streets throughout Britain and the loyal anthem "God Save the King," which audiences began singing in London theaters during the Jacobite Rebellion of 1745. In the words of one enthralled pamphleteer, the king had "won the Hearts of his Subjects" by risking "his Life, to raise the *British* Nation to the highest pitch of Glory." If anything, Lord Perceval was even more effusive, casting George as the worthy descendant of Henry V,

> who has sacrificed every private Interest to the Interests of Great Britain,—who has supported his Ally with that Steadiness, Sincerity, and good Faith, which would have rendered a private man an Ornament to the Society in which he lived,—who, in this Just, and Necessary Cause, has exposed his Person to the Dangers of War, as much as the meanest private Soldier in his Armies,—and is now at the Head of his Troops, in a Foreign Country, animating the Courage of the British nation, and restoring the Antient Glory of the Royal Race of Plantagenants from which he is descended.[36]

35. Voltaire, *Letters on England*, trans. and ed. Tancock, 41.

36. Christopher Hogwood, *Handel* (London, 1984), 184; [Perceval], *Faction Detected*, 172; "God Save the King," in *Gentleman's Magazine and Historical Chronicle*, XV (1745), 552; *The Present Measures Proved to Be the Only Means of Securing the Balance of Power in Europe, as well as the Liberty and Independency of Great-Britain* (London, 1743), 30. For the memory of Dettingen, see the posthumous account of George II's reign in the *Annual Register*, III (1760), 41.

FIGURE 7
The British Jubilee. *1748. The conclusion of the Treaty of Aix-la-Chapelle*
spawned widespread celebration in Britain. The king's newfound popularity
reflected his personal bravery at Dettingen and the predominantly loyal response
to the Jacobite rebellion of 1745. © *The British Museum*

For all the parallels with England's martial past, though, the most
enduring image of the king at Dettingen was that of a prince whose
limited objectives represented the antithesis of the Bourbon norms of
absolutism and universal monarchy. Indeed, George II frequently appeared as a latter-day Augustus, judiciously observing the boundaries of
his power at home and along the frontiers of his empire while he set
boundaries to the lawless pretensions of a barbarous tyrant abroad. It was
in this spirit, for example, that the Scottish earl of Stair claimed that a
British prince could wish for nothing greater than "the glory of procuring a very good peace for Europe." In the words of the Whig historian
Richard Rolt, the king's decision to come to the assistance of the European balance of power had "appeared more agreeable to his own royal
glory, and the illustrious figure the British nation was accustomed to
make among the neighbouring potentates" on the Continent. As another polemicist put matters, the king had returned the nation to its first
principles by demonstrating

I. That it is the Duty of every Administration to make the Nation's Figure Abroad a principal object of their Attention. II. That our Figure Abroad must depend upon our holding the Balance of Power, and being at the head of that Interest, which opposes universal Monarchy. III. That in order to do this, we must lay aside all particular and party Prejudices, and consider the Interests of our Neighbors, so far as they regard the common Cause, as much as we do our own.[37]

It would be difficult to exaggerate the appeal that this rhetoric held for men and women in England and among the outlying realms and provinces of Britain's maritime empire. As every British schoolchild knows, of course, Dettingen turned out to be the last occasion when a British monarch personally led his subjects into battle on the Continent. Indeed, for reasons that we shall explore more fully below, the middle decades of the eighteenth century witnessed a growing unwillingness on the part of the British public to match this general commitment with more tangible undertakings in the way of troops and subsidies for their European allies. Still, even after the British began to shift their attention toward the western Atlantic and Asia, they remained convinced that they were fighting to defend both themselves and the rest of Europe from the lawless ambition of an arbitrary and potentially barbarous power. The self-styled "Country-Gentleman" was treading a well-trod path when he assured his readers at the start of the Seven Years' War that "to be thoroughly apprized of the Designs of *France,* must tend to rouse the Indignation of every Lover of Peace, Justice, his Country, and its Rights and Privileges; and induce every Prince to unite for crushing this

37. Stair to Lord Loudoun, The Hague, Sept. 24, 1742, in Papers of the earl of Loudoun, LO 7659, Huntington Library, San Marino, Calif.; Richard Rolt, *An Impartial Representation of the Conduct of the Several Powers of Europe, Engaged in the Late General War,* 4 vols. (London, 1749), III, 485; *Observations on the Conduct of Great-Britain,* 12. For Augustan references to Dettingen, see [James Fortescue], *The Expedition: A Poem, on the Duke's Going to Flanders* (London, 1747), 9:

Shew yourselves, Britons, worthy such a Race;
Let not your future, His late Acts disgrace:
But learn from him the common Cause to serve;
T'enjoy his Honours, go, like Him deserve.
Be these your Arts, enlarge Britannia's Sway;
Make Tyrants tremble; Kings protection pray;
Raise the Oppress'd; the stubborn Foe o'ercome;
Be GEORGE Augustus, and His Albion, Rome.

ambitious, perfidious, restless, bigoted, persecuting, plundering Power, which has long been the common Disturber of the western World, and as long struggled for Universal Monarchy." For most readers, the validity of this sort of rhetoric was self-evident, and only served to reassure them that they belonged to an empire of liberty more perfect than any the world had ever seen.[38]

38. *The Progress of the French, in Their Views of Universal Monarchy* . . . (London, 1756), iii, 2.

The Blue Water Vision

BRITISH IMPERIALISM AND THE
SEVEN YEARS' WAR

For an apparently minor incident with implications of the first importance, few Georgian controversies can match the imbroglio caused by the Hanoverian soldier who walked off with one too many handkerchiefs from a Maidstone haberdasher in September 1756. Brought over during the French invasion scare of the previous spring, the fifteen thousand Hessians and Hanoverians on the Kentish coast had already aroused the suspicions of a public searching for someone to blame for a string of humiliating French victories in North America and the Mediterranean. Amid this tense situation, the story of the stolen handkerchief quickly took on a life of its own. In publications ranging from the seditious writings of the Tory pamphleteer (and possible Jacobite) John Shebbeare to lighter satires like the anonymous "English maiden's" *Lamentation for the Departure of the Hanoverians,* critics seized on the government's resort to such unreliable forces as evidence of a much wider pattern of negligence in managing the opening phase of the Seven Years' War. Ever sensitive to the vagaries of public opinion, the opposition leader, William Pitt, even attempted to make the unfortunate soldier's prosecution a condition for accepting office in October, and the owners of inns and lodging houses across Kent flatly refused to provide winter quarters for any of his countrymen. "I cannot believe the facts

FIGURE 8

The Kentish Out-Laws. *1756. The Hanoverian troops stealing the handkerchief
in Kent are compared to the Norman soldiers of William the Conqueror.*
© *The British Museum*

alleged are true," remarked Frederick II of Prussia upon learning of the
controversy, "unless the genius of England be entirely changed."[1]

For people who knew anything about British politics, however, the
affair of the Hanoverian and the handkerchief must have sounded all too
familiar. As we have seen, the British people took tremendous pride in
their government's role as a principal guarantor of the European balance
of power. Notwithstanding such apparently cosmopolitan sentiments,
though, they frequently appeared to distrust their allies almost as much
as they did natural enemies like France and Spain. Nowhere were these
suspicions more conspicuous than in matters involving the electorate of
Hanover, the king's north German principality, with which Britain had
been permanently allied since the accession of George I in 1714. Although ministerial apologists liked to claim that the dynastic alliance
complemented Britain's interests in northern Europe and the Holy Roman Empire, the general public was capable of taking almost any diplo-

1. *A Lamentation for the Departure of the Hanoverians; Being an Epistle from an
English Maiden to Her German Sweetheart* (London, [1757]); [John Shebbeare], *A
Fourth Letter to the People of England, on the Conduct of the M——s, in Alliances, Fleets,
and Armies . . .* , 6th ed. (London, 1756), 30–37. For a brief account of the Maidstone
affair as well as Frederick's observation, see O. A. Sherrard, *Lord Chatham: Pitt and the
Seven Years' War* (London, 1955; reprint, Westport, Conn., 1975), 133, 177.

matic mishap as evidence that the governing Whigs cared more for the welfare of the royal family's native electorate than for Britain and its valuable overseas empire. Despite the apparent insignificance of the Hanoverian soldier's offense, the government thus recognized that "the present temper and disposition makes every caution necessary," as William Murray, the future Lord Mansfield, warned Secretary at War Lord Barrington in mid-October. Although the king refused to permit the poor man to be tried under English law, a Hanoverian court-martial duly sentenced him to three hundred lashes. Meanwhile, rather than risk a confrontation with the innkeepers of Kent, the government opted—in clear violation of eighteenth-century practice—to leave the troops in the field to face the worsening elements without adequate shelter. Finally, upon taking office as prime minister in November, William Pitt brought the unfortunate affair to a close by making good on his promise to have the entire contingent shipped back to Germany.[2]

So ended one of the less heartening chapters in Britain's dealings with its allies. In one important respect, however, the episode's effects lasted long after the Hanoverian and Hessian auxiliaries had set sail for home. Although the specifics were soon forgotten, the Maidstone affair heralded a new, increasingly isolationist phase in British attitudes toward the Continent. Largely in order to safeguard Hanover from a French invasion, the wartime ministry of William Pitt and the duke of Newcastle (1757–1761) remained actively involved in the European dimensions of the Seven Years' War, dispatching troops to Germany and approving subsidies for the benefit of Britain's principal ally, Frederick II of Prussia. For a substantial—and growing—body of metropolitan opinion, however, the most efficient and cost-effective way to prosecute the war appeared to lie in reducing these European commitments and pursuing an independent, "blue water" policy calculated to strengthen Britain's imperial power by seizing French possessions in North America, India, and the Caribbean. The appeal that this colonial and maritime vision held for the general public helps explain why the British public greeted colonial victories like the capture of Quebec (1759) with such overwhelming approval. But as we shall see, this determination to withdraw from Europe and rely exclusively on Britain's Atlantic and Asiatic empire also

2. William Murray to Lord Barrington, Oct. 13, 1756, Papers of William Wildman, Viscount Barrington, Suffolk Record Office, Ipswich, HA 174/1026/3a/61. The politics of hiring German auxiliaries is treated in Jeremy Black, "Parliament and Foreign Policy in the Age of Walpole: The Case of the Hessians," in Black, ed., *Knights Errant and True Englishmen: British Foreign Policy, 1660–1800* (Edinburgh, 1989), 41–54.

had several less-welcome consequences. Although people could hardly have foreseen it at the time, the strategy that Britain adopted during Pitt's "great war for empire" helped set the stage for the various attempts at imperial reform that culminated in the American Revolution.

I. "THE SEPULCHRE OF BRITISH INTEREST"

For the Court Whigs who had dominated British politics since the reign of George I, the reasons for the outcry against the government's involvement in Europe often seemed hard to fathom. Not only did the British gain a sense of moral satisfaction from their activities on the Continent, but subsidizing allies like Hanover also enabled the government to raise auxiliary troops at a fraction of the cost required to recruit comparable numbers in Britain. In addition, France's vulnerability along its northern and eastern frontiers meant that even a small army of observation in Germany or the Netherlands could limit the Bourbon monarchy's ability to challenge British power on the high seas, let alone threaten England itself with the horrors of invasion and civil war. As anyone could see, Continental strategies required substantial military and financial resources—which otherwise might have gone to defend colonial outposts in North America and Asia. Nonetheless, the British reaped some considerable advantages from their role as the arbiter of Europe.[3]

Although contemporary observers were certainly aware of these benefits, the ruling Whigs' involvement in Continental affairs suffered from several potentially serious weaknesses. The first involved the financial burdens of waging war in Europe. Not only did Britain's commitment to the balance of power require the government to employ a peacetime army of some twelve thousand regulars, but the taxes and deficits necessary to maintain these forces weighed heavily on ordinary men and women. Furthermore, because so much of the king's revenue came from taxes on consumer goods like beer, candles, soap, and clothing, a disproportionate share of this burden fell on the humblest ranks of English

3. The argument here owes a good deal to Daniel Baugh, "Withdrawing from Europe: Anglo-French Maritime Geopolitics, 1750–1800," *International History Review*, XX (1998), 1–32; I am grateful to the author for allowing me to see an earlier version of his article. For more on the relationship between European and colonial strategies, see Richard Pares, "American versus Continental Warfare, 1739–63," *English Historical Review*, LI (1936), 429–465; Baugh, "Great Britain's 'Blue-Water' Policy, 1689–1815," *International History Review*, X (1988), 33–58; H. M. Scott, "'The True Principles of the Revolution': The Duke of Newcastle and the Idea of the Old System," in Black, ed., *Knights Errant and True Englishmen*, 55–91.

society—small farmers, shopkeepers, artisans, small-scale manufacturers, and the like. Despite the benefits that the British gained from fielding armies and forming alliances in Europe, the Court Whigs' management of foreign policy thus exposed them to increasing criticism during the middle years of the eighteenth century, and nowhere more so than among the middle-class inhabitants of London and expanding provincial centers like Bristol, Newcastle, and Norwich, many of whom provided clamorous support for Pitt's patriotic program. Indeed, the very success of the governing Whigs' foreign and domestic policies probably increased these political difficulties, for as people began to worry less about the receding threat of Jacobitism and civil war, they became ever bolder in their willingness to criticize measures whose other benefits were often difficult to discern.[4]

At the same time, the inconclusive peace that followed the War of the Austrian Succession produced doubts over whether Britain's activities in Europe really were worth the costs. Although few people denied the need for allies on the Continent, the government's Tory and Patriot Whig opponents in Parliament and the press claimed with increasing urgency that the "common cause" that such confederations were pledged to uphold merely fostered an impression of high moral purpose while disguising the sacrifices that Britain was all too often expected to make in return. Indeed, such allegations were so prevalent before the fall of 1756, when the king reluctantly invited William Pitt to form the first of his two wartime administrations, that politicians like the new prime minister's brother-in-law, Lord Temple, affected to believe that the government's regard for the liberties of Europe made it all but impossible for Britain to prosecute a war "in the defence of her most essential interests, her commerce, and her colonies." "To be the Head of a great Confederacy sounds big," wrote another of the Whigs' many critics, "to

---

4. For popular resentment of Whig foreign policy, see esp. Kathleen Wilson, *The Sense of the People: Politics, Culture, and Imperialism in England, 1715–1785* (Cambridge, 1995), chap. 3. See also Lucy S. Sutherland, "The City of London and the Pitt-Devonshire Administration, 1756–1757," *Proceedings of the British Academy,* XLVI (1960), 148–193; Paul Langford, "William Pitt and Public Opinion, 1757," *English Historical Review,* LXXXVIII (1973), 54–79; Marie Peters, *Pitt and Popularity: The Patriot Minister and London Opinion during the Seven Years' War* (Oxford, 1980), 24–31. Although political historians have generally given this "popular" support an instrumental part in Pitt's appointment as prime minister in both 1756 and 1757, note the dominant role of the king and Court Whig grandees like the duke of Newcastle in J. C. D. Clark's *The Dynamics of Change: The Crisis of the 1750s and English Party Systems* (Cambridge, 1982).

command a great combined Army in the Field, is a fine Rare Show; and
to poize the European Balance of Power is a fine Piece of speculative
Honour," but such "visionary Advantages" had rarely compensated the
nation for "the Loss of Blood, Treasure, Trade, and perhaps Liberty."⁵

This criticism had its roots in the long-running debate over the peace
that the Tory ministry of Lord Bolingbroke and the earl of Oxford
negotiated at the end of the War of the Spanish Succession (1702–1713).
As far as most Whigs were concerned, the Peace of Utrecht (1713) represented nothing less than a seditious betrayal of Britain's original war
aims, the foremost of which was to prevent a Franco-Spanish union.
Not only did the treaty appear to compromise this objective by permitting Louis XIV's grandson to be named Philip V of Spain, but the
government also deserted allies like the Holy Roman Emperor, the
Dutch Republic, and Britain's future monarch, Prince Georg Ludwig of
Hanover. For the peace's Tory supporters, however, Britain's imperial
and commercial gains far outweighed whatever moral and legal principles they had sacrificed in Europe. By stipulating that the French and
Spanish crowns would never be held by the same ruler, the peace barred
a future union between the two powers, effectively shielding Britain
from the danger of another Bourbon universal monarchy. At the same
time, the Tories claimed that they had rescued the nation from becoming what Bolingbroke referred to as "a province of the confederacy"—in
this case, a confederacy driven by Emperor Charles VI's stubborn refusal
to make peace until he was recognized as the rightful Habsburg heir to
the throne of Spain. Indeed, it became something of a Tory common-
place during the first half of the eighteenth century that the wars against
Louis XIV had turned the Whigs into incorrigible enthusiasts who
cared more for abstract, unattainable, and (often) undesirable objectives
in Europe than they did the welfare of the people they governed.⁶

5. "Protest by Earl Temple against Support for the Electorate of Hanover, 13 November 1755," in Joel H. Wiener, ed., *Great Britain: Foreign Policy and the Span of
Empire, 1689–1971: A Documentary History*, 4 vols. (New York, 1972), I, 95; *Seventeen
Hundred Forty-two: Being a Review of the Conduct of the New Ministry the Last Year,
with regard to Foreign Affairs* . . . (London, 1743), 42.

6. Henry St. John, Viscount Bolingbroke, *Letters on the Study and Use of History*
(1752), in *The Works of Lord Bolingbroke* . . . , 4 vols. (1844; New York, 1967), II, 324. For
the Tories' criticism of Whig foreign policy, both before and after the Peace of Utrecht,
see Bolingbroke, *Letters on History*, in *Works of Bolingbroke*, II, 313, 330–331; [Jonathan
Swift], *The Conduct of the Allies* (1711), in Herbert Davis, ed., *The Prose Works of
Jonathan Swift*, VI (Oxford, 1951), 1–65; Isaac Kramnick, *Bolingbroke and His Circle:
The Politics of Nostalgia in the Age of Walpole* (Cambridge, Mass., 1968), 181–187; Linda

As the Whigs never tired of pointing out, this represented a rather partial view of the last great struggle with Louis XIV, a view that failed to take account of their own role in seizing French territory in Nova Scotia, Newfoundland, Hudson Bay, and the Caribbean, as well as the part that British victories on the Continent played in gaining the commercially vital strongholds of Gibraltar and Minorca from Spain. With some justification, however, Bolingbroke insisted that, had it not been for the Tories' determination to offer France reasonable terms, these gains might just as easily have fallen victim to the Whigs' subservience to their allies. Moreover, even though both George I and George II proved willing to abide by Utrecht's terms, Bolingbroke was sure that Sir Robert Walpole and the Court Whigs who returned to power in 1714 had continued to squander British resources with grandiose schemes like the Quadruple Alliance (1718), whereby Britain joined with France, the Holy Roman Emperor, and the Dutch Republic in pledging to uphold the peace of Europe, and the Treaty of Hanover (1726), which brought both Britain and Europe to the verge of a general war that nobody wanted. In short, one effect of Whig rule had been to produce the appearance of lawful war and diplomacy while disguising an alarming reality of domestic corruption and impoverishment—a kind of theatrical politics where the gratifying illusion of grandeur served to obscure consequences that were as detrimental to Britain's own interests as they were to the rest of Europe.[7]

Colley, *In Defiance of Oligarchy: The Tory Party, 1714–60* (Cambridge, 1982), 13–16, 57, 94, 178–185; Joachim Muelenbrock, "Alexander Pope's *Windsor Forest* (1713): Genre and Political Propaganda," *Studi settecentri,* 11–12 (1988–1989), 9–15. The general discussion of British foreign policy in this paragraph and the ones that follow is based on W. F. Reddaway, "Rivalry for Colonial Power, 1714–1748," "The Seven Years' War," both in J. Holland Rose et al., eds., *The Cambridge History of the British Empire,* I (Cambridge, 1929), 346–376, 460–484; D. B. Horn, *Great Britain and Europe in the Eighteenth Century* (Oxford, 1967); Jeremy Black, *British Foreign Policy in the Age of Walpole* (Edinburgh, 1985); Black, *Natural and Necessary Enemies: Anglo-French Relations in the Eighteenth Century* (Athens, Ga., 1986); Paul Langford, *A Polite and Commercial People: England, 1727–1783* (Oxford, 1989), chaps. 2, 5; Mark Kishlansky, *A Monarchy Transformed: Britain 1603–1714* (London, 1996), chap. 13.

7. The complementary relationship between Britain's European and colonial interests was the subject of numerous Whig pamphlets during the 1740s and 1750s; see, for example, *The Important Question Discussed; or, A Serious and Impartial Enquiry into the True Interest of England, with respect to the Continent* (London, 1746); *An Answer to a Pamphlet, Called, A Second Letter to the People: In Which the Subsidiary System Is Fairly Stated, and Amply Considered* (London, 1755). For Bolingbroke on the tendencies of

This was clearly a Tory language, one that betrayed the role the party's leaders had played in negotiating a controversial peace. By the time of Bolingbroke's death in 1751, though, his views on international relations were beginning to enjoy a much broader acceptance not just among the rump of his own Tory cohort but also among a younger generation of Patriot Whigs like William Pitt, George Townshend, Lord Temple, and their mercantile and middle-class supporters. One reason for this Whig embrace of Tory principle involved the perception that the British gained almost nothing from their efforts on the Continent during the later 1740s—nothing, that is, beyond a renewed sense of how fervently they wished for France's humiliation. At the same time, despite Whig claims about the security that came from European alliances, the British were unable to prevent France from landing Charles Stuart in Scotland during the summer of 1745 and mounting an invasion of England. To make matters even worse, the War of the Austrian Succession ended up confirming the Holy Roman Empire's reduction to a pale shadow of the unified confederation that the Whigs had long regarded as the fulcrum of the European balance of power. Indeed, because the British ministers who negotiated the Treaty of Aix-la-Chapelle (1748) were the same men who had originally opposed Prussia's unprovoked annexation of Silesia, their subsequent willingness to recognize Frederick's claim to the Austrian province appeared to condone the waning significance of the hereditary rights and liberties upon which the "public law" and general peace of Europe had historically been thought to depend. No self-respecting Whig dared suggest that such concepts had ceased to matter entirely, but the Tory determination to leave the Continent's warring powers to their own devices no longer seemed quite so heretical.[8]

The full effects of this new reality were slow to dawn on George II and the duke of Newcastle, both of whom spent the early 1750s attempting to restore the "old system" through measures like the carefully orchestrated

British foreign policy since the Glorious Revolution, see "Letter VIII," in Bolingbroke, *Letters on History,* in *Works of Bolingbroke,* II, 276–334.

8. For the often indistinguishable nature of Tory and Patriot Whig perspectives on the War of the Austrian Succession, see, for example, *German Politicks; or, The Modern System Examined and Refuted . . .* (London, 1744), 54; *The Natural Interest of Great Britain, in Its Present Circumstances* (London, 1748), 8, part 2 of *The Present Condition of Great Britain . . .* (London, 1746); *A General View of the Present Politics and Interests of the Principal Powers of Europe . . .* (London, [1747]), 52–55; *A Letter to a Noble Negotiator Abroad, on the Present Prospect of a Speedy Peace . . .* (London, 1748), 58–59; *Pasquin and Marforio on the Peace: Being a Discussion, by These Celebrated Statues at Rome . . . ,* 3d ed. (London, [1749?]), 35–36.

election of Maria Theresa's son to the imperial crown and sizable Russian and Hessian subsidies designed to check the Prussian king's apparently boundless appetite for additional conquests. For the government's critics, however, it was no longer clear whether maintaining the balance of power in this manner was even possible, let alone at an acceptable cost. Indeed, the opening phase of the Seven Years' War produced what looked like a stunning confirmation of Britain's declining influence, as Austria rebuffed the Whigs' overtures in favor of an agreement with France while George II was compelled to ally with the same monarch whose cynical invasion of Silesia had done more than anything else to undermine the public law of Europe. Thanks to several brilliant—and unexpected—Prussian victories, this "Diplomatic Revolution" eventually came to seem like a stroke of genius, one that helped Britain achieve its own annus mirabilis in 1759 with triumphs over France in every quarter of the globe. In the short term, however, the main effect of subsidizing Frederick's ambition was to confirm the Tory maxim that four decades of Whig foreign policy had turned concepts like "the Ballance of Power, the Independency of Europe, [and] the Protestant Cause" into empty phrases that had ceased to "have any Meaning at all." As patriot Israel Mauduit remarked in 1761, the "whole system of Europe" seemed to have changed so thoroughly that "those grand alliances by which Britain gained so many *real* victories on the continent" were now "no longer to be hoped for." Given this state of affairs, even the government's supporters found themselves hard-pressed to explain what the British stood to achieve by diverting supplies from their own beleaguered possessions and making yet another attempt to shore up the balance of power in Europe.[9]

Another—and in some ways, even more serious—reason for the growing isolationism of the 1750s involved the way that waging war on the Continent tended to complicate Britain's relationship with Hanover. According to the Act of Settlement (1701), Britain's Hanoverian kings were required to maintain a sharp distinction between their royal and electoral capacities. As the actions of the first two monarchs repeatedly demonstrated, however, keeping the affairs of Britain and Hanover separate proved far easier to articulate in principle than to establish in practice. Within months of his accession, for example, George I dispatched a British fleet to the Baltic in order to prevent Sweden from expelling his electoral troops from the German bishoprics of Bremen and

9. *A Modest Enquiry into the Present State of Foreign Affairs* . . . (London, [1745]), 3–4; [Israel Mauduit], *Occasional Thoughts on the Present German War,* 2d ed. (London, 1761), 47.

Verden. Still mindful of how Hanover had been abandoned at Utrecht, the king also proceeded to exact his revenge on anyone who had been even remotely involved, including the Tories who negotiated the despised peace and—briefly, it was rumored—German composer George Frederick Handel, whose misfortune it had been to compose a *Te Deum* celebrating the treaty's ratification. Furthermore, it was well known that both George I and George II took their responsibilities as prince-electors of the Holy Roman Empire every bit as seriously as they did their royal duties in Britain. As George II is alleged to have declared to his wife, Queen Caroline, after an especially tumultuous parliamentary session in 1736, "the devil take the Parliament, and the devil take the whole island, provided I can get out of it and go to Hanover."[10]

Although this royal concern for Hanover was hardly popular, most Whigs accepted such outbursts as an inevitable, if unfortunate, consequence of having a king of Great Britain who gave equal weight to his affairs in Germany. During the opening phase of the War of the Austrian Succession, for example, the threat of a combined invasion of Hanover by Prussia and France prompted George II to declare himself officially neutral in his electoral capacity—despite the fact that his British ministers were pledged to defend the Habsburg claim to the imperial crown from the same coalition. Much the same thing happened at the start of the Seven Years' War, when the king's ministers dutifully sent troops and supplies to Hanover even though such resources were badly needed to defend Britain's own embattled outposts in the Atlantic and Mediterranean. Indeed, following the battle of Dettingen, the government was compelled to refute Tory and Patriot Whig reports that the king had taken the field wearing the "yellow sash" of Hanover, that he had shown undue favor to his Hanoverian officers, and that the army had failed to capitalize on the victory out of deference to his fears for the

---

10. E. Neville Williams, ed., *The Eighteenth-Century Constitution, 1688–1815: Documents and Commentary* (Cambridge, 1960), 59; John J. Murray, *George I, the Baltic, and the Whig Split of 1717: A Study in Diplomacy and Propaganda* (Chicago, 1969); Donald Burrows, *Handel* (1994; Oxford, 1996), 71–72, 76–77; George II to Caroline, quoted in Reddaway, "Rivalry for Colonial Power," in Rose et al., eds., *History of the British Empire*, I, 350. Burrows argues that there is no reason to accept accounts of Handel's temporary disgrace by George I; however, the composer's two eighteenth-century chroniclers, John Mainwaring and John Hawkins, both report a brief estrangement, ending with the public performance on the royal barge of *Water Music* in 1717 (Burrows, 76–77). No doubt both authors included the story because it downplayed the German origins of a composer who, by the time of his death in 1759, had metamorphosed into a representative of all that was best in English culture.

FIGURE 9

The H——v——n Confectioner General. *1743. Mocking Whig claims about
George II's courage at Dettingen, a white horse, symbolizing Hanover, rides a
prostrate British lion as mounted Hanoverian officers look on. The German officer
hides behind a tree and boasts that he "has saved our men"—referring to
widespread allegations that the king's electoral troops stayed safely in the rear
while British regular soldiers bore the brunt of the French attack.*
© *The British Museum*

safety of his beloved electorate. The duke of Richmond even complained
that he had been forced to endure the "barbarous and cruel" slight of being offered a rear-facing seat in the royal chaise after the battle. "While
Britain dared France," quipped the earl of Chesterfield, "the monarch
trembled for his Hanover." "*Your* America, *your* lakes, *your* Mr. Amherst
might ruin *you* or make *you* rich" was how the king himself described
these Hanoverian apprehensions to his British ministers, "but in all
events *I* shall be undone."[11]

11. Richmond to Newcastle, Aug. 10, 1743, BL Add. MSS 32,702, 5–8; John Carswell
and Lewis Arnold Dralle, eds., *The Political Journal of George Bubb Dodington* (Oxford,
1965), 203 (entry for Feb. 8, 1753); remarks of George II, as quoted in Reddaway, "Seven
Years' War," in Rose et al., eds., *History of the British Empire*, I, 463.

While the governing Whigs were usually willing to resign themselves to this state of affairs, however, the king's regard for Hanover invariably met with a much harsher reception in Parliament and among the wider public, many of whom saw in the electorate a ready explanation for Britain's otherwise inexplicable involvement in Europe. In the words of a protest lodged in the House of Lords during the spring of 1746, "the undue Influence of foreign Interests" (meaning Hanover) represented one of the chief reasons why Britain had repeatedly been "unnecessarily embroiled in endless Jealousies and Contests, and engaged in impracticable Treaties and fruitless Subsidies." In his *Letters to the People of England* (1755), John Shebbeare went even further, declaring that the accession of George I had reduced the English to the same status "as the Gladiators of old Rome, doomed to sell and sacrifice yourselves for the Entertainment and Advantage of the Elector of Hanover." Indeed, despite the frequently articulated fear that restoring the Catholic Stuarts would make Britain a "province of France," the repeated occasions when Hanoverian needs seemed to dictate British policy helped keep the hopes of James II's exiled heirs alive, at least until the duke of Cumberland's victory at Culloden Moor (1746) ended any realistic chance for a Jacobite coup de main. "Did not the Elector of *Hannover* disdain to wear a *British* Sash on the memorable Day at *Dettingen?*" urged a typical Jacobite broadside during the Rebellion of 1745. As Prince Charles Stuart himself put the issue in his manifesto from Edinburgh's Holyrood Palace: "Who has the better chance to be independent on foreign powers"—a king who was also a "tributary prince" in Germany or "an independent monarch" whose only concern involved the welfare of his British subjects?[12]

For most Britons, of course, this was merely a hypothetical question. However, despite the gradual subsiding of the Jacobite threat, the widespread resentment over George II's loyalty to Hanover ultimately reinforced the growing skepticism about the benefits of using British resources to maintain the balance of power in Europe. There was simply no reason, wrote an anonymous Tory in 1743, for the British to assist their Hanoverian monarch in "seeking the alliance of the Powers on the Continent, nor of prying with too great Eagerness into their Councils,

---

12. *The Lords Protest on a Motion to Address His Majesty for the Keeping Our Forces at Home, Till the Dutch Has Declared War against France* (London, 1746), 7–8; [John Shebbeare], *A Sixth Letter to the People of England, on the Progress of National Ruin . . . ,* 2d ed. (London, 1757), 58; [Britannus], *Considerations Addressed to the Publick* (n.p., 1745), 12; proclamation of Charles Stuart [printed], Dec. 2, 1745, P.R.O., S.P., 36/76/i/78.

Treaties, and Designs." Elsewhere critics like the Whig earl of Chesterfield continued to affirm a British interest in European diplomacy while
nonetheless insisting that the government's efforts in Germany and the
Netherlands had all too often ended up favoring "those foreign Dominions, in which it was . . . a Condition in the Act of Settlement, that we
should have no Concern." Indeed, by the time of Pitt's appointment in
1756, this kind of rhetoric had become so widespread that some Court
Whigs feared that public animosity toward Hanover might prompt the
new ministry to make the grave mistake of attempting to abandon the
Continent altogether. Thanks to the Prussian king's uncanny ability to
wrest glittering triumphs from certain catastrophe, such fears proved
groundless, at least in the short run. Nonetheless, the mounting perception that Hanover represented the sole reason for intervening in the
affairs of Europe helps explain why the popular demand for ending this
involvement seemed so pervasive on the eve of Pitt's elevation to office.[13]

Along with these misgivings over the external effects of Whig foreign
policy, most commentators gave as a final reason for reducing Britain's
involvement in Europe the tendency of such commitments to distort the
course of politics at home. As we have already seen, the Whigs liked to
claim that one benefit of waging war on the Continent was to free the
British people from the sort of sustained political and military vigilance
that would have been necessary to guarantee the stability of a more
vulnerable regime. From the standpoint of the government's Tory and
Patriot Whig critics, however, the indirect, sedentary patriotism that
was the inevitable result of this kind of complacency actually represented
one of the Hanoverian state's greatest potential weaknesses. Not only did
the alleged passivity of the British people make them less able to respond
to a domestic crisis like the Rebellion of 1745, but it also left them
powerless to oppose the "large and dreadful strides" of French ambition
on the high seas, in the "Empire of the Mediterranean," and in Britain's
"Forts and Colonies in America"—as Newcastle vicar John Brown argued in his famous *Estimate* of 1757. Indeed, for both Patriot Whigs
like Brown and Tories who inclined to the views of Lord Bolingbroke,
the "luxurious effeminacy" and "regulated selfishness" that the Court
Whigs' Eurocentric foreign policy seemed to encourage among ordinary
men and women ultimately represented at least as grave a danger to

13. [Philip Dormer Stanhope, fourth earl of Chesterfield], *The Interest of Hanover
Steadily Pursued since the Accession . . .* (London, 1743), 46; [Chesterfield], *The Case of the
Hanover Forces in the Pay of Great-Britain, Impartially and Freely Examined* (London,
1743), 1–2.

Britain's security as the more obvious threat from untrustworthy allies and avowed enemies on the Continent.[14]

There were actually two parts to this criticism of Whig rule. The first of these concerned the way forty years of administering to the needs of Hanover and the European balance of power had distracted Britain's rulers from what ought to have been their primary duty to provide effective government at home. Once again, Bolingbroke played a crucial role in shaping this argument with works like his *Idea of a Patriot King* (1738), the famous panegyric to Frederick, Prince of Wales, in which he sketched the sort of reformist agenda that he expected to attend the accession of a British monarch who shared none of George II's concern for his German electorate. "A Patriot King will neither neglect, nor sacrifice his country's interest," wrote the Tory peer. "No other interest, neither a foreign nor a domestick, neither a public nor a private, will influence his conduct in government." Indeed, both Bolingbroke and his many imitators during the early 1750s envisioned severing—or at least reducing—Britain's ties to Europe as the first stage in a new era of virtuous government, whereby the British would achieve the domestic and imperial prosperity that the Whigs and their Hanoverian masters had supposedly allowed to languish. As Bolingbroke himself described this enticing prospect: "To give ease and encouragement to manufactory at home, to assist and protect trade abroad, to improve and keep in heart the national colonies, like so many farms of the mother country, will be principal and constant parts of the attention of such a prince." Freed from the burden of needless wars and endless negotiations on the Continent, Britain would at long last become the world's preeminent maritime power, as content at home as it was feared and respected abroad.[15]

14. [John Brown], *An Estimate of the Manners and Principles of the Times,* 2d ed. (London, 1757), 143.

15. Bolingbroke, *The Idea of a Patriot King,* in *Works of Bolingbroke,* II, 416. Bolingbroke's general influence among both Tories and Patriot Whigs during the later 1740s and 1750s is the subject of a large literature, but see esp. J. G. A. Pocock, *The Machiavellian Moment: Florentine Political Thought and the Atlantic Republican Tradition* (Princeton, N.J., 1975), 424–496, 507–531; Pocock, "The Varieties of Whiggism from Exclusion to Reform: A History of Ideology and Discourse," in Pocock, *Virtue, Commerce, and History: Essays on Political Thought and History, Chiefly in the Eighteenth Century* (Cambridge, 1985), 240–253; J. C. D. Clark, *English Society, 1688–1832: Ideology, Social Structure, and Political Practice during the Ancien Regime* (Cambridge, 1985), 179–185; Eliga H. Gould, "To Strengthen the King's Hands: Dynastic Legitimacy, Militia Reform, and Ideas of National Unity in England, 1745–1760," *Historical Jour-*

Although Bolingbroke was notoriously vague about the specific measures that he expected a patriot ruler—or minister—to implement, those who invoked his ideas frequently betrayed a decidedly paternalistic bent, one that was often tinged with a surpising admiration for the superior efficiency of absolutist states like Prussia and France. Indeed, among the more striking features of this opposition rhetoric was the willingness of many Tories and Patriot Whigs to countenance measures that seemed to threaten the negative liberty that most Court Whigs took as the benchmark of their rule. In his tract on patriotic kingship, for example, Bolingbroke claimed that his final desire was to see the "intimate" blending of "things so seldom allied as empire and liberty." Elsewhere, self-styled patriots linked the accession of a virtuous ruler with intrusive measures like the reformation of manners and the closer policing of crime and domestic unrest. As the Patriot Whig George Lyttleton put the issue in his *Letter to the Tories* (1747), the ministers in such an administration "might, without any danger, exert with spirit and vigour the full power of legal government, check and even suppress the infamous licence of the press . . . whet the blunted sword of justice, and make all disloyal subjects feel or fear the edge of it." In a development ripe with potential problems, the mid-1750s even witnessed a sudden burst of interest in finding new ways to mobilize the military and fiscal resources of Britain's North American colonies, with one of the more popular proposals involving taxes raised by authority of Parliament.[16]

Such unsettling ideas were an important—and, from the standpoint of modern scholarship, much neglected—part of the rhetoric that helped make the Whigs' concern for Europe seem increasingly untenable at the start of the Seven Years' War. What gave Pitt's appointment the appearance of a popular mandate, however, was the second, more libertarian part of this Tory and Patriot Whig critique, which held that

---

nal, XXXIV (1991), 329–348; David Armitage, "A Patriot for Whom? The Afterlives of Bolingbroke's *Patriot King*," *Journal of British Studies*, XXXVI (1997), 397–418.

16. Bolingbroke, *Idea of a Patriot King*, in *Works of Bolingbroke*, II, 428; [George Lyttleton], *A Letter to the Tories* (London, 1747), 17. John Brown was quite explicit in his respect for France (*An Estimate of Manners*, 143–144), and Frederick II of Prussia received praise as an appropriate ally in *An Appeal to the Sense of the People, on the Present Posture of Affairs* . . . (London, 1756), 11–12; see also Malachy Postlethwayt, *Great-Britain's True System* . . . (London, 1757), cxlii–cl; John Leland, *Serious Reflections on the Present State of Things in These Nations* (London, 1758), ix–x. The proposals for imperial reform, including taxing the American colonists, are discussed more fully later in this chapter.

withdrawing from Europe would enable Britain's rulers to implement domestic reforms like abolishing the hated game laws and decreasing the size of the regular army. Of these promised reforms, none appeared more popular than the assurance that reducing Britain's involvement on the Continent would end the practice of using foreign troops to defend England's own coasts from invasion. Not only did the presence of such forces on British soil look like a sure sign that the government was bent on depriving the king's loyal subjects of the means to defend themselves, but there were also more than a few among the government's opponents who claimed that placing such heavy reliance on the soldiers of allies like Denmark, the Dutch Republic, Hesse-Cassel, and—of course—Hanover was tantamount to courting a foreign occupation. Even though the use of such auxiliaries required the approval of Parliament, who was to say that they might not someday make Britain a "province" of the same kind of European confederacy that Bolingbroke had cautioned against forty years before?[17]

For many people during the summer of 1756, the presence of Hessian and Hanoverian troops on the coast of Kent lent fresh validity to such fears. Coupled with the debacles in North America and the Mediterranean, the ministry's employment of German auxiliaries suggested at the very least that the Whigs' long history of catering to the whims of even the most insignificant states on the Continent had left them incapable of protecting Britain's legitimate maritime and colonial interests. For many patriots, though, the presence of so many troops on the southern coast of England conjured up still darker fears of a deliberate betrayal of the British people—what a contributor to the *London Evening Post* termed "a certain Event of the Treachery, Negligence, or Incapacity of those who were entrusted with Power." One pamphleteer even warned that the Whigs' inexplicable and unjustifiable concern for events in Germany might lead the British to attempt "an Insurrection . . . on the Account of so much of their Money being spent in [Hanover's] Defence, whilst . . . their own Affairs are but little minded." There were not many readers

17. The libertarian dimensions of Pitt's program—at home as well as abroad—are treated fully in Peters, *Pitt and Popularity*, 24–31, and Peters, "The *Monitor* on the Constitution, 1755–1765: New Light on the Ideological Origins of English Radicalism," *English Historical Review*, LXXXVI (1971), 706–727. See also Langford, "William Pitt and Public Opinion, 1757," *English Historical Review*, LXXXVIII (1973), 54–79; Colley, *In Defiance of Oligarchy*, chap. 10; Wilson, *Sense of the People*, chap. 3; Robert Donald Spector, *English Literary Periodicals and the Climate of Opinion during the Seven Years' War* (The Hague, 1966), chap. 1.

who would have missed the implied threat in John Shebbeare's question of why "the Sons of those who placed William on the throne of England" in 1689 should now passively entrust their welfare to a cabal of corrupt ministers, backed by an army of "Russian Savages and German Bloodsuckers."[18]

Such allegations certainly did not go unanswered. But the most striking feature of the uproar over the use of German troops was the ministry's apparent powerlessness in the face of this onslaught. As the controversy ran its course, Whig apologists mounted a concerted defense of Continental strategies while the government initiated proceedings that eventually resulted in prosecutions against the most flamboyant polemicists, including John Shebbeare and Joseph Shepheard, a London printer charged with distributing a tract entitled *German Cruelty* in order to influence the jury in a case involving one of the last remaining rights of way through the royal deer park at Richmond. But the Whigs' longstanding insistence on Britain's interest in expending its own military and financial resources on the Continent was increasingly difficult to maintain. Indeed, the ministry proved unable to prevent Pitt and his supporters from organizing hostile addresses in such bastions of Whig loyalism as Norwich, Bristol, and Yorkshire. In the words of the address from Yorkshire, Britain's misfortunes in the war with France stemmed entirely from the government's "servile dependence" on Hanover and its pursuit of "foreign and pernicious" measures like the domestic employment of German mercenaries and the creation of an "enlarged public debt" in order to support its allies in Europe. As an anonymous informer warned at the end of August, seditious publications like Shebbeare's *Letters to the People of England* and the Beckford brothers' *Monitor* "are readily devoured by the people in general." It is hardly surprising that the duke of Newcastle—the Whig prime minister who had served in nearly

18. *A Constituent's Answer to the Reflexions of a Member of Parliament upon the Present State of Affairs at Home and Abroad*... (1755; London, 1756), 15–17; *London Evening Post* (Aug. 24–26, 1756), quoted in Wilson, *Sense of the People*, 183 (the passage quoted is also discussed for possible prosecution as seditious libel in Sharpe to Newcastle, Aug. 28, 1756, BL Add. MSS 32,867, 135–136); *England's Warning; or, The Copy of a Letter, from a Hanoverian Officer, in England, to His Brother, in Hanover*. . . . (London, [1756]), 4; [John Shebbeare], "Letter III: On Liberty, Taxes, and the Application of the Public Money," in *Three Letters to the People of England*, 6th ed. (London, 1756), 71. The allusion is to the treaties that George II negotiated with Russia and Hesse-Cassel to protect Hanover during the summer of 1755. The first edition of the pamphlet appeared in response to the ensuing controversy in Parliament and the press.

every government since the accession of George I—wondered how long it would be before "the violence without doors" came "within."[19]

Historians generally agree that the diplomatic changes that the start of the Seven Years' War produced in Britain's relations with Europe turned out to be nothing short of "revolutionary," with the Prussian alliance enabling the government to abandon its historic commitment to Austria's preeminence in Germany and to concentrate instead on the nation's own commercial and imperial interests in the Atlantic and Asia. As an indication of these changes, Newcastle resigned as the king's first minister at the end of October 1756. Although he returned to power the following spring and eventually served as an equal partner in William Pitt's second ministry (1757–1761), the war on the Continent clearly represented nothing more than an expedient of diminishing importance. By the fall of 1756, even Newcastle had become convinced that the course of events—at home as much as abroad—had left the British no choice but to prosecute a blue water war against France without regard either to expense or the likely consequences in Europe. To be sure, British troops continued to help protect Hanover's western flank from the armies of France, and Pitt himself would eventually boast to the House of Commons that the victories that secured Britain's conquests in North America had been won on the plains of Germany. But no one doubted which strategy mattered more. "Ungrateful Germany," insisted Yorkshire's predominantly Whig freeholders in their address of 1756, had long been "the sepulchre of British interest." As a Tory commentator expressed the point three years later, "Germany is not only . . . the Gulph of our Treasures, but the grave of our People." "Let Nature, as well as Politicks, deter us from this Land of Slaves."[20]

---

19. *King v. Joseph Shepheard*, King's Bench, Feb. 20, 1758, P.R.O., T.S. 11/347/1083 (Shepheard was also charged with printing and circulating a pamphlet with the title *A Tract on the National Interest, and Depravity of the Times . . . Being a Supplement to German Cruelty* [London, 1757], the first five pages of which summarized the arguments against the Whigs' alleged Hanoverian bias); Wilson, *Sense of the People*, 182–185; "Yorkshire Address," quoted in John Entick, *The General History of the Late War . . .* , 5 vols. (London, 1763–1764), I, 426–428; anon. letter from "E. F.," Warwickshire, Aug. 21, 1756, P.R.O., S.P. 36/135/191–192; Newcastle to Hardwicke, Aug. 28, 1756, BL Add. MSS 32,867, 111–122.

20. Newcastle to Fox, July 24, 1756, BL Add. MSS 51,379, 30–31; "Yorkshire Address," in Entick, *History of the Late War*, I, 426–428; *The Honest Grief of a Tory, Expressed in a Genuine Letter from a Burgess of ——, in Wiltshire, to the Author of the Monitor, Feb. 17, 1759* (London, 1759), 20–21.

II. OCEANS, INDIANS, AND COLONISTS

This hostility to the Whigs' involvements in Europe certainly helps explain why the British greeted William Pitt's commitment to the campaigns in North America and the West Indies with such overwhelming approval after 1756. But it was by no means the only reason for this shift in emphasis. According to many of the new ministry's Tory and Patriot Whig supporters, the case for withdrawing from the Continent had at least as much to do with Britain's perceived ability to destroy France's own maritime and colonial power—and at far less cost than the European strategies favored by the Court Whigs. Not only was Britain's Atlantic empire a place of extraordinary wealth, but the British were increasingly aware of the strategic possibilities of a burgeoning settler population in North America of some three million inhabitants, many of whom shared their own desire to humble France. Furthermore, most Britons also assumed that they were free to exploit these imperial advantages without having to worry about the sorts of moral and legal considerations that constrained the actions of even the most powerful states on the Continent. Of course, Britain's imperial potential often seemed to be just that—a tremendous source of wealth and strength that decades of Whig neglect had kept the British from developing to the full. Even so, when Tory and Patriot Whig writers directed their gaze out to the Atlantic during the early 1750s, most saw one more reason why it finally seemed possible to disengage from the costly wars and European alliances that had been the legacy of so many uninterrupted decades of Whig governance, and a chance to achieve the lasting victory over France that had eluded Britain since the great struggles against Louis XIV.

One reason for this conviction involved long-standing assumptions that Britain's demonstrated success as a maritime power made it especially well situated to acquire what poet Richard Glover styled a "boundless empire" on the high seas and in the entrepôts that adjoined them. As the British were well aware, their dominion of the sea was hardly an empire in the conventional sense of the word. Although Parliament claimed jurisdiction over the commodities that British ships conveyed around the world, jurists regarded the ocean over which this traffic passed as a global common governed by the universal laws of nature rather than by the laws of any state in particular. In fact, the only place outside the British Isles where the government enjoyed anything like full imperial sovereignty was in the ports and along the shores of its overseas

FIGURE 10

Power of Great Britain by Land *and* Power of Great Britain by Sea. *Attributed
to James Thornhill. Early 18th century. In the painting above, a captive is brought
in chains before Britannia, who prepares to free him, symbolizing Britain's
military efforts in Europe. The painting on the right shows Britannia*

colonies. In other words, Britain's supremacy over what Whig authors
John Trenchard and Thomas Gordon aptly termed "that coy element"
was tenuous and provisional. Polemicists might boast that "Britannia
ruled the waves," but most recognized that the dominion that sustained
such extensive claims had far more to do with the competitive advantages that British merchants and privateers had managed to wrest from
their European rivals over the last century—and that they might just as
easily lose—than it did with any recognizable legal right.[21]

21. *London; or, The Progress of Commerce* (1738?), quoted in Richard Koebner, *Empire*
(Cambridge, 1961), 83; John Trenchard and Thomas Gordon, "Trade and Naval Power
the Offspring of Civil Liberty and Cannot Subsist without It" (Feb. 3, 1721), in Trenchard and Gordon, *Cato's Letters, or Essays on Liberty, Civil and Religious, and Other
Important Subjects*, 2 vols., ed. Ronald Hamowy (1755; Indianapolis, 1995), I, 449. For an

*and Neptune looking on as a British warship destroys an enemy vessel. The
paintings distinguish Britain's limited objectives in Europe from its boundless
ambition at sea and in its colonies. Courtesy of the Yale Center for British Art,
Paul Mellon Collection*

If the British admitted that the ocean they aspired to rule represented
an inherently lawless, brutally competitive realm, most of those who
joined the chorus demanding a blue water strategy in 1756 were convinced that they had far less to dread from its ungovernable nature than
any other state in Europe, including both France and Spain. This was
partly because of the seemingly limitless wealth generated by Britain's
prodigious maritime commerce. As Voltaire had noted nearly thirty
years before:

---

especially insightful analysis of the British "mercantile system," see Daniel Baugh,
"Maritime Strength and Atlantic Commerce: The Uses of 'a Grand Marine Empire,'"
in Lawrence Stone, ed., *An Imperial State at War: Britain from 1689 to 1815* (London,
1994), 185–223.

Posterity will perhaps learn with surprise that a small island which has no resources of its own except a little lead, some tin, some fuller's earth and coarse wool has through its commerce become powerful enough to send, in 1723, at one and the same time, three fleets to three extremities of the world, one before Gibraltar, conquered and held by its forces, another to Porto-Bello to cut off the treasures of the Indies from the King of Spain, and the third into the Baltic to prevent the Northern Powers from fighting.

Even writers who doubted the benefits of overseas expansion recognized that the wealth that came from Britain's impressive seaborne trade was one of the principal reasons why its rulers had become the masters of a maritime dominion without historical parallel. In the words of Trenchard and Gordon's *Cato's Letters* (1720–1723), trade and credit, when properly managed, "will turn deserts into fruitful fields, villages into great cities, cottages into palaces, beggars into princes, convert cowards into heroes, blockheads into philosophers; will change the coverings of little worms into the richest brocades, the fleeces of harmless sheep into the pride and ornaments of kings, and by a further metamorphosis will transmute them again into armed hosts and haughty fleets."[22]

The British were mindful that they also owed their command of the sea to the simple fact that they possessed the largest, most formidable navy in Europe. During the final years of the War of the Austrian Succession, for example, the Royal Navy achieved a series of stunning victories in the North Atlantic, giving rise to widespread expectations that Britain would be able to use its undisputed command of the seas to compensate for the inability of its allies to check the dramatic conquests that France's armies had made in the Netherlands. "I believe no body will deny," predicted a typically confident polemicist in 1747, "but that our own commerce is in a thriving Way, and the *French* on the decline; nor that it is in our Power, with very moderate Care and Skill, to entirely ruin that of *France*." As the Grub Street journalist William Horsley explained in the *Daily Gazetteer* of January 2, 1748, "Two great points to be considered in this war, are the preservation of our Trade, and Ruin of that of the Enemy." That France abandoned its conquests in the Netherlands during the peace conference at Aix-la-Chapelle certainly did nothing to dampen these expectations. As an observer put matters in 1749, only "our Indolence, our Inattention, our Want of Publick Spirit,

22. Voltaire, *Letters on England* (1733), trans. and ed. Leonard Tancock (New York, 1980), 51; "Trade and Naval Power," in Trenchard and Gordon, *Cato's Letters*, ed. Hamowy, I, 442–443.

can prevent us from reaping such Advantages as . . . offer themselves to our View, and our Possession."[23]

Indeed, the paeans to blue water empire that inundated the metropolitan press during the later 1740s and 1750s frequently betrayed a kind of buccaneering exhilaration over the way the abstract goals and treaty obligations that the British felt compelled to honor in Europe had little bearing on their operations at sea. For example, it was not unusual for British pamphleteers to urge the government to grant wider scope not just to the navy's own raids on enemy shipping but to the activities of privateers as well. Even the dubious wartime practice of searching neutral ships for enemy goods received virtually no comment in the metropolitan press, although it was widely resented by the other maritime powers of Europe. When Frederick II of Prussia raised the issue in 1753, the British Solicitor General, William Murray—soon to be elevated to the bench as Lord Mansfield—responded predictably enough that the government was well within its rights by permitting such activities. British patriots liked to think that the ultimate goal of such high-handed policies was to make the oceans safe for peaceful commerce. But they were equally sure that the sea belonged to whichever power could master it. "Let your Navies prove that France can be humbled without mercenary Assistance," insisted John Shebbeare in 1755. In the words of another pamphlet, Britain was "the only country in the world" whose power could "never be subverted" by anyone but its own people: "We are, of any nation, the best situated for trade; we are the best-provided with good harbours; and we have all the conveniences necessary to become the general mart of the world, and to prescribe laws upon the ocean; whereon, did we only exert our power, we are capable of giving maritime laws to the world." Given this extraordinary potential, any minister who refused to make Britain's maritime power his chief concern had to be guilty of serious negligence, if not outright treason.[24]

23. *The State of the Nation Consider'd, in a Letter to a Member of Parliament* (London, [1748]), 50 (the pamphlet went through a total of four editions within the first year of publication); *Daily Gazetteer* (Jan. 2, 1747/8), quoted in Robert Harris, *A Patriot Press: National Politics and the London Press in the 1740s* (Oxford, 1993), 221; *Miscellaneous Reflections upon the Peace, and Its Consequences* (London, 1749), 33. Despite such popular assumptions, it is actually not clear whether Britain's naval supremacy played much of a role in forcing France to come to terms; see M. S. Anderson, *The War of the Austrian Succession, 1740–1748*, 189; Langford, *Polite and Commercial People*, 209–210.

24. Percy E. Corbett, *Law in Diplomacy* (1959; Gloucester, Mass., 1967), 30–31; [Shebbeare], "Letter II: On Foreign Subsidies, Subsidiary Armies, and Their Consequences to This Nation," in *Three Letters to the People of England*, 62; [J. Payne], *The*

In voicing their support for the war at sea, of course, the British were also calling for a war with an important territorial dimension, especially in North America. Because of the emphasis that they placed on maritime strategies, imperial advocates of Bolingbroke's generation had often paid scant attention to the mainland colonies, thinking instead of the sugar islands in the West Indies as the more important and indispensable of the crown's American possessions. During both the War of the Austrian Succession and the Seven Years' War, however, Britain and France came into conflict along a vast, inland arc stretching from the western reaches of Virginia to the mouth of the Saint Lawrence River. Indeed, by the time Pitt formed his first administration in November 1756, the two powers had been waging an undeclared war in this region for over two years, with Britain, in particular, making unprecedented commitments in the form of several thousand regular soldiers and subsidies for nearly as many provincial troops. Because of setbacks like General Edward Braddock's disastrous attempt to capture Fort Duquesne in western Pennsylvania (1755), the British had little to show for their efforts on the eve of Pitt's appointment, but there was no denying that their bid for maritime dominion was also one for a swath of territory "greater than a fourth part of Europe," as Samuel Johnson exclaimed to readers of the *Literary Magazine*.[25]

That this territorial dimension did nothing to diminish public sup-

---

French Encroachments Exposed; or, Britain's Original Right to All That Part of the American Continent Claimed by France Fully Asserted . . . (London, 1756), 26–27. On the question of neutral rights, see Corbett, *Law in Diplomacy*, 139–140; A. Pearce Higgins, "The Growth of International Law, Maritime Rights, and Colonial Titles," in Rose et al., eds., *History of the British Empire*, I, 547–558; John B. Hattendorf, "Maritime Conflict," in Michael Howard et al., eds., *The Laws of War: Constraints on Warfare in the Western World* (New Haven, Conn., 1994), 106–107.

25. Samuel Johnson, "Review of Lewis Evans, Analysis of a General Map of the Middle British Colonies in America," *Literary Magazine*, I, no. 6 (Sept. 15–Oct. 15, 1756), in Donald J. Greene, ed., *Political Writings* (New Haven, Conn., 1977), 210–211, vol. X of *The Yale Edition of the Works of Samuel Johnson*. The growing importance of the North American mainland in British thinking is discussed in Baugh, "Maritime Strength and Atlantic Commerce," in Stone, ed., *An Imperial State at War*, 210–212; see also Kurt William Nagel, "Empire and Interest: British Colonial Defense Policy, 1689–1748" (Ph.D. diss., Johns Hopkins University, 1992). For the early phase of the Seven Years' War in North America, see Stanley McCrory Pargellis, *Lord Loudoun in North America* (New Haven, Conn., 1933); Lawrence Henry Gipson, *The British Empire before the American Revolution* (New York, 1936–1970), VI, *The Years of Defeat, 1754–1757;* Ian K. Steele, *Betrayals: Fort William Henry and the "Massacre"* (Oxford, 1990).

port for the maritime war with France reflected two related perceptions. First, most people thought of the land beyond the Appalachian Mountains as a region whose indigenous inhabitants enjoyed only limited rights under the European law of nations. As a result, British polemicists tended to envision much of North America in the same way that they did the waters of the Atlantic, that is, as a zone where the government did not need to worry about the finer points of treaties or international law. To be sure, relations with the Native Americans often entailed a complex process of negotiation where both imperial agents and indigenous leaders had to make all sorts of accommodations and compromises. Nonetheless, the metropolitan depiction of Britain's encounters on this "middle ground" invariably emphasized the superiority and unilateral nature of the government's position. At times, the resulting impression was devastatingly negative, as in Samuel Johnson's comment in 1756 likening the contest between Britain and France in the Ohio Valley to "the quarrel of two robbers for the spoils of a passenger." On other occasions, publicists used relations with the Indians as a way to underscore the benevolent effects of extending British power over the whole region. In an early manifestation of this tendency, English poet Thomas Tickell recalled the sensational London visit of the four Mohawk "kings" in 1710 as a clear example of Britain's determination "to teach th'untam'd barbarian laws":

> Did not the painted kings of India greet
> Our Queen and lay their sceptres at her feet . . .
> Her pitying smile accepts their suppliant claim,
> And adds four monarchs to Christian name.

Likewise, evangelical ventures like the Anglican Society for the Propagation of the Gospel derived much of their domestic support from the widespread assumption that the inhabitants of the North American interior represented empty vessels waiting to be filled by the Church of England's version of the Christian message.[26]

---

26. Samuel Johnson, "Observations on the Present State of Affairs," *Literary Magazine*, no. 4 (July 15–Aug. 15, 1756), in Greene, ed., *Political Writings*, 188, vol. X of *Works of Samuel Johnson; The Prospects of Peace* (1712), quoted in Koebner, *Empire*, 94. More work needs to be done on British perceptions of Indians, but see Eric Hinderaker, "The 'Four Indian Kings' and the Imaginative Construction of the First British Empire," *William and Mary Quarterly*, 3rd Ser., LIII (1996), 487–526. For encounters between British and Indians in America, see James Axtell, *The Invasion Within: The Contest of Cultures in Colonial North America* (Oxford, 1985); James H. Merrell, "'The

But whatever view writers took of such interactions, the important point was that they occurred in a hypothetical "state of nature," a wild, untamed interior where the British believed themselves free to prosecute the war with France with the same moral and legal impunity that they enjoyed on the high seas. This is not to suggest that North America represented a place entirely devoid of legal standards, since commentators usually regarded the competing territorial claims of France and Spain as sufficiently legitimate to merit rebuttal, often in the form of lengthy references to boundaries set by earlier treaties or rights established by explorers like Henry Cabot and Sir Francis Drake. But when it came to dealings with the continent's indigenous peoples, these same writers acknowledged almost no constraints on Britain's actions, or rather none beyond considerations of expediency and whatever principles the British voluntarily chose to respect. "*America*," read a typical discussion in 1755, "is divided between the *English, French* and Natives; the latter possessing very little, as to Power, Riches—but much as to Extent of Land—a natural Consequence of their Strength being absorbed by the other two potent Adversaries." Another pamphleteer observed of Britain's final triumph in 1761:

> Our Conquests in the present War can never create any Rivalship, much less endanger our Independency.—they are so remote, and divided from all Connections with this Part of the World, that they cannot stir up any reasonable Jealousy in our Neighbours, by giving us either Power or Inclination to disturb them, as Conquests in *Europe* would naturally do.

Whatever rights jurists conceded to its native inhabitants, North America was, from the standpoint of European diplomacy, *terra nullius*— empty space that the British might conquer and govern according to their own notions of justice.[27]

Customes of Our Countrey': Indians and Colonists in Early America," in Bernard Bailyn and Philip D. Morgan, eds., *Strangers within the Realm: Cultural Margins of the First British Empire* (Chapel Hill, N.C., 1991), 117–156; Richard White, *The Middle Ground: Indians, Empires, and Republics in the Great Lakes Region, 1650–1815* (Cambridge, 1991); Eric Hinderaker, *Elusive Empires: Constructing Colonialism in the Ohio Valley, 1673–1800* (Cambridge, 1997).

27. *A Letter from a Member of Parliament to . . . the Duke of —— upon the Present Situation of Affairs* (London, 1755), 16; *The Crisis; or, Considerations on the Present State of Affairs . . .* (London, 1761), 11. For the breadth of British territorial claims, which often included legal title to the entire continent of North America, see *The Conduct of*

In many ways, this perception was deeply ironic, for the vast, un-charted character of the Indian territory between the Great Lakes and the Ohio and Mississippi Rivers would shortly provide one of the central reasons for keeping British troops in North America and taxing the colonists to support them. Indeed, there were some observers during the 1750s who regarded the sheer extent of this disputed wilderness as cause for concern. "The Idea of securing yourself, only by having no other Nation near you," wrote Edmund Burke's cousin William in 1760, "[is] an idea of *American* Extraction. It is the genuine Policy of Savages; and it is owing to this Policy, that *England* and *France* are able at this Day to dispute the Sovereignty of Deserts in *America;* to which neither of us would otherwise have had any right." Yet for most commentators, the prospect of a successful war in the North American interior promised to place Britain's Atlantic empire on a far more durable foundation than any previous government had ever been able to achieve. Far from antic-ipating the difficulties likely to attend such extensive conquests, most Britons saw the war in North America as a justifiable action over unoc-cupied territory that was theirs to govern as they saw fit. "Tho' the Country of *Canada* be neither the Property of the *French* nor of *Britain* on the Principle of original Right," one pamphleteer wrote following the capture of Quebec, "Experience" showed that "it should now be ours by Right of Security."[28]

The second reason for the popularity of the war in North America involved the heightened expectations that characterized British thinking about the colonies on the eastern seaboard. As historians have often

---

the *Ministry Impartially Examined: In a Letter to the Merchants of London* (London, 1756), 3–24; *Considerations on the Importance of Canada, and the Bay and River of St. Lawrence* (London, 1759).

28. [William Burke], *Remarks on the Letter Address'd to Two Great Men: In a Letter to the Author of That Piece* (London, [1760]), 27; *A Candid and Fair Examination of the Remarks on the Letter to Two Great Men...*, 2d ed. (London, 1760), 9. On the perceived "defensive" nature of the American strategy advocated by both the Newcastle-Fox ministry and William Pitt, see Richard Middleton, *The Bells of Victory: The Pitt-Newcastle Ministry and the Conduct of the Seven Years' War, 1757–1762*, (Cambridge, 1985), intro., chap. 1; Baugh, "Maritime Strength and Atlantic Commerce," in Stone, ed., *An Imperial State at War*, 211–213; W. A. Speck, "The International and Imperial Context," in Jack P. Greene and J. R. Pole, eds., *Colonial British America: Essays in the New History of the Early Modern Era* (Baltimore, 1984), 384–407. But see O. A. Sher-rard, *Lord Chatham: Pitt and the Seven Years' War* (1955; Westport, Conn., 1975), 74–76, 172–175, who emphasizes Pitt's early commitment to taking Quebec. The decision to leave British regulars in North America is discussed in Chapter 4, below.

noted, the expanding potential of Britain's North American colonies was slow to impress itself on the metropolitan public. Upon receiving a report during the opening phase of the Seven Years' War, for example, the duke of Newcastle, who had spent most of his career overseeing the disposition of patronage in the colonies, is alleged to have exclaimed: "Annapolis, Annapolis! oh! yes, Annapolis must be defended; to be sure Annapolis should be defended—where is Annapolis?" By the time Newcastle uttered these words, however, his lack of knowledge was sufficiently unusual to merit specific comment and ridicule. Not only were the colonies well established in the public mind as growing and integral parts of Britain's own prosperity, but the British were also increasingly aware of their strategic potential. Ellis Huske, the New Hampshire merchant and publisher of the *Boston Post-Boy*, was invoking a familiar refrain when he explained to British readers in 1755:

> It is from the American colonies our Royal Navy is supplied in a great Measure with Masts of all Sizes and other Naval Stores . . . ; it is from them our Men of War in the American World are on any Occasion man'd, and our Troops there augmented and recruited; it is from them we have most of our Silver and Gold either by their Trade with Foreigners in America, or by the Way of Spain, Portugal, and Italy. . . . Consider then, if you ought not to direct the whole of your Counsels and Arms to support a War, wherein, with the Being of your State, you assert the Dignity of your Reputation, the Safety of your Friends, the best Branches of your Revenue, and the Properties of your Fellow Subjects.[29]

Once again, the latter stages of the War of the Austrian Succession, when British arms threatened to sweep France from Canada and the North Atlantic, played an important role in strengthening the general public's awareness of these immense strategic advantages. Indeed, dur-

---

29. Horace Walpole, *Memoirs of King George II*, ed. John Brooke, 3 vols. (London, 1985), II, 16; [Ellis Huske], *The Present State of North-America, Etc.*, 2d ed. (London, 1755), 56–58. This pamphlet is sometimes attributed to Huske's brother and to his son, both of whom were named John Huske; see the discussion of Huske's role as a newspaperman in Charles E. Clark, *The Public Prints: The Newspaper in Anglo-American Culture, 1665–1740* (Oxford, 1994), 162, 166, 188, 199, 203. For Britain's growing awareness of its Atlantic empire, see Wilson, *Sense of the People*, chap. 3; Nagel, "Empire and Interest"; Jacob M. Price, "Who Cared about the Colonies? The Impact of the Thirteen Colonies on British Society and Politics, circa 1714–1775," in Bailyn and Morgan, eds., *Strangers within the Realm*, 395–436.

ing the summer of 1745—at roughly the same moment when Charles Stuart was summoning the clans to his standard in Scotland and the armies of Louis XV were consolidating their position in the Netherlands—a force of New England provincials organized by the governor of Massachusetts, William Shirley, commanded by Kittery merchant William Pepperell, and supported by a British squadron under Admiral Peter Warren, managed to capture Louisbourg, the principal French citadel on Cape Breton Island at the mouth of the Saint Lawrence River. To the dismay of patriots on both sides of the Atlantic, Britain's emissaries at Aix-la-Chapelle agreed to return the fortress, giving rise to predictable denunciations of the Whig ministry's readiness to permit "that valuable Acquisition . . . [to] fall a Sacrifice to the Ambition or Avarice of our Allies." Nonetheless, the effect of using the strategic superiority that the New Englanders had gained in the North Atlantic to reverse France's conquests in the Netherlands provided incontrovertible evidence that one expedition by Britain's American colonists had achieved what nearly a decade of supporting the Whigs' allies in Europe had not. As Governor Shirley recollected in 1757, the provincial forces that captured Cape Breton had "accelerated the Extinction of a most expensive War to *Great Britain*," and, as such, deserved a good deal of the credit "for restoring . . . the public Tranquillity of Europe."[30]

By the start of the Seven Years' War, this interest in North America's strategic potential had developed to the point where some commentators were even beginning to think of the crescent of settlements stretching from Georgia to New Hampshire as a possible substitute for the grand alliances that the Whigs had maintained since the Glorious Revolution. Not surprisingly, this was an argument that New Englanders like William Shirley and Ellis Huske tended to make with particular vigor. As Huske insisted in 1755, the Cape Breton expedition demonstrated that, even if "we and our Allies should be beat and distressed upon the

---

30. *The Groans of B——n; or, A Pathetical Display of the Many Hardships, Miseries, and Oppressions to Which This Distressed Nation is Become Subjected . . .* (London, [1747?]), 14; [William Shirley], *Memoirs of the Principal Transactions of the Last War between the English and French in North America* (London, 1757), vii. For more on the British sense of Cape Breton's importance, see *Considerations on the State of the British Fisheries in America, and Their Consequence to Great Britain . . .* (London, 1745); [Philip Durell], *A Particular Account of the Taking Cape Breton from the French, by Admiral Warren, and Sir William Pepperell, the Seventeenth of June, 1745* (London, 1745); *The Importance of Cape Breton to the British Nation . . .* (London, 1745); [Sir William Pepperrell, bart.], *An Accurate Journal and Account of the Proceedings of the New-England Land-Forces . . .* (Exeter, 1746).

FIGURE 11

The Congress of the Brutes. *1748. Satirizing the Treaty of Aix-la-Chapelle,*
the principal belligerents quarrel over the spoils of war; only the lion (Britain) is
willing to continue sacrificing for the common cause, in this case by returning
Cape Breton to France. © *The British Museum*

Continent of Europe, it is only [by] giving up some one or other of our
Conquests in America . . . [that] we may whenever we please, or the
general State of Europe requires it, reconcile jarring Interests and purchase Repose." Although such views were especially well suited to the
colonists' needs, plenty of people in Britain agreed that supporting the
efforts of their fellow subjects in North America was far preferable to
"trusting to the *Inactivity* of *subsidiary Armies*" in Europe. As one pamphleteer put matters, protecting "our Colonies" and relying on "ourselves" represented the surest way to guarantee that Britain was "never
again . . . deceived with false insignificant Quotas, and treacherous and
evasive Embassies." Ever the controversialist, John Shebbeare made a
similar point in the fourth of his *Letters to the People of England,* praising
the efforts of the provincial troops that accompanied General Braddock
on his march against Fort Duquesne in 1755. In a probable reference to
the capture of Fort Beauséjour in Nova Scotia, Shebbeare also noted that
"the only Advantages" won during the dismal campaigns of the beginning of the Seven Years' War had been "effected by a General, unknown

to the B——sh Minister, and a Militia of Americans, and by an Expedition planned by the Provinces of New England."[31]

Of course, the notion of using a colonial war to disengage altogether from European political affairs represented an untenable position, one that Pitt himself was quick to disavow upon assuming office at the end of 1756. Nonetheless, the imperial unity upon which these hopes rested provides some revealing clues to the benefits that the British expected to realize from the war in North America. First and foremost, the metropolitan public—or at least those men and women who affected to speak for it—seemed sure that aiding the mainland colonies would enhance the prosperity of the empire as a whole. Indeed, many commentators went so far as to claim that the massive subsidies and military supplies that Parliament began approving for the American theater from 1756 onward would further the oceanic trade that was so essential to maintaining Britain's command of the sea. Thus a pamphleteer noted during the summer of 1756 that the Americans' place among Britain's principal trading partners meant that the colonial dimensions of the war could "be carried on . . . at as little Expence as a Russian Subsidy, but with a very different kind of profit." As Shebbeare explained, "whatever is expended in the Defence of English plantations, returns to England again." In the words of another observer:

> Our plantations . . . in North America, are very extensive, and as good a country as any in the world. Whatever expences we are at, in keeping and defending [them], are so far from being a loss to us, that . . . what money is laid out this way, may be considered as expended all among ourselves, as it will return to us with Double interest; the consequences to us are not like those of a war in Europe, for, in that case, we send men and money that never return to us.[32]

---

31. [Huske], *Present State*, 62–63; *Answer to the Reflexions of a Member of Parliament*, 11; *The Parallel; or, The Conduct and Fate of Great Britain in regard to Our Present Contest with France: Exemplified from the Histories of Macedon and Athens . . .* (London, 1756), 43; [John Shebbeare], *A Fourth Letter to the People of England on the Conduct of the M——rs, in Alliances, Fleets, and Armies . . .*, 6th ed. (London, 1756), 11–12.

32. "Speech by King George II on Opening the Session of Parliament, 2 December 1756," in Wiener, ed., *Great Britain*, I, 97–98; *An Enquiry into the Present System* (London, 1756), 40–41; [Shebbeare], "Letter II," in *Three Letters to the People of England*, 60; Payne, *The French Encroachments Exposed*, 5–6. For more on the commercial benefits of a blue water strategy, see [John Jones], *A Letter to a Friend in the Country, upon the News of the Town* (London, [1755]), 21–25; *Proposals for Carrying On the War*

For many people, the Anglicized character of Britain's colonies in North America conjured up the even grander prospect of a vast English-speaking empire founded on a shared religious, patriotic, and cultural heritage. As the English merchant and philanthropist Jonas Hanway wrote the year after Quebec had fallen, "the stability" of an empire based on a similarity "in *religion, politics, manners, language,* and *laws*" was bound to be far more enduring than the *"fluctuating* friendship" that the British had enjoyed with even the closest of their allies in Europe. Indeed, during the later 1750s, the war in North America occasionally assumed the dimensions of an explicitly "national" struggle, where the British claimed to be fighting for a "Possession" that was "as much Part of national Property as any County in *England"* and for colonies that were "peopled by our Brethren, *Englishmen* as we are, our own Flesh and Blood, and for that reason . . . infinitely dear to us." As the Scottish adventurer Peter Williamson warned his English readers in 1758, the atrocities that he claimed to have witnessed at the hands of Indians along the Susquehanna River—including instances of rape, murder, torture, scalping, and even cannibalism—were carried out against their fellow subjects and thus represented a mere foretaste of what they could expect from a French invasion at home: "For the same will certainly be the Case with *Great-Britain,* if we don't unanimously agree, and join together as one Man, exerting our united Efforts like valiant Soldiers, in behalf of our King and Country."[33]

The most fascinating—and problematic—prospect of all, though, involved the metropolitan belief that Parliament's ability to govern this greater British nation was as extensive as the sovereignty that it exercised at home. To be sure, anyone who had experience dealing with colonial affairs was likely to know better. At the famous Albany Congress of 1754, for example, Britain's attempt to persuade the Americans to pool their

---

with *Vigour, Raising the Supplies within the Year, and Forming a National Militia . . .* (London, 1757), 3–4; *A Letter to the Right Honourable W. P., Esq.* (Exeter, 1758), 41–42, 90–91. On the evolution of Pitt's thinking about the need for allies in Europe, see Sherrard, *Pitt and the Seven Years' War,* 155–161.

33. [Jonas Hanway], *An Account of the Society for the Encouragement of the British Troops, in Germany and North America* (London, 1760), 52n–53n; *Reflections upon the Present State of Affairs, at Home and Abroad . . .* (London, 1755), 29; *A Letter from Sir William —— Deputy Lieutenant of the County —— to His Tenants and Neighbors . . .* (London, 1757), 10; Peter Williamson, *Some Considerations on the Present State of Affairs. . . .* (York, 1758), 7–8. See also Peter Williamson, *French and Indian Cruelty; Exemplified in the Life and Various Vicissitudes of Fortune, of Peter Williamson, a Disbanded Soldier,* 2d ed. (York, 1758), 10–21.

resources in the coming war with France collapsed, in part because the assembled delegates feared creating a precedent that might open the way for greater metropolitan involvement in their internal affairs. Likewise, the large number of regular troops that Westminster began sending to North America were frequently the object of colonial resentment. Indeed, during the spring of 1756, the regular army's policy of enlisting indentured servants without compensating their masters touched off a wave of protest in the middle colonies that included the arrest and imprisonment of several of the king's recruiting officers, an address from the Pennsylvania assembly objecting "to the very great Oppression of the said Masters, and Injury to the Province," and a series of riots that prompted the governor of Maryland, Horatio Sharpe, to warn the British commander in chief that "an Insurrection of the People is likely to ensue." As Governor Shirley duly noted, the colonists' unruly behavior threatened "the nature of Government in general, and is contrary to the Practice of it in the English Constitution." Yet none of this shook the metropolitan public's confidence that the government possessed the authority to resolve such matters to Britain's advantage.[34]

Indeed, during the 1750s a growing literature urged the crown—with or without Parliament's assistance—to tighten the administration of Britain's North American colonies. In some instances, these writings were the work of men like Archibald Kennedy, Henry McCulloh, and James Abercromby, people whose thoughts on the need for reform reflected decades of experience in colonial politics; in other cases, those who called for a new rigor in imperial governance were either relative newcomers like Arthur Young or pamphleteers whose identities have long been forgotten. But whatever their background, all partook of a conviction that the British finally had it within their grasp to establish an enduring empire on the North American mainland. As the English political economist Malachy Postlethwayt noted in a particularly reveal-

34. Sharpe to William Shirley, Feb. 2, 1756, address of the Pennsylvania House of Representatives to Robert Hunter Morris, Feb. 11, 1756, Shirley to Morris, Feb. 29, 1756, Shirley to Henry Fox, Mar. 8, 1756, all in Papers of the earl of Loudoun, LO 793, 819, 867, 890, Huntington Library, San Marino, Calif. (hereafter cited as Loudoun Papers). On the constitutional conflicts between provincial and metropolitan authorities, see Jack P. Greene, *Peripheries and Center: Constitutional Development in the Extended Polities of the British Empire and the United States, 1607–1788* (Athens, Ga., 1986), chaps. 3, 4. For the tensions that characterized relations between British regulars and the American populace, see Alan Rogers, *Empire and Liberty: American Resistance to British Authority, 1755–1763* (Berkeley, Calif., 1974); Fred Anderson, *A People's Army: Massachusetts Soldiers and Society in the Seven Years' War* (Chapel Hill, N.C., 1984).

ing treatise, Britain's colonies had often "acted independently of her, as it were, though supported by her"—in effect, mimicking the behavior of the nation's subsidiary allies in Europe. But where Britain could not check the ambitions of its "confederates" in Europe, Postlethwayt had no doubt that it was within Parliament's power "to determine upon such a union in government and constitution . . . as may tend to strengthen the whole British empire." "Let us revive the consideration of our ancestors, and grow wise by their misfortunes," Postlethwayt enjoined his readers. "If the English colonies in America were wisely consolidated into one body, and happily united in one common interest . . . ; if their united forces were framed to act in concert for the common safety, and their commercial councils regulated for their general prosperity; would not such political concord and harmony establish invincible strength and power?"[35]

On the eve of the Seven Years' War, the British thus conceived of their maritime empire as a system with three interconnected parts—one involving the Atlantic and its adjacent seas and islands, another the wilderness of the trans-Appalachian interior, and a third the increasingly Anglicized colonies along the eastern seaboard. Of these, the first was the most familiar. But it was the two images of North America that made a deeper impression. For the men and women who rallied to Pitt's blue water standard, the Indian lands of the Ohio Valley and Great Lakes summoned fantasies of war unencumbered by considerations of international law, and the colonies to the east seemed to contain many of the resources necessary to master this chaotic periphery. In neither case did these perceptions convey more than a partial understanding of the actual situation in North America. Indeed, the exaggerated power that metropolitan writers thought Britain could bring to the interior almost cer-

---

35. Archibald Kennedy, *Serious Considerations on the Present State of the Affairs of the Northern Colonies* (London, [1754]); [Henry McCulloh], *Proposals for Uniting the English Colonies on the Continent of America so as to Enable Them to Act with Force and Vigour against Their Enemies* (London, 1757); Jack P. Greene et al., eds., *Magna Charta for America: James Abercromby's "An Examination of the Acts of Parliament Relative to the Trade . . ."* (Philadelphia, 1986); [Arthur Young], *Reflections on the Present State of Affairs at Home and Abroad* (London, 1759); *An Appeal to the Sense of the People*, 40–50; *Fatal Consequences of the Want of System in the Conduct of Public Affairs* (London, 1757), 39–40, 55; Malachy Postlethwayt, *Britain's Commercial Interest Explained and Improved . . .* (London, 1757), 469, 474; Postlethwayt, *Great-Britain's True System*, xxviii. Postlethwayt did not make the comparison with Britain's continental allies directly in *Britain's Commercial Interest*. But see the virtually identical discussion of the pitfalls of relying on European alliances in *Great-Britain's True System*, xxviii–xxix.

FIGURE 12

The Contrast. *1749. A prosperous Dutch merchant and a gaunt Englishman
impoverished by the recent war in Europe. During the War of the Austrian
Succession, the metropolitan press criticized Holland for failing to shoulder its
share of the war effort. The palace and fireworks suggest a response to* The British
Jubilee *(Figure 7). Significantly, the Englishman obscures the inscription to
George II that appears in Figure 7.* © *The British Museum*

tainly contributed to the equally unrealistic expectations about the government's authority over the English-speaking settlements on the coast. Although both misperceptions carried ominous implications for the future, however, they nonetheless contributed to the prevailing view that Britain finally had the means to withdraw from Europe and secure the permanent victory over France that half a century of Whig and Hanoverian neglect had prevented.

III. THE LEGACY OF WILLIAM PITT

These attitudes toward Britain's efforts in Europe and America had a far-reaching effect on Pitt's appointment as prime minister, first during the fall of 1756 and again the following spring in a broad-based coalition with the duke of Newcastle and the Court Whigs. Not only did both administrations enjoy explicit Tory support, but the terms upon which the "patriot minister" took office appeared to vindicate Bolingbroke's argument that Britain's proper role in Europe was to act as an impartial arbitrator, intervening, when absolutely necessary, to preserve the balance of power, but steering as clear as possible of the petty squabbles that seemed to erupt with such depressing regularity on the other side of the English Channel. As his detractors never failed to note, Pitt himself found it impossible to make this his only guiding principle, and during the spring of 1758, he agreed to a Prussian subsidy worth more than £600,000, an amount roughly comparable to Britain's own peacetime revenue. Yet even this extraordinary sum paled in comparison to the millions lavished on the war in the colonies. Pitt might have boasted of conquering America in Germany, but his reputation ultimately depended on colonial and naval victories like Louisbourg, Plassey, Guadeloupe, and Quebec. Although Britain had no choice but to continue the war in Europe while George II lived, few people could have been surprised when his grandson, George III—the first "truly British" monarch in nearly half a century—decided two years after his accession in 1760 to end the Prussian subsidy rather than risk Britain's colonial gains by prolonging the fighting in Germany. Nor was it terribly remarkable that, even with crises like France's annexation of Corsica (1768) and the first partition of Poland (1772), the British ended up waiting another thirty years before making a comparable military effort on the Continent.[36]

As significant as this diplomatic transformation was, however, the domestic consequences of Pitt's elevation arguably mattered even more. Not only did the Whigs' vulnerability during the agitations of 1756 appear to confirm the growing political importance of the great commercial centers whose middle-class inhabitants had been the loudest in demanding a change of measures, but Pitt's ability to maintain this extraparliamentary support once he was in office also suggested that a war for trade and empire could be popular to a degree that the Hanoverian regime's involvement in Europe never had been. As a result, the Seven Years' War ended up consolidating the relationship between overseas imperialism and domestic popularity in ways that lasted long after Pitt's resignation in 1761. During the protracted crisis over colonial taxation, each of George III's successive ministers sought to maintain this public support by projecting his policies as a natural extension of the blue water imperialism that had served the Newcastle-Pitt ministry so well

36. Reddaway, "The Seven Years' War," in Rose et al., eds., *History of the British Empire*, I, 478; Michael Roberts, *Splendid Isolation, 1763–1780* (Reading, 1970); Jonathan R. Dull, *A Diplomatic History of the American Revolution* (New Haven, Conn., 1985), chaps. 2, 3; H. M. Scott, *British Foreign Policy in the Age of the American Revolution* (Oxford, 1990), chaps. 3–7.

during the later 1750s. Although Pitt himself opposed each of Parliament's various attempts to raise an American revenue, his success at translating his regard for Britain's maritime and colonial interests in places like North America into political power at home ultimately provided an important impetus for the policies that eventually drove the colonists to open rebellion.

But of all Pitt's various legacies, perhaps the most important involved the costs generated by his war for trade and empire. Although the rhetoric of Pitt's supporters often suggested otherwise, waging war on the high seas and in the colonies turned out to be every bit as expensive as leading grand alliances in Europe. Indeed, even before the war had ended, ordinary men and women found themselves confronted with a number of new pressing financial burdens, including mounting taxes, a potentially debilitating deficit, and an unpopular reform designed to turn the English militia into an effective force for home defense—all of which gave the lie to the Tory and Patriot Whig contention that fighting in places like North America would be cheaper than concentrating on campaigns in Europe. As befit a nation of armchair patriots, however, the troubling question of how these burdens should be distributed caused fewer anxieties than we might suppose during the last years of George II's reign. Although someone would eventually have to pay the bill, most Britons preferred to concentrate on the short term and to think about the heady victories that the king's forces were gaining in nearly every region of the globe.

Patriotism Established

THE CREATION OF A "NATIONAL MILITIA" IN ENGLAND

To anyone who had followed the twists and turns of British politics in recent years, George II's review of the Norfolk militia at Kensington Palace on July 17, 1759, must have had an air of unreality about it. For the better part of the last half-century, the moribund state of England's county militia had been one of the more conspicuous symbols of the Whig regime's dependence on European allies and foreign mercenaries. Now, however, with a French fleet in the Channel and the war in North America yet to be decided, the militia's presence at Kensington suggested that the days of requisitioning Hessians and Hanoverians for home defense were finally over. According to a description in the *Norwich Mercury*, the aging monarch asked the name of every officer, doffing his hat as each marched by and calling out, "'they are brave fellows,' 'they are fine fellows,' etc." As the officers insisted in the address that they presented in response, the regiment stood ready "to obey your Majesty's commands, in any part of the kingdom, with the alacrity and vigour of subjects, who have no interest separate from that of their Prince, and of soldiers, who are determined to hazard their lives in opposing all attempts, that shall be made against your Majesty, your royal house, and the happy constitution, upon which your throne is established."[1]

The review at Kensington was clearly an act of political theater, one meant to show that the government of William Pitt and the duke of Newcastle would pursue the war in America with as little influence and assistance from Britain's European allies as possible. "What a charming account of our militia!" wrote Hester Pitt on learning of the event from her husband; the review demonstrated that "a military figure" could be "acquired out of the army and without long practice—the true British soul will give the rest." According to one pamphleteer, the decision to embody the militia during the summer of 1759 sent an unmistakable message that the English were no longer expected "to fight . . . battles for other princes or people, no battles but what are really and properly their own, and . . . absolutely necessary for the defence and security of their own wives and children, their king and country, their religion, laws and liberty." As the Scottish memoirist and Presbyterian minister Alexander Carlyle observed the following year:

> *England,* who but the last war trembled in her very capital at a highland rabble, beheld for the first time since the days of Elizabeth, the preparations of her enemies with firmness and dignity. Fifteen thousand of her inhabitants, led by the gentlemen of property, were in arms in a few days; her credit remain'd unshaken, and her troops, every where victorious, pursued their operations.[2]

What no one bothered to mention was that the measure that had made all this possible—the English Militia Act of 1757—was deeply unpopular. Only a week before the Norfolk militia passed muster, an armed crowd in Kent "composed chiefly of Labourers and Servants in husbandry" registered a very different opinion of the new corps by forcibly entering a meeting of the county lieutenants, seizing the lists

1. J. R. Western, *The English Militia in the Eighteenth Century: The Story of a Political Issue, 1660–1802* (London, 1965), 159; John Entick, *The General History of the Late War,* 5 vols. (London, 1763–1764), IV, 280n.

2. Marie Peters, *Pitt and Popularity: The Patriot Minister and London Opinion during the Seven Years' War* (Oxford, 1980), 144–146; Kathleen Wilson, *The Sense of the People: Politics, Culture, and Imperialism in England, 1715–1785* (Cambridge, 1995), 196–198, 407–408; Western, *English Militia,* 159; *A Letter to the Right Honourable William Pitt, Esq.: Wherein the Utility and Necessity of a Well-Regulated Militia, during the French War, Is Clearly Demonstrated . . .* (London, 1760), 16; [Alexander Carlyle], *The Question Relating to a Scots Militia Considered . . .* (Edinburgh, 1760), 1.

of potential recruits, and promising to pull down the house of any gentleman who persisted in attempting to implement the new law. Although hardly enough to disturb the heady scene at Kensington, the
incident was nonetheless an important reminder that the "national militia" that Pitt and his supporters had worked so hard over the last
two years to turn into an effective fighting force also represented an
extraordinarily intrusive domestic institution. From the standpoint of
the Pittite press, militia reform had shown the English people that
they were "governed by a wise and moderate king," who was every bit
as committed to Britain's imperial project as his patriot minister. But
to humble men who were actually eligible for service, the new act looked
more like yet another scheme to force "the poor . . . to defend the
rich."[3]

The hostile response to Pitt's militia is an important reminder of the
unprecedented burdens generated by the Seven Years' War. Although
the resulting victories proved to be every bit as popular in England as in
the rest of the British Atlantic, they were also victories that exacted a
high price. Not only did the annual costs of Pitt's "great war for empire"
come to a staggering average of £13.7 million—more than twice the
figure for the War of the Austrian Succession and nearly triple that for
the wars against Louis XIV—but the government also fulfilled a considerable share of its wartime responsibilities through regressive measures
like increasing excise taxes on strong beer and cider and reviving the
militia. Indeed, in organizing the semiprofessional force that made such
a splash at Kensington, the Tories and Patriot Whigs who supplied Pitt's
domestic support came dangerously close to undoing the limited military obligation that had represented one of the mainstays of Britain's
matchless constitution since the Glorious Revolution. As we shall see,
the ordinary men and women who refused to accept this change ensured
that the government ultimately had to recruit the English militia in
much the same way as it did the regular army. Nonetheless, the same
body that provided such a compelling symbol of Britain's new imperial
commitments during the annus mirabilis of 1759 was also a reminder of

3. Lewis Watson and the Deputy Lieutenants of East Kent, Canterbury, July 10,
1759, P.R.O., S.P., 41/30/175–176; *Letter to the Right Honourable William Pitt*, 14; letter from G. Lane, York, Oct. 1, 1757, P.R.O., S.P. 36/138/43–44. See also Eliga H.
Gould, "To Strengthen the King's Hands: Dynastic Legitimacy, Militia Reform, and
Ideas of National Unity in England, 1745–1760," *Historical Journal*, XXXIV (1991),
329–348.

the high costs of waging an avowed war of conquest for acquisitions in distant places like North America.[4]

I. THE POWER OF POPULARITY

What made the popular objections to Pitt's militia reform so ironic was that Tories and Patriot Whigs alike had long depicted the absence of such an institution as one of the more conspicuous emblems of the Hanoverian regime's disregard for the liberties of the English people. Indeed, as their critics liked to note, the governing Whigs' hostility to the militia was difficult to square with their stated commitment to the Revolution Settlement and especially the English Declaration of Rights (1689), which included a universal right to bear arms among the fundamental laws that no future monarch might revoke. As always, the Tory polemicist John Shebbeare drew out the populist dimensions of the issue with particular vigor, arguing in his *Letters to the People of England* that "Liberty . . . is the Birthright of every Englishman" and that only the most corrupt minister could object to an institution that made it possible for such rights "to be defended by all." In the words of the preface to a published set of addresses from 1756, there was no reason to doubt the "popularity" of a reform that would enable the British to reduce "the immense expense of our regular forces" and to eliminate "the danger to our peace and liberties from the introduction of foreign troops." Apologists for the governing Whigs might argue that relying on professional soldiers and foreign auxiliaries represented a far less burdensome form of national defense, but their opponents were sure that denying ordinary subjects the right to defend themselves threatened the very foundations of their constitution.[5]

One reason for apprehension involved the conviction that a viable militia was essential for safeguarding Britain's standing as one of the

4. The comparative figures for the costs of the Seven Years' War come from Paul Langford, *A Polite and Commercial People: England, 1727–1783* (Oxford, 1989), 346.

5. [John Shebbeare], "Letter III: On Liberty, Taxes, and the Application of Public Money," in *Three Letters to the People of England*, 6th ed. (London, 1756), 70; *The Voice of the People: A Collection of Addresses to His Majesty, and Instructions to Members of Parliament by Their Constituents* . . . (London, 1756), ix. For the English right to bear arms, see Joyce Lee Malcolm, *To Keep and Bear Arms: The Origins of an Anglo-American Right* (Cambridge, Mass., 1994), 114–122. See also J. G. A. Pocock, *The Machiavellian Moment: Florentine Political Thought and the Atlantic Republican Tradition* (Princeton, N.J., 1975), chaps. 12–14.

principal maritime powers of Europe. Although the Court Whigs obviously saw things differently, most of those who backed the successive bills that Parliament considered between 1755 and 1757 did so for the same reason they supported Pitt's blue water strategy in North America and Asia. By enabling the English to protect their own coasts without the assistance of foreign auxiliaries, an effective militia promised to reaffirm Britain's independence in its dealings with the Continent. At the same time, most advocates claimed that reforming the militia would free the army and navy for offensive operations beyond the vicinity of western Europe and the British archipelago. Thus the English jurist Richard Burn explained in his analysis of the English Militia Bill of 1757 that a "proper internal defense" was all Britain needed to give "laws to the world" as both Queen Elizabeth and Oliver Cromwell had done. "Our navy will preserve our superiority at sea; our army maintain and extend our conquests abroad; and our Militia be sufficient to frustrate any attacks that may be made by invasions or rebellions." In the words of another proponent of reform:

> The terror of such an armament would not only preserve us from any attack of an enemy, but also give great weight to our ministers in every foreign negotiation; this would enable them to act in a manner suitable to the dignity of the English nation; instead of purchasing allies, they would command them; and instead of meanly soliciting assistance at a monstrous expence, and of being refused by those, upon whom they had the greatest reason to depend, they would let all the nations, with whom they treated, know, that England was secure at home, and in a condition of granting, not of wanting, assistance.[6]

For many of those who supported the attempt to reform the militia, the so-called Diplomatic Revolution of 1756, whereby Maria Theresa deserted her long-standing alliance with Britain for an agreement with France, provided an especially compelling illustration of the need to revive England's militia. Although the two former allies did not formally declare war, the reversal nonetheless gave the forces of Louis XV access to the very ports and garrisons in the Austrian Netherlands that the Brit-

---

6. [Richard Burn], *Observations on the New Militia Bill, Now under the Consideration of Parliament* (London, [1757]), 25–26 (a copy of Burn's pamphlet is in the papers of British lord chancellor Philip Yorke, earl of Hardwicke, in BL Add. MSS 35,877, 332–345); *An Address to the Electors of England* (London, 1756), 28–29.

ish had historically regarded as one of their principal bulwarks against a foreign invasion. Lest anyone question the significance of this development, the final years of the War of the Austrian Succession, when Prince Maurice's brilliant campaigns brought French forces to the gates of Amsterdam, provided a vivid reminder of just how easily a foe who controlled the towns on the Flemish coast might threaten Britain's own shores—and weaken its efforts in places like North America. According to William Thornton, the Yorkshire Whig whose *Counterpoise* (1752) helped build support for the Militia Act of 1757, Britain had been almost powerless during the French invasion scares of 1744 and 1745. "We . . . stand singly against a powerful neighbor" was how the Patriot Whig Charles Jenkinson described England's renewed vulnerability in 1757; "numerous and unemployed troops are now ready to take every opportunity that may offer to invade our country." Given the possibility of a French landing at almost any point from the ports on England's southern coasts to the Essex flats and Thames estuary, even Court Whigs could see the advantages in adding some thirty thousand effectives to the regular army's normal establishment in South Britain.[7]

As if the loss of England's traditional barrier in the Netherlands were not alarming enough, the Jacobite Rebellion of 1745 provided an equally disturbing reminder of the dangers of entrusting the internal defense of the realm to soldiers who fought for pay alone. Not only had the regular army been unable to prevent Charles Stuart's Highland band from marching as far as the English town of Derby, but many of the Dutch, Swiss, and German auxiliaries brought over to help quell the insurrection had refused to undertake offensive operations, thereby forcing the government to withdraw troops from Britain's hard-pressed allies in the Netherlands. Although no one claimed that the Scottish and English militia had been any more effective against the Jacobites, the fact that professional soldiers had fared so poorly led more than a few observers to conclude that a militia under proper regulation might provide a far more dependable form of defense, whether from a French invasion, an insurrection in a neighboring province, or a coup by the troops of an allied state like Hanover. "If we had such a Militia," wondered one commentator in early 1746, would "this Rebellion . . . ever have happen'd?" "The

---

7. [William Thornton], *The Counterpoise: Being Thoughts on a Militia and a Standing Army* (London, 1752), 50–51; [Charles Jenkinson, first earl of Liverpool], *A Discourse on the Establishment of a National and Constitutional Force in England* (London, 1757), 11–12.

truth is," wrote another, that the Jacobites had come so close to succeed-
ing because none of the king's loyal British subjects had it "in their Power
to appear in Arms either in their own Defence, or in Defence of the
Government." In the concise words of a bill that the Tories proposed at
the height of the crisis, "A well-constituted militia is the natural and
constitutional defence of this Kingdom and the best security for both
King and people."[8]

More than anything else, though, the militia's popularity came from
the belief that such a corps would enable the government to place the
defense of the realm in the hands of men who were not only English but
also of a different class from the idle fellows who tended to enlist in
Britain's own regular army. To be sure, the supporters of the Militia Act
of 1757 took care to avoid any suggestion that the new militia might
eventually rival—or even supersede—the professional establishment. As
Lord George Sackville told the House of Commons, he intended to vote
for the "present Bill not as a Counterpoise to the Army, but as an
additional strength for the Security of the Nation." Nonetheless, it was
understood among the militia's projectors that having an able force in
the counties of England and Wales would rectify one of the worst effects
of a standing army by permitting men from the "middling" and more
respectable of society's "lower" ranks to acquire the training necessary to
defend themselves, their families, and, of course, their king and country.
Indeed, the case for militia reform ultimately rested on the proposition
that men whose position in society gave them a vested interest in preserving Britain's constitution would fight with much greater conviction
than soldiers who enlisted for life terms and served for pay alone. "I
speak to the nobility and gentry, the traders and yeomanry of this kingdom, to all those who are possess'd of property, and have something to
lose," was the way Edward Wortley Montagu envisioned the militia in
1759. As an anonymous pamphleteer had explained during the Jacobite
Rebellion a decade and a half before:

8. Gould, "To Strengthen the King's Hands," *Historical Journal*, XXXIV, 335–336,
338–346; *An Enquiry into the Causes of Our Late and Present National Calamities, and
Some Methods Proposed to Remove Them, and Prevent the Like for the Future* (London,
[1745/6]), 26; *An Enquiry into the Causes of the Late Rebellion, and the Proper Methods for
Preventing the Like Misfortune for the Future* (London, 1746), 24; draft legislation,
[1745–1746], Papers of Francis Dashwood, Lord Dispencer, Bodleian Library, Oxford,
MS. D.D. Dashwood (Bucks) (hereafter Dashwood MSS), C.4/B8/2/11a. For the
printed version of the bill, see *A Bill for the Better Regulation of the Militia in That Part
of Great Britain Called England* (n.p., [1746]).

The Hireling, who goes to the Field only to earn his daily Wages, has but weak Motives to risk his Life in the Defence of his Country. His Notions of Liberty are but confused and cold; whereas, the Housekeeper's must be supposed to be animated with a Different Spirit; his Knowledge of the Happiness he enjoys under our happy Establishment, fires him with Zeal for its Preservation; the Thoughts of his Property, his Wife and Family, animate his Courage in their Defence.[9]

The problem, of course, was that it was not at all clear whether men like this would actually be willing to make the sacrifices that militia duty was bound to entail. The Court Whigs who had long opposed efforts to revive the militia in England were especially quick to point out the institution's authoritarian potential. As the duke of Argyll assured the House of Lords during the 1730s, "The militia of a country may be brought under such exact discipline, as to make them almost equal to any regular troops," but the Scottish peer was also confident that "laying the whole militia of the kingdom under a necessity of marching to exercise once or twice every week, would raise a most terrible disaffection against the government." The Whig dean of Gloucester, Josiah Tucker, struck an equally critical note in his lengthy polemic on the dangers inherent in Pitt's blue water rhetoric, warning that the gentry who officered the militia would have to assume broad *"discretionary,* nay *military* Powers" in order to prevent it from becoming a "headless Mob." In the words of Robert Henley Ongley, member of Parliament for Bedford, it seemed "that many Persons [had] of late been captured by the Sound of the Word, without duly attending to the Nature of the thing."[10]

While events would bear out such concerns, however, the most notable feature of these remarks was how little effect they had on prospects for the militia's revival. At times, the Tories and Patriot Whigs who

9. Lord Dupplin to Newcastle, Jan. 26, 1757, BL Add. MSS 32,870, 115–116; E[dward] W[ortley] Montagu, *Reflections on the Rise and Fall of the Antient Republicks: Adapted to the Present State of Great Britain* (London, 1759), 380; *The Folly and Danger of the Present Associations Demonstrated, with Some Proposals for Rendering the Zeal for Liberty . . .* (London, 1745), 18.

10. William Cobbett, ed., *Parliamentary History of England from the Norman Conquest to the Year 1803,* 36 vols. (London, 1806–1820), VIII, 1244; [Josiah Tucker], *The Important Question concerning Invasions, a Sea-War, Raising the Militia, and Paying Subsidies for Foreign Troops . . .* (London, 1755), 26; [Robert Henley-Ongley], *An Essay on the Nature and Use of the Militia; with Remarks on the Bill Offered to Parliament Last Session . . .* (London, 1757), iii.

THE ENGLISH LION DISMEMBER'D
Or the Voice of the Public for an enquiry into the loss of Minorca - with Adl. Byng's plea before his Examiners.

FIGURE 13

The English Lion Dismember'd. *1756. A lion (England) prepares to avenge the
recent loss of Minorca. Three farmers defy German mercenaries, one of whom
carries a flag bearing the white horse of Hanover. In a statement meant to signal
popular willingness to serve in the militia, the farmer in the middle laments:
"Our enemies have Guns. Our Arms are only Rakes and Flails."*
Colonial Williamsburg Foundation

favored reforming the militia cast the issue in voluntaristic terms, insisting that men with families would welcome military service as a way to
ensure that "Mercenary Foreigners . . . shan't enter your Houses, ravish
your Wives, deflower your Daughters and eat up your Property." As an
anonymous pamphleteer claimed in 1756, the English had every reason
to urge Parliament to pass a law that would entrust "the brave and
warlike natives of this island with arms to defend themselves, their
Wives, their Children, their Properties, and every thing else, that can be
dear to freeborn men." On other occasions, militia supporters conceded
that the common men of England might not willingly take up arms in
defense of king and country—at least not at first—but insisted that forcing them to would nonetheless produce salutary effects. Indeed, there
were more than a few self-styled patriots who looked on militia duty as a
kind of compulsory civic education, which would eventually make the
common men of England and Wales less "profligate, irreligious and

debauched in their manners," and more like "the temperate and indus-
trious Switzers, or the Jersey and Guernsey men, who are every Sunday
under arms . . . [to] defend what GOD and nature have bestowed." As
Pitt's brother-in-law, Lord Temple, claimed in the upper house of Parliament, serving in a well-regulated militia would be a test of public
spirit among the landed gentry and a training in it for the poor. The
Newcastle vicar John Brown argued the same point in his influential
Estimate (1757): there were no braver soldiers than "the *common people* of
this Nation," provided they were placed under a proper discipline.[11]

One of the clearest indications of this imperviousness to the personal
wishes of the militia's likely opponents involved the preoccupation of
many patriots with the paired categories of "manliness" and "effeminacy." As scholars have frequently noted, the often misogynistic use of
such terms can be understood partly as an attempt to reaffirm traditional
gender relationships in the face of widespread anxieties over the changing role of women in contemporary English society.[12] At the same time,
discussing matters of national politics in terms of a generalized crisis of
masculinity was no less capable of constraining the conduct of men.
Although patriotic tribunes like Brown and Shebbeare were confident
that a militia would eventually meet with general approval, they effectively removed the legitimate grounds for opposition by insisting that
the only reason why a man might decline to serve his country was that he
did not care for the safety of his wife, children, and property. In the
words of a pamphlet ostensibly addressed to the common men of Norfolk during the fall of 1757, "those who would at such a Time call upon
Substitutes, to defend their Sweethearts, their Wives and Families, deserve richly, that my pretty Countrywomen should find Substitutes to

11. *German Cruelty: A Fair Warning to the People of Great Britain* (London, 1741), 33; *A Modest Address to the Commons of Great Britain, and in Particular to the Free Citizens of London . . .*, 2d ed. (London, 1756), 26–28; Cobbett, ed., *Parliamentary History*, XV, 767–768; [John Brown], *An Estimate of the Manners and Principles of the Times*, 2d ed. (London, 1757), 88.

12. The literature on gender and British political culture during the eighteenth cen-
tury is vast, but see G. J. Barker-Benfield, *The Culture of Sensibility: Sex and Society in Eighteenth-Century Britain* (Chicago, 1992), chap. 3; Laura Brown, *Ends of Empire: Women and Ideology in Early Eighteenth-Century English Literature* (Ithaca, N.Y., 1993); Elaine Chalus, "'That Epidemical Madness': Women and Electoral Politics the Late Eighteenth Century," in Hannah Barker and Elaine Chalus, *Gender in Eighteenth-Century England: Roles, Representations, and Responsibilities* (London, 1997), 151–178; Dror Wahrman, "*Percy's* Prologue: From Gender Play to Gender Panic in Eighteenth-Century England," *Past and Present*, no. 159 (May, 1998), 113–160.

serve for them in a more pleasing Duty." Elsewhere, writers predicted that, once a reformed militia took hold, the English would lose their "effeminacy," and "the military virtues, and the manly exercises, [would] become fashionable, and the nation . . . [would] think seriously and be once more, what it has often been, the terror of Europe." As the author of a drill manual for the militia insisted in 1760, "the man who professes himself a soldier, yet behaves like an old woman" deserved "to be condemn'd to the society of old women, have his sword converted into a distaff, his sash into a bunch of flax, and his gorget into a waterpot, to moisten his thread."[13]

This effeminate construction of the English commoner provides an important clue to why even the Court Whigs who had dominated British politics for the better part of the last forty years ultimately found the demand for a national militia "too popular to be withstood"—as Horace Walpole remarked in his memoirs from the reign of George II. During the public debates preceding Parliament's final approval of the Militia Act of 1757, any opposition to the measure was easily dismissed as yet another example of the passivity that the government had encouraged among the people in general, and particularly among the Whig gentry and urban middle class upon whom the fate of Britain's empire ultimately depended. "Will ye, degenerate Men," wrote John Shebbeare in the second of his *Letters to the People of England,* "behold Britannia, like Prometheus, chained to a Rock, whilst the German Eagle is devouring her Vitals, and yield her no Assistance?" Indeed, the patriotic diatribes that accompanied the outbreak of the Seven Years' War often betrayed a distrust of the inclinations and abilities of Britain's own social and political leaders almost as pronounced as the suspicion with which they regarded the nation's allies in Europe. In the words of the *Monitor* (the London journal edited by William Beckford, a West Indian Planter, London alderman, and Tory member of Parliament), it was easy to see why "a German prince who traffics in human flesh, and has no other market but Great-Britain, might with great propriety" oppose the formation of a national militia, but there was no reason for a British legislator "to support an interest destructive to our country." John Brown made a similar argument in his *Estimate,* lambasting the "better sort" for encouraging a "vain, *luxurious,* and *selfish* EFFEMINACY" that had left

13. *A Plain Address to the Farmers, Labourers, and Commonalty of the County of Norfolk* (n.p., 1757), 16; *Motives for a Peace with England, Addressed to the French Ministry . . .* ([London], 1757), 4; *The Complete Militia-Man; or, A Compendium of Military Knowledge . . .* (London, 1760), 74–75.

the English incapable of defending either themselves or their overseas possessions.[14]

Although some critics questioned their motives, both Pitt and his supporters thought they had good reason to seize on militia reform during the opening stages of the Seven Years' War. Following the humiliating loss of Minorca at the end of May 1756, the Patriot Whig and Norfolk grandee George Townshend took what many Court Whigs regarded as the "most unwarrantable" step of circulating a printed letter to towns and counties across England urging them to petition the government for a new militia law. In the words of the address submitted by the city of Bristol, "the establishment of a well-regulated MILITIA" represented "the surest and most permanent guard of his majesty's sacred person, and this now-endangered kingdom," both in securing the nation "from any alarm of invasions" and for the "free scope" that it promised to give "to our maritime force abroad." A petition from Cheshire struck a similar note, lamenting "with the deepest sorrow" the sight of "foreign troops unavailingly imported, and expensively maintained within this kingdom, while your Majesty's faithful subjects are unarmed and rejected." Indeed, the electors of Yorkshire—who made a point of mentioning the leading role that they had taken in opposing Charles Stuart's Jacobite army in 1745—went so far as to "advise" the king to "oppose (unless exigencies change) all future schemes of receiving foreign mercenaries into this land," and the petition hoped the king would urge Parliament to create a "constitutional militia" in order to "supply the occasions, for which aliens were imported." Although events would show that there were sound reasons to question the popularity of such proposals, the broad-based support for Pitt's imperial war rendered the case against the militia almost impossible to make.[15]

II. THE MILITIA RIOTS OF 1757

If militia reform seemed irresistibly popular to Pitt's urban and middle-class supporters, however, the plebeian riots that greeted the Militia Act of 1757 supplied a vivid reminder of the other side to eighteenth-century

14. Horace Walpole, *Memoirs of King George II*, ed. John Brooke, 3 vols. (London, 1985), II, 91; [Shebbeare], "Letter II: On Foreign Subsidies, Subsidiary Armies, and Their Consequences to This Nation," in *Three Letters to the People of England*, 61; *The Monitor; or, British Freeholder*, no. 43 (May 29, 1756); [Brown], *Estimate*, 29.

15. Lord Hardwicke to Lord Royston, Aug. 26, 1756, BL Add. MSS 35,351, 347–348 (a copy of Townshend's circular letter, dated Aug. 6, 1756, is at BL Add. MSS 32,866, 376); *Voice of the People*, xii; Entick, *General History of the Late War*, I, 423, 427–428.

patriotism. To be sure, the good of the country could easily serve—in Samuel Johnson's apt words—as the last refuge for scoundrels of all sorts, including those bent on reminding Britain's rulers of their duty to safeguard the rights of the people, whether at home or abroad. Indeed, it is no accident that John Wilkes, soon to gain a reputation as the most famous scoundrel of them all, made one of his first popular gestures as a signatory of the Bedfordshire petition seconding Townshend's call for a new militia law. As the riots of 1757 demonstrated, however, the patriotism that Pitt rode to power was no less notable for its potential to strengthen the hands of government in novel and unprecedented ways. In fact, for all its popular and libertarian resonance, the measure that the new prime minister's Tory and Patriot Whig supporters virtually compelled Parliament to approve during the spring of 1757 resembled nothing so much as a calculated attempt to use the war on the high seas and in North America to justify enhancing the reach of the British "military-fiscal state" in England.[16]

This authoritarian potential was readily apparent from the militia act's formal provisions, the most objectionable of which subjected all able-bodied men to a compulsory ballot regardless of their social position or personal wealth. As a number of witnesses were quick to note, this represented a substantial departure from the seventeenth-century militia laws, which placed the militia's primary burden on the landed gentry and which, despite decades of neglect, were still in force at the start of the Seven Years' War. Although men with little or no real property were also expected to contribute under the existing statutes, they did so, not by serving in person or individually assuming the full expense of hiring a substitute, but by pooling their resources in small groups to pay the costs of a single soldier. By contrast, both the Militia Act of 1757 and its various successors shifted the main responsibility for the militia squarely onto the shoulders of those least able to afford it. Because both Tories and Patriot Whigs held the humble to be as capable of serving their country as their superiors, the new laws made every able-bodied man equally

16. Royston to Hardwicke, Aug. 24, 1756, BL Add. MSS 35,351, 343–344. For the authoritarian potential of rhetorical appeals to patriotism and popularity, see Pierre Bourdieu, *Language and Symbolic Power*, ed. John B. Thompson and trans. Gino Raymond and Matthew Adamson (Cambridge, Mass., 1991), 90–102; Gould, "To Strengthen the King's Hands," *Historical Journal*, XXXIV, 329–348; Gould, "'What Is the Country?': Patriotism and the Language of Popularity during the English Militia Reform of 1757," in Gerald MacLean et al., eds., *The Country and the City Revisited: England and the Politics of Culture, 1550–1850* (Cambridge, 1999), 119.

eligible for the militia ballot. Furthermore, despite a provision that permitted anyone whose lot happened to be drawn to find a substitute, the landless laborer had to pay the same ten-pound penalty for doing so as the broad-acred gentleman. For a middling farmer whose income came to several hundred pounds per annum, this might seem like an acceptable expense. But there were many more men—and families—for whom the militia ballot meant making a difficult choice between the possible hardship of losing three years of wages and the certainty of having to pay a particularly onerous wartime tax.[17]

By a cruel twist, the passage of the militia act came on the heels of one of the worst subsistence crises of the eighteenth century, with rising food prices during the fall of 1756 and widespread grain riots across northern and western England. Not surprisingly, the new law received an overwhelmingly hostile response from people who were already struggling to make ends meet. During the summer and fall of 1757, nearly every parish where the local magistrates attempted to raise the militia produced some sort of violent demonstration. At Berkhamsted in Hertfordshire, for example, a crowd of several hundred armed with clubs and staves surrounded a meeting of the deputy lieutenants, engaged them in a long and heated argument, and eventually forced them to surrender the lists of eligible men. The same thing happened several days later in Cambridgeshire, where a gathering of both men and women attacked the house of a magistrate who had attempted to ballot men at Royston, refusing to leave until he agreed to give them three guineas and insisting that he sign a pledge promising not to enforce the militia laws for the rest of the year. In November, a belated attempt to draw up lists of eligible men in Gloucestershire threw the entire countryside "for eight or ten miles" around Cirencester into "the utmost confusion . . . with the sounding of horns, and hollowing, the signals for calling the riotous together." And crowds in Yorkshire proved so successful at intimidating

17. The provisions of both the seventeenth-century militia laws and the English Militia Act of 1757 are discussed in detail in Gould, "To Strengthen the King's Hands," *Historical Journal*, XXXIV, 330–331, 346–348; Western, *English Militia*, 17–18; Charles M. Clode, *The Military Forces of the Crown: Their Administration and Government*, 2 vols. (London, 1869), I, 33–42; Linda Colley, "The Reach of the State, the Appeal of the Nation: Mass Arming and Political Culture in the Napoleonic Wars," in Lawrence Stone, ed., *An Imperial State at War: Britain from 1689 to 1815* (London, 1994), 167–168. For contemporary remarks about the inegalitarian character of the new militia law, see, for example, Lord Hardwicke's observations in his letter to Charles Yorke, Sept. 8, 1757, BL Add. MSS 35,353, 222–225.

the parish constables that the county's superior magistrates despaired of ever bringing the leading perpetrators to justice.[18]

In many ways, the riots triggered by the Militia Act of 1757 resembled what students of English popular culture would regard as a familiar conflict between long-standing custom and an innovative parliamentary statute. This is certainly how the men and women who resisted the militia ballot seem to have regarded their own actions. During the riot that thwarted the attempt to ballot men at Royston, for example, the crowd forced two constables to accompany them in their march, an act probably meant to suggest that, by defying the deputy lieutenants, they were upholding the customary law of England. Several days later, an identical encounter took place in Lincolnshire, where a crowd entered the county seat, "compell'd the Chief and Petty Constables to deliver up all their Lists," and proceeded to shred them, "forcing some of the Constables to joyn" in the destruction. And no fewer than twenty-eight constables appeared at the head of a large crowd in Yorkshire, the members of which all "expressed great Loyalty to his Majesty" but also insisted that they looked upon the present "Bill as taking their Liberties from them" and "that they would not consent to this Law." There were even reports that rioters in the East Riding had raised what amounted to their own posses—or militias—by holding meetings, signing associations "to stand by each other," and raising "contributions" from anyone who refused to "go with them."[19]

18. Letter from Charles Gore, Sept. 5, 1757, letter from Sir John Chapman, Cockinhatch, Sept. 6, 1757, both in Chatham Papers, 30/8/77/2, 168–169, 172–173, 178–179 (account of events in Cambridgeshire also based on Hardwicke to Newcastle, Wimple, Sept. 7, 1757, BL Add. MSS 32,873, 510–511; Hardwicke to Lord Royston, Wimple, Sept. 9, 1757, BL Add. MSS 35,531, 407–409); letter from G. Lane, York, Oct. 1, 1757, letter from Gabriel Hanger, Dryffield, Nov. 6, 1757, both in P.R.O., S.P. 36/138, 43–44, 117–118. The riots are treated extensively in Gould, "'What is the Country?'," in MacLean et al., eds., The Country and City Revisited, 124–128; Western, English Militia, 290–302; Ian Gilmour, Riots, Risings, and Revolution: Governance and Violence in Eighteenth-Century England (London, 1992), 295–300; Nicholas Rogers, Crowds, Culture, and Politics in Georgian Britain (Oxford, 1998), chap. 2 (I am grateful to the author for permitting me to read an earlier version of this chapter).

19. Hardwicke to Royston, Sept. 9, 1757, BL Add. MSS 35,351, 407–409; Nathaniel Cholmley to Newcastle, Hawsham, Sept. 14, 1757, W. Osbaldeston to Lord Irwin, Kunmanby, Sept. 15, 1757, Duke of Ancaster to Newcastle, Sept. 19, 1757, all in BL Add. MSS 32,874, 46–47, 90–91, 157–158. According to a separate account of the Yorkshire riot, "several" of the constables participated under the threat of having their houses pulled down; see Osbaldeston to Newcastle, Kunmanby, Sept. 16, 1757, BL Add. MSS 32,874, 88–89. The classic formulation of the English crowd is, of course, E. P. Thomp-

In the eyes of Britain's rulers, of course, popular challenges to a parliamentary statute were always cause for alarm. The disturbances that convulsed the English countryside during the fall of 1757 were no exception, producing a predictable litany of warnings over the likely effects of "suffering a giddy and riotous populace to stand in opposition to an Act of Parliament." As Lady Jane Allgood, wife of the Tory magnate Sir Lancelot Allgood, reminded him shortly after the bloody riot at Hexham four years later, "attempting the breach of one law is attempting the whole subversion of government." What was unusual about the resistance to the new militia was that it cast the government in the role of having to compel the men who were supposed to serve in it to undertake an action that ultimately depended on their voluntary consent. Indeed, the more perceptive observers were quick to apprehend that the attempt to reform the English militia was inconsistent with the Whig understanding of liberty as the right to conduct one's personal affairs with as little interference from the civil and religious authorities as possible. Lord Chancellor Hardwicke pointed out in a revealing letter to his son:

> This is a law, which it is impossible to cram down the people's throats by force. You can never raise a militia by the compulsion of a standing army. . . . It differs from other cases. Troops may defend, and keep up a turnpike. But, in this instance, the final acts are to be done by the people themselves, personally. They are to *subscribe* their names and *take oaths* before the Deputy-Lieutenants. No force can make them do that, if they stand out; nor can any body do it for them. They may indeed be convicted, and be imprisoned or fined, for their refusal, but is it possible to imprison or prosecute 1000 or 500 men in a county at once? . . . Force must support it at last; and force is inadequate to the present case.[20]

There were actually two separate parts to the problem that Hardwicke described. The first was that the landed gentry responsible for drawing up lists and balloting men on the parish and county level could imple-

---

son, "The Moral Economy of the English Crowd in the Eighteenth Century," *Past and Present*, no. 50 (Feb. 1971), 76–136; Thompson, *Customs in Common: Studies in Traditional Popular Culture* (New York, 1991).

20. Bedford to Pitt, Woburn Abbey, Sept. 1, 1757, P.R.O., S.P. 36/138, 1–2; Lady Jane Allgood to Sir Lancelot Allgood, Mar. 13, 1761, in W. Percy Hedley, "An Episode of the Hexham Riots, 9th March, 1761," Society of Antiquaries of Newcastle upon Tyne, *Proceedings*, 4th Ser., X (1945), 233; Hardwicke to Charles Yorke, Wimple, Sept. 8, 1757, BL Add. MSS 35,353, 222–225.

ment the Militia Act only at great risk to themselves and their property. Even those who had opposed the measure while it was still under consideration as a bill in Parliament recognized that, once the militia had been enacted into law, they were under a general obligation to try to enforce it. Nonetheless, few gentlemen relished the idea of taking steps that were likely to result in disturbances like the ones that occurred during the fall of 1757. Indeed, at the height of the riots, the earl of Hardwicke was startled to discover that his part in defeating an earlier version of the militia bill in the House of Lords had made him one of the only politicians in England with a legitimate claim to be popular. While denying that he had done anything to cultivate such a reputation, he nonetheless cautioned that, "if it is fancied, in London, that even the most zealous Friends of the Bill will suffer their Houses to be pulled down, their Persons to be insulted, and their Election-Interests in their Counties to be lost, for the sake of this Bill, they are much mistaken."[21]

As a result, the new ministry had to rely on a language of patriotic obligation and national duty to encourage English gentlemen to undertake those actions that the law alone could not compel. Indeed, in some rather fundamental ways, the innovations wrought by the Militia Act of 1757 helped forge a new unity among the upper reaches of English society, where both the Court Whigs and their Tory and Patriot Whig opponents found themselves drawn—often quite reluctantly—into the common task of implementing an unpopular reform that was nonetheless perceived as vital for the war in the colonies. In one of the more blatant attempts to enforce this sense of obligation, the Whig earl of Leicester, whose position as lord lieutenant of Norfolk required him to take the lead in organizing the militia, narrowly avoided having to fight a duel with George Townshend because he had "endeavour'd . . . to hinder it from being popular." Although Townshend eventually withdrew the challenge, he reminded the aging peer that he had "known many respectable Families, in Days which I am sure your Lordship approved of, deemed and treated as Jacobites, for talking with no more freedom against a General Excise, before it had passed, than your Lordship has now used against a Militia, after it had received the solemn sanction of King, Lords and Commons." Elsewhere, those charged with implementing the militia opted for gentler methods, yet such efforts often

21. Hardwicke to Newcastle, Wimple, Sept. 11, 1757, BL Add. MSS 32,874, 1–6. See also Hardwicke to Newcastle, Wimple, Sept. 19, 1757, BL Add. MSS 32,874, 144–147: "Tho' I was originally against the Bill, yet now it is a Law, I talk as much for it, and against the opposition to the execution of it, as anyone. But I cannot say with effort."

produced the same reluctant compliance with the new law. During the summer of 1758, Lord Poulett enjoined his deputy lieutenants in Somerset to "animate the gentlemen of this county, to shew themselves Englishmen," and he pointedly reminded the farmers and gentry who attended a meeting two weeks later of the militia petition they had submitted during the summer of 1756, and of the zeal that other counties had already displayed. As the historian Edward Gibbon would later recall of his service in the Hampshire Grenadiers, it was the ministry's ability to manipulate this sort of patriotic language that induced his Tory father and him to enroll as officers. "When the king's order for our embodying came down," Gibbon noted dryly, "it was too late to retreat and too soon to repent."[22]

Indeed, one of the more lasting consequences of the effort to implement Pitt's reformed militia was to reduce considerably the differences that often still divided Whig and Tory squires in jurisdictions across England and Wales. For members of the Whigs' "old corps," this shared sense of purpose might have reflected nothing deeper than a familiar determination to keep the peace and uphold the law as Parliament had determined it. But for Tories like Sir Francis Dashwood, Sir Lancelot Allgood, Sir Humphrey Monoux, and the Gibbons, père et fils—men who had spent the better part of the last forty years in the political wilderness—taking an active role in the military affairs of the realm provided them with their first appreciation of what it felt like to oppose a crowd rather than lead one. "The whigs and tories have had a fair and open eclaircissement," wrote one observer shortly before George II's death; "they now see there is not half that difference between them, as the leaders of their respective parties would make them believe." As Lord Poulett reported from Somerset in January 1759, enforcing the new militia law had

> in a great measure destroyed all distinction of parties in this county, for none who voluntarily enlist in His Majesty's service and take up arms in his defence can go any longer under any other denomination than friends to this Government. And gentlemen now associate and act together who were very shy lately and scarce knew one another before. Mr. Balch at the head of rigid Dissenters did not scruple travelling to London with Mr. Palmer, member for the uni-

22. Leicester to Townshend, Townshend to Leicester, [Jan. 1759], both in BL Add. MSS 35,893, 198–202, 203–205; Poulett to Pitt, July 29, Aug. 19, 1758, Chatham Papers, 30/8/53/1, 105–106, 111–112; Dero A. Saunders, ed., *The Autobiography of Edward Gibbon* (New York, 1961), 132.

versity of Oxford, tho' I believe his friends are not entirely pleased with it.[23]

As for the ordinary men and women who objected so strenuously to the new law, many of the militia's staunchest supporters seem to have hoped that this carefully cultivated, sometimes-grudging patriotism would eventually produce the same results among the lower classes as it had among their landed superiors. Indeed, the government initially responded to the riots with what amounted to a series of attempts to encourage the good opinion of those who were expected to serve in its ranks. During the spring of 1758, Parliament took the unusual step of enacting a new law, a principal goal of which involved simplifying the oaths of allegiance in order to make the militia's purely defensive function more readily apparent to the enlisted men. At the same time, the militia's supporters embarked on a sustained campaign in the London and provincial press in order to allay the public's concerns. "Would you not rather spare Twenty Days in a year for the Exercise of arms, though it were at the Price of your Days Work, than labour all your Life for a Tyrant?" inquired one pamphleteer. "Would you not give Three Half Crowns for insuring your Wives—your Daughters, from the Brutality of Tygers, yourselves from Death, and your Posterity from Popery and Slavery?" Another piece addressed to the "farmers, labourers, and commonalty" of Norfolk reminded readers that "we are engaged in a War with the *French*, our old and implacable Enemies; they hate us both on Account of our Religion, and because we are rich, happy, and free." Elsewhere, commentators spoke of the devastation that the French and their Indian allies had inflicted on the American colonists—"our Brethren, Englishmen as we are, our own Flesh and Blood, and for that reason . . . infinitely dear to us."[24]

23. Linda Colley, *In Defiance of Oligarchy: The Tory Party, 1714–60* (Cambridge, 1982), 275–276; *Letter to the Right Honourable William Pitt*, 13; Poulett to Pitt, Jan. 29, 1759, Chatham Papers, 30/8/53/1, 115–116. It is not entirely clear how much weight should be attached to reports like this. In 1761, Poulett lamented "that there are still some [in the militia], who having a view to party Distinctions, which I endeavour to break, and which ought never to take Place in a Body of Men who are under military Discipline" (letter dated Dec. 26, 1761, P.R.O., S.P. 41/31, 21).

24. Western, *English Militia*, 142–143; *A Letter to the People of England, upon the Militia, Continental Connections, Neutralities, and Secret Expeditions* (London, 1757), 5 (although sometimes attributed to John Shebbeare, this pamphlet appears to have been written by an anonymous imitator); *A Plain Address to the Farmers of Norfolk*, 17; *A Letter from Sir William —— Deputy Lieutenant of the County of —— to His Tenants and Neighbours . . .* (London, 1757), 10.

Along with such generalized statements, local gentlemen frequently responded to the riots by publishing their own written explanations. In Hertfordshire, for example, the superior magistrates had a broadsheet printed and distributed to farmers attending local markets in order to counter "false representations of the Act." Likewise, during the fall of 1757, the *Gloucester, Cambridge,* and *Ipswich Journals* all published manifestoes from the county lieutenants meant to reassure the general public that service would be limited to three-year terms, that the enlisted men would receive adequate pay and clothing, and that Parliament had specifically prohibited the government from sending the militia to fight "romantic" wars on the Continent. Elsewhere, magistrates referred rioters to the text of the act itself, and in at least one instance persuaded a crowd to disperse after they acknowledged "that an Act of Parliament never had deceiv'd them, nor was likely ever to do so." Indeed, Pitt himself was quite sure—or so he claimed in the Privy Council—that "a proper disposition in the Lord Lieutenant and Deputy Lieutenants to explain the Act" was all that was necessary to persuade the people to serve in the regiments of their constituent counties. In the words of a pamphlet allegedly meant to reassure potential recruits in Norfolk of the militia's character:

> You don't depend for this upon the Word of any Man, not even of the King: You have an ACT of PARLIAMENT, that is the LAW for your Security; as good a Title as any Man has to his Estate, or even the King has to his Crown; which he holds by Virtue of the Act for *Settling the Succession in the House of Hanover,* as you will see by the Oath you are to take as Militia men.[25]

The problem was that ordinary English men and women already understood the militia's central provisions perfectly well. In Lincolnshire, angry rioters claimed that the new law demonstrated "that the gentlemen just kept Poor men alive to fight for them," and several magistrates received an anonymous letter wondering "which of you Buntin' Ars'd Coated fellows" were prepared to maintain the families of those

25. Letter from Lord Cowper, Sept. 7, 1757, Chatham Papers, 30/8/77, 172–173; Western, *English Militia,* 301–302; Lawrence Monck, "Representation" to the Duke of Ancaster, Lincolnshire, Sept. 9, 1757, BL Add. MSS 38,874, 159–160; Newcastle to Hardwicke, Sept. 10, 1757, BL Add. MSS 32,873, 541–549; *A Plain Address to the Farmers of Norfolk,* 30. On the other hand, Lord Poulett reported in 1761 that the common people of Somerset had "so little Faith and Reliance . . . in the Promises of the Government" that they did not believe they could obtain any "legal Security for their Liberties from an express Act of Parliament" (letter dated Nov. 2, P.R.O., S.P. 41/32, 18).

whose "ticket" happened to be drawn in the militia ballot. In a similar manner, an anonymous note posted at Halifax warned potential recruits that "you [are] soon to be trepann'd out of your liberty and all that is Dear," and crowds elsewhere insisted that the Militia Act placed unfair burdens on the poor, that the new law would reduce honest countrymen to the same condition as regular soldiers, and that they would "rather be hanged in England, than scalped in America." As the author of a pamphlet observed in early 1758, "our daily bread being dear, husbandry work very cheap, and the labourers required to fight, or learn to form the hollow-square, for little or nothing,—are [all] esteemed intolerable hardships!" "The friends of the Bill cannot now say, that, the Gentry have been the authors of its failure," Lord Royston noted with evident satisfaction, "for *it is* the work of their *favorites and friends* the *[oi polloi]*—the *People.*"[26]

In the final analysis, the disturbances caused by the Militia Act suggested that the patriotism of ordinary English people was not all that different from the remote forms of participation favored by the Court Whigs. In the East Riding, for example, the crowds that forced the deputy lieutenants to suspend the Militia Act during the fall of 1757 took care to maintain a "dutifull Loyalty to his Majesty," and they insisted that they were ready "to serve him in any other way against all enemys whatsoever." Likewise, observers frequently noted that the common men claimed to be "willing in time of publick danger to fight for their King and country," though they objected to being compelled "to desert their families" in order to serve for extended periods of time on the same terms as soldiers in the regular army. Even after Parliament had removed some of the main popular grievances in 1758, the militia's emphasis on personal service remained the subject of recurring complaint. In the words of an anonymous note addressed to the constables of Hambleden in Buckinghamshire in the mid-1760s, "supose we are farmer leaber or wat not, we must leaves our wives and familys and all our callings for that one damd wimse of yours when there is leteren [loitering] felers enouf

26. Anon. letter to James Bateman and Samuel Dashwood, n.d., BL Add. MSS 32,874, 161–162, included in Duke of Ancaster to Newcastle, Sept. 19, 1757, David Hansfeld to Lord Rockingham, Halifax, Sept. 24, 1757, both in BL Add. MSS 32,874, 157–158, 274–275; letter from G. Lane, York, Oct. 1, 1757, P.R.O., S.P. 36/138, 43–44; J. S. Charlton to Newcastle, Staunton, Aug. 27, Lord Dupplin to Newcastle, Brodsworth, Sept. 3, 1757, both in BL Add. MSS 32,873, 311–312, 444–447; John Railton, *Proposals to the Public, Especially Those in Power* . . . (London, 1758), 13; Royston to Hardwicke, Wrest, Sept. 15, 1757, BL Add. MSS 35,351, 415–416.

goes about the country such as Jipses and others trampers." British patriots might decry the Whigs' dependence on standing armies and foreign auxiliaries, but given the chance to speak for themselves, the common people obviously preferred to leave the unwelcome burden of defending the nation to the "leteren felers" who presumably had nothing better to do than accept the king's bounty.[27]

Largely as a result of this popular opposition, the original emphasis on appealing to plebeian voluntarism and patriotic duty gradually ceased to be a distinguishing feature of the English militia reform. One indication of this change involved an increasing willingness on the part of local authorities to treat those who openly resisted the militia ballot as lawless criminals, rather than men who might be willing to listen to "reason" or whose complaints merited a "civil" response. The decisive moment in this transition occurred at the Northumberland market town of Hexham on March 9, 1761, where several companies of the Yorkshire Militia engaged a crowd of some eight thousand miners in a pitched battle that left nearly a hundred dead or wounded. "No words would pacify them" was how the militia's commanding officer justified his own role in the bloodiest provincial riot of the century. Lady Jane Allgood was even more resolute, warning that the "hot headed runagadoes" who took part deserved to "have a regiment of soldiers . . . drive them to their slaughter and teach them what it is to go to fight." In the fray's immediate aftermath, a number of pamphlets and published sermons appeared, each designed to reaffirm what constituted acceptable behavior among the "lower" reaches of society and what did not. One clergyman pointedly inquired of the lower class by what authority "Men of your Rank" presumed to judge "what is, or is not, expedient, for the Good and Wellbeing of the whole Community?" In a similar manner, the Reverend William Totton asked a congregation at Hexham: "How can he get Wisdom that holdeth the Plough, and that glorieth in the Goad; that driveth oxen, and is occupied in their labours; and whose Talk is of Bullocks?" Even that most patriotic Whig of all, the Reverend John Brown, whose *Estimate* had helped catalyze extraparliamentary support for the militia in 1757, preached a sermon at his church in Newcastle in which he recast the "natural duty" of personal service as an obligation that the government had a "right" to expect from "*every member* of the

27. Lord Irwin to Newcastle, Sept. 17, 1757, BL Add. MSS 32,874, 121–122; George Townshend to Pitt, Feb. 28, 1758, Chatham Papers, 30/8/64, 151–152; "To the Constables of the Parish of Hambledon," [1765–1766?], Dashwood Papers, C.4/B82/2a.

FIGURE 14

A Militia Meeting. *1773. The typical militia recruit increasingly was represented
as a truculent yokel like the one depicted here. The magistrates on the left argue
over the Militia Bill on the table, and the adjutant in the center looks on the
plight of the recruit on the right with amusement.* © *The British Museum*

State," rather than one that "inclination" alone could be expected to
prompt the "inferior Ranks" to undertake.[28]

At the same time that they cast people who forcibly resisted the ballot
as common criminals, the militia's supporters also quietly abandoned the
ballot as the preferred mode for recruiting the county regiments. Although some people claimed to lament this development, the period
from 1757 onward witnessed the proliferation of clubs, societies, and
charitable associations across England and Wales, all designed to shield
their members from either having to serve or pay the full cost of a
substitute in the event any of them were balloted. In some instances,
these organizations consisted entirely of humble men like the Sussex

28. Gilmour, *Riot, Risings, and Revolution,* 299; Lady Jane Allgood to Sir Lancelot
Allgood, Mar. 10, 1761, in Hedley, "An Episode of the Hexham Riots," *Proceedings of
the Society of Antiquaries,* 4th Ser., X (1945), 230; *A Serious Address to the Common People
on Account of the Late Insurrection at Hexham, March 9, 1761,* 3d ed. (Newcastle, 1761), 11–
12; William Totton, *On the Important Duty of the Subjection to the Civil Powers: A
Sermon, Preached at Hexham . . .* (London, [1780]), 32; John Brown, *On the Natural Duty
of a Personal Service in Defence of Ourselves and Country . . .* (London, 1761), 16–19.

shopkeeper Thomas Turner, who entered into an agreement with the other male inhabitants of East Hoathly in 1762 in order "to indemnify any of the society from serving in the militia by raising a fund to pay the money charged upon anyone by Act of Parliament." In other cases, the initiative came from the gentry and wealthier members of the middle class, as in Norwich where a group of gentlemen announced a charitable subscription in December 1759 to pay the costs of substitutes for poor men with wives and children. On still other occasions, such ventures were the work of commercial enterprises like the Colchester firm that maintained offices in the principal market towns of Essex and promised subscribers that, in exchange for premiums ranging from 4s. 6d. for one year's coverage to nine shillings for three, it would find "strong and active young fellows who have spirit and resolution to serve King and Country as substitutes." Whether organized for profit or charity, the cumulative effect of societies like these was to free those with families and trades from actual militia duty and to turn the detested ballot into a new form of taxation, one that remained the subject of widespread resentment but that the English people ultimately proved willing to pay.[29]

As an indication of the prevalence of such attitudes, the ballot's unpopularity in England played a key role in defeating efforts on two subsequent occasions during the Seven Years' War to extend the laws to Scotland. Although both bills enjoyed broad support among the gentry and moderate clergy who controlled the Presbyterian Church and Scottish universities, opponents included the governing corporations of the principal commercial centers north of the Tweed as well as a substantial number of lesser farmers who feared—in the words of a manifesto adopted in East Fife—that a Scots militia would institute a sort of "perpetual legal slavery." Citing the popular hostility to the militia in England, the author of a letter to the *Edinburgh Courant* warned in 1762 that "the labourer must be taken from his plough, and the manufacturer from his loom." In addition, it seemed "evident" to a group of farmers who met at Edinburgh later that same year that a militia would "be more and more hurtful, not only to the farmer, but to every other person concerned in trade and manufactures." According to the royal chaplain

29. David Vaisey, ed., *The Diary of Thomas Turner, 1754–1765* (Oxford, 1984), 251; Western, *English Militia*, 252; John William Burrows, *The Essex Militia*, vol. IV of *Essex Units in the War, 1914–1919* (Southend-on-Sea, 1929), 141. This sort of charitable undertaking often represented a fairly direct response to the militia riots, as in the subscription pledged in 1758 by the principal farmers in the Cambridgeshire parish of Gamingay, which had witnessed some of the most violent disturbances the year before; see Royston to Hardwicke, Cambridge, Oct. 26, 1758, BL Add. MSS 35,352, 57–59.

Edmund Pye, the "Scotch Militia" ultimately failed because "the English ditto" had been "scouted out of all credit, as a most ridiculous, expensive, and to the common men (as to morals and industry) ruinous project."[30]

The upshot of all this was that the English militia that took the field to such apparently universal acclaim during the summer of 1759 actually resembled nothing so much as the regular army whose worst effects it was meant to correct. Indeed, as ordinary men like Thomas Turner of Sussex insured themselves against having to serve in person—in effect, turning the cost of a substitute into yet another of William Pitt's wartime taxes—the actual burden of militia duty fell to drifters, unemployed laborers, and the like, men who might otherwise have enlisted in the regular army but wanted to avoid having to serve overseas. It is hardly surprising that some of the most persistent complaints came from the king's regular officers, who resented the added competition from a force that, by the time George II reviewed the Norfolk regiment at Kensington, numbered nearly fifteen thousand effectives. Lord Temple reported in August 1759 that the cost of raising the militia in his own county of Buckinghamshire had driven "the price of a substitute . . . from 4 guineas to ten pounds," making it unlikely that the army's recruiting parties would meet with success "in this part of the world." Similarly, the Secretary at War, Lord Barrington, lamented that the demand for substitutes in the militia "keeps men from inlisting in the Army." Such difficulties even led Barrington to suggest on more than one occasion that recruiting parties be permitted to "beat up among the Militia," and during the spring of 1760, Yorkshire militia officer William Thornton went so far as to recommend (unsuccessfully, it should be noted) that Parliament empower the crown to send individual regiments overseas. "This lure of a

---

30. John Robertson, *The Scottish Enlightenment and the Militia Issue* (Edinburgh, 1985), 115–116, 120; O. A. Sherrard, *Lord Chatham: Pitt and the Seven Years' War* (London, 1955; reprint, Westport, Conn., 1975), 361. See also Richard B. Sher, *Church and University in the Scottish Enlightenment: The Moderate Literati of Edinburgh* (Princeton, N.J., 1985), 213–235. But see the reply to the letter in the *Edinburgh Courant* in *Letter from a Gentleman in East-Lothian, to His Friend in Town, on the Subject of Militia* (Edinburgh, Feb. 13, 1762), 7:

> Although many of the English, at first from mistaken notions, or from effeminacy contracted behind the counter or on the loom, opposed that salutary law, and obstructed the execution of it; yet time and experience had enlarged their views, envigorated their minds, furnished satisfying answers to every objection, and made them at last unanimous in the pursuit of that manly and constitutional measure.

militia was hung out, or toss'd about, for several years, and the public adopted it with the utmost raptures," noted William Guthrie shortly after Pitt's resignation in 1761. "Little, however, did they know what it meant; and that the whole boasted patriot's scheme of militia, in contradistinction to a standing-army, must end in rendering that militia, to all intents and purposes, a standing-army."[31]

For all the discomfort this realization caused, however, there is every reason to think that the abandonment of the patriotic commitment to personal military service ultimately suited most members of British society. As the Yorkshire magnate and militia officer Sir George Savile argued in an influential pamphlet published in 1762, subjecting all able-bodied men to a lottery without respect to "rank or fortune" amounted to an unequal form of taxation, as well as a dangerous policy for "carrying an Utopian idea of property and patriotism into the ranks." According to Savile, there was no question that every state possessed "an absolute and indefeasible right" to call on "every subject, capable of personal service, to stand forth in defence of his country in its distress." It was equally clear, however, that this right should usually remain "dormant" and that during the normal course of affairs—including most foreign wars—subjects should fulfill their military obligations through the payment of taxes levied according to the value of their property. Savile had been roughed up by a crowd in Lincolnshire during the riots of 1757, an experience that may help explain why he objected to the ballot's "inequitable" burden on the poor. But he was also bothered by the subversive effects of placing middling shopkeepers and small farmers under the same obligation as landed gentlemen. "The men of property in a country, have doubtless a right to act a principal part in its defence," Savile said. "It is doubtless their duty, their bounden duty." At the same time, broadening this duty to include every member of English society, something many of the militia's projectors still claimed to favor, struck him as a certain way to make the county regiments militarily ineffective and politically dangerous:

31. Temple to Pitt, Stowe, Aug. 26, 1759, Chatham Papers, 30/8, 37–38; memorandum, [Nov.–Dec. 1759], Papers of William Wildman, Viscount Barrington, Suffolk Record Office, Ipswich (hereafter cited as Barrington Papers), HA 174/1026/3c/236; Barrington, memorandum, [1766–1775], Barrington Papers, HA 174/1026/3b/289; Barrington to Pitt, Jan. 21, 1761, Chatham Papers, 30/8/18, 209–210; Charles Townshend to George Townshend, May 15, 1760, English Historical MSS, Bodleian Library, Oxford, D.211, 9–10; [William Guthrie], *A Third Letter to the Right Honourable the Earl of B——* . . . (London, 1762), 40.

The yeoman, the man of property, is not in the ranks; nor do I wish
him there. The last man, I desire to have the command of, is the substantial tenant or freeholder; and ask, if I am singular; it were an un-
gracious business to bring a constituent to the halberds, or too bit-
terly to animadvert on *him* for getting drunk to day, whom courte-
ously I entreated, and invited by example, to do the same yesterday.[32]

The attempt to revive the militia in England and Wales thus ended by
confirming the effectiveness of a system of political obligation that permitted most people to fulfill their patriotic obligations by paying others
to fight their country's battles for them. To be sure, the militia ballot remained the subject of recurring complaint, both as a potential vehicle for
compulsory service and because of the high costs of purchasing a substitute. Thanks to Pitt's reform, the Seven Years' War added yet another
popular grievance to the expanding list of so-called improvements in
Georgian Britain, measures (like market deregulation, turnpike construction, and field enclosure) that invariably commanded broad support
among the country's aristocratic rulers and their middle-class followers
but that were widely detested by those who had to bear the primary
burden. Much as they disliked the whole militia business, however, most
English families ultimately found the costs of hiring a substitute far
preferable to the prospect of having to participate in person. "Every one
of us cannot shine *in deeds of arms*," remarked Jonas Hanway in 1760, "but
we may demonstrate our inclinations to do so, by showing our respect for
military virtue." No doubt words like this struck the more ardent of the
militia's supporters as anathema. But for anyone who had experienced
the ballot directly, they must have rung true indeed. Ultimately, Georgian patriotism remained a public spectacle or artifact for mass consumption, not a virtue to be sustained by widespread personal participation.[33]

III. THE PRICE OF VICTORY

Perhaps the most unexpected part of Pitt's militia reform, however, was,
not that its provisions requiring personal military service turned out to

32. [Sir George Savile], *An Argument concerning the Militia* (London, 1762), 6–9, 15,
17. For similar statements on the ballot's inegalitarian character, see *A Letter to the Right
Hon. Charles Townshend, Secretary at War: Being Thoughts on the Militia Laws . . .*
(London, 1762), 20; *Directions for the More Faithful Execution of the New Militia Act . . .*
(London, [1762]), 13–14.

33. [Jonas Hanway], *An Account of the Society for the Encouragement of the British
Troops, in Germany and North America* (London, 1760), 20.

be so unacceptable, but that this failure did so little to tarnish its public reputation. By the time the king reviewed the Norfolk regiment at Kensington, there cannot have been many people who thought militia duty held much appeal for the common people of England and Wales. Nonetheless, Pitt's apologists continued to insist on the militia's character as a kind of popular array, a mobilization of ordinary Englishmen that showed his imperial efforts still enjoyed the support of the British people. "Let it not be said," urged one of the patriot minister's anonymous correspondents during the fall of 1757, "that the national honour and credit, are matters of no concern, to the common people." Indeed, throughout the three years that the county regiments spent encamped on the southern coasts of England, many of the militia's supporters continued to speak of a general revival of martial virtue among the "lower orders." As an American who served as an officer in the Wiltshire battalion wrote in 1760: "The Knowledge of Arms will grow fashionable, and the lower Sort of People, now so into Ease and Luxury, will awake as from a Dream, and be familiariz'd to a military Spirit." According to another piece, also written during the last year of George II's reign, the example of the Dorset regiment suggested that the restoration of virtue for which patriots had waited so long had at last arrived:

> They have in the Militia of this single county a hundred thousand pounds, that is, one thousand pounds a man; they are the sons of our farmers, shop-keepers, clothiers, serge-makers, etc., etc. men that have wives and children and real property of their own to defend; and, on a more particular enquiry, I find them to be a healthful, vigorous and robust people; they are not enervated by pleasure, but inured from their infancy to virtue and sobriety,—not accustom'd to a soft, effeminate, and luxurious life.—No, Sir, they despise death, and would rather lose their lives, than those civil and religious liberties they now enjoy, under so wise and moderate a king, who they believe reigns only to make reason and justice reign.[34]

The prevalence of language like this clearly owed something to the selective manner in which the London and provincial press reported on the militia. As Charles Yorke remarked at the height of the rioting in

34. Anon. letter to Pitt, Oct. 28, 1757, Chatham Papers, 30/8/77/2/214; [Young?], *A Letter from a Militia-Man to His Colonel: Representing the Inconveniencies That May Attend a Deviation from the Regular Establish'd Exercise of the* ARMY . . . ([London?], [1760?]), 11; *Letter to the Right Honourable William Pitt*, 8–9.

1757, "My newspaper (I observe) studiously conceals from me every disorder which tends to affect the credit of the Militia Bill." Indeed, once the crown started to embody the county regiments two years later, it became almost impossible to read anything but positive accounts of the new corps. Where the county leaders managed to raise the requisite number of officers and men, regimental gatherings frequently took on the features of carefully staged spectacles. Following the first successful training session by the Norfolk militia, for example, George Townshend reported that "the behaviour of the private men" was so impressive that "in many places the farmers and spectators collected sixpence a piece for each man." What did not appear in print were private reports of fatigue in the ranks, of tensions with regular soldiers, of discontent over being kept under canvas during harvest, and—occasionally—of opposition among the enlisted men to marching beyond the borders of their home counties. Even the men in the celebrated Norfolk regiment were rumored to "murmur and complain much in their march" during the summer of 1759. Not surprisingly, when a serious mutiny by the Devonshire Militia at Plymouth Dock received no comment at all in the London press, the militia's critics began to suspect "that some industry is used to restrain the publication of such incidents." "As the Militia seems to be the Fashion of the Year," wrote a perceptive observer in 1760, "it is but a common Degree of Complaisance in Government . . . not to obstruct its Operation."[35]

If the patriotic writers who dominated the wartime press played an important role in perpetuating such images, however, the course of events also helped buttress the militia's reputation. Not only did the closing months of 1759 bring news of Britain's stupendous series of victories in Canada, India, Africa, and the West Indies, but county regiments like the one that George II reviewed at Kensington also played a role in thwarting France's last, desperate attempt to reverse these successes with an invasion of southern England. As critics duly noted, the militia's role

35. Yorke to Hardwicke, Sept. 15, 1757, BL Add. MSS 35,353, 226–229; Townshend to Pitt, Oct. 5, 1758, Chatham Papers, 30/8/64/1, 159–160; William Beckford to Pitt, Sept. 18, Oct. 5, 1759, Chatham Papers, 30/8/19/1, 51–54; Lord Clanricarde to Lord Holdernesse, June 10, 1759, P.R.O., S.P. 36/142, 64–65; Lord Shaftesbury to [Pitt], [May 29, 1759], Chatham Papers, 30/8/56/1, 15–16; letter from Lord Cowper, July 27, 1759, P.R.O., S.P. 41/30, 157–159; Hardwicke to Royston, July 24, 1759, BL Add. MSS 35,352, 99–100; Hardwicke to Royston, Sept. 1, 1759, BL Add. MSS 35,351, 118–119; *Reflections without Doors on What Passes within: Recommended to the Perusal of All Friends to the Militia* . . . (London, 1760), 9–10.

proved more symbolic than real, because a series of naval victories by Admirals Hawke and Rodney eventually dashed the projected invasion before it could get underway. Nonetheless, the presence of fifteen thousand militia men on England's southeastern coast ensured that there would be no need to withdraw British troops from abroad, let alone any pretext for employing foreign auxiliaries like the despised Hanoverians and Hessians. "The better capacity we are in to defend ourselves at home," wrote Jonas Hanway at the height of the threatened invasion, "the more force we can spare to secure his Majesty's AMERICAN dominions." No matter how considerable the differences between the semi-professional force of 1759 and the patriotic body that Parliament had envisioned two years before, the English militia ultimately appeared to fulfill its primary purpose by freeing the king's fleets and armies for remote operations in every corner of the globe.[36]

Indeed, once the government embodied the county regiments, the militia helped provide the metropolitan public with a sense of connection to the regular troops whose exploits heralded Britain's apotheosis as the greatest imperial power since the fall of Rome. During the latter years of the war, the effort to train the county regiments produced a remarkable array of printed manuals and drill books based on those used by regular soldiers. Some of these were meant for both the army and the militia, as in the regular army's own official *Manual Exercise;* others were written for the use of specific militia battalions, among them the Warwickshire, Dorsetshire, and West Kent regiments, but all were designed to familiarize both the general public and the landed gentlemen charged with officering the militia with the regulations, practices, and customs of the professional troops that were triumphing in places like Guadeloupe and Quebec. "I am pretty certain," wrote the author of one such manual, "that by the help of this book it will be very easy for any man, by his own fire-side, to make himself tolerably well acquainted with the common duties of a solider." The military officer William Windham made much the same claim in the influential *Plan of Discipline* that he and George Townshend composed for the use of the Norfolk regiment. Although Windham conceded that soldiers in the militia would probably never know the full "reality" of combat, he was nonetheless sure that teaching them the rudiments of military science would help forge a new constituency capable of appreciating what he described as "the superior

36. [Jonas Hanway], *Thoughts on the Duty of a Good Citizen, with regard to Apprehensions of Invasion,* 2d ed. (London, 1759), 20.

merit and ability" of those regular officers who were capable of "doing their country service" in the most distant regions of Britain's far-flung empire.[37]

In view of the popular opposition to serving in the county regiments, claims of this sort clearly reflected an element of wishful thinking. By the final years of the war, however, even Pitt's critics thought the English militia had played an important role in maintaining popular support for the war in North America and Asia. According to a growing number of observers (including apologists for the earl of Bute, who replaced Pitt as prime minister at the end of 1761) the militia's popularity with the reading public raised the terrifying possibility that British opinion had become so militarized that the government would find it difficult to offer France and Spain equitable terms of peace. In his lengthy polemic on the detrimental effects of waging war to expand trade, for example, Josiah Tucker worried that Britain stood in danger of being impoverished by an unholy alliance of "mock-patriots" in Parliament, "hungry pamphleteers" and "news-writers" in the press, warmongering colonial merchants, and land and sea officers. Sir James Marriott struck an equally alarming note in his own pamphlet on "the national rage of perpetuating war." "By a thirst of military glory," Marriott cautioned, "we seem to have intirely forgot that moderation and equity which always gave this nation the greatest weight in Europe." And William Guthrie claimed to fear that the effusive praise for "our brave soldiers and our brave sailors" was beginning to obscure public awareness that Britain had prospered most fully "when the character of her arms and power was the least conspicuous." As Tucker explained in an especially scathing passage on the enthusiastic tendencies of modern patriotism:

> Heroism is the Wish and Envy of all Mankind; and to be a Nation of Heroes, under the Conduct of an heroic Leader, is regarded, both by Prince and People, as the Summit of all earthly Happiness.

37. *New Manual Exercise as Performed by His Majesty's Dragoons, Foot-Guards, Foot Artillery, Marines, and by the Militia . . .* (London, 1757); *An Explanation of the Manual Exercise. . . . Composed for the Use of the Militia of the County of Warwick* (Coventry, 1758); *The Manual Exercise, for the Dorsetshire Regiment of Militia* (London, 1759); Sir Edward Fage, *A Regular Form of Discipline for the Militia, as It Is Perform'd by the West-Kent Regiment* (London, 1759); *The Complete Militia-Man*, x; William Windham and George Townshend, *A Plan of Discipline for the Use of the Norfolk Militia*, 2d ed. (London, 1768), "Advertisement," xxx. Windham and Townshend's manual quickly became something of a classic on both sides of the Atlantic, running to at least nine separate editions in America between 1768 and 1774; see J. A. Houlding, *Fit for Service: The Training of the British Army, 1715–1795* (Oxford, 1981), 207n.

It is really astonishing to think with what Applause and Eclat the Memoirs of such inhuman Monsters are transmitted down, in all the Pomp of Prose and Verse, to distant Generations: Nay let a Prince but feed his Subjects with the empty Diet of military Fame, it matters not what he does besides . . . ; for their Lives and Liberties, and every Thing that can render Society a Blessing, are willingly offered up as a Sacrifice to this Idol, GLORY.[38]

Of course, the concerns of writers like Tucker turned out to be more than a little exaggerated. Although the peace that the Bute ministry concluded at the end of 1762 confirmed Britain's dominance among the European powers in North America and southern Asia, it demonstrated just enough leniency toward France and Spain for George III's apologists to lay claim to the same "Wisdom" and "Moderation" that Whigs had used to justify every foreign initiative since the Glorious Revolution. In one important respect, though, such criticism turned out to be very much on target. Despite the prevailing tone of optimism and hope, the British found themselves weighted down with a crushing financial obligation. Furthermore, much of this burden fell, not on the aristocratic and middle-class tribunes who had been in the rhetorical vanguard of Pitt's great war for empire, but on the same kinds of people who had been so active in opposing the English Militia Act of 1757. Indeed, even after Parliament solved the problems associated with the reformed militia, the duties necessary to finance Britain's spiraling deficit continued to trigger plebeian unrest, like the riots that convulsed London in 1760 over the increased excise on strong beer and the West Country disturbances occasioned by the Cider Tax of 1763. In a sense, the patriotic unity generated by the Seven Years' War hastened the end of one set of divisions based on the old Tory-Whig rivalry while simultaneously sowing the seeds of future conflict over how to pay for the war's exorbitant costs.[39]

38. [Josiah Tucker], *The Case of Going to War, for the Sake of Procuring, Enlarging, or Securing of Trade, Considered in a New Light . . .* (London, 1763), 13–14, 42–50; [Sir James Marriott], *Political Considerations: Being a Few Thoughts of a Candid Man at the Present Crisis . . .* (London, 1762), 55; [William Guthrie], *Third Letter to the Earl of B——,* 38.

39. *An Address to the People of Great-Britain and Ireland, on the Preliminaries of Peace, Signed November 3, 1762, between Great-Britain, France, and Spain* (London, 1763), 7. The political changes wrought by the Seven Years' War in England—both within Parliament and among the wider political nation—are the subject of a vast literature, but see Langford, *A Polite and Commercial People,* chap. 8; Colley, *In Defiance of Oligarchy,* chap. 10; John Brewer, *Party Ideology and Popular Politics at the Accession of*

FIGURE 15
Sic Transit Gloria Mundi. *1762. To universal acclaim, William Pitt soars
upward, borne aloft by bubbles that he has inflated. The print captures
growing fears at the close of the Seven Years' War that his achievements
were not likely to prove either lasting or beneficial.*
Courtesy of the John Carter Brown Library at Brown University

One obviously would not want to press this conclusion too far, not
least because of considerable evidence that, despite their resentment over
the war's burdens, humble men like East Hoathly's Thomas Turner
shared fully in the sense of pride generated by Britain's apparent ascent
to greatness. As we shall see below, however, the metropolitan conflicts
surrounding the taxing of the Americans often betrayed an underlying
guilt over the costs that William Pitt's wartime ministry had placed on
ordinary men and women in Britain. It was certainly no accident that the

George III (Cambridge, 1976); J. C. D. Clark, *The Dynamics of Change: The Crisis of the
1750s and English Party Systems* (Cambridge, 1982); J. G. A. Pocock, "The Varieties of
Whiggism from Exclusion to Reform: A History of Ideology and Discourse," in
Pocock, *Virtue, Commerce, and History: Essays on Political Thought and History, Chiefly
in the Eighteenth Century* (Cambridge, 1985), 253–264.

defenders of Parliament's fiscal rights in North America saw in the English militia laws an obvious way to illustrate the heavy obligations that the king's metropolitan subjects had borne during the Seven Years' War. Nor was it surprising to find the Stamp Act's supporters invoking characters like John Ploughshare, a fictitious tenant farmer from Hertfordshire who paid his taxes—"tho' I wish they were not so many"—and who consequently saw no reason why the Americans who benefited equally from the protection of Britain's troops and ships should not also help carry part of the cost. Despite its extraordinary popularity, Pitt's great war for empire thus ended by generating new responsibilities that weighed heavily on ordinary men and women. Given this unwelcome reality, the British were bound to look favorably on any measure that promised to shift some of this load onto someone else's shoulders.[40]

40. Vaisey, ed., *Diary of Turner*, 191; "John Ploughshare," *London Chronicle* (Feb. 20, 1766), in Edmund S. Morgan, ed., *Prologue to Revolution: Sources and Documents on the Stamp Act Crisis, 1764–1766* (New York, 1973), 102. For the connection between the justice of taxing the Americans and the burdens of militia service and wartime taxation in Britain, see [John Lind], *An Answer to the Declaration of the American Congress* (London, 1776), 52–53; John Shebbeare, *An Essay on the Origin, Progress, and Establishment of National Society*, 2d ed. (London, 1776), 137; [John William Fletcher], *American Patriotism Farther Confronted with Reason, Scripture, and the Constitution . . .* , 2d ed. (London, 1777), 33.

4

The Nation Abroad

THE ATLANTIC DEBATE OVER
COLONIAL TAXATION

Britain's prospects had never seemed brighter than they did in 1763. In every quarter of the globe, France's ambitions were in ruins while the British had made substantial acquisitions in Africa, India, the Caribbean, and—most importantly of all—North America, where the crown had gained control over French Canada, Spanish Florida, and the immense wilderness bounded by the Appalachian Mountains and the Mississippi River. As William Pitt boasted in the House of Commons, Britain "had over-run more world" in three years than the Romans had "conquered in a century." Thomas Turner was only slightly more circumspect, noting in his diary the "pleasure" that it gave "every true Briton to see with what success it pleases Almighty God to bless His Majesty's arms with, they having success at this time in Europe, Asia, Africa and America." Oliver Goldsmith even claimed that France was now "sensible of one truth, which, however seemingly inconsistent, is founded on reason and experience; we mean, that Great Britain is stronger, fighting by herself and for herself, than if half Europe were her allies." "It is enough to read the Treaty of Paris," concluded the comte de Vergennes, "to realize the ascendancy which England has acquired over

FIGURE 16

British North America, 1763. *Drawn by Richard Stinely*

France and to judge how much that arrogant nation savours the pleasure of having humiliated us."[1]

For all the public elation over Britain's triumph, however, the restoration of peace also brought with it a host of new expectations and anxieties. According to many observers (including, it was rumored, some of

1. R. C. Simmons and P. D. G. Thomas, eds., *Proceedings and Debates of the British Parliaments respecting North America, 1754–1783*, 6 vols. (Millwood, White Plains, N.Y., 1982–1986), I, 305; David Vaisey, ed., *The Diary of Thomas Turner, 1754–1765*

the new king's closest advisers) the most pressing challenge confronting the nation in 1763 was to disengage from the Continent in the manner envisioned by patriots during the first half of the eighteenth century, using the strategic advantages gained during the Seven Years' War. Although no one denied the importance of remaining on good terms with the other states of Europe, more than a few commentators hoped Britain's rulers would finally make the affairs of the empire their primary concern and, in so doing, adopt "a plan of policy, which is neither Austrian, Prussian, nor even Hanoverian, but English." The fact that the British possessed in George III a young and vigorous monarch who shared none of his predecessors' affection for Hanover only heightened these patriotic expectations. Indeed, the king himself appeared to promise as much when he brashly claimed in his first speech to Parliament in 1760 "to glory in the name of Briton." As an indication of this concern for Britain's welfare, the king's first two prime ministers—Lord Bute and George Grenville—soon began formulating measures like the Sugar Act (1764), the Currency Act (1764), and the American Mutiny Act (1765), all of which were meant to remedy decades of neglect by enhancing Whitehall's administrative efficiency on the far shores of the Atlantic. Although the day might come when Britain would once again be called to defend the liberties of Europe, the new king's subjects could hope that a proper attention to imperial affairs would free them to fulfill their obligations, not through endless negotiations and useless alliances on the Continent, but as the metropolitan head of a self-sufficient maritime empire.[2]

(Oxford, 1984), 191; [Oliver Goldsmith], *The Martial Review; or, A General History of the Late Wars . . .* (London, 1763), 237; C. B. A. Behrens, *The Ancien Régime* (London, 1967), 158.

2. *The Political Balance, in Which the Principles and Conduct of the Two Parties Are Weighed* (London, 1765), 61; The King's Speech, as quoted in the *Annual Register,* III (1760), 248. According to some accounts, the king said "Britain" rather than "Briton." For a contemporary interpretation of the speech as an explicit rejection of the first two Hanoverian monarchs' Continental policies, see *A Letter to the Whigs, with Some Remarks on a Letter to the Tories* (London, 1762), 15: "What terrors can the most wayward imagination form of predilection and partiality to any foreign interests in the bosom of a Sovereign, who has so sensibly expressed his affection for this country, when he boasted of his being born a Briton?" For the blue water commitments of George III's court, see Nicholas Tracy, "The Gunboat Diplomacy of the Government of George Grenville, 1764–1765: The Honduras, Turks Island, and Gambian Incidents," *Historical Journal,* XVII (1974), 711–731; Philip Lawson, *George Grenville: A*

If the British were to realize these new goals, though, one issue demanded the government's immediate attention: how to defray the costs of defending an empire that was no longer confined to colonies governed by Protestant settlers from Britain and Ireland but that now included a Catholic majority in Quebec, a large indigenous population in the lands west of the Appalachians, and the Indian province of Bengal. Indeed, within a month of the war's end, the government announced that it would expand the army in order to create an unprecedented peacetime establishment of some ten thousand regulars in North America. Although few people doubted that the British ought to bear most of this new burden, a growing number of observers worried that the military and naval expenditures necessary to secure their overseas dominions would eventually bankrupt the Treasury without some contribution from the other members of the empire, particularly the older English-speaking colonies in the West Indies and on the North American seaboard. With the grand purpose of raising such a revenue, the ministry of George Grenville enacted the Stamp Act in 1765, committing the British to a fateful series of attempts to tax the colonies in Parliament without their explicit consent. As we shall see, the public support in Britain for Grenville's reform, as well as for the Townshend Revenue Act (1767), reflected a widespread perception that the neglect of colonial affairs under the first two Hanoverian monarchs had been anything but salutary and that the victories of the Seven Years' War had brought their maritime empire to a critical juncture that no true patriot could afford to leave unresolved.[3]

Political Life (Oxford, 1984), 203–207; H. M. Scott, *British Foreign Policy in the Age of the American Revolution* (Oxford, 1990), chaps. 3–5. As Scott rightly notes, the Bute and Grenville administrations remained committed to the "Old System" of cultivating Continental alliances in order to resist French ambitions in Europe (41–50). As he also points out, though, none of George III's early ministries proved willing to renew the peacetime subsidies that had undergirded Whig diplomacy during the 1740s and 1750s and that blue water patriots like Bolingbroke had found so repulsive (50). This alone represented a substantial departure from the Continental policies of George II.

3. The definitive account of the British army in North America is still John Shy, *Toward Lexington: The Role of the British Army in the Coming of the American Revolution* (Princeton, N.J., 1965). For the decision on the peacetime army in 1763, see also John L. Bullion, "'The Ten Thousand in America': More Light on the Decision on the American Army, 1762–1763," *William and Mary Quarterly*, 3rd Ser., XLIII (1986), 646–657; Bullion, "Security and Economy: The Bute Administration's Plans for the American Army and Revenue," *William and Mary Quarterly*, 3rd Ser., XLV (1988), 499–509.

I. THE ORIGINS OF THE STAMP ACT (1765)

As both Grenville and his supporters were well aware, raising a colonial revenue by parliamentary appropriation represented a significant innovation. Although Parliament had used port duties to regulate the colonies' external trade since the first Navigation Act (1652), metropolitan responsibility for most areas of provincial administration—including the management of colonial defense—still resided, as it had since the seventeenth century, in the relatively powerless hands of the king, his privy councillors, and the governors of the various colonies in America. An unintended effect of this dependence on the royal prerogative was to give colonial legislatures extraordinary control over matters like raising troops and levying taxes. Yet few people doubted that it was within Parliament's authority to change this relationship, nor were there many metropolitan observers, least of all among Grenville's colleagues at Westminster, who questioned the wisdom of doing so in order "to reconcile the regulation of commerce with an increase of revenue." As Grenville assured the House of Commons on presenting his initial proposal in March of 1764, "We have expended much in America. Let us now avail ourselves of the fruits of that expence."[4]

There were several reasons why the metropolitan public found Grenville's request so "unexceptional"—as "Anti-Sejanus" described the Stamp Act to readers of the *London Chronicle* toward the end of 1765. The first was the extent of Britain's conquests in North America and the perception that preserving the strategic gains of the Seven Years' War would require a larger naval and military establishment than the crown had maintained before the war. Although the army's overall size occasioned some comment during the early 1760s, a broad section of the British public, within Parliament as well as without, appeared to accept without question the wisdom of using ten thousand regulars to defend

4. P. D. G. Thomas, ed., "Parliamentary Diaries of Nathaniel Ryder, 1764–7," *Camden Miscellany*, XXIII (Camden 4th Ser., VII) (London, [1969]), 234 (hereafter cited as Thomas, ed., "Diaries of Ryder"). The genesis of the Stamp Act is the subject of a considerable literature, including P. D. G. Thomas, *British Politics and the Stamp Act Crisis: The First Phase of the American Revolution, 1763–1767* (Oxford, 1975), chap. 3; John L. Bullion, *A Great and Necessary Measure: George Grenville and the Genesis of the Stamp Act, 1763–1765* (Columbia, Mo., 1982), chap. 1; Lawson, *George Grenville: A Political Life*, 187–202. For the imperial relationship before 1763, see Jack P. Greene, *Peripheries and Center: Constitutional Development in the Extended Polities of the British Empire and the United States, 1607–1788* (Athens, Ga., 1986), 7–76.

the lands seized from France and Spain.[5] As Thomas Whately, Grenville's treasury secretary and chief political confidant, explained in his defense of the government's military policy, "the Addition of an immense Territory in *North America,* and a very valuable one in the *West Indies*" had expanded the army "a little beyond former Peace Establishments," but he was sure that the nation had "all the reason in the World to hope the burthen will be well compensated both in Profit and Security, and that it will grow lighter every Day." In the words of another pamphlet, the "present army" was not only "suitable to our situation in Europe" but was "likely to prevent any insults, and to maintain an honourable and advantageous peace." As an indication of the prevalence of such views, the most serious criticism of the proposed establishment came from William Pitt, now in opposition, who worried, not that "the American force" was too numerous, but that it was "hardly sufficient for so large an extent of country."[6]

These attitudes had a good deal to do with the expectation that placing troops in North America would bring stability to the vast frontier beyond the borders of the older American colonies, including Quebec, Nova Scotia, East and West Florida, and—most significantly of all—the Indian lands of the trans-Appalachian interior, from which new settlers were excluded by the Proclamation of 1763. In keeping with contemporary European attitudes, the British tended to think of the territory to the west of the Proclamation Line as *terra nullius*—empty space, inhabited by Indians, French trappers, and British traders, none of whom had much appreciation for the finer points of English jurisprudence or the

5. Letter by "Anti-Sejanus", *London Chronicle,* XVIII, 523 (Nov. 28–30, 1765), in Edmund S. Morgan, ed., *Prologue to Revolution: Sources and Documents on the Stamp Act Crisis, 1764–1766* (New York, 1973), 100; Thomas, *British Politics and the Stamp Act Crisis,* 100. For the tendency in the press to criticize the general size of the peacetime establishment but not the deployment of troops in America, see esp. [David Hartley], *The Budget: Inscribed to the Man, Who Thinks Himself Minister . . . ,* 6th ed. (London, 1764), 5, 9; see also *A Letter to the Right Hon. the Earl of Temple, on the Subject of the Forty-fifth Number of the North-Briton . . .* (London, 1763), 17; [John Butler], *Serious Considerations on the Measures of the Present Administration . . .* (London, 1763), 15–18; [Butler], *An Address to the Cocoa-tree, from a Whig, and a Consultation on the Subject of a Standing-Army . . .* (London, 1763), vii, 25, 30–31, 50–52.

6. [Thomas Whately], *Remarks on the Budget; or, A Candid Examination of the Facts and Arguments Offered to the Public in That Pamphlet* (London, 1765), 6; *A Second Letter to the Right Honourable Charles Townshend, Occasioned by His Commendation of the Budget . . .* (London, 1765), 13–14; Simmons and Thomas, eds., *Proceedings and Debates,* I, 441.

FIGURE 17

The Indians Delivering up the English Captives to Colonel Bouquet. *By
Benjamin West. 1769. A benevolent British colonel restores two English children
to their natural families. Courtesy of the Yale Center for British Art,
Paul Mellon Collection*

European law of nations. As both the Americans and their English apologists were quick to point out, the individual colonies had traditionally managed relations in this extensive marchland, negotiating treaties with neighboring Indians, raising temporary levies in time of war, and relying on local militias for their other defensive needs. According to the proponents of imperial reform, however, it was inconceivable that such policies could bring order to the unsettled territories for which the British government was now responsible. Not only did the European settlers in this region seem to be "the outcasts of all Nations, and the refuse of Mankind" (as the British commanding officer at Detroit, Major Henry Bassett, assured a correspondent in 1769) but most people also assumed that only a standing army could fulfill remote obligations like occupying conquered and potentially hostile territory, ensuring that relations with the Indians remained peaceful, and garrisoning distant points in the immense wilderness between the Gulf of Mexico and the Great Lakes.[7]

Furthermore, despite the legendary prowess of colonial Indian fighters like Major Robert Rogers and his dissolute Rangers, most commentators insisted that British regulars were essential for securing the older colonies and those parts of North America designated for immediate settlement. "I am of opinion," declared an anonymous pamphleteer in 1763, that "there ought to be a proper force kept in our new acquisitions, for the protection of the settlers." As Thomas Whately put the issue, the presence of regular troops was certain to "promote the Settlement of the new Colonies; for Planters will value Property there much higher, and be more sollicitous to acquire it, when they observe that . . . measures are taken for putting those Provinces in a State of Defence." For many

7. On the adequacy of existing defensive strategies in America, see [James Otis], *Considerations on Behalf of the Colonists, in a Letter to a Noble Lord* (London, 1765), 29; [William Bollan], *The Mutual Interest of Great Britain and the American Colonies Considered* . . . (London, 1765), 10–11; [John Fothergill], *Considerations relative to the North American Colonies* (London, 1765), 9. The quote by Major Bassett comes from Jack M. Sosin, *Whitehall and the Wilderness: The Middle West in British Colonial Policy, 1760–1775* (Lincoln, Nebr., 1961), 218. Sosin's book is still the best treatment of British policy toward the new dominions, but see also the Report of the Board of Trade, June 18, 1763, in Adam Shortt and Arthur G. Doughty, eds., *Documents Relating to the Constitutional History of Canada, 1759–1791*, 2d ed. rev., 2 vols. (Ottawa, 1918), I, 139–140, 143; Fernand Ouellet, "The British Army of Occupation in the St. Lawrence Valley, 1760–74: The Conflict between Civil and Military Society," trans. A. Kern, in Roy Prete and A. Hamish Ion, eds., *Armies of Occupation* (Waterloo, Ont., 1984), 17–54; Philip Lawson, *The Imperial Challenge: Quebec and Britain in the Age of the American Revolution* (Montreal, 1989).

people, the central part that British regulars played in the conquest of Canada only enhanced this impression, suggesting that personal military service was no more popular in the settled regions of North America than it was in England, Scotland, and Wales. Likewise, the colonists' largely ineffective response to Pontiac's Rebellion (1763–1766)—the Indian insurrection that took hundreds of lives in Pennsylvania, New York, and the Ohio Valley—provided additional evidence that the Americans were neither willing nor able to assume primary responsibility for their own defense. Although people were willing to concede the military prowess of Americans when they were placed under regular discipline, professional soldiers now seemed to be every bit as necessary for the security of Britain's European settlements as they were on the near shores of the Atlantic.[8]

Finally, according to many, having troops in America promised to discourage both France and Spain from avenging their recent losses. Although not all Britons accepted Pitt's belief that the recent peace amounted to little more than a "temporary truce," many assumed that they would eventually have to fight another colonial war with one or both of the Bourbon powers.[9] Indeed, in the years immediately following the Treaty of Paris (1763), both Versailles and Madrid gave ample evidence of their warlike intentions, with imperial reforms that included raising new colonial taxes, replacing militias with regular troops, and rebuilding their decimated navies. Although such activities were cause for concern, however, many Britons remained hopeful that the combination of their naval superiority in the West Indies and the army in North America would enable the government to treat the neighboring possessions of both rivals as hostages for their good behavior. "Should the Enemy presume, in future, to disturb us in our legal Possession in any Quarter of the Globe," observed one defender of the ministry's colonial policy, "with what Facility may we pour Vengeance upon them, when our *American* Continent [is] conveniently placed . . . to controul the

8. *An Address to Sir John Cust, Bart., Speaker of the House of Commons; in Which the Characters of Lord Bute, Mr. Pitt, and Mr. Wilkes, Appear in a New Light* (London, 1761), 39; [Thomas Whately], *The Regulations Lately Made concerning the Colonies . . .* (London, 1765), 22. On the role of Pontiac's Rebellion in persuading British officials of the need for troops in America, see esp. Shy, *Toward Lexington,* 121–125.

9. The persistence of such tensions is covered in Scott, *British Foreign Policy,* 48–50. As Scott notes, Britain's rivalry with France and Spain was at least as intense after 1763 as it had been in the period before the war. The most serious confrontations included France's occupation of the Turks Islands in the West Indies in 1764, its seizure of Corsica in 1768, and the Falkland Islands dispute with Spain in 1771.

Islands of the *West-Indies?*" "The definitive Treaty is now Public," wrote another pamphleteer; "the many new countries in *America*, added to what we formerly had, will in Time secure us from the future Insult of *France* or *Spain*." Few people doubted that Britain's European rivals would eventually recover from their current "distress," as George Grenville reminded the House of Commons upon presenting his initial proposal for a colonial stamp tax. With adequate defensive arrangements in North America, however, the British might finally bring lasting security to their Atlantic empire.[10]

In other words, there were sound blue water arguments for keeping a standing army in North America, which explains why both George Grenville and his apologists were so quick to invoke the patriotic rhetoric of the early 1750s to justify their colonial policies. In the opening sections of *The Regulations Lately Made*, for example, Thomas Whately presented the government's activities in North America as a tangible sign that the corrupt Hanoverianism of earlier reigns had finally yielded to a virtuous attention to matters of national concern. Using the same logic, William Knox, the Irishman whose five years as an official in Georgia apparently gave him authority in such matters, claimed that Britain's dominance in North America had "put it in our power to wage another war with equal efficacy, and with infinitely less expence." By improving the trade and security of the crown's overseas possessions, the Grenville administration could plausibly claim to have ended what yet another apologist termed *"the age of treaties and guarantees,"* and to be substituting "the resources of a strict oeconomy" for the Continental system of *"guarantees, subsidies, extras, quotas,* and *dedommagements"* that had characterized Whig foreign policy since the Glorious Revolution. Although Britain would undoubtedly remain active in the affairs of Europe, the defenders of Grenville's policies hoped that its rulers would do so without falling back on the discredited strategies of the last half-century.[11]

---

10. *Reflections on the Terms of Peace . . .* (London, 1763), 31; *Impartial Observations, to Be Considered on by the King, His Ministers, and the People of Great Britain* ([London?, 1763]), 26 (inscribed in hand on the cover of the copy at the Huntington Library [Pamphlet 32435]: "Wrote 25th March 1763 for Lord Egremont [President of the Board of Trade]"); Thomas, ed., "Diaries of Ryder," 234. The author of *Impartial Observations* took it as a matter of course that the government's plans for North America ought to include maintaining regular troops and that these forces should be paid through an increase in tariffs (13).

11. [Whately], *The Regulations Lately Made*, 31 ("There have been Ministers ignorant of the Importance of the Colonies; others, have impotently neglected their Concerns; and others again have been diverted by meaner Pursuits from attending to them: But

Given these claims, the lack of English opposition to the government's plan to help finance the costs of the American establishment with a colonial revenue is not surprising. As Soame Jenyns, then in his eleventh year at the Board of Trade, put the question during Parliament's final consideration of the Stamp Act: "Can there be a more proper Time to force [the colonies] to maintain an Army at their Expence, than when that Army is necessary for their own Protection, and we are utterly unable to support it?" Thomas Whately struck a similar note: the growing costs of imperial defense, the perpetual nature of the public debt, and the disproportionate burden that both placed on ordinary people in Britain made it inconceivable that the colonists who benefited from this system should not assume some of the expense. Although the few members with colonial experience—notably William Beckford and the cashiered army officer Isaac Barré—raised some telling objections, the parliamentary debates that preceded the measure's final approval revealed broad support for the course of reform charted by the king's ministers. By attempting to tax the American colonists, the British government was obviously departing from the policies of earlier reigns. But it was doing so on the assumption that the troops this revenue would help support were essential if the British were to secure the strategic advantages that they had just fought an expensive war to preserve.[12]

The second reason many of Grenville's supporters gave for taxing the Americans involved the supposition that a perpetual revenue of some sort, whether based on tariffs, the land tax, or excise duties, represented an unavoidable political obligation. This belief reflected the nature of the fiscal bargain that the English had struck with the crown during the second half of the seventeenth century and that half a century of Whig rule had turned into one of the main foundations of Parliament's metro-

---

happily for this country, the Real and Substantial, and those are the Commercial Interest of Great Britain, are now preferred to every other Consideration"); [William Knox], *The Present State of the Nation: Particularly with respect to Its Trade, Finances, Etc. Etc.* (London, 1768), 12; *The Political Balance,* 34, 46, 60–61. For a trenchant critique of these claims, see *The Late Occurrences in North America, and Policy of Great Britain, Considered . . .* (London, 1766), 30–31.

12. [Soame Jenyns], *The Objections to the Taxation of Our American Colonies, by the Legislature of Great Britain, Briefly Consider'd* (London, 1765), 12; [Whately], *The Regulations Lately Made,* 56–57. The consensus in Parliament on the need to raise an American revenue is established in Thomas, *British Politics and the Stamp Act Crisis,* 55–57, 61, 85–100. For the objections of Beckford and Barré, see Simmons and Thomas, eds., *Proceedings and Debates,* II, 11–17.

politan authority. As William Blackstone described it in the first volume of his *Commentaries on the Laws of England* (1765), the current "perfection" of the British constitution was in large measure a result of the Restoration Parliament's decision to provide Charles II with a more certain revenue in exchange for the abolition of personal military tenures. In keeping with his own Tory background, Blackstone lamented the way this system of finance had enhanced the crown's informal power, enabling every monarch since William III to borrow apparently limitless funds in order to wage "long wars" for goals that often had little to do with Britain's own maritime and imperial interests. Because servicing this debt required a constant revenue, however, the crown had come in turn to depend "on the liberality of parliament for it's necessary support and maintenance." In other words, the dynamics of deficit finance and perpetual taxation fostered a symbiotic relationship between king and Parliament, which created obligations that were in practice mandatory. With careful management, the government might reduce some of this fiscal burden, but the idea of "the total abolition of taxes" struck Blackstone as "the height of political absurdity."[13]

Whether Blackstone was thinking of the developing controversy over colonial taxation when he wrote these words is hard to say. To many Britons, though, the political imperatives that made permanent taxation compulsory in Britain created equally pressing obligations in America. In *The Regulations Lately Made,* for example, Whately insisted that the protection that the British state bestowed on American shipping throughout the world had given rise to fiscal obligations that were every bit as extensive. Two years later, Grenville's secretary Charles Lloyd based his own defense of the Stamp Act on the fact that "the Americans, under the shade and protection of Great-Britain, have made rapid advances in population, commerce and wealth." In fact, some people argued that Parliament was under no obligation to confine the proceeds from the Stamp Act to the defense of the American frontier but might just as readily use colonial funds to meet general costs like the naval estimates that benefited the British Empire as a whole. In the words of the former governor of Massachusetts Thomas Pownall:

13. William Blackstone, *Commentaries on the Laws of England,* 4 vols. (1765–1769), ed. Stanley N. Katz et al. (Chicago, 1979), I, 296–297, 315, 323, 325. For more on Blackstone's analysis of English constitutional development, see Eliga Hayden Gould, "War, Empire and the Language of State Formation: British Imperial Culture in the Age of the American Revolution" (Ph.D. diss., Johns Hopkins University, 1993), 127–130.

It cannot but be observed, that as there are in each respective colony
services which regard the support of government, and the special
exigencies of the state and community of that colony, so there are
general services which regard the support of the crown, the rights
and dominions of Great Britain in general:—That as lands, tene-
ments, and other improved property within the colony, considered
as the private especial property of that community, should be left to
the legislatures of those colonies unincumbered by parliament . . .
so revenues by imposts, excise, or a stamp duty, become the proper
fund whereon the parliament of Great Britain may, with the utmost
delicacy and regard to the colonies power of taxing themselves,
raise those taxes which are raised for the general service of the
crown.[14]

What made the Stamp Act seem so urgent, however, was the crushing
debt that commentators were sure would otherwise descend on the British themselves. Indeed, according to many of the Stamp Act's defenders,
the signs of economic hardship that followed the war's end—including
labor unrest in London, massive resistance to the cider tax in the West
Country, and grain riots across much of northern England—signaled
that the common people of "Great Britain [were] sufficiently exhausted
already." During the debates over the Stamp Act's repeal, Lord Lyttleton
claimed that only an American revenue could alleviate the "dreadful"
burdens on "the gentry and people of this Kingdom." Using the same

14. The *Commentaries* make no mention of the specific issue of colonial taxation;
Blackstone's parliamentary statements on the question all concerned Parliament's legal
right to impose taxes rather than the necessity or utility of doing so (see esp. Black-
stone's speech of Feb. 3, 1766, in Simmons and Thomas, eds., *Proceedings and Debates*,
II, 140, 147–148); [Whately], *The Regulations Lately Made*, 51–52, 57; [Charles Lloyd],
The Conduct of the Late Administration Examined, relative to the American Stamp Act, 2d
ed. (London, 1767), 136; Thomas Pownall, *The Administration of the Colonies*, 2d ed.
(London, 1765), 90. The passage concludes:

> Because these kind of taxes are (if I may be permitted the expression) coincident
> with those regulations which the laws of the realm prescribe to trade in general; to
> manufactures—and to every legal act and deed;—because they are duties which
> arise from the general rights and jurisdiction of the realm, rather than from the
> particular and special concerns of any one colony . . . (90–91)

For the broader uses of the proceeds from the stamp tax, see the parliamentary speeches
of Grenville and Charles Townshend during the debate of Feb. 6, 1765, in Simmons
and Thomas, eds., *Proceedings and Debates*, II, 10, 13; [Whately], *The Regulations Lately
Made*, 56, 101–104.

logic, Whately spoke of the need to safeguard "the Consumption of the Poor," and William Knox was sure that the effects of failing to tax the colonies "already begin to shew themselves in the increased price of labour and the necessities of life." There were even writers for whom the attempt to tax the colonists demonstrated the government's paternal concern for the welfare of ordinary people. In the words of the fictitious John Ploughshare, it was "neither fair nor honest" for the colonists to refuse to make a modest contribution toward maintaining "that army which defends them against the savages." "If the Americans . . . would judge with candour," another British polemicist put the issue in 1769, "they would readily acknowledge that their brethren on this side the Atlantic lie under much more pressing burdens than themselves."[15]

In addition to such concerns, most apologists gave as a final reason for taxing the colonists their firm belief that Parliament's authority was every bit as extensive in the settled regions of North America and the West Indies as it was in England, Scotland, and Wales. The definitive statement came from Whately, who argued in *The Regulations Lately Made* that Parliament "virtually" represented the American colonists in the same manner that it represented those Britons—including all women and most men—who did not have a direct say in choosing its members. Indeed, because Parliament theoretically spoke for the nation as a whole, Whately maintained, "all *British* Subjects are really in the same [condition]; none are actually, all are virtually represented in Parliament; for every Member of Parliament sits in the House, not as Representative of his own constituents, but as one of that august Assembly by which all the Commons of *Great Britain* are represented." Whately acknowledged that the existence of provincial legislatures meant that Parliament would "not often have occasion to exercise its Power over the Colonies." When it came to matters that concerned the welfare of the whole, however, Britain and America together constituted "one Nation" whose subjects all had to "be govern'd by the same supreme Authority."[16]

15. *The Justice and Necessity of Taxing the American Colonies, Demonstrated . . .* (London, 1766), 10; *Protest against the Bill to Repeal the American Stamp Act, of the Last Session* ([London], 1766), 9; [Whately], *The Regulations Lately Made*, 56–57; [Knox], *The Present State of the Nation*, 30; John Ploughshare, "I Am for Old England," *London Chronicle* (Feb. 20, 1766), in Morgan, ed., *Prologue to Revolution*, 103; *The True Constitutional Means for Putting an End to the Disputes between Great-Britain and the American Colonies* (London, 1769), 31.

16. [Whately], *The Regulations Lately Made*, 40, 109, 112. The last passage quoted concludes: "Their connexion would otherwise be an Alliance, not a Union; and they would be no longer one State, but a confederacy of many: Local Purposes may indeed

The most striking feature of this formulation was Whately's assumption that the colonists were subject to Parliament by virtue of a common nationality that owed nothing to the exercise of positive political rights. Although not everyone was quite so confident that Westminster could tax the colonies without allowing for some sort of consultation, the fact that active participation played so little role in the patriotism of ordinary men and women in Britain made the denial of such rights to America seem much less anomalous. During the debates that preceded the Stamp Act's eventual repeal, both the measure's supporters and many of its opponents pointed to the numerous occasions in English history when Parliament had taxed individuals and groups that did not have a direct vote for its members. Until the second half of the seventeenth century, Grenville's defenders claimed, the counties palatinate of Durham and Chester had both been taxed by Parliament without sending representatives to the House of Commons. In a similar manner, the succession of wars since the Glorious Revolution had turned the taxation of those without a direct vote into a permanent feature of Parliament's metropolitan sovereignty. "There were twelve millions of people in England and Ireland who were not represented," noted Lord Mansfield during the debates over the Stamp Act, yet every one of them paid taxes levied in Parliament. William Knox made the same point with a series of rhetorical questions:

> When the tax was laid upon hops, did the people who were to pay the tax, viz. the hop-growers, consent to it, either by themselves or their distinct representatives? Did the people in the cyder counties, or their distinct representatives, consent to the tax upon cyder? Is the land-tax kept up at three shillings with the consent of all the land-owners in the kingdom, or that of all the knights of shires, their distinct representatives? What tax is it indeed to which those who pay it, or their distinct representatives, have all consented? . . . If this be the case, he must be a patriot indeed who pays any tax whatever, since he can so easily discharge himself from it, by only saying he does not choose to pay it.[17]

---

be provided for by local Powers, but general Provisions can only be made by a Council that has general Authority; that Authority vested by indefeasible right in Parliament over all the Subjects of Great-Britain."

17. Thomas Pownall, *The Administration of the Colonies*, 4th ed. rev. (London, 1768), 140; Simmons and Thomas, eds., *Proceedings and Debates*, II, 129–133, 568; [William Knox], *The Controversy between Great-Britain and Her Colonies Reviewed* . . . (London,

Even after reports of the massive riots that greeted the Stamp Act began to appear in the metropolitan press, British observers continued to use such arguments. During the winter of 1765–1766, pamphlets frequently compared the protests in America with the initial unpopularity of the excise in the outlying regions of England and Scotland.[18] Similarly, both Lord Mansfield and Fletcher Norton reminded their colleagues of the plebeian crowds that had defied Parliament over the English Militia Act less than a decade before; by taxing the colonists without their consent, Norton insisted, "we use North America as we use ourselves." Indeed, many members of Parliament acquiesced in the gradual move toward using military force that began during the summer of 1768, on the assumption that regular troops would be able to deal with the popular opposition to taxation in America in the same way they did excise riots in Britain. No less a figure than the Secretary at War, Lord Barrington, held this view. As he assured Sir William Draper:

> The present commotions at Boston are such as we see almost every day in our own country: in both there are always men who prefer their own interest to the obedience which every good subject owes to the laws, and factious people who avail themselves of every clamour which arises. . . . For a time the laws are without efficacy, unless supported by a proper degree of legal force: when such a force appears at Boston, I am persuaded the Magistrates will be easily enabled to do their duty; and wholesome example will secure future obedience to the laws in all parts of America.[19]

1769), 87–88. Some members of Parliament—notably Edmund Burke and the Rockingham Whigs—opposed the Stamp Act for pragmatic reasons but nonetheless accepted the principle of parliamentary sovereignty; see Paul Langford, "Old Whigs, Old Tories, and the American Revolution," *Journal of Imperial and Commonwealth History*, VIII (1980), 106–130. On the parallels between the American colonies and England's counties palatinate, see Lord Mansfield's speech in the upper house on Feb. 3, 1766 (Simmons and Thomas, eds., *Proceedings and Debates*, II, 129–133); Pownall, *The Administration of the Colonies*, 4th ed., 140.

18. *Considerations on the American Stamp Act, and on the Conduct of the Minister Who Planned It* (London, 1765), 30–31; [William Knox], *A Letter to a Member of Parliament, Wherein the Power of the British Legislature, and the Case of the Colonists, Are Briefly and Impartially Considered* (London, 1765), 1–2; *The Justice and Necessity of Taxing the American Colonies, Demonstrated . . . , Together with a Vindication of the Authority of Parliament* (London, 1766), 13.

19. Simmons and Thomas, eds., *Proceedings and Debates*, II, 169 (for Mansfield's reference to the militia, see 130); Barrington to Draper, Sept. 1, 1768, Papers of William Wildman, Viscount Barrington, Suffolk Record Office (hereafter Barrington Papers),

Events would soon show just how mistaken such assumptions were. As the full extent of Grenville's miscalculation impressed itself on the British public, the Stamp Act began to draw criticism from many of the same groups that had rallied to William Pitt's imperial standard a decade before: middle-class patriots, merchants and manufacturers with interests in North America, and parliamentary politicians bent on cultivating a reputation for popularity. Long after the difficulties of raising a colonial revenue had become clear, however, Grenville's apologists continued to insist that, in attempting to secure the gains of the Seven Years' War, the government had asked for nothing from America that the Whig regime did not already expect as a matter of course at home. Moreover, although members of Parliament had adopted the Stamp Act with only the vaguest sense of what their constituents thought, such arguments carried weight with the general public. Indeed, the principal reason why the standoff between Parliament and the colonies proved so intractable was the continued assumption that the various conditions that made for the perfection of the British constitution in England, Scotland, and Wales operated in equal measure throughout the other settled regions of the empire. As the governor of Massachusetts, Sir Francis Bernard, reminded the members of the provincial assembly during the summer of 1765:

> In an empire, extended and diversified as that of Great Britain, there must be a supreme legislature, to which all other powers must be subordinate. It is our happiness that the supreme legislature, the parliament of Great Britain, is the sanctuary of liberty and justice; and that the prince, who presides over it, realizes the idea of a patriot King. Surely then, we should submit our opinions to the determinations of so august a body; and acquiesce in a perfect confidence, that the rights of the members of the British empire will ever be safe in the hands of the conservators of the liberty of the whole.[20]

HA 174/Acc 1026/107, 112–113. See also Barrington to General Thomas Gage, Aug. 1, 1768, Barrington Papers, HA 174/Acc 1026/107, 107–108, in which he reminded the commander of the British forces in America that "Riotous Englishmen in New England must be treated as their fellows in Old England, they must be compelled to obey the law and the civil magistrate must have troops to enforce that obedience."

20. [John Almon, ed.], *A Collection of Papers relative to the Dispute between Great Britain and America, 1764–1775* (1777; New York, 1971), 8–9 (hereafter cited as Almon, ed., *Prior Documents*).

II. AN AMERICAN THEORY OF EMPIRE

If officials like Bernard regarded the creation of an American revenue as a natural expression of Parliament's authority, Grenville's reforms struck the colonists (and their metropolitan sympathizers) in an entirely different light. Following the lead of the Virginia House of Burgesses, most assemblies insisted on their own competence in matters of "internal Polity and Taxation" and denied the legality of any revenue measure that had not received "their own Consent." At the same time, merchants in ports up and down the North American seaboard organized boycotts of British goods, and more radical groups began planning the popular resistance that convulsed Boston, New York, and a number of other ports during the summer of 1765. "It is enough to break the heart of the Patriot," wrote a contributor to the *New York Mercury,* "to find [his country] fainting and despairing, hourly expecting to be utterly crush'd by the iron rod of power." In the words of the resolves adopted by the Sons of Liberty in Wallingford, Connecticut, "the late act of Parliament called the Stamp-Act, is unconstitutional, and intended to enslave the true subjects of America." And the town of Wilmington, North Carolina, warned that "moderation ceases to be a virtue, when the liberty of British subjects is in danger." "I mean not . . . to exaggerate things," wrote Pennsylvania attorney John Dickinson in an open letter to William Pitt, but it was "certain, that an unexampled and universal Jealousy, Grief and Indignation [had] been excited in the Colonists by the Conduct of the Mother Country since the Conclusion of the last War."[21]

Although American historians have tended to emphasize the "radical" character of the Stamp Act crisis of 1765, colonial polemicists were quick to assert that their opposition did not mean they disputed the general principle of Parliament's imperial sovereignty; nor, they insisted, did they object to contributing to the costs of government in Britain. In fact, throughout the imperial crisis, one of the mainstays of the American response was the large, though indirect, subsidies that the crown's overseas dominions already made through their compliance with the navigation laws. In the words of the declaration that John Dickinson drafted for the Stamp Act Congress, Britain's monopoly on the "trade of

21. "The Virginia Resolves" (May 30, 1765), in Jack P. Greene, ed., *Colonies to Nation, 1763–1789: A Documentary History of the American Revolution* (1967; New York, 1975), 61; *New-York Mercury,* Oct. 21, 1765; *Connecticut Courant* (Hartford), Dec. 30, 1765; "Address of the Mayor and Gentlemen of Wilmington to Governor Tryon," July 28, 1766, in Almon, ed., *Prior Documents,* 112; Dickinson to Pitt, in Morgan, ed., *Prologue to Revolution,* 119.

FIGURE 18

Virtual Representation. *1775. Two colonists, the second and third figures from the right, view parliamentary taxes as robbery while a blinded Britannia runs headlong into a "pit prepared for others."* © The British Museum

these colonies" meant that "they eventually contribute very largely to all supplies granted there to the crown." Benjamin Franklin made the same point in his famous testimony before the House of Commons: although the colonists denied Parliament's right to impose internal taxes, they readily conceded that "the sea is yours." "You maintain, by your fleets, the safety of navigation in it, and keep it clear of pirates; you may have therefore a natural and equitable right to some toll or duty on merchandizes carried through that part of your dominions." As John Morgan explained in an essay that won him the College of Philadelphia's Sargent Prize in 1766:

> The whole trade of America to all parts of the globe employs, one year with another, above two thousand sail of English ships, by which treasures of greater wealth are conveyed to Britain, than are derived [by Spain] from Mexico or Peru. . . . From the commodities of America, chiefly manufactured in England, and conveyed through innumerable channels of trade to every quarter of

the globe, Great-Britain acquires immense wealth, keeps up a spirit of industry among her inhabitants, and is enabled to support mighty fleets, great in peace and formidable in war.[22]

One reason for this emphasis on the navigation laws was to refute charges that colonists opposing the Stamp Act had committed acts of rebellion or were in any way challenging the British constitution. "Nothing can be more cruel and absurd," commented a sympathetic pamphleteer in England, "than to pronounce a whole people rebellious, because a few unavowed rioters get together and burn a coach." Indeed, American polemicists insisted that they were, in the main, a loyal and patriotic people. "If I have one ambitious wish," wrote Massachusetts assemblyman James Otis, "it is to see Great-Britain at the head of the world, and to see my King, under God, the father of mankind." John Dickinson echoed these sentiments in his public letter to the planters of Barbados, insisting that "every drop of blood in my heart is *British*." As Franklin assured the House of Commons, the Americans had long regarded the British constitution as "the best in the world":

> They submitted willingly to the government of the crown, and paid, in all their courts, obedience to acts of parliament. Numerous as the people are in the several old provinces, they cost you nothing in forts, citadels, garrisons or armies, to keep them in subjection. They were governed by this country at the expence only of a little pen, ink and paper. They were led by a thread. They had not only a respect, but an affection for Great-Britain, for its laws, its customs and manners, and even a fondness for its fashions, that greatly increased the commerce.[23]

While demonstrating their allegiance to the present regime, the colonists' compliance with the Navigation Acts also enabled their apologists

22. "Declaration of the Stamp Act Congress" (Oct. 19, 1765), in Greene, ed., *Colonies to Nation,* 64; "Examination of Benjamin Franklin" (Feb. 13, 1766), in Almon, ed., *Prior Documents,* 73; John Morgan, "Dissertation I," *Four Dissertations, on the Reciprocal Advantages of a Perpetual Union between Great-Britain and Her American Colonies . . .* (London, 1766), 17.
23. *Considerations on the American Stamp Act,* 30; James Otis, *The Rights of the British Colonies Asserted and Proved,* 2d ed. (London, 1766), 61; [John Dickinson], *An Address to the Committee of Correspondence in Barbados . . .* (Philadelphia, 1766), in Paul Leicester Ford, ed., *The Writings of John Dickinson,* I, *Political Writings, 1764–1774* (Historical Society of Pennsylvania, *Memoirs,* XIV), (Philadelphia, 1895), 267; "Examination," in Almon, ed., *Prior Documents,* 67.

to draw attention to the part that the monopoly on American commerce had played in making Britain the preeminent maritime power in Europe. As William Pitt reminded the House of Commons, profits from "the trade of the colonies" currently amounted to some "two millions a year" and had provided the bulk of the "fund that carried you triumphantly through the last war." In the words of another observer, there were some that had "treated the Americans with great freedom and contempt, yet it should be remembered that Britain owes her present importance and power to them alone." Perhaps betraying an early indication of the madness that would end his career, James Otis even predicted that "the next universal monarchy" would be British and that the world was about to witness "the highest scene of earthly power and grandeur that has been ever yet displayed to the view of mankind." Indeed, the Stamp Act's opponents frequently noted that the Americans already contributed far more to maintaining British naval power than the sixty thousand pounds that Grenville had expected the new measure to yield. "As long as this globe continues moving," wrote John Dickinson in 1766, "may [Great Britain] reign over its navigable part"—adding, for good measure, "and may she resemble the ocean she commands, which recruits without wasting, and receives without exhausting."[24]

The following decade would show that the American distinction between Parliament's sovereignty over their external trade and its right to tax internally for revenue was unsustainable. Within months of the Stamp Act's repeal, in fact, a new ministry led by none other than William Pitt, now earl of Chatham, was once again considering measures for raising an American revenue, this time through the commercial tariffs that polemicists like Franklin had insisted the colonists did not

24. [William Pitt, earl of Chatham], *The Celebrated Speech of a Celebrated Commoner,* [London, 1766], 15; *The Necessity of Repealing the American Stamp-Act Demonstrated; or, A Proof That Great-Britain Must Be Injured by That Act* . . . (London, 1766), 29; [Dickinson], *An Address to the Committee in Barbados,* in Ford, ed., *Writings of Dickinson,* 267. The passage containing Otis's quote merits citation in full:

The cards are shuffling fast through all Europe. Who will win the prize is with God. This however I know, *detur degniori.* The next universal monarchy will be favourable to the human race, for it must be founded on the principles of equity, moderation and justice. No country has been more distinguished for these principles than Great Britain, since the revolution.

Otis, *The Rights of the British Colonies,* 61. See also [John Dickinson], *The Late Regulations, respecting the British Colonies on the Continent of America Considered* . . . (London, 1766), 32: "I think it may justly be said, that THE FOUNDATIONS OF THE POWER AND GLORY OF GREAT BRITAIN ARE LAID IN AMERICA."

Worthy of Liberty. Mr. Pitt scorns to invade the Liberties of other People.

FIGURE 19

Worthy of Liberty, Mr. Pitt Scorns to Invade the Liberties of Other People.
*By Charles Willson Peale. 1766. Pitt holds a copy of the Magna Carta in one
hand while he points with the other to a representation of British liberty
trampling on the American Congress's petition for repeal of the Stamp Act.*
Colonial Williamsburg Foundation

mind paying.[25] Yet even after the Townshend Revenue Act touched off a fresh round of protests in the colonies, American patriots continued to insist that they had no objection to the substantial benefits that the British gained from Parliament's regulation of their maritime trade. As the Massachusetts House of Representatives assured Lord Chancellor Camden in early 1768: "The subjects in this province, and undoubtedly in all the colonies, however they may have been otherwise represented to his Majesty's ministers, are loyal: They are firmly attached to the mother state: They always consider her interest and their own as inseparably interwoven, and it is their fervent wish that it may ever so remain."[26]

Although no one doubted that the colonists were obligated to contribute to the British crown directly, however, Americans were sure that their own provincial assemblies were the only legislative bodies with the right to approve such financial grants. In the words of the petition that the Stamp Act Congress presented to George III, the colonists readily conceded a general duty "to grant to your Majesty such Aids as are required for the Support of your Government over them, and other public Exigencies," but the only way they could give their consent was through the assemblies of their respective provinces. Even the crowds in American ports, whose anger over parliamentary taxation occasionally betrayed an impatience with their own elected leaders, signaled their acceptance of this principle by limiting their violence to politicians who refused to denounce the Stamp Act. Benjamin Franklin explained the colonists' position on taxation and representation to the House of Commons:

> Their opinion is, that when aids to the crown are wanted, they are to be asked of the several assemblies, according to the old established usage, who will, as they always have done, grant them

25. Thomas, *British Politics and the Stamp Act Crisis*, chap. 16; Lawrence Henry Gipson, *The Coming of the Revolution, 1763–1775* (New York, 1962), chap. 11. The notion that Americans would accept "external" taxes, which ministerial apologists used to justify the Townshend duties, reflected a widespread misunderstanding of what Franklin had actually said in his testimony to Parliament. According to the published version of his statement, Franklin only claimed that it was "the opinion of every one [in the colonies], that we could not be taxed in a parliament where we were not represented. But the payment of duties laid by act of parliament, as regulations of commerce was never disputed" (Almon, ed., *Prior Documents*, 68).

26. Letter dated Jan. 29, 1768, in [Thomas Hollis, ed.], *The True Sentiments of America. . . . Contained in a Collection of Letters Sent from the House of Representatives of the Province of Massachusetts Bay to Several Persons of High Rank in this Kingdom. Together with Certain Papers relating to a Supposed Libel on the Governor of That Province* (London, 1768), 36.

freely. . . . The granting aids to the crown, is the only means they have of recommending themselves to their sovereign, and they think it extremely hard and unjust, that a body of men, in which they have no representatives, should make a merit to itself of giving and granting what is not its own, but theirs, and deprive them of a right they esteem of the utmost value and importance, as it is the security of all their other rights.[27]

As Franklin's choice of words suggested, colonial polemicists assumed that their assemblies enjoyed such exclusive powers of taxation partly as a matter of right. In order to substantiate this point, Americans often drew on the history of England's relations with the outlying regions of the British Isles, noting—as Maryland attorney Daniel Dulany did in 1766— that English monarchs had customarily secured the consent of provincial representatives before asking them "to perform or pay anything extrafeudal." As Lord Camden observed during the debates over the Stamp Act's repeal, there was "not a blade of grass" anywhere in Britain "which when taxed, was not taxed by the consent of the proprietor," and Camden insisted, despite contrary assertions by the Stamp Act's supporters, that neither the Welsh nor the inhabitants of counties palatinate like Durham and Chester had been subject to parliamentary taxation before they were granted representation in the House of Commons. Indeed, where Grenville's defenders claimed that the Glorious Revolution had given Parliament unlimited authority over the rest of the empire, American apologists virtually took it for granted that the same settlement that had secured the principle of legislative sovereignty in England provided equally firm guarantees for their own provincial assemblies. In the words of the Declaration of Rights and Grievances adopted by the Stamp Act Congress in October 1765, it was "inseparably essential to the freedom of a people, and the undoubted rights of Englishmen, that no taxes should be imposed on them, but with their own consent, given personally, or by their representatives."[28]

27. "A Petition to the King from the Stamp Act Congress" (Oct. 19, 1765), in Ford, ed., *Writings of Dickinson*, 194; "Examination," in Almon, ed., *Prior Documents*, 72. For the constitutional principles of rioters protesting the Stamp Act, see Pauline Maier, *From Resistance to Revolution: Colonial Radicals and the Development of American Opposition to Britain, 1765–1776* (1972; New York, 1991), chap. 3; Gary Nash, *Urban Crucible: The Northern Seaports and the Origins of the American Revolution* (Cambridge, Mass., 1979), chap. 6.

28. [Daniel Dulany], *Considerations on the Propriety of Imposing Taxes in the British Colonies for the Purpose of Raising a Revenue . . .* (Annapolis, 1765), in Bernard Bailyn

For all their certainty, however, the colonists did not claim the right to be taxed by their own representatives only as a matter of principle. As American commentators never tired of pointing out, this decentralization of fiscal authority owed at least as much to the colonies' well-documented history of providing for their own defensive needs through temporary levies and provincial militias. "I cannot help remarking," wrote the former Massachusetts agent William Bollan in 1765, "that, for one hundred years past, whilst Canada and Louisiana were in the hands of France, the colonies wanted no such defence or security from England; but, on the contrary, they defended themselves." According to the governor of Rhode Island, Stephen Hopkins, there was no precedent for either a standing army or a parliamentary revenue in America, since most colonies had been settled entirely "at the expence of the planters themselves" and had been left "to the protection of heaven and their own efforts" during the long wars with the French and Indians. During Parliament's preliminary consideration of the Stamp Act, Isaac Barré went even further, urging the House of Commons to consider whether the colonies really had been "planted by your care," "nourished by *your* indulgence," and "protected by *your* arms"—or whether settlers had gone to America because of "your oppressions," had grown "by your neglect," and now merited nothing more than Britain's thanks for remaining "as truly loyal as any subjects the King has." As Jared Ingersoll of Connecticut, who witnessed Barré's performance from the Commons gallery, later confided, "I own I felt Emotions that I never felt before."[29]

These alone were adequate reasons to oppose paying a tax that the Stamp Act's supporters depicted as necessary to provide a peacetime army for the colonies' defense. But most commentators carried the issue

and Jane N. Garrett, eds., *Pamphlets of the American Revolution, 1750–1776* (Cambridge, Mass., 1965–), I, 613; Simmons and Thomas, eds., *Proceedings and Debates*, II, 322; "Declaration," in Greene, ed., *Colonies to Nation*, 64. For a fuller discussion of the "imperial constitution" as the colonists understood it, see Greene, *Peripheries and Center*, chaps. 4, 5.

29. [Bollan], *The Mutual Interest of Great Britain and the American Colonies Considered with respect to an Act Passed Last Session of Parliament for Laying a Duty on Merchandise, Etc. with Some Remarks on a Pamphlet, Intitled, "Objections to the Taxation of the American Colonies, Etc. Considered." In a Letter to a Member of Parliament*, 10; [Stephen Hopkins], *The Grievances of the American Colonies Candidly Examined . . .* (London, 1766), 38–39; Simmons and Thomas, eds., *Proceedings and Debates*, II, 16; *The Fitch Papers: Correspondence and Documents during Thomas Fitch's Governorship of the Colony of Connecticut, 1754–1766*, II (Jan. 1759–May 1766), (*Collections of the Connecticut Historical Society*, XVIII) (1920), 322–323.

FIGURE 20

The Parricide: A Sketch of Modern Patriotism. *1776. An Indian (America)
prepares to stab a staggering Britannia while John Wilkes (to America's
immediate left) and his fellow "patriots" in the burgeoning radical movement
look on approvingly. The figure on the far left represents faction:
The irresponsible behavior of the Wilkites at home is linked to the enthusiasm of
the Americans' defiance of parliamentary taxation.
Courtesy of the John Carter Brown Library at Brown University*

further still by insisting that the colonists' military self-sufficiency had
ultimately made them far more effective participants in Britain's wars
with France than if they had been reduced to supporting a permanent
revenue of the sort that Grenville's apologists had in mind. The achievements of the New England provincials during the Cape Breton expedition of 1745 often featured with particular prominence in such accounts.
"Everyone knows the importance of *Louisbourg,* in the consultations of
Aix la Chapelle," wrote James Otis, and Massachusetts clergyman Amos
Adams insisted that the "success of the New-England arms" had supplied the "*single* equivalent for all the conquests of France" and Cape
Breton "the price that purchased the peace of Europe."[30] In addition,

30. Otis, *The Rights of the British Colonies,* 87; Amos Adams, *A Concise, Historical
View of the Difficulties, Hardships, and Perils Which Attended the Planting and Progressive*

polemicists argued that the level of American participation during the Seven Years' War was comparable to that within Britain itself. "This house may appeal to the nation, that the utmost aid of the people has been chearfully given when his Majesty required it" was the way the members of the Massachusetts assembly put the issue in their famous 1768 letter to Lord Chatham. "Can there then be a necessity for so great a change, and in its nature so delicate and important that instead of having the honour of his Majesty's requisitions laid before their representatives here, as has been invariably the usage, the parliament should now tax them without their consent?"[31]

Probably the most striking feature of this account of Westminster's relations with the colonies was the emphasis that American apologists placed on personal military service. As William Bollan argued in 1765, Americans would be only too "glad to see those red coats embark for England, since they can be of no use to the colonies, whose real defence and protection is received from the British navy, and the valour of their own native militia." Elsewhere, polemicists insisted that, although a standing army might be the appropriate way to secure a conquered province like Quebec, the right of self-defense represented one of the chief benchmarks of English liberty in the older colonies. Indeed, because the regular army was entirely subject to the fiscal control of Parliament, the only legal way for the colonists to fulfill their military obligations was by maintaining local militias and raising temporary levies in times of emergency. As observers described it, the result was a system

---

Improvements of New England (London, 1770), 49. For additional references to the Cape Breton expedition, see [Bollan], *The Mutual Interest of Great Britain and the American Colonies Considered*, 10; [Hopkins], *Grievances of the American Colonies*, 38–39; Massachusetts House of Representatives to the earl of Chatham, Feb. 2, 1768, in [Hollis, ed.], *The True Sentiments of America*, 39; [Stephen Sayre], *The Englishman Deceived: A Political Piece, Wherein Some Very Important Secrets of State Are Briefly Recited* . . . (London, 1768), 34–35; [John Erskine], *Shall I Go to War with My American Brethren?* . . . (London, 1769), 31; *A Brief Review of the Rise and Progress, Services and Sufferings, of New England, Especially the Province of Massachuset's-Bay* (London, 1774).

31. Letter dated Feb. 2, 1768, in [Hollis, ed.], *The True Sentiments of America*, 39. On the alleged levels of American participation in the Seven Years' War, see [Israel Mauduit], *Some Thoughts on the Method of Improving and Securing the Advantages Which Accrue to Great-Britain from the Northern Colonies* (London, 1765), 13–14; *Four Dissertations on the Reciprocal Advantages of a Perpetual Union*, 18, 86–87; *The Crisis; or, A Full Defence of the Colonies* (London, 1766), 21–22; *The Necessity of Repealing the American Stamp-Act*, 8; [Dulany], *Considerations on Imposing Taxes*, in Bailyn and Garrett, eds., *Pamphlets of the American Revolution*, 622.

of military obligation that guaranteed North America would remain a ready source of recruits even as it made Parliament's attempts at taxation both unnecessary and inadvisable. "How easily are Fleets or Armies recruited for an *American* or *West Indian* Expedition, from two Millions of People just upon the Spot?" asked the English Quaker and royal physician Dr. John Fothergill in 1765. In the words of another essayist:

> Here is a fund of hardy, brave soldiers, inured to fatigue and frugality, ready to engage in the service of *Great-Britain*, whenever she thinks proper to require them. From this fruitful, this increasing source, her armies and navies may receive constant supplies, not of mercenary hirelings ready to engage in the service of the highest bidder, but faithful, dutiful children, animated with becoming fortitude, freedom and loyalty. These, if encouraged, cherished and protected, will indeed prove "Of *Britain's* empire the support and strength."[32]

The American response to the Stamp Act thus highlighted a fundamental schism between metropolitan and provincial definitions of patriotism. Although Grenville and his supporters had insisted otherwise, their attempt to tax the colonists demonstrated that the conditions that made it possible for Parliament to assume final responsibility for all questions of political obligation in Britain simply did not exist in the colonies. Not surprisingly, the Townshend Revenue Act (which included paying the salaries of royal governors among the purposes for which Parliament might tax the colonists) only intensified this conflict. As William Johnson, who acted as the agent for Connecticut in London during the later 1760s, wrote on learning of the new measure, empowering Parliament to assume such extensive responsibilities would eventually deprive the colonists of any political influence whatever, making it

---

32. [Bollan], *The Mutual Interest of Great Britain and the American Colonies Considered,* 11; [Fothergill], *Considerations relative to the North American Colonies,* 8; *Four Dissertations, on the Reciprocal Advantages of a Perpetual Union,* 87. On the relationship between militias and colonial autonomy, see also Massachusetts House of Representatives to Dennis DeBerdt, Jan. 12, 1768, in [Hollis, ed.], *The True Sentiments of America,* 72–74; William Pitkin to William Samuel Johnson, June 6, 1768, in "Letters of Dr. William Samuel Johnson," *Trumbull Papers* (Massachusetts Historical Society, *Collections,* 5th Ser., IX [1895]), 276–284 (hereafter cited as *Trumbull Papers*); Sir Francis Bernard to Lord Hillsborough, Sept. 16, 1768, in *Letters to the Ministry, from Governor Bernard, General Gage, and Commodore Hood* . . . (London, 1769), 72–74; [Dulany], *Considerations on Imposing Taxes,* in Bailyn and Garrett, eds., *Pamphlets of the American Revolution,* I, 642–643; *The Necessity of Repealing the American Stamp-Act,* 12–13.

unnecessary for "an American Governor . . . [to] know whether his government is in that country or in Indostan, in Bengal or at the Cape of Good Hope." John Dickinson made the point even more forcefully in his celebrated *Letters from a Farmer in Pennsylvania* (1768), warning—in a pointed response to Governor Pownall—that once Parliament assumed such powers colonial assemblies would cease to enjoy even the "puny privileges of French parliaments."

> When the charges of the "administration of justice," the "support of civil government," and the expenses of "defending, protecting and securing" us, are provided for, I should be glad to know, upon *what occasions* the crown will ever call our assemblies together. Some few of them may meet of their own accord, by virtue of their charters. But what will they have to do, when they are met? To what shadows will they be reduced? The men, whose deliberations here-tofore had an influence on every matter relating to the *liberty* and *happiness* of themselves and their constituents, and whose authority in domestic affairs at least, might well be compared to that of *Roman* senators, will *now* find their deliberations of no more conse-quence, than those of *constables*.[33]

Largely as a result of these concerns, a growing number of observers insisted that the only way to safeguard the principle of voluntary obliga-tion in the colonies was to reconceptualize Britain's Atlantic empire as a confederation of sovereign states bound together, not by Parliament's unlimited authority, but by allegiance to a common monarch. In some ways, of course, this shift amounted to little more than a belated recogni-tion that Britain's relations with the colonies were not all that different from those with subsidiary allies like Portugal or Hanover. "If Britain has protected the property of America," wrote a pamphleteer in 1769, "it does not constitute her the owner of that property. She has, for her own sake, protected, in their turns, almost every country in Europe, but that does not make her the proprietor of those countries, or give her a power of taxation over them." At the same time, though, introducing the law of nations into what British theorists continued to depict as a civil dispute carried undeniably subversive implications. In a reply to William Knox's "review" of the imperial controversy, for example, Edward Bancroft, an American-born physician resident in London, argued that, because En-

---

33. Letter to Governor William Pitkin, July 13, 1767, in *Trumbull Papers*, 239; [John Dickinson], *Letters from a Farmer in Pennsylvania, to the Inhabitants of the British Colonies* (Philadelphia, 1768), in Ford, ed., *Writings of Dickinson*, 369, 373.

gland's title to North America during the first age of settlement had been vested in the person of Queen Elizabeth, the colonies owed allegiance to "the *English* Crown" but were under no obligation to obey any act of Parliament, *"even for regulating our Commerce."* Thomas Jefferson employed a similar argument in his famous appeal to George III to "resume the exercise of his negative power" by checking the despotic pretensions of Parliament. As Jefferson insisted in an analogy that English readers must have found particularly offensive, the confederal nature of the crown's imperial authority gave provincial assemblies the same right to prevent the king's ministers from stationing British regulars in the colonies that Parliament exercised when it required the king (as German elector) to obtain its consent before deploying Hanoverian troops in Britain.[34]

Even as chances for reaching a mutually satisfactory resolution to the standoff over colonial taxation receded, most American polemicists continued to affirm the need for an imperial union to safeguard what John Dickinson termed "the common good of all." With growing determination, however, the colonists also insisted on preserving the consensual basis of the two most important powers of government, the right to levy taxes and the right to raise troops. Speaking in 1774 of the colonial requisition system that the Stamp Act destroyed, Franklin's convictions on this score were only too clear:

> Had this happy method been continued (a method which left the King's subjects in those remote countries the pleasure of shewing their zeal and loyalty, and of imagining that they recommended themselves to their Sovereign by the liberality of their voluntary grants) there is no doubt but all the money that could reasonably be expected to be raised from them, in any manner, might have been obtained from them, without the least heart-burning, offence, or breach of the harmony of affections and interest that so long subsisted between the two countries.

Despite the palpable sense of loss and regret, Franklin's words highlighted the extent to which Parliament's attempt to tax the Americans without their consent had given rise to a theory of empire fundamentally

---

34. *The Case of Great Britain and America, Addressed to the King, and Both Houses of Parliament*, 2d ed. (London, 1769), 29; [Edward Bancroft], *Remarks on the Review of the Controversy between Great Britain and Her Colonies . . .* (London, 1769), 40, 119; [Thomas Jefferson], *A Summary View of the Rights of British America* (London, 1774), 28, 39–42.

different from the one that most Britons had envisioned from their
triumphant perch in 1763.[35]

III. THE PLUNGE OF LEMMINGS

By the time Franklin wrote this passage, of course, Britain's position no
longer seemed nearly as unassailable as at the close of the Seven Years'
War. Not only was there the prospect of armed insurrection in Boston—
to say nothing of the rest of the American seaboard—but a vocal group
of "disaffected patriots" in the environs of London and Westminster
seemed bent on making the colonists' cause their own. Furthermore,
despite the widespread hope that George III's accession would end the
party divisions of his predecessor's reign, the period from 1768 onward
witnessed the emergence of a new, extraparliamentary opposition cen-
tered on the notorious libertine and former militia officer John Wilkes.
Given the gravity of these problems, the government's refusal to make
any real concession to the colonists' wishes has often looked like an
inexplicable act of self-destruction, a stubbornness in the face of disaster
that the great twentieth-century historian Sir Lewis Namier likened to
the plunge of lemmings hurtling blindly toward the ocean and certain
death. If most Britons failed to grasp the full extent of their predicament,
however, growing numbers—including many who continued to accept
Parliament's imperial authority—feared that the government was losing
its hold over the very possessions that the British had just fought a costly
war to protect.[36]

These concerns reflected several related developments, the first being
the increasingly coercive methods with which the ministers of George III
seemed determined to enforce Parliament's colonial requisitions in
North America, especially Massachusetts. Although there was nothing
unusual about professional troops' assisting the civil magistrates at home,
many people regarded the army's occupation of Boston during the summer of 1768 as an especially troubling demonstration of Britain's inability
to fulfill even the most rudimentary functions of government in North

35. [Dickinson], *Letters from a Farmer in Pennsylvania*, in Ford, ed., *Writings of
Dickinson*, 312; [Benjamin Franklin], *The Causes of the Present Distractions in America
Explained*. . . (New York, 1774), 2.

36. Sir Lewis Namier, *England in the Age of the American Revolution*, 2d ed. (New
York, 1961), 41. See also Thomas, *British Politics and the Stamp Act Crisis*, 364–371;
J. G. A. Pocock, "1776: The Revolution against Parliament," in *Virtue, Commerce, and
History: Essays on Political Thought and History, Chiefly in the Eighteenth Century*
(Cambridge, 1985), 73–88.

America—let alone raise the sort of revenue envisioned by politicians like George Grenville and Charles Townshend. As John Wilkes wrote the Boston Sons of Liberty in 1769, the king's ministers seemed to be treating the city "as if it were the capital of a province belonging to our enemies, or in the possession of rebels." "Asiatic despotism," Wilkes assured his correspondents, "does not present a picture more odious in the eye of humanity." Elsewhere, those sympathetic to the colonists' situation charged that the British were governing them "as a conquered people," that the army in Boston was acting independently of the civil magistrates, even—as the earl of Chatham warned the House of Lords in early 1775— that Britain had "changed her civil power and salutary laws for a *military code*" and was on the verge of transferring "her seat of empire to Constantinople." History showed, insisted the London politician and Virginia native Arthur Lee, that "the liberties of the subject, which [ought to be] the constant care and provision of the Law and Constitution, could not exist" under such a regime; Chatham went so far as to mention the possibility of amending the English Declaration of Rights to prohibit either the crown or Parliament from maintaining regular troops in any colony without the consent of its representative assembly.[37]

As if the situation in America were not bad enough, commentators also worried about the increasingly tumultuous nature of England's own politics. Nothing caused greater concern on this score than the House of Commons' expulsion of John Wilkes following his election to Parliament in March 1768. Although Wilkes was technically a fugitive from the law when he stood for the London constituency of Middlesex, he already enjoyed a reputation as a popular champion. For those who worried about developments in America, the government's response to the election—including throwing Wilkes in jail and "massacring" a dozen of his riotous supporters at St. George's Field in London—seemed to con-

37. John Wilkes to the Committee of the Sons of Liberty in Boston, Mar. 30, 1769, BL Add. MSS 30,870, 135; John Hope, *Letters on Certain Proceedings in Parliament during the Sessions of the Years 1769 and 1770* . . . (London, 1772), 16; Simmons and Thomas, eds., *Proceedings and Debates*, III, 270–296; [William Pitt], *The Speech of the Right Honourable the Earl of Chatham, in the House of Lords, on Friday the 20th of January 1775* . . . (London, 1775), 13; [Arthur Lee], *A Speech, Intended to Have Been Delivered in the House of Commons, in Support of the Petition from the General Congress at Philadelphia* . . . (London, 1775), 2; William Pitt, first earl of Chatham, *A Plan Offered by the Earl of Chatham, to the House of Lords, Entitled, A Provisional Act, for Settling the Troubles in America* . . . (London, 1775), 6–7. Having raised the possibility of amending the Declaration of Rights, Chatham immediately rejected it as an unacceptable encroachment on parliamentary sovereignty.

firm a disturbing authoritarian trend. Indeed, the House of Commons' repeated refusal in early 1769 to recognize the results of the Middlesex election and its controversial decision to seat one of the losing candidates struck even Wilkes's detractors as an unwarranted abuse of parliamentary privilege no less likely to weaken Britain's liberal underpinnings than what was happening on the far shores of the Atlantic. In the words of a petition submitted by the county of York (one of dozens of English addresses that together garnered some fifty-five thousand signatures), Parliament's treatment of Wilkes "threaten[ed] to impair that equal state of Legal Liberty for which this Nation has long been respected abroad and by which it hath been made Happy at Home." Elsewhere, pamphleteers and publicists claimed that Wilkes's expulsion was but the latest manifestation of a sinister plot to make Parliament absolute, the first signs of which had appeared with Parliament's approval of the Stamp Act. "The government of England is a government of law," declared the celebrated Junius to readers of the *Public Advertiser* in 1771. "We betray ourselves, we contradict the spirit of our laws and we shake the whole system of English jurisprudence, whenever we intrust a discretionary power over the life, liberty or fortune of the subject, to any man, or set of men whatsoever."[38]

On top of everything else, Britain's rulers appeared to be pursuing these misguided policies to the exclusion of all other considerations, including the need to remain vigilant against the reviving ambitions of France and Spain. From the standpoint of the government's critics, the summer of 1768 provided an especially disturbing illustration of this trend, as the king's ministers refused—at the very moment when they were sending troops to Boston and preparing the case against Wilkes— to take firm action against France for its flagrant annexation of the Mediterranean island of Corsica. "What has been your enemy's conduct, what your own?" demanded Colonel Isaac Barré in the House of Commons. "You have been confining yourself to the lowest business, that of pursuing little, low criminals, instead of giving laws to the world." According to Francis Webb, Britain's internal difficulties had made it im-

---

38. John Brewer, *Party Ideology and Popular Politics at the Accession of George III* (Cambridge, 1976), 179; "Petition of the County of York," presented Jan. 5, 1770, P.R.O., H.O. 55/2/2; Letter XLVII to the *Public Advertiser* (May 25, 1771), in John Cannon, ed., *The Letters of Junius* (Oxford, 1978), 243. For connections between Wilkes and the government's actions in America, see *A Letter to the Right Honourable George Grenville, Occasioned by His Publication of the Speech He Made in the House of Commons* . . . (London, 1769), 46–49; [Matthew Dawes], *A Letter to Lord Chatham, concerning the Present War of Great Britain against America* . . . (London, 1776), 58.

possible for the king to "stand forth as the defender of his people's violated rights, and his own dignity." A few commentators even claimed during the Corsica crisis that the Bourbon powers were actively encouraging the British government's despotic tendencies—that, in the words of Stephen Sayre of New York, Britain's foreign rivals had embarked on a policy of "forming dissentions, stirring up prejudices, disaffection, disagreement, and divisions" in order to "bring us to a fatal civil war." "Let us not say we do not feel the discontent in America," warned Sir Hercules Langrishe. "We feel it in the insults of our natural enemies; we feel it in our impotence or our fear to check the progress of their usurpation, and the extension of their empire;—we feel it in the sacrifice of our generosity and of our glory,—we feel it in the wounds of an illustrious people, and the contempt of all Europe."[39]

Wherever they looked during the later 1760s and early 1770s, the British thus found cause for concern. There were even people who affected to believe Parliament's actions threatened to reduce Britain's "empire of liberty" to the same condition of slavery that had characterized the "universal monarchies" of despots like Emperor Charles V, Philip II of Spain, and Louis XIV. To the ministry's supporters, of course, this sounded like an irresponsibly wild, self-serving allegation. For some Britons, though, the parallels with these historic tyrants seemed compelling enough. As Arthur Lee insisted in 1774, those who defended the government's policies in America seemed to have forgotten there was "no magic or efficient power in the world" that could make the laws of Parliament sovereign "in all cases whatsoever." The English naval officer John Cartwright went even further in his precocious call for American independence, noting darkly that, "while Lewis the XIVth was intoxicated with the drunken fancy of universal monarchy, his courtiers did not fail to satisfy him . . . that he had an undoubted right" to the same sort of authority in Europe that Britain was now claiming in America. Indeed,

39. Simmons and Thomas, eds., *Proceedings and Debates*, III, 227; [Francis Webb], *Thoughts on the Constitutional Power, and Right of the Crown, in the Bestowal of Places and Pensions* . . . (London, 1772), 62; [Stephen Sayre], *The Englishman Deceived: A Political Piece, Wherein Some Very Important Secrets of State Are Briefly Recited* . . . (London, 1768), 3; [Sir Hercules Langrishe], *Considerations on the Dependencies of Great Britain, with Observations on a Pamphlet Intitled, the Present State of the Nation* (London, 1769), 83. See also the editorial remarks of Francis Blackburne in his *Memoirs of Thomas Hollis, Esq. F.R. and A.S.S.*, 2 vols. (London, 1780), I, 180: "British administration have reaped this advantage from not interfering with the French in their attempts on Corsica, that they may say to them, 'We left you to complete your conquest of Corsica at your leisure: why will you obstruct our conquest of America?'"

the Welsh Presbyterian minister, Richard Price, whose *Observations on the Nature of Civil Liberty* sold approximately sixty thousand copies during the first half of 1776, claimed to see no difference between Britain's imperial pretensions in America and the pope's claim to be "the supreme head on earth of the Christian church." For a reading public that would shortly make Edward Gibbon's *Decline and Fall of the Roman Empire* (1776) one of the century's best-selling histories, it went without saying that rulers who succumbed to such pernicious temptations invariably ended by squandering the very dominions they so desperately sought to preserve and expand.[40]

Historians of the American Revolution have devoted a good deal of attention to those Britons who shared these libertarian sentiments. Convinced of its own invincibility and limitless authority, the British government seemed bent on its own destruction in ways right-minded men and women could only lament. For all the evident concern on this account, however, the British were no less troubled by what might happen if Parliament relented on the question of colonial taxation. As even the colonists' critics admitted, safeguarding Westminster's fiscal rights was bound to unsettle a people accustomed to thinking of themselves as the freest in the world—a people, after all, who were supposed to be as solicitous of the liberties of friends and neighbors in Europe and beyond as they were of their own rights and privileges. Yet most Britons also feared that weakening Parliament's imperial authority would give rise to an unacceptable degree of colonial autonomy. Indeed, just as the government's actions in Boston raised the specter of universal monarchy, the Americans' increasingly radical response threatened to turn Britain's Atlantic empire into a loose-knit confederation not unlike the ineffective alliances from which its people had only recently begun to extricate themselves in Europe. If they bowed to the colonists' demands, the

40. [Arthur Lee], *An Appeal to the Justice and Interests of the People of Great Britain . . .* (London, 1774), 32; [John Cartwright], *A Letter to Edmund Burke, Esq., Controverting the Principles of American Government, Laid Down in His Lately Published Speech on American Taxation . . .* (London, 1775), 21; Richard Price, *Observations on the Nature of Civil Liberty, the Principles of Government, and the Justice and Policy of the War with America,* 8th ed. (1776), in Richard Price, *Two Tracts on Civil Liberty, the War with America, and the Debts and Finances of the Kingdom* (1778; New York, 1972), 36, 44–45; the estimate of the pamphlet's sales comes from Bernard Peach, ed., *Richard Price and the Ethical Foundations of the American Revolution: Selections from His Pamphlets, with Appendices* (Durham, N.C., 1979), 9. For the American acceptance of this perception, see Bernard Bailyn, *The Ideological Origins of the American Revolution* (Cambridge, Mass., 1967); Maier, *From Resistance to Revolution.*

British might well purchase a brief period of prosperity and repose—but it was a repose that people feared would come with the long-term cost of escalating deficits and crushing taxes.

This impression was enhanced by Britain's growing preoccupation with the racially diverse territories gained at the end of the Seven Years' War. In the case of the Indian lands to the west of the Appalachian Mountains, for example, the Stamp Act crisis carried implications for Britain's imperial authority that were no less grave than the unrest in Boston or New York. According to the plan formulated by the Bute and Grenville ministries, the proceeds from the new taxes had been meant for the use of the regular troops stationed in the Ohio and Mississippi Valleys. In the wake of the act's repeal, however, the British faced a difficult choice between bearing the costs of this army themselves or pulling back their garrisons. Although successive ministries from 1766 onward opted for the latter course, British officials routinely warned against the effects of leaving the Indians and frontier settlers at each other's mercy—and of leaving such extensive lands vulnerable to French or Spanish encroachments.[41] Furthermore, Whitehall maintained just enough of a military presence in the Great Lakes region—chiefly at Fort Niagara and Detroit—to make it seem as though the colonists were giving the British sole responsibility for what should have been the "common cause" of all. Within an empire defined by ethnically diverse and geographically remote territories, the American insistence on regarding taxes as voluntary contributions—which their assemblies might refuse whenever they saw fit—increasingly looked like nothing more than a selfish scheme to avoid the most fundamental national obligation of all.[42]

To compound matters, the Americans' resistance to parliamentary taxation stood in stark contrast to the government's relations with the East India Company, whose proprietors reluctantly agreed in 1767 to award the crown an annual subsidy of £400,000 in exchange for Parliament's recognition of their new role as de facto rulers of the Mughal emperor's northeastern province of Bengal. Although there were impor-

41. Army officers routinely referred to the European settlers and traders that increasingly encroached on Indian rights as "banditti" and "vagabonds," and often complained of their "licentiousness" in dealings with native representatives (Sosin, *Whitehall and the Wilderness*, 218).

42. For the general problem, see Sosin, *Whitehall and the Wilderness*, esp. chaps. 3, 4, 6–9; Shy, *Toward Lexington*, 52–68, 192–204, 223–231; Lawson, *Imperial Challenge*, chaps. 2, 5, 6; Peter Marshall, "Colonial Protest and Imperial Retrenchment: Indian Policy 1764–1768," *Journal of American Studies*, V (1971), 1–17.

tant differences between the London-based company's governing board
and the colonial assemblies in North America, English jurists generally
regarded both as "corporations" with special rights and privileges, but
nonetheless subject to Parliament's controlling authority. As such, the
company's landmark agreement made the American position on taxation look that much more exceptional. In the words of Alexander Dalrymple, the East Indian subsidy showed that no "part of this Nation,
whether in a Corporate or Individual Capacity, is independant of the
Supreme Jurisdiction of Parliament." As William Knox stated in 1769,
Parliament's unlimited sovereignty extended to all British subjects, regardless of their political condition or distance from the metropolis:

> There is no material difference between the grant of the crown to
> the proprietor of Maryland, and the grant to the proprietors of the
> countries to the East of the Cape of Good Hope, save in the article
> of trade. The inhabitants, therefore, of the East-India company's
> possessions, are equally bound with the people of Maryland to
> contribute to the burdens of the state; and the sovereign's power
> over the whole empire, is equally obliged to require them so to do,
> according to their ability.[43]

For most Britons, though, what sealed the case for colonial taxation
was the widespread belief that the colonies along the North American
seaboard together constituted an increasingly important part of the
greater British nation and that surrendering Parliament's fiscal rights in
Massachusetts and Virginia would set a dangerous precedent for the
government of English settlers in places as scattered as Ireland, Jamaica,
and Bengal. In the words of the aging John Shebbeare, the controversy
over colonial taxation ultimately turned on the question of whether "all
the subjects of the same realm should, according to their respective abilities, pay their *legal* contributions." "Should the parliament give way to
the pretensions of the Americans," wrote Matthew Wheelock in 1770,
"the national credit would be immediately affected, as then great Britain *alone* would become responsible for the national debt." Indeed, na-

43. [Alexander] Dalrymple, *A General View of the East-India Company, Written in
January, 1769* . . . (London, 1772), 61; [Knox], *The Present State of the Nation*, 39–40
(pagination sequence repeats for two pages in original). For the relationship between
Parliament's scrutiny of the East India Company and the attempt to tax the American
colonies, see H. V. Bowen, *Revenue and Reform: The Indian Problem in British Politics,
1757–1773* (Cambridge, 1991), 24–27, 85, 187–188; P. J. Marshall, "Britain and the World
in the Eighteenth Century: I, Reshaping the Empire," *Transactions of the Royal Historical Society*, 6th Ser., VIII (1998), 1–18.

tional ties between Britain and America seemed so pronounced that even friends of America like John Wilkes claimed that it was hard to differentiate "between an inhabitant of Boston in Lincolnshire, and of Boston in New England." According to the colonists' metropolitan sympathizers, of course, this common nationality tended to reinforce the case for allowing them to fulfill their fiscal obligations by obeying the navigation laws and approving wartime requisitions. For a broad swath of the British public, however, the fact that even the colonists' friends in England regarded them as "British subjects" only strengthened the prevailing impression that freeing them from the duty to pay parliamentary taxes would constitute "a system of misgovernment not to be paralleled."[44]

Given the extent of Britain's obligations in the Atlantic and Asia, many people naturally concluded that the Americans' refusal to contribute directly to the national revenue would eventually make the unacceptable costs long associated with war in Europe a permanent feature of British politics. Even Adam Smith, whose defense of free trade in *Wealth of Nations* (1776) gave him a measure of sympathy for the colonists, found the idea of surrendering Parliament's fiscal supremacy indefensible on these grounds. Although Smith hardly shared the polemical purposes of court apologists like Whately or Knox, his analysis of the imperial crisis seconded many of their positions, including the need to maintain professional troops in outlying provinces like Scotland and the American colonies, the inevitability of deficit finance in times of war, and the unavoidable obligation to pay taxes levied by a centrally constituted sovereign. Smith also insisted on the benevolent effects of modern military and fiscal practice, noting how borrowing funds against future revenue had enabled the governments of Europe to wage expensive wars without imposing extortionate taxes or universal military service on their subjects. But most important of all, he was sure that, unless such debts were serviced by an adequate revenue, they bred enthusiasm of the worst sort, permitting governments to lay out vast expenditures even in times of peace, frequently on the most ephemeral projects and far-fetched schemes. It seemed to Smith that, in the absence of a colonial revenue,

44. John Shebbeare, *An Essay on the Origin, Progress, and Establishment of National Society . . .* , 2d ed. (London, 1776), 127; [Matthew Wheelock], *Reflections Moral and Political on Great Britain and Her Colonies* (London, 1770), 41; Wilkes to Junius, Nov. 6, 1771, BL Add. MSS 30,881, 27; [John Gray], *The Right of the British Legislature to Tax the American Colonies Vindicated, and the Means of Asserting That Right Proposed . . .* (London, 1774), 37–38.

Britain's empire in America had become just such a costly project, an imaginary dominion that the general public mistakenly thought contributed to the general prosperity but that actually cost them millions in uncompensated expenditures. As he wrote in the treatise's concluding paragraph:

> The rulers of Great Britain have, for more than a century past, amused the people with the imagination that they possessed a great empire on the west side of the Atlantic. This empire, however, has hitherto existed in imagination only. It has hitherto been, not an empire, but the project of an empire; not a gold mine, but the project of a gold mine; a project which has cost, which continues to cost, and which, if pursued in the same way as it has been hitherto, is likely to cost, immense expense, without being likely to bring any profit.[45]

For a handful of observers—Smith included—this realization was enough to make them ponder whether keeping the colonists in the empire was worth the expense.[46] But for the vast majority of Britons, the spiraling debts, unrealistic expectations, and general lack of direction that the nation's experience with confederations in Europe had invariably produced simply reinforced the case for preserving Parliament's jurisdiction over every aspect of colonial finance. As William Knox insisted in his review of the imperial controversy, "There is no alternative: either the Colonies are a part of the community of Great Britain, or they are in a state of nature with respect to her." Samuel Johnson was equally scathing in his savage attack on the Americans and the self-styled patriots who defended them in Britain. "To suppose," wrote Dr. Johnson, that colonists did not have to "contribute to their own defense, but at their own pleasure" and that they should be freed from "the general system of

45. Adam Smith, *An Inquiry into the Nature and Causes of the Wealth of Nations* (1776), ed. Edwin Cannan, 2 vols. (1904; Chicago, 1976), II, 85, 103, 212–228, 442–465, 483, 486. See also John Robertson, *The Scottish Enlightenment and the Militia Issue* (Edinburgh, 1985), 212–215.

46. Two other notable members of this group were Josiah Tucker and Richard Price. For the emergence of a sustained critique of empire during the 1770s, see Bernard Semmel, *The Liberal Ideal and the Demons of Empire: Theories of Imperialism from Adam Smith to Lenin* (Baltimore, 1993), chaps. 1–4; Peter N. Miller, *Defining the Common Good: Empire, Religion, and Philosophy in Eighteenth-Century Britain* (Cambridge, 1994), chap. 6; Anthony Pagden, *Lords of all the World: Ideologies of Empire in Spain, Britain, and France, c. 1500–c. 1800* (New Haven, Conn., 1995), chaps. 6, 7.

representation" as it existed in Britain involved "such a degree of absurdity, as nothing but the shew of patriotism could palliate." Even Edmund Burke, no friend of taxing the Americans, dismissed the idea of colonial requisitions, remarking that "the empire of Germany" raised "the worst revenue and the worst army in the world" in just such a manner. As the king's Scottish painter Allan Ramsay observed in 1776, there were "sixteen separate Provinces, upon the continent of America, and about the same number of governments in the American islands," all of which could claim the right to tax themselves. If the British permitted the colonists to exercise this right, it was entirely possible that "the East might be at war, while the West was out of danger; and the North might be lost, for want of the assistance of the South." "This would create a general weakness in the state" was Ramsay's depressing conclusion; "separate interests would actuate every part of the British empire, and nothing but confusion, and destruction, would ensue."[47]

For the same reasons that they had found the patriotic, blue water rhetoric of the 1750s so compelling, the British thus chose to reaffirm the empire's unitary character by giving the fiscal authority of Parliament priority over all other considerations.[48] No doubt this is why the ministry of Lord North took such care in early 1775 to depict the impending war in America as an internal contest over the colonists' obligations to contribute to the national revenue. According to the conciliatory proposi-

47. [Knox], *Controversy between Great-Britain and Her Colonies Reviewed*, 50–51; [Samuel Johnson], *The Patriot: Addressed to the Electors of Great Britain* (London, 1774), 22–23; Edmund Burke, *The Speech of Edmund Burke, Esq., on Moving His Resolutions for Conciliation with the Colonies, March 22, 1775*, 3d ed. (London, 1775), 99; [Allan Ramsay], *A Plan of Reconciliation between Great Britain and Her Colonies . . .* (London, 1776), 49–51. See also Smith, *Wealth of Nations*, ed. Cannan, II, 134: "The assembly of a province, like the vestry of a parish, may judge very properly concerning the affairs of its own particular district; but can have no proper means of judging concerning those of the whole empire."

48. To be sure, commentators often conceded the existence of important differences between the Americans' political condition and that of their fellow subjects in England, Scotland, or Wales. As an indication of this, Thomas Pownall, Adam Smith, and William Knox each argued that the surest way to secure Parliament's imperial sovereignty would be to grant the colonists the privilege of sending representatives to the House of Commons. Even without such a representation, however, all three continued to think of the Americans as integral parts of a greater British nation that Parliament could tax. For proposals to create an American representation, see Pownall, *The Administration of the Colonies*, 4th ed., 174; Smith, *Wealth of Nations*, ed. Cannan, II, 471; [Knox], *The Present State of the Nation*, 39–40.

tion that the government laid before the House of Commons on February 20, the ministry stood ready to rescind all penalties from any colony whose legislature came forward with a regular subsidy for the common defense of the empire, the only stipulation being that the disposition of such grants be left entirely to the discretion of Parliament. As Lord North himself admitted, such a proposal was not likely to meet with approval in America. According to the *London Evening Post*, though, the prime minister claimed that the mere fact that the offer had been extended would not *"fail of doing Good in England"*: first by standing "as an eternal monument of the wisdom and clemency, of the humanity and justice, of British Government"; second, by demonstrating the moderation of Parliament to "the traders and manufacturers of England"; and finally, by animating "the officers and soldiers we send out to America to a vigorous and manly exertion of their native courage, without doubt or scruple, when they are assured they no longer fight for a phantom, and a vain, empty point of honour, but for a substantial benefit to their country, which is to relieve her in her greatest exigencies."[49]

As Bernard Bailyn observed some two hundred years later, the "ideological origins" of the American Revolution ultimately lay in an inexorable "logic of rebellion," which led the colonists to believe that Parliament's actions were so diabolical and menacing that their only chance for lasting freedom and prosperity was to sever all remaining ties to the British people and their government. To a greater extent than is sometimes realized, the Revolution's British origins reflected an equally terrifying set of fears and apprehensions, some that could be traced back to the military and fiscal bargain the English had struck at the close of the seventeenth century, others that arose from more recent developments like the growing animus toward Britain's European allies. Whether these made the American Revolution inevitable is impossible to say. For most Britons who sought to make sense of the looming imperial crisis, however, the government seemed to have little choice. In a letter describing the terms of the Boston Port Act (1774), which Parliament was currently debating, Arthur Lee confessed to Benjamin Franklin, "The highest and lowest Ranks of People in this Country [seemed] so totally debauched and dissipated" that the vast majority accepted the necessity of taking a firm line against the Americans. But according to John Shebbeare, the war in America was likely to be the first ever under-

---

49. Simmons and Thomas, eds., *Proceedings and Debates*, V, 435–436; *London Evening Post*, Feb. 25, 1775, quoted in Simmons and Thomas, eds., *Proceedings and Debates*, V, 436.

taken solely for the benefit of "the common people." Although the wisdom of attempting to coerce the colonies would come to seem a good deal less obvious, Britons were sure that a contest for the preservation of Parliament's independent authority in the fullest sense possible was pre-eminently for the welfare of the nation.[50]

50. Bailyn, *Ideological Origins,* chap. 4, "The Logic of Rebellion"; Lee to Franklin, London, June 1, 1774, P.R.O., C.O. 5/118/27 (Lee observed that the one exception to this support for the government was in "the middling ranks, where you have many friends"); Shebbeare, *Essay on the Origin, Progress, and Establishment of National Society,* 127.

The Revolution
in British Patriotism

THE FRIENDS OF GOVERNMENT AND
THE FRIENDS OF AMERICA

During the spring of 1780, while standing for a parliamentary seat at Oxford that he stood no chance of winning, William Jones made what must have sounded like an unusually candid admission to his friend and benefactress, Lady Georgiana Spencer:

> Those, who call me [an American], do me great injustice . . . but I fairly confess, that I rejoice, as an Englishman, in the success of America, that I detest the war from its beginning to this hour, and that I think the form of government, which the American states have established, manly, sensible, rational, and as perfectly adapted to them, as long as they continue virtuous, as it would be improper for a nation so depraved by luxury as the English. Discretion and good breeding have forbidden me from supporting these sentiments in all companies; but I never disavowed them, nor would deny them with my lips, while I entertained them in my heart, for twenty seats in parliament.[1]

1. William Jones to Lady Spencer, London, May 24, 1780, in Garland Cannon, ed., *The Letters of Sir William Jones*, 2 vols. (Oxford, 1970), I, 388.

Jones, who already enjoyed a reputation as Britain's foremost Orientalist, had just received a letter from Lady Spencer advising him to withdraw from the Oxford election, so perhaps he was looking for a way to explain his failure to garner more support among the university's voters. Yet Jones's sense of "discretion" and his reluctance to express his views in "all companies" also speak to the larger difficulties that the Revolution created for the colonists' metropolitan sympathizers. Although few people relished a civil war with their fellow subjects in America, fewer still were willing to relent on the question of Britain's imperial authority.

For a brief period during the spring of 1780, of course, it looked as though this situation was starting to change. Although the last five years had tended to marginalize people who shared the views of Jones and Lady Spencer, Britain seemed to be at a turning point. Buffeted by a series of humiliating defeats in the colonies, a nascent independent movement in Ireland, and an impending Franco-Spanish invasion at home, associations demanding fiscal and electoral reform gathered in cities and counties across England. Meanwhile, an emboldened opposition pursued an ever more radical agenda in the House of Commons, culminating in John Dunning's nearly successful motion in early June opposing the dissolution of Parliament without a royal redress of grievances. At the height of the agitations, even Lord North, who early on had promised the nation an easy victory, began to despair of Britain's chances of winning the war, and it was with difficulty that George III persuaded him to remain in office. "Let us not any longer amuse ourselves with the thoughts of the conquest of America," implored a pamphleteer as the crisis unfolded. "She has now acquired experience; she is assisted by powerful nations, and the people look no longer towards Britain."[2]

Yet predictions of the war's end turned out to be sadly premature. Although the opposition that surfaced during the spring of 1780 was certainly genuine, it was not enough to prevent Lord North's supporters from carrying the general election at the end of the summer, nor could it stop the government from continuing the war in the colonies for another year. Indeed, for all the soul-searching occasioned by the war, the American Revolution ultimately did little to alter imperial sentiments at

2. *An Essay on the Interests of Britain, in regard to America; or, An Outline of the Terms on Which Peace May Be Restored to the Two Countries* (London, 1780), 10–11. For the political crisis, see H. Butterfield, *George III, Lord North, and the People, 1779–80* (London, 1949); Ian R. Christie, *Wilkes, Wyvill, and Reform: The Parliamentary Reform Movement in British Politics, 1760–1785* (London, 1962), chap. 3.

home. Although the inconclusive contest required the British people to make enormous sacrifices, Lord North's defenders succeeded in casting the war in the colonies as a patriotic struggle for the integrity of Britain's blue water empire. Moreover, despite the costs generated by so many distant campaigns, the government managed to avoid making the sorts of military and fiscal demands that might have triggered a more sustained popular backlash. As the general tone of Jones's remarks to Lady Spencer suggests, one consequence for the war's opponents was a sense of powerlessness verging on despair. Yet even with the impending dissolution of Britain's North American empire, most men and women—including all but the most disaffected friends of America—opted for a course of moderation and grudging loyalism. No matter what people thought of the issues at stake, the American Revolution ultimately seemed remote, something that obviously carried implications of the first importantce for Britain and its empire, but that the British were also willing to see resolved by the government and their fellow subjects on the far shores of the Atlantic.[3]

I. AMBIVALENT PATRIOTS

The government's ability to withstand the various crises wrought by the American Revolution was certainly impressive. Not only did Lord North and his ministers sustain seven demoralizing campaigns in the colonies, but the intervention of France in 1778—joined over the next two years by Spain and the Dutch Republic—transformed the conflict into a desperate struggle that threatened the destruction of British power in places as scattered as Gibraltar, the Caribbean, and northeastern India. With the exception of a few subsidiary allies in western Germany, moreover, the British were forced to prosecute this global war without the assistance of any of Europe's other major powers. "When I look upon

3. The literature on the response of British radicals to the American Revolution is vast, but see Butterfield, *George III, Lord North, and the People;* J. H. Plumb, "British Attitudes to the American Revolution," in Plumb, *In the Light of History* (Boston, 1973); David Brion Davis, *The Problem of Slavery in the Age of Revolution, 1770–1823* (Ithaca, N.Y., 1975), chaps. 8, 9; John Brewer, *Party Ideology and Popular Politics at the Accession of George III* (Cambridge, 1976), chap. 10; Colin Bonwick, *English Radicals and the American Revolution* (Chapel Hill, N.C., 1977), esp. chaps. 5–7; John Sainsbury, *Disaffected Patriots: London Supporters of Revolutionary America, 1769–1782* (Montreal, 1987); Linda Colley, *Britons: Forging the Nation, 1707–1837* (New Haven, Conn., 1992), 352–355; Peter N. Miller, *Defining the Common Good: Empire, Religion, and Philosophy in Eighteenth-Century Britain* (Cambridge, 1994), chaps. 4–6.

this little island in the map," remarked an observer of Britain's plight in 1783, "I can scarcely think it is the same country that has extended its empire from the St. Lawrence to the Gulf of Mexico; given law to the kingdoms upon the Ganges; trampled under foot, in our own memory, the united force of France and Spain; and spread the treasures of its commerce through every region of the globe." As conspicuous as Britain's losses were, however, the most striking feature about the War of American Independence was how little it had done to disrupt the ordinary course of politics at home. "Even now," the writer concluded, "how great do you appear even in your calamity?"[4]

At no point was this resilience the result of universal support for the government's actions in America. As a crude measure of political divisions in England, the king and Parliament together received as many addresses in 1775 urging a negotiated solution to what the Bristol petition called a "ruinous civil war" as they did statements endorsing the use of force. Dissenters and Deists were especially active on the Americans' behalf, delivering sermons, sponsoring petitions, and writing pamphlets, among them Richard Price's widely read *Observations on the Nature of Civil Liberty* (1776). There was likewise evidence in some places of an unusual level of popular hostility to the recruiting efforts of the army and navy, with scattered anti-impressment riots, including one that involved hundreds of tinners in Cornwall and left several dead and many more injured. Even after France's intervention, which enabled the government to redefine the war as a contest with Britain's ancient enemy, people still appeared reluctant to give their full support. Significantly, in its political review for 1776, the *Annual Register* remarked on the "unusual apathy" with which the English public seemed to view the hostilities in America. "Accounts of many of the late military actions, as well as of political proceedings of no less importance, were received with as much indifference, and canvassed with as much coolness and unconcern, as if they had happened between two nations with whom we were unconnected."[5]

4. [Powis], *A Dialogue on the Actual State of Parliament* . . . (Dublin, 1783), 2–3.

5. "The Humble Petition of the Merchants, Traders, Manufacturers, and Others, Citizens of Bristol" (n.p., [1775?]), P.R.O., H.O. 55/11/64; *Annual Register,* XIX (1776), 39. The addresses of 1775 are the subject of James E. Bradley, *Popular Politics and the American Revolution in England: Petitions, the Crown, and Public Opinion* (Macon, Ga., 1986); for the response of English Dissenters to the Revolution, see esp. Richard Price, *Observations on the Nature of Civil Liberty, the Principles of Government, and the War with America* . . . , 2d ed. (London, 1776), as well as Bradley, *Religion, Revolution, and English Radicalism: Noncomformity in Eighteenth-Century Politics and Society* (Cam-

If some Britons had doubts about what the North ministry was doing in the colonies, however, enough remained silent or muted their criticism to give the government's supporters the rhetorical advantage, at least until the spring of 1780. Even in places with a long tradition of opposition politics, observers often noted a reluctance to speak out. As the English abolitionist William Richards recalled, the war produced a grudging silence among his friends and neighbors in the Norfolk borough of Lynn, many of whom had vigorously supported the cause of John Wilkes during the late 1760s but who declined to make any public gesture "towards the oppressed and much injured Americans." According to another account, probably written by an American resident in England, it was almost impossible to guess "the real sentiments of People" during the early years of the Revolution. "The interested on each side declare themselves, but the bulk of the Nation is perfectly silent." As Andrew Kippis, one of the more radical of the government's many Dissenting opponents, recollected in his comments on the preliminary peace negotiations in 1782:

> There was a time . . . when the American War was popular. . . . Many encouraged the contest, and others looked upon it with a supine indifference. Had public bodies of men more generally interfered, had the country gentlemen been sooner awakened, had the principal merchants vigorously interposed, a wiser policy might have taken place, and many evils have been prevented. But through interested or mistaken views, the measures of our governors received too much acquiescence and support.[6]

The government owed this acquiescence and support to several factors. First, the commencement of hostilities enabled the North administration to mobilize groups in England who had often held back from endorsing wars earlier in the century. Foremost among these was the Tory wing of the Anglican Church. English clerics displayed a rare unanimity

---

bridge, 1990); J. C. D. Clark, *The Language of Liberty, 1660–1832: Political Discourse and Social Dynamics in the Anglo-American World* (Cambridge, 1994), 328–335; for the riots against naval impressment, see Nicholas Rogers, *Crowds, Culture, and Politics in Georgian Britain* (Oxford, 1998), 101–119.

6. William Richards, *The History of Lynn, Civil, Ecclesiastical, Political, Commercial, Biographical, Municipal, and Military . . .* , 2 vols. (Lynn, 1812), II, 954; —— to Robert Carter Nicholas, Sept. 22, 1775, P.R.O., C.O. 5/40/1/22; [Andrew Kippis], *Considerations on the Provisional Treaty with America, and the Preliminary Articles of Peace with France and Spain* (London, 1783), 9–10.

throughout the war, delivering loyal sermons, signing petitions against the rebellion, and rebutting the arguments of radicals in England. Oxford University, which was notorious for its Jacobite and High Church sympathies, was especially active in denouncing the Americans, but even Whig Cambridge showed little support for a policy of conciliation. The same pattern was evident in Tory strongholds like Manchester, which had been the only English town to provide significant numbers for Charles Stuart's army in 1745, and which was unswerving in its affirmations of Lord North's colonial policies. Indeed, according to some observers, the strength that the government derived from this revanchist fringe represented the clearest indication of the despotic tendencies of its policies in America. In the words of one, the conflict seemed to have revived the Tory and Whig divisions of earlier generations, with "the Jacobites and Nonjurors addressing for coercive measures, the Merchants and Manufacturers petitioning for conciliation, while the Counties and large Cities in general . . . remain unmov'd."[7]

If Lord North could count on Tory acquiescence, however, his apologists also insisted on the Whig underpinnings of his administration's policies. Indeed, in the eyes of many Britons, the American Revolution was manifestly a contest for blue water empire, something even people who questioned the wisdom in the government's resort to violence continued to see as a cause worth fighting for. Throughout the war's early years, the North ministry's defenders routinely maintained that Britain was at war to protect the maritime supremacy that it had expended so much to acquire during the previous two wars with France. As one writer put the matter in 1776, defeat in North America promised nothing less than the "dismemberment" of Britain's empire by "inclosing us within the confined seas of England, Ireland and Scotland." Elsewhere, polemicists placed the war in a European context, warning not only that the destruction of Britain's North American empire would disrupt the international balance of power but that recognizing the legitimacy of Congress's claims would set a dangerous precedent for the colonies of the Continent's other imperial powers, including natural enemies France and

---

7. —— to Robert Carter Nicholas, Sept. 22, 1775, P.R.O., C.O. 5/40/1/22. The Anglican clergy are the subject of Paul Langford, "The English Clergy and the American Revolution," in Eckhart Hellmuth, ed., *The Transformation of Political Culture: England and Germany in the Late Eighteenth Century* (Oxford, 1990), 275–308; see also Clark, *The Language of Liberty*, chap. 2; James J. Sack, *From Jacobite to Conservative: Reaction and Orthodoxy in Britain, c. 1760–1832* (Cambridge, 1993), chap. 2.

Spain. As Alexander Carlyle admonished his congregation in the Scottish parish of Inveresk, the gravity of the issues made the war's outcome a matter of the first importance for men and women everywhere:

> In the wars usual in Europe, when rival nations have contended with each other, it has often been on points of small importance, and the parties have gained nothing in the end by the contest, but the exercise of arms. In such wars the interests of mankind are safe. . . . But, in the present war, we are to retain, or lose forever, not our new provinces, that are hardly yet a part of the state, but our antient colonies that are coeval with our navigation and commerce, those great branches that are deeply engrafted into the commonwealth, which have grown with our growth, and cannot now be lopt off, without hazard that the tree shall perish.[8]

As part of these claims, ministerial writers continued to insist that the English-speaking colonies in North America represented integral parts of the British nation and as such ought to be subject to Parliament's unlimited authority. According to John William Fletcher, Methodist vicar of Madeley in Shropshire, it was self-evident that "all those who share in the protection and dignity of the empire should contribute in due proportion towards defraying the national expence." If Britain caved in to the colonists' demands, quipped another commentator in 1777, the inhabitants of Yorkshire or Devonshire might decide that they, too, should be free of Parliament's authority, "till in the end we should have as many constitutions as parishes." Even after France's entry had made the prospect of complete victory unlikely, there were still people who supported the government's efforts in the hope that "the whole nation, English, Scotch, Irish and American, will unite, assume its character; recover its reason and affections; and act with that impetuous justice and generous resentment for which it has been ever dreaded by its envious and insidious foes." Such ideas were popular, at least before the full extent of American disaffection became clear. Restore Westminster's authority in the colonies—the reasoning went—and Britons on both

8. *The Duty of King and Subject, on the Principles of Civil Liberty: Colonists Not Intitled to Self-Government, or to the Same Privileges with Britons . . .* (London, 1776), 13; Alexander Carlyle, *The Justice and Necessity of the War with Our American Colonies Examined: A Sermon, Preached at Inveresk, December 12, 1776* (Edinburgh, 1777), 45–46. For British concerns over the Revolution's threat to the liberties of Europe, see Eliga H. Gould, "American Independence and Britain's Counter-Revolution," *Past and Present*, no. 154 (February 1997), 112–121.

sides of the Atlantic would once again join in defending the nation's rightful place as the preeminent maritime power in Europe.[9]

More than anything else, however, British support for the war reflected the government's success in enlisting the general public in the same evocative displays of patriotism that had served the Newcastle-Pitt ministry so effectively twenty years before. As they had in every war since the Glorious Revolution, of course, foreign auxiliaries played a key role in the crown's strategy overseas, with Hessians and Brunswickers accounting for over a third of the total British establishment in North America and Hanoverians helping safeguard potentially vulnerable outposts in the Mediterranean and India. Likewise, it was well known that the king's American forces drew much of their strength from racially and ethnically suspect groups like Irish Catholics, runaway slaves, and Native Americans. In order to stave off the predictable outcry in Parliament and the press, the North ministry took care to counterbalance these policies with visible signs of the British public's willingness to assist in the war effort at home. Early on, these included organizing loyal addresses and petitions from local bodies across Britain—including, significantly, the officer corps of half a dozen militia regiments in England. As the conflict dragged on, the government also encouraged local elites to become more actively involved in finding recruits to help meet the extraordinary demands that the war placed on the army and the navy. But most important, the king's advisers cast the war as a contest for the welfare of the people by entrusting the defense of Britain and Ireland entirely to national levies made up of British regulars and—following France's intervention in 1778—English militia, Scottish "fencibles," and Irish volunteers. Although the resort to such semiprofessional forces meant risking the sorts of unrest that had nearly undone Pitt's militia reform twenty years before, it also enabled the government to muster the support of the people as a whole, including more than a few who opposed its actions on the far shores of the Atlantic.[10]

9. John Fletcher, *A Vindication of the Rev. Mr. Wesley's "Calm Address to Our American Colonies"* . . . (London, 1776), 2; *Essays Commercial and Political, on the Real and Relative Interests of Imperial and Dependent States, Particularly Those of Great Britain and Her Dependencies* . . . (Newcastle, 1777), 1; [David Williams], *Unanimity in All Parts of the British Commonwealth, Necessary to Its Preservation, Interest, and Happiness* (London, 1778), 35–36.

10. Overviews of the British war effort can be found in Piers Mackesy, *The War for America, 1775–1783* (1964; Lincoln, Nebr., 1993); Stephen Conway, *The War of American Independence, 1775–1783* (London, 1995). See also A. T. Patterson, *The Other Armada: The Franco-Spanish Attempt to Invade Britain in 1779* (Manchester, 1960); Rodney

FIGURE 21
A Visit to the Camp. *1779.* © *The British Museum*

Nothing demonstrated the success of this mobilization more vividly than the huge force that the government was able to concentrate from 1778 onward in southeastern England, most notably at the great army and militia encampments on Coxheath and Warley Common. As we might expect, the soldiers themselves often found life in these camps dull and unremarkable. For the general public, however, the spectacle of the nation in arms was irresistible. "I was in hopes that your letter about the camp would have been longer" was Samuel Johnson's response upon receiving a report from his friend Hester Thrale. Even William Jones could barely conceal his interest, inquiring of his former student Vis-

Atwood, *The Hessians* (Cambridge, 1980); John Robertson, *The Scottish Enlightenment and the Militia Issue* (Edinburgh, 1985), chap. 5; Sylvia R. Frey, *Water from the Rock: Black Resistance in a Revolutionary Age* (Princeton, N.J., 1991); Colin G. Calloway, *The American Revolution in Indian Country: Crisis and Diversity in Native American Communities* (Cambridge, 1995). According to Secretary at War Charles Jenkinson, the domestic establishment that resulted from the government's effort to involve the British public was "vastly superior, and much more effective than the Force that was thought necessary for our Home Defence, during any part of the last, or any other former war in which we have been engaged" (Jenkinson to Lord Amherst, Dec. 21, 1779, BL Add. MSS 38,212, 307–308).

THE THREE GRACES OF COX—HEATH.

FIGURE 22

The Three Graces of Cox-Heath. *1779. The duchesses of Gordon,
Devonshire, and Grafton.* © *The British Museum*

count Althorp, "How shall I express the delight which your letter from
Warley camp has given me?" With more than fifteen thousand troops in
quarters that stretched for three and a half miles, Coxheath proved to be
an especially popular destination for visitors from London, a fact duly
celebrated in several West End comedies, including, notably, *The Camp*,
by Irish playwright Richard Brinsley Sheridan. So many women visited
the camp that Lady Spencer's daughter, Georgiana, duchess of Devonshire, spent the summer of 1778 with her husband in the Derbyshire
Militia, where she donned regimental colors and established a ladies'
mess, to which only officers of military distinction were invited. "As
many of our modern dames want the modesty of women, I hope they
will have the courage of men" was Elizabeth Montagu's arch comment
on the latest fashion. "I must own . . . I was sorry to see them striding
about the walks at Tunbridge with their arms akimbo, dressed in martial
uniform."[11]

11. Johnson to Thrale, Oct. 24, 1778, Montagu to Duchess of Portland, [1779], both in
Ernest Sanger, ed., *Englishmen at War: A Social History in Letters, 1450–1900* (Dover,

As Mrs. Montagu's disapproving tone suggests, this *rage militaire* was only partly the result of official encouragement. Nonetheless, both the king's ministers and the camp commanders were only too happy to endorse it. In the four and a half years that the militia spent under canvas, George III paid repeated visits to the great encampments, prompting the radical duke of Richmond to grumble in the House of Lords that "many ignorant persons" might be led to suppose "that parading at Coxheath or at Warley Common, and being reviewed by his Majesty, was all that they had to do." When the royal entourage came to Coxheath in November 1778, however, Lord Althorp, though no supporter of the ministry's war in the colonies, was clearly delighted to have been "taken notice of," and he happily reported to his mother that "my Sister with the Duchess of Gordon and Grafton, Lady Cranbourne and L[ad]y Jane Aston stood with the Q[ueen] in her marquee" while the officers were presented to the king. As an indication of the importance that the militia attached to such occasions, a number of units formed wind bands comprised of professional and semiprofessional musicians, often with funds raised by local subscription. "In the Gen'l Salute," reads a typical order lodged with the Buckinghamshire Militia during its stay at Coxheath, "those Reg'ts that have musick, must allways play God save Great Geo[rge], our King once quite through, the music beginning, on the word being given present your arms." For good measure, the bands were instructed not "to play there to slow."[12]

Not surprisingly, Lord North's apologists were quick to capitalize on the loyal implications of such displays. According to some polemicists,

---

N.H., 1993), 186–187; Jones to Lord Althorp, Oct. 19, 1779, in Cannon, ed., *Letters of Jones*, I, 274; J. R. Western, *The English Militia in the Eighteenth Century: The Story of a Political Issue, 1660–1802* (London, 1965), 387–388; *The Camp*, in Cecil Price, ed., *Sheridan Plays* (London, 1975), xxiii–xxiv (*The Camp* was performed during the fall of 1778 at the Drury Lane Theatre). For the debate over British gender relations during the American Revolution, see Dror Wahrman, "Percy's Prologue: From Gender Play to Gender Panic in Eighteenth-Century England," *Past and Present*, no. 159 (May, 1998), 113–160.

12. William Cobbett, ed., *Parliamentary History of England from the Norman Conquest to the Year 1803*, 36 vols. (London, 1806–1820), XX, 981–982; Lord Althorp to Lady Spencer, Nov. 5, 1778, BL Althorp Papers, F8 (unfoliated) (the sister to whom Althorp referred was the duchess of Devonshire); M. J. Lomas, "Militia and Volunteer Wind Bands in Southern England in the Late Eighteenth and Early Nineteenth Centuries," *Journal of the Society for Army Historical Research*, LXVII (1989), 154–166; "Buckinghamshire Militia Orderly Book," II (July 3–Sept. 13, 1779), Stowe Papers, Huntington Library, 144.

the great encampments were an unambiguous affirmation of the same national purpose that had carried the British through previous struggles in Europe. "Genius of Britain! to thy office true, / On Cox-Heath rear'd the waving banners view," one poet envisioned the mobilization in 1778. "A spirit of unanimity, vigour, and exertion, begins to pervade the whole kingdom," concurred the Scottish author of *Ossian*, James MacPherson, at the height of the invasion scare the following summer. At the opening of Parliament in November 1778, even the king expressed his pleasure at witnessing "that public spirit, that steady ardour, and that love of their country, which animate and unite all ranks of my faithful subjects, and which cannot fail of making us safe at home, and respected abroad." Indeed, so widespread was the response to France's involvement that it swept up many of those who doubted the legitimacy of Parliament's claims in the colonies. As an anonymous pamphleteer urged the gentry of Durham in 1779:

> Whatever may be our Sentiments with respect to our Armaments abroad; whether we consider them as enforcing lawful Claims, or as spreading wanton Destruction, it is time for Animosities to sub-side, when we are threatened with an invasion, and when national Honour and Welfare are at stake. Whether our situation at present be the effect of Mismanagement, or the result of Causes which baffle human Prudence, matters not the least. The object which should engross our attention at present is, our present situation, such as we find it, and the very alarming apprehensions of its becoming still worse.[13]

Although historians have often remarked on this apparent unity of purpose, the patriotism occasioned by France's intervention often be-trayed the same underlying ambivalence that had characterized British attitudes toward the imperial crisis since the later 1760s. This was espe-cially evident within the militia. During the threatened French invasion of 1779, William Eden, North's lieutenant at the Treasury, claimed with typical confidence that the "leading men" encamped in the regiments across southern England would "not rest satisfied with having prevented

13. [William Tasker], *An Ode to the Warlike Genius of Great Britain* (London, 1778), 7 (Tasker noted the significance in Coxheath's proximity to Maidstone where "German hireling troops . . . [had] disgrac'd the state, and sham'd the land"); [James MacPher-son], *A Short History of the Opposition during the Last Session of Parliament* (London, 1779), 56; "His Majesty's Most Gracious Speech to Both Houses of Parliament" (Nov. 25, 1778), in *Annual Register*, XXII (1779), 337; *An Address to the Gentry of the County of Durham* . . . (Newcastle, 1779), 7.

the invasion of external enemies." As far as many of those same officers were concerned, however, defending their country from a French invasion was not to be confused with sanctioning the government's war in America. Shortly after being embodied as a major in the Nottinghamshire Militia, John Cartwright, who had resigned his naval commission at the war's outset, wrote his niece that his willingness to use his "sword against either Frenchman or American who shall invade this country" did not mean that he had come to doubt the enormity of Parliament's actions in the colonies.

> Offensive war, by which I mean a war not entered into through necessity and for self-defence, is always wicked and foolish; and when we have brought ourselves into the necessity of engaging in a new war for self-defence, by first wantonly engaging in an offensive war of the most unnatural and criminal nature, it seems to me to be an aggravation of our crime.

William Jones dispensed similar advice to Lord Althorp, drawing a sharp distinction between the imperative "to unite all the force of the kingdom against the house of Bourbon" and the need for reconciling "with America on terms of liberty and reciprocal advantages." As Cartwright's dissenting protégé, the Reverend George Walker, put the issue to the Nottinghamshire regiment in January 1779, "You are the Soldiers of the People, more than of the Crown. . . . When we speak of Loyalty and Obedience to the Prince, we mean in consistence with the Constitution and the Law."[14]

The prevalence of such attitudes was certainly public knowledge. Throughout the five years that the militia spent in the field, Secretary at War Charles Jenkinson acknowledged the dubious allegiance of many of its officers by confining especially arduous or unpopular tasks to regi-

---

14. [William Eden], *Four Letters to the Earl of Carlisle*, 2d ed. (London, 1779), 31; Cartwright to Miss D[ashwood], Mar. 26, 1778, in F. D. Cartwright, ed., *The Life and Correspondence of Major Cartwright*, 2 vols. (London, 1826), I, 118–119; Jones to Althorp, July 18, 1779, in Cannon, ed., *Letters of Jones*, I, 299; [George Walker], *The Duty and Character of a National Soldier . . .* (London, 1779), 28. Walker's remarks were consistent with Cartwright's own view of the militia as a defensive force, which "by its institution is not intended to spread the dominion or to vindicate in war the honour of the crown, but it is to preserve our laws and liberties, and therein to secure the existence of the state" (letter to unspecified correspondent, Sept. 4, 1775, in Cartwright, ed., *Life and Correspondence of Major Cartwright*, I, 54–55). For the unifying effects of French intervention, see Plumb, "British Attitudes to the American Revolution," in Plumb, *In the Light of History;* Bonwick, *English Radicals and the American Revolution*, 107–113.

ments commanded by men of unquestionable loyalty. There were likewise rumors of party divisions within the large encampments on the English coast, as militia officers disputed issues ranging from the prosecution of the war at sea to the legality of the government's actions in America. The initial organizers of the county associations were well aware of the popularity of such views, and several even expressed a private wish during the winter of 1779–1780 that "the Militia would join in the Petition." As an anonymous writer observed in a pamphlet dedicated to the pro-American commander of the Yorkshire Militia, Sir George Savile, "The soldier has an absolute right to the free exercise of his opinion, notwithstanding his particular engagements to the Prince." Indeed, although he was firmly opposed to the government's actions in America, the opposition leader, Lord Shelburne, found such discussions of the militia's loyalty to be sufficiently serious to congratulate the Wiltshire Association in March 1780 for resisting any temptation "to have Recourse to other Means than those purely civil as well as strictly constitutional." "I still have that Confidence in our Army as well as Militia," Shelburne explained, "that I hope neither are yet so estranged from a Love of the Constitution, as to give any just Apprehension of Danger."[15]

When he wrote these words, Shelburne was probably thinking of his native Ireland, where some of the sixty thousand volunteers who had mustered in response to the threatened French invasion of the previous summer were starting to demand the same sort of independence from the British Parliament that had driven the Americans into open rebellion in 1775. In England, however, such concerns proved to be without foundation. Indeed, even as the militia's mobilization gave wider scope to loyal patriots like the officers of the Devonshire regiment—who had

15. Lewis to Charles Jenkinson, July 24, 1780, BL Add. MSS 38,214, 109–110 (Jenkinson pointedly barred several battalions commanded by the opposition leaders, Sir George Savile and Sir James Lowther, from assisting in enforcing the naval press laws; by contrast, the Carmarthenshire battalion "with our friend Johnes at their head" was thought to be sufficiently trustworthy); Lord Althorp to Lady Spencer, Oct. 23–27, 1778, BL Althorp Papers, F8 (unfoliated); Sir William Anderson to Christopher Wyvill, Nov. 30, 1779, in Christopher Wyvill, ed., *Political Papers, Chiefly respecting the Attempt of the County of York, and Other Considerable Districts, Commenced in 1779 . . .*, 6 vols. (York, [1794–1802]), III, 119 (hereafter cited as *Wyvill Papers*) (see also General George Cary to Wyvill, Nov. 30, 1779, *Wyvill Papers*, III, 115: "I am glad to hear the East-Riding Militia are soon to be at York; as I am informed *most* of the Officers think as we do"); *A Letter to the English Nation, on the Present War with America* (London, 1777); Shelburne to William Salmon, clerk of the Committee, Mar. 26, 1780, in *Copies of the Proceedings of the General Meetings of the County of Wilts . . .* (Salisbury, 1780), 55.

petitioned the king in 1775 affirming their willingness to help "reestablish the violated Supremacy of the British Legislature over every part of your Majesty's Dominions"—it also enabled the North ministry to make use of the services of ambivalent patriots like John Cartwright and Sir George Savile. Had there been a French invasion, or had there been a serious breach between the king and Parliament, the divided loyalties of those encamped on the English coast might have created difficulties. By drawing them into a popular show of support for the crown, however, the government effectively turned the "friends of America" who served at places like Warley Common and Coxheath into unwitting agents for the increasingly desperate and costly war on the opposite shores of the Atlantic. Whatever the officers in the militia actually thought of the issues at stake, the North ministry faced few obstacles in its efforts to dramatize the legitimacy of the war overseas with such convincing demonstrations of national unity at home.[16]

Moreover, the government's ability to use ambivalent officers like Cartwright and Savile was mirrored by a corresponding ability to enlist the services of ordinary people without triggering disturbances like those that had nearly undone Pitt's militia reform twenty years before. As Attorney General Alexander Wedderburn reminded the House of Commons in 1779, national emergencies entitled Parliament to call "every man to the aid of the state," preferably through bounties and other incentives but by compulsion if less drastic means proved insufficient. Probably the most striking feature of the government's recruiting efforts during the American Revolution, however, was that service in both the army and the militia (though not the navy) remained voluntary. Although more Britons served in the armed forces of the crown than in any previous foreign war in British history, the means by which the enlisted men were raised differed from that of earlier conflicts only in degree. Insofar as recruiting officers resorted to compulsion in England, Scotland, and Wales, the victims were seamen and other "idle fellows," whose brutal treatment by naval press gangs rarely elicited much public comment or sympathy, even from groups that styled themselves friends of liberty. By contrast, the government generally opted for gentler methods with the army and militia, both of which could also be recruited by conscription, but affected a far broader (and more visible) swath of English society. Indeed, despite scattered reports of reluctance to serve and disturbances like the impressment riots in Cornwall, many observers

16. "The Humble Address of the Officers of the First Regiment of the Devonshire Militia" (Oct. 11, 1775), P.R.O., H.O. 55/11/17.

took the popular willingness to volunteer for the king's forces as evidence of loyal sentiments among even the humblest people. "Lookee, lads," enjoins a captain addressing potential recruits in George Downing's musical farce on the militia, "I have no inclination to force any man into my company—they must all be volunteers." Although doubtless an idealized view of the treatment of potential recruits, the men whom the army and militia sought to enlist remained legally free to refuse their service, if they so desired.[17]

For most people, of course, the most pressing compulsory wartime obligation remained what it had been since the struggles against Louis XIV—the duty to pay taxes. By the time support for the war finally began to falter, the duties on ordinary men and women had reached harrowing levels, with the rates on consumer goods like soap, salt, and alcohol weighing especially heavily on the poor. Likewise, the war economically devastated those parts of Britain—notably ports like Liverpool and the expanding textile centers of Lancashire—that depended most on overseas commerce. To Sir George Savile, who spent the fall of 1779 with the Yorkshire Militia protecting cotton mills from machine breakers, popular resentment over the war's disruptions in the Midlands seemed to have given rise to "a kind of invisible Potentate with whom we can neither fight nor treat." The anti-Catholic Gordon Riots, which paralyzed London for a week the next spring, produced even graver concerns over the possibility of widespread popular unrest. But when the radical physician John Jebb suggested that the best way for the British to register their opposition to the war would be to refuse pay their taxes, he was engaging in hyperbole. Ordinary men and women turned out to be no more willing than their reputed superiors to forswear the habits bred by nearly a century of obedience to constitutional government. In a sense, the armchair patriotism that had enabled the governing Whigs to

17. Cobbett, ed., *Parliamentary History*, XX, 963; [George Downing], *The Volunteers; or, Taylors to Arms! A Comedy of One Act, as it is Performed at the Theatre-Royal in Covent Garden* (London, 1780); see also the injunction by the sergeant in Sheridan's comedy, who reminds potential recruits at Maidstone that they "may have the Credit of a Volunteer, and the Bounty money too" by enlisting (*The Camp*, in Price, ed., *Sheridan Plays*, 315). Parliament passed press acts in 1778 and 1779, which empowered civil magistrates to draft "vagabonds" into the regular army, but observers like Sir John Fielding doubted whether they had much effect (Fielding to Charles Jenkinson, Apr. 3, 1779, BL Add. MSS 38,211, 4–5). For the validity of Fielding's observation, as well as general patterns for recruiting the army, see Conway, *The War of American Independence*, 34–40, 43–54; for the muted response of the English radicals to naval impressment, see Rogers, *Crowds, Culture, and Politics in Georgian Britain*, 119–121.

withstand so many earlier foreign crises effectively carried the North ministry through one of the least successful wars in British history.[18]

II. THE COUNTY ASSOCIATIONS (1780)

The clearest indication of the government's political strength in Britain was the relatively short period during which Lord North's opponents were able to seize the initiative. Historians have used various terms to describe the county association movement of 1780, ranging from an early attempt at "bureaucratic rationalization" to a great "national revival" and the "revolution we escaped." But whatever characterization is preferred, the campaign of petitions and extraparliamentary agitations that the Yorkshire parson Christopher Wyvill began organizing at the end of 1779 clearly threatened the government's standing in England. Born of rising concerns over Britain's increasing isolation in Europe and America, the nearly forty associations that formed in England and Wales drew much of their support from self-styled moderates, many of them landed gentlemen whose main interest was to find an honorable exit from an unwinnable war and in so doing to reduce the tax burden that the contest had done so much to expand. At the same time, the movement also enabled a small but influential group of radicals in London and Westminster to demand far more sweeping changes, including equalizing the size of electoral districts, implementing universal male suffrage, and organizing local militias that ordinary people might use to defend their rights in the same manner as the Irish and the Americans. But the most prominent feature of the county association movement was its sheer brevity. For a few months during the spring of 1780, Christopher Wyvill and his associates appeared to speak for a majority of the political nation. By the summer's end, however, the public outrage had subsided, leaving the government in a domestic position at least as strong as it had occupied over the previous five years.[19]

18. Savile to John Hewitt, Oct. 17, 1779, Foljambe of Osberton Papers, Historic Manuscript Commission Report (typescript), National Registry of Archives, London (hereafter cited as Foljambe Papers [NRA]) 20442, III, XI.D(ii), 128–129; Jebb to Capel Lofft, Dec. 23, 1781, in John Disney, ed., *The Works Theological, Medical, Political, and Miscellaneous, of John Jebb, M.D. F.R.S., with Memoirs of the Life of the Author,* 3 vols. (London, 1799), I, 171. The mounting burden of taxation in Britain is discussed in Paul Langford, *A Polite and Commercial People: England, 1727–1783* (Oxford, 1989), 543.

19. John Torrance, "Social Class and Bureaucratic Innovation: The Commissioners for Examining the Public Accounts 1780–1787," *Past and Present,* no. 78 (February 1978), 56–71; Joanna Innes, "Jonathan Clark, Social History, and England's 'Ancien

One of the main reasons for the county association movement's sudden popularity—and, one suspects, for its equally rapid demise—was that many of its supporters shared the government's view about the need for preserving some sort of imperial presence in North America. Of course, many Britons who opposed the war did so because they claimed to favor granting the Americans independence. As Cartwright put the matter in 1775, the principles of justice dictated treating the colonies as sovereign states bound to Britain, not by uniform "civil or political, obligations," but by the "voluntary good offices" characteristic of relations between allies. Although this was a far cry from the ministry's commitment to maintaining Parliament's unlimited authority, those who thought Britain should accept American independence generally did so on the assumption that relaxing Parliament's claims would open the way toward some sort of permanent union or alliance between the two belligerents. In his treatise on American independence, for example, Cartwright argued that the government might readily "cement a lasting union" by recognizing the North American and West Indian colonies as "sister kingdoms" bound to Britain by virtue of their allegiance to the crown. The radical Presbyterian Richard Price took the same position in his *Observations on Civil Liberty:* "Had we, like a liberal and wise people, rejoiced to see a multitude of free states branched forth from ourselves, all enjoying independent legislatures similar to our own, there is nothing so great or happy that we might not have expected." Indeed, advocates for this sort of colonial "independence" routinely argued that renouncing Parliament's sovereignty would actually ensure the imperial unity that the king's ministers mistakenly thought they could achieve by more coercive means. "To suppose the Colonies to think they have no longer occasion for the protection of Great-Britain," wrote the author of one such proposal in 1775, "is to suppose them entirely unacquainted with the present state of Europe."[20]

Regime,'" *Past and Present,* no. 115 (May 1987), 190; Butterfield, *George III, Lord North, and the People,* vi. For more on the county associations, see Eugene Charlton Black, *The Association: British Extraparliamentary Organization, 1769–1793* (Cambridge, Mass., 1963), chap. 2; Philip Harling, *The Waning of "Old Corruption": The Politics of Economical Reform in Britain, 1779–1846* (Oxford, 1996), 32–42.

20. [John Cartwright], *American Independence the Interest and Glory of Great Britain: A New Edition* (1774; New York, 1970), 13, 20; Richard Price, *Observations on the Nature of Civil Liberty, the Principles of Government, and the Justice and Policy of the War with America* (1776), in Price, *Two Tracts on Civil Liberty, the War with America, and the Debts and Finances of the Kingdom* (1778; New York, 1972), 69; *A Proposition for the*

By the winter of 1779–1780, of course, it was highly unlikely that Americans who accepted the Declaration of Independence would be willing to consider a proposal to reconstitute Britain's North American empire as a consortium of independent states, each governed by a separate assembly but still subject to the crown of George III. "Surely there was never a more preposterous chimera conceived in the brain of a minister" was how Benjamin Franklin characterized Lord Shelburne's last-ditch attempt to preserve such a connection in 1782. For the British themselves, though, it was not always clear exactly what "American independence" meant. Did it necessarily mean complete separation? Or, as the duke of Richmond put the issue in the House of Lords in early 1778, was it possible that Congress might still agree to a peace treaty "upon the ground and footing of dependency?" Because the precise meaning of "independence" remained vague, the possibility of forming some sort of confederation or "friendly league" with the Americans continued to strike many commentators as the best way to end the imperial crisis. Indeed, following France's alliance with the United States, even the ministry's opponents wondered just how committed the Americans were to achieving full independence, especially if doing so meant placing themselves under the permanent protection of the most powerful Catholic monarch in Europe. "Will the people of America enjoy more happiness or more dignity, under the sovereignty of a Congress, allied to France," inquired the member of Parliament for Shrewsbury, William Pulteney, in 1779, than they would as subjects "of the limited Monarch of Great Britain?" In the words of another pamphleteer:

> It may be supposed that the Americans will not yield up that material point of sovereignty to the King of Great Britain, the power of making peace and war; and that they will not choose to be involved in every quarrel in which our Sovereign may choose to be engaged. It is likely, however, that after so long a course of warfare, America will be inclined to relinquish this point, especially if they find that France is no longer able to protect them; besides, they can hardly suspect that Great Britain, so burthened with taxes, will be disposed wantonly to distress America, by engaging in groundless quarrels, which must prove oppressive to herself.[21]

Present Peace and Future Government of the British Colonies in North America (London, 1775), 21–22.

21. Benjamin Franklin, *Two Letters from Dr. Franklin, to the Earl of Shelburne* (London, [1782]), 21; Viscount Mahon to the earl of Chatham, Feb. 11, 1778, in William

Perhaps because the British government eventually recognized American independence on the terms stipulated by Congress in 1776, historians have never paid much attention to the political implications of these alternative solutions. Until the end of 1782, however, when George III's peace commissioners finally renounced all claims to sovereignty over the United States, the British friends of America remained as committed as the government's own apologists to finding some way to salvage what one polemicist referred to as a "FAMILY COMPACT between Great Britain and America." Because of these convictions, those who opposed the war—including many who supported the county associations—sought to appeal to the same blue water patriotism as Lord North's defenders. In his pamphlet of 1779 urging the freeholders of Middlesex to associate, for example, John Jebb insisted that there was yet hope for "a FOEDERAL UNION with the American States"—though only if the government ceased employing "the arts, that have been used to inflame the minds of the People of England, against their Brethren on the other side of the Atlantic." The following spring, David Hartley, member of Parliament for Kingston upon Hull, held out the same prospect of a "federal Alliance" in a letter that Christopher Wyvill subsequently presented to the Yorkshire Association. "There is every rational ground of argument to hope," wrote Hartley, "that by generous and temperate management on the part of this Nation, America may be reconciled to this Country, and prevented from forming any perpetual Alliance with France." Indeed, as late as the summer of 1782, Charles James Fox had "no doubt"—or so he assured the middle-class electors of Westminster—that "a solid, permanent, and advantageous Treaty [might] still be formed" with the United States.[22]

The prevalence of such ideas helps explain why the leaders of the

---

Stanhope Taylor and John Henry Pringle, eds., *Correspondence of William Pitt, Earl of Chatham*, 4 vols. (London, 1838–1840), IV, 503 (hereafter cited as *Chatham Correspondence*); [William Pulteney], *Considerations on the Present State of Public Affairs, and the Means of Raising the Necessary Supplies* (London, 1779), 10; *An Examination into the Conduct of the Present Administration, from the Year 1774 to the Year 1778, and a Plan of Accommodation with America . . .* (London, 1778), 58–59.

22. [Joseph Cawthorne], *A Plan of Reconciliation with America; Consistent with the Dignity and Interests of Both Countries, Humbly Inscribed to the King* (London, 1782), 48; [John Jebb], *An Address to the Freeholders of Middlesex . . .* (London, [1779]), 17n; Hartley to Wyvill, Mar. 22, 1780, in *Wyvill Papers*, III, 187 (for Wyvill's presentation of the letter to the Yorkshire Association, see minutes of debate at York, Mar. 28, 1780, in *Wyvill Papers*, I, 163); "Proceedings at a General Meeting of the City of Westminster, Held in Westminster Hall, on the 17th day of June, 1782," in *Wyvill Papers*, II, 180.

county associations were briefly able to seize the political initiative during the spring of 1780. Although the news later in the summer that Charleston, South Carolina, had fallen to British troops revived hopes for a military solution, the notion that Britain might retain its North American empire through peaceful negotiation and generous concessions was bound to appeal to a public grown tired of so many ineffective and expensive campaigns. "While this war lasts," wrote William Jones to Lord Althorp, "England neither will enjoy, nor ought to enjoy, prosperity"; however, Jones also continued to hope for "a family-compact between us and the United States." As the members of the Dorset Association put the issue in their resolutions of April 1780, there was no question that Britain's present "unhappy state" was a direct result of "the rash and imprudent contest so long and so unprosperously pursued with North-America"; but they nonetheless remained confident that the government might yet negotiate "a reunion with that country, on beneficial, just, and honourable terms." Although their preferred methods differed, the metropolitan friends of America were no less committed to maintaining Britain's Atlantic empire than Lord North's most ardent supporters.[23]

What distinguished the county associators from the ministry's apologists was their stated conviction that the gravity of the crisis facing Britain demanded a thorough reformation of the existing system of representation at Westminster, preferably through parliamentary legislation, but if necessary by extralegal agitation. The roots of this willingness to defy Parliament lay in the growing frustration felt across England over the way the domestic mobilization of the previous two summers had enabled the government to prolong the war in America. Although many Britons eagerly participated in the county meetings, patriotic associations, and local subscriptions that the North ministry encouraged as part of its search for recruits to resupply the king's forces in the colonies, such gatherings were also the occasion for deliberate opposition and heated argument. In Birmingham, for example, a meeting in early 1778 elicited angry complaints in the press about the way the town's magistrates were "raising regiments and encouraging warfare." Elsewhere, the response to such initiatives ranged from outright obstruction (as in the earl of Abingdon's unsuccessful attempt during the summer of 1779 to disrupt a recruiting meeting at Oxford) to more subtle forms of opposition like the hisses with which "many [men and women] of the middling

23. Jones to Althorp, in Cannon, ed., *Letters of Jones,* I, 349; "Proceedings at the Adjourned General Meeting of the County of Dorset," Apr. 25, 1780, in *Wyvill Papers,* I, 202–203.

class" greeted the archdeacon of Lincoln when he "moved a Subscription to strengthen the hands of government." As the pottery manufacturer Josiah Wedgwood discovered when he attended a meeting in Lancashire, the government's opponents even turned such gatherings to their own purposes on several occasions by urging that their neighbors petition the king "to grant [the Americans] such terms . . . *as freemen may accept.*" After witnessing such an exchange at Norwich, one observer concluded that a "regiment may perhaps be raised here, before many years are passed, of a different sort from that proposed at present."[24]

As long as the government controlled events in the cities and counties of England, such words amounted to little more than talk. With the emergence of Christopher Wyvill's county associations, however, the threat of a popular backlash became much less innocuous. Petitioning Parliament for a redress of popular grievances was hardly a novel step, let alone a revolutionary one, even during times of war or national emergencies. What was unprecedented about the group of gentlemen gathered in the York Assembly Rooms at the end of 1779 was their decision to formalize their meeting as an "association." Although Wyvill himself insisted that he meant nothing "which is not pacific, and agreeable to Law and Constitution," the term suggested at the very least a desire to establish an extralegal alternative to the government's own county meetings, and some critics claimed that the movement's organizers were bent on imitating the violent example of the radical patriots in America. As one of Wyvill's more moderate supporters cautioned in early 1780, " 'An Association upon legal and constitutional grounds,' with one set of men, means one thing; with other men, it has a different signification." Indeed, upon presenting the Yorkshire Association's initial petition for economical reform in the House of Commons, Sir George Savile admitted as much. "I make no threats . . . this petition is not presented by men with swords and muskets." Concurred James Fox, "The people are not in arms, they do not menace civil war."[25]

24. *Aris's Birmingham Gazette,* Feb. 9, 1778, in John Money, *Experience and Identity: Birmingham and the West Midlands, 1760–1800* (Manchester, 1977), 208; Lord Macclesfield to Charles Jenkinson, Sherburn Castle, July 29, 1779, BL Add. MSS 38,212, 40–42; A. William Boucherett to John Hewett, Aug. 14, 1779, Foljambe Papers (NRA), XI.A.i.41–42 (the letter refers to men and women); Josiah Wedgwood, in Plumb, "British Attitudes to the American Revolution," in Plumb, *In the Light of History,* 82; W. W. to John Almon, Norwich, Jan. 14, 1778, BL Add. MSS 20,733, 132. Significantly, the government referred to these meetings as associations; see Charles Jenkinson to Lord Amherst, Parliament Street, Jun. 24, 1779, BL Add. MSS 38,306, 157.

25. Wyvill to Dr. A. Hunter, Burton-Hall, Jan. 7, 1780, Dr. A. Hunter to Wyvill,

FIGURE 23

Association Meeting at York. *1780. The delegates at York are approached by the
various national blessings of the county associations' reforms, including hope,
public virtue, commerce, and manufacturing. The painting at the top shows
Britannia and America embracing in reconciliation; in the foreground, France
and Spain (the rooster and the peacock) flee as a soldier and sailor unchain the
British lion. Courtesy of the John Carter Brown Library at Brown University*

Despite the conviction in Savile's and Fox's statements, the county
associations' specific claims and objectives occasionally gave the impression that, like Hamlet's mother, their apologists protested too much.
This was readily apparent from the associations' contention that the war
in America threatened a dissolution of government at home. Although
even moderates within the movement agreed "that much of our unhap-
piness arose from the American war," the published statements of some
committees betrayed a sense of impending collapse that verged on the
apocalyptic. At their London meeting in March 1780, delegates representing nearly forty boroughs and counties in England and Wales insisted, "We are arrived at the crisis which the wisest of political writers
have uniformly marked for the downfall of Britain, when the Legislative

York, Jan. 9, 1780, both in *Wyvill Papers,* III, 175, 177; Cobbett, ed., *Parliamentary
History,* XX, 1375, 1379.

body shall become as corrupt as the executive and dependent upon it." The Westminster Committee made much the same point in its own report in May, arguing that Britain's only hope for redemption from the present crisis lay in *"the interposition of the great collective body of the nation."* Indeed, in his pamphlet seconding Wyvill's call for nationwide associations, Jebb even suggested that the misfortunes brought on by the war in America had given the "people" of England an absolute right "to new-model the Constitution, and to punish with exemplary rigour every person, with whom they have entrusted power, provided, in their opinion, he shall be found to have betrayed that trust."[26]

The inflammatory potential of such words was only heightened by suggestions that the county associations might assume for themselves the authority that Parliament seemed in danger of abdicating. Here again, Christopher Wyvill went to great lengths to avoid appearing to favor such a possibility, but some of his followers were a good deal less careful. According to the Westminster Committee, it required no "extraordinary degree of sagacity" to see that Britain's present difficulties all stemmed from the fact that the House of Commons "is no longer obedient to the will, or speaks the language of the great constituent body of the people." Jebb was even bolder, describing the members of the prospective associations as the "delegates of a state, chosen according to forms, which not law and custom, but necessity or expedience shall prescribe." "In such assembly alone," Jebb explained, "I acknowledge the SOVEREIGN power to reside. To such alone, the tremendous name of MAJESTY may with propriety be attributed."[27]

Both Jebb and his compatriots in the Westminster Committee hoped that the county associations would use their "authority" not only to press for a federal alliance with the Americans but also to bring about the adoption of an electoral system in Britain based on universal male suffrage. Again, there was nothing terribly new or inherently subversive about criticizing the existing mode of representation in the House of Commons. Although the issue had acquired radical overtones during the Wilkite disturbances of the late 1760s, even moderate Whigs and

26. Speech of General Hale, in "Substance of the Debate at the Meeting at York on the 28th of March 1780," in *Wyvill Papers,* I, 163; "Memorial," in "Report of the Deputies of the Committees of Association" (St. James, Mar. 11–20, 1780), in *Wyvill Papers,* I, 428; *Report of the Sub-Committee of Westminster, Appointed April 12, 1780, to Take into Consideration All Such Matters, relative to the Election of Members of Parliament* . . . ([London], 1780), 2; [Jebb], *Address to the Freeholders of Middlesex,* 9.

27. *Report of the Sub-Committee of Westminster,* 2; [Jebb], *Address to the Freeholders of Middlesex,* 9.

Tories like Josiah Tucker, William Paley, and Sir William Blackstone were willing to entertain at least the possibility of broadening the right to vote for members of Parliament. By insisting that every man deserved to participate in this right without respect to wealth or education, however, the leaders of the county associations underscored the fact that they found Parliament's present authority in England, Scotland, and Wales to be as arbitrary as it was in Ireland and America. As the Westminster Committee contended during the war's final years, those who were denied the vote at home enjoyed no more liberty than the most abject slaves in America. Elsewhere, proponents of extending the vote noted that the "*people* now bear the whole burden and expence both of the civil government and of war," as John Horne Tooke observed in his widely read pamphlet on the American crisis. "Listen to no proposal, adopt no plan, formed upon partial grounds" was how John Cartwright put the case for electoral reform in an open letter to the county associations. According to such democratic proposals, any scheme of electoral reform that fell short of giving every adult male the vote represented—in the words of Major Cartwright—"an exclusion unwise as it is unjust," which would only teach "the strong to oppress the weak, the rich to despise the poor, and the poor to have no feelings for the public weal."[28]

For some Westminster radicals, this challenge to parliamentary authority even extended to the government's monopoly on armed force. This was especially evident during the destructive riots that Lord George Gordon's campaign against the Catholic Relief Act triggered in London and several other English cities during June 1780. Because the members

28. *Report of the Sub-Committee of Westminster*, 3–4; minutes of the meeting of the Westminster Committee of Association, July 5, 1784, BL Add. MSS 38,595, 43–44; [John Horne Tooke], *Facts: Addressed to the Landholders, Stockholders, Merchants, Farmers, Manufacturers, Tradesmen* . . . (London, [1780]), 11 (Tooke was speaking in support of Burke's proposal for economical reform, but his argument here was consistent with his advocacy of universal suffrage); [John Cartwright], *An Address to the Gentlemen, Forming the Several Committees of the Associated Counties, Cities, and Towns* . . . ([London, 1780]), iii–iv. For less radical ideas of reform, see Josiah Tucker, *A Treatise concerning Civil Government* . . . (London, 1781), 276–278, 284–292; William Paley, *The Principles of Moral and Political Philosophy* (1785), in *The Works of William Paley, D.D.* . . . (Philadelphia, [1857]), 127; William Blackstone, *Commentaries on the Laws of England* (1765–1769), ed. Stanley N. Katz et al., 4 vols. (Chicago, 1979), I, 166. See also John Cannon, *Parliamentary Reform, 1640–1832* (Cambridge, 1973), esp. chaps. 1–4; J. G. A. Pocock, "Josiah Tucker on Burke, Locke, and Price: A Study in the Varieties of Eighteenth-Century Conservatism," in Pocock, *Virtue, Commerce, and History: Essays on Political Thought and History, Chiefly in the Eighteenth Century* (Cambridge, 1985), 184.

of the Protestant Association shared the county associations' opposition to the war in America, some of the government's most prominent critics, including, notably, John Wilkes (now a London alderman), went out of their way to differentiate their own activities from those of the Gordon rioters. At the height of the insurrection, in fact, Wilkes set a conspicuous example in helping the army and militia defend the Bank of England from repeated assaults by the frenzied crowd. In the riots' aftermath, however, there were confrontations between regular army officers and the local posses that had formed in towns across England. In London, for example, groups of armed tradesmen met the army's efforts to prevent them from patrolling the streets with angry insistence on the constitutional right of every Protestant Englishman to bear arms in his own defense. In other localities, nervous gentlemen greeted similar activities with recommendations that the magistrates invoke the Riot Act and call in the army. During the summer of 1780, the ministry's determination to check the spread of such groups even prompted the Yorkshire Association to adopt a resolution denouncing any attempt to "disarm peaceable subjects" who were Protestant as "contrary to the natural right of self-defence, contrary to the positive law of the land, and directly tending to the utter ruin of our liberties, by the introduction of a military government."[29]

The right of every man—and woman—to own firearms had been part of the English constitution since the Glorious Revolution. Yet by conceiving of this right, not just in individual terms, but as a justification for the formation of what amounted to autonomous popular militias, the radicals who took issue with the crown's prosecution of the war in the colonies came dangerously close to sanctioning the very sort of political violence that they claimed to abhor. Probably the most explicit and controversial statement of this sort occurred in the anonymous *Dialogue between a Scholar and a Peasant* (1782), which William Jones wrote while visiting Benjamin Franklin in Paris and which was subsequently published for free distribution by the radical, Westminster-based Society for Constitutional Information. In the pamphlet, a patriot agitator persuades a common farmer not only that he is entitled to the full rights of citizenship but that it is his "legal and rational" right as a freeborn

29. T. Wilson to John Wilkes, June 12, 1780, P. Thompson to John Wilkes, Aug. 6, 1780, both in BL Add. MSS 30,872, 196, 199–200; Col. Thomas Twisleton to Lord Amherst, June 14, 1780, P.R.O., S.P. 37/20/166; Lord Macclesfield to Charles Jenkinson, June 23, 1780, BL Add. MSS 38,214, 39; "Resolutions at a Meeting of the Committee of Association, for the County of York" (Aug. 2, 1780), in *Wyvill Papers*, I, 260. See also Nicholas Rogers, "Crowd and People in the Gordon Riots," in Hellmuth, ed., *Transformation of Political Culture*, 39–55.

Englishman to resist any minister who attempts to employ the force of government "against the nation." Having made his point, the scholar provides his humble friend with a spare musket and enjoins him to "spend an hour every morning for the next fortnight in learning to prime and load expeditiously, and to fire and charge with bayonet firmly and regularly." As Jones commented in a letter to John Cartwright, "It is my deliberate (though private) opinion, that the people of England will never be a people in the majestic sense of the word, unless two hundred thousand of the *civil* state be ready, before the first of next November, to take the field, without rashness or disorder, at twenty-four hours' notice."[30]

The incendiary tone of such comments was unmistakable. Yet as the speed of the North ministry's recovery suggests, we should not exaggerate the number of people who were prepared to carry their patriotism to the extreme suggested in tracts like Jones's *Dialogue*. Historians agree that two main reasons accounted for the county association movement's rapid disintegration during the summer of 1780. The first was the capture of Charleston, which enabled the government to claim that the war in North America was going better than Wyvill and his supporters contended. At the same time, many of the people who initially accepted the associations' methods abandoned them amid the growing intolerance that the Gordon Riots bred for extralegal activities of all sorts. As Jones himself reported shortly after the insurrection had been quelled, "many of the best-intentioned men, well inclined till now to our mixed constitution, are continually saying, 'How much more secure we should have been in France!'" This was an obvious exaggeration; however, the riots' aftermath witnessed the movement's rapid desertion by many of the same landed gentlemen who only months earlier had eagerly flocked to Christopher Wyvill's reformist standard. "All such associations should be suppressed and strictly forbidden in future," exclaimed a typically hostile commentator following Lord North's electoral triumph in September. As the Essex parson Thomas Twining remarked with satisfaction in July 1780, support for his county's association was bound to wane as the violence of Lord George Gordon's fanatical adherents opened "the eyes of many well-meaning people who had before joined in them." Indeed, even Jones had to admit, "the word *people* [is so] equivocal in our

30. [William Jones], *The Principles of Government, in a Dialogue between a Scholar and a Peasant* . . . (London, 1782), 6–7; Jones to Cartwright, May 23, 1782, in Cartwright, ed., *Life and Correspondence of Major Cartwright*, I, 152. The "first of November" is a clear reference to the opening of Parliament. The English right to bear arms (for women as well as men) is the subject of Joyce Lee Malcolm, *To Keep and Bear Arms: The Origins of an Anglo-American Right* (Cambridge, Mass., 1994).

NO POPERY or NEWGATE REFORMER.

Tho' He Says he's a Protestant, look at the Print,
The Face and the Bludgeon, will give you a hint,
Religion he cries, in hopes to deceive,
While his practice is only to burn and to thieve.
Publifhd as the Act Directs, June 9.1780 by I. Catch of Stoiles.

FIGURE 24

No Popery; or, Newgate Reformer. *By James Gillray. 1780. The aftermath of the Gordon Riots.* © *The British Museum*

language" that "a crafty politician" might easily twist its meaning in order to cast the blame for the popular excesses of the London mob on the Westminster radicals and the county associations.[31]

Of course, broad-acred gentlemen whose families had reaped the benefits of parliamentary government for the better part of the last century were unlikely to take more than a passing interest in extralegal agitation. But this tendency to pull back from the brink was not confined to the more moderate of the county associations' supporters. John Cartwright, for one, remained careful to balance the unambiguous opposition that he mounted as a founding member of the Westminster Committee and the Society for Constitutional Information with his loyal activities as an officer who bore the king's commission in the Nottinghamshire Militia. Likewise, when one considers the anonymous publication of Jones's *Dialogue* and the "private" character of his subsequent communication to Cartwright, even this affirmation of a popular right of resistance loses some of its force—although it was not enough to prevent the pamphlet's Welsh translation from exposing Jones to charges of libel and sedition. In many ways, the moderate norms that figures like Cartwright and Jones continued to observe in their actual conduct mattered more than the radical principles they espoused in theory. The day before Sir George Savile laid the first petition before the House of Commons, one of the Yorkshire Association's organizers confessed that he could not "help being afraid of things going to great lengths, as many People are too violent and there is no preventing them." As the success that the county associations and Westminster radicals briefly enjoyed suggests, appealing to the people could take on a life of its own—if only in the world of speech, print, and conversation. In the end, though, even the county associations' radical fringe remained sufficiently moderate to check the movement's more extreme tendencies.[32]

Indeed, London-based radicals like John Cartwright, Richard Price,

---

31. Jones to Lady Spencer, Temple, June 9, 12, 1780, both in Cannon, ed., *Letters of Jones*, I, 404, 409 (both passages cited come from this letter); *A Letter to the New Parliament, with Hints of Some Regulations Which the Nation Hopes and Expects from Them* (London, 1780), 5; Twining to Charles Burney, July 14, 1780, in Ralph S. Walker, ed., *A Selection of Thomas Twining's Letters, 1734–1804*, 2 vols. (Lewiston, N.Y., 1991), I, 184–185.

32. St. Andrew Warde to John Hewett, Hooton Pannell, Foljambe Papers (NRA), XI.A.i.63–64. The Welsh translation of Jones's pamphlet was published by the Flintshire Committee on its own initiative. For the legal difficulties that resulted, see Jones to Lloyd Kenyon, Lamb Building, Mar. 28, 1783, in Cannon, ed., *Letters of Jones*, II, 607–610.

and John Jebb ultimately showed themselves every bit as committed as the rest of British society to a kind of armchair politics—where the stirring rhetoric of heroic struggle was mitigated by an equally conspicuous predilection to leave the actual business of revolution to others. Nowhere did this fascination with someone else's heroism appear more fully than in the admiration that many professed for their "brothers and sisters" in Ireland and America. Throughout the 1780s, the Society for Constitutional Information routinely ended its dinners with toasts to "the Rights of the Subject to the Possession and the Use of Arms, as secured to us by the Revolution—and as asserted by the Irish Volunteers." "I confess," John Cartwright wrote a colonel in the volunteers during the summer of 1783, "that in England we have not yet had, at any period, a prospect of effecting a complete Reform; but in Ireland, your Volunteer Army—the most glorious production of public virtue that ever adorned a nation!—have perfection or imperfection wholly in their option." The same thing was true of the United States, which many radicals hoped might serve as a model for democratic reform in England. As an indication of such attitudes, the Society for Constitutional Information continued well into the 1780s to advocate the "antient friendship" between Great Britain and the United States. In a similar manner, long after the crisis of 1780 had subsided—and long after the danger of any sort of violent upheaval in England had passed—both the Society for Constitutional Information and the remnants of Wyvill's county associations continued to congratulate themselves on having supported the cause of armed revolution in America.[33]

Yet however genuine such expressions might have been, Britain's radicals remained no more willing to undertake actions that could "lead to violence and commotion" at home than the government's own loyal supporters. As a result, the British friends of America ultimately played almost no role in determining the Revolution's final outcome—or rather, none beyond drawing attention to mounting war weariness among the general public. Furthermore, even before the final defeat at Yorktown freed Britain from what surely would have been the heavy burdens of conquest, the declarations of the colonists' metropolitan sympathizers

33. "Minutes of the Society for Constitutional Information" (Dec. 9, 1785), P.R.O., T.S. 11/961, 119; Cartwright to Colonel Sharman, Aug. 26, 1783, in *A Collection of the Letters Which Have Been Addressed to the Volunteers of Ireland on the Subject of a Parliamentary Reform* . . . (London, 1783), 99; *The Speech of the Hon. C. J. Fox Delivered at Westminster on Feb. 2, 1780* (London, 1780), quoted in Butterfield, *George III, Lord North, and the People*, 226; Daniel Adams to John Lathorp at Boston, July 24, 1784, as entered in "Minutes of the Society for Constitutional Information," P.R.O., T.S. 11/961/58.

FIGURE 25
Volunteers at Dublin as They Met 4 November 1779. *By Joseph Collyer*
(after Francis Wheatley). 1784. Courtesy of the Yale Center for British Art,
Paul Mellon Collection

frequently betrayed a theatrical air at odds with the war's obvious gravity.
As the dissenting clergyman Thomas Northcote lamented in an open
letter to the Irish Committee for Parliamentary Reformation, "An Englishman, without a *vote* or a *Musket,* is stripped more naked and defen-
celess than the Savage in the Desart." Likewise, after reading a copy of
John Wilkes's first parliamentary performance on the Americans' behalf,
Catherine Macaulay is alleged to have compared it—without even a
trace of irony—to "some of her favourite Speeches in 1639 etc." No
matter what other opinions Reverend Northcote and the redoubtable
Mrs. Macaulay might have held, the crisis of the American Revolution
was clearly something to be experienced as only events encountered at a
distance could be.[34]

34. "Letter Address[ed] to the Freeholders of Yorkshire by the Rev. Christopher
Wyvill," Dec. 30, 1783, in *Wyvill Papers,* III, 48; Northcote to the Committee of
Parliamentary Reformation, Oct. 15, 1783, in *A Collection of Letters to the Volunteers of
Ireland,* 94; Thomas Wilson to Wilkes, Bath, Nov. 4, 1775, BL Add. MSS 30,871, 248.

III. A PEOPLE ABOVE REPROACH

Although few Britons could have foreseen it in 1775, one of the great ironies of the American Revolution was that the loss of such an important part of Britain's Atlantic empire not only failed to disrupt in any permanent way the ordinary pattern of domestic politics but arguably left the Whig regime of George III at least as secure as it had been twenty years before. In a number of important respects, of course, the war proved a chastening experience for a public perhaps grown too accustomed to military success. "It is not above *twenty years* since this kingdom was the envy of the world," lamented one of the government's critics in 1780. "Great in commerce, in arts, in arms, in liberty; universally revered, and held up as a model to surrounding nations: but now alas! how great the change!" Yet for all the sense of humiliation and regret in some quarters, Britain remained remarkably unaffected by the eight-year struggle that nearly everyone feared would bring ruin in its wake. As the English abolitionist William Richards recollected of his compatriots' response to the war's end, "we sat down very demurely and composedly, without the least apparent feeling of contrition, sorrow or self-reproach; like Solomon's adulterous woman, who eat, and wiped her mouth, and said, 'I have done no wickedness.' "[35]

One explanation for this resilience was that Britain's international situation at the war's end was actually less dire than doomsayers had predicted. Although the loss of the thirteen colonies was a terrible blow, members of the British public—including many who had supported Wyvill's associations in 1780—could take comfort that the defenses of Gibraltar had held, that Bengal was secure, and that Admiral Rodney's victory at the Saints had ensured Britain's continued dominance in the West Indies. Even Ireland looked like less of a problem than it had just a few years before, and commentators like Josiah Tucker were starting to wonder how long it would be before its parliament requested "to be incorporated with *Great-Britain*" in the same manner as Scotland. As the English historian of manners John Andrews reminded his readers in 1783, Britain had withstood "the brunt of the most powerful confederacy that was ever formed against any State," and Baptist Noel Turner went so far as to speak of "a war, more truly glorious than any thing Lewis XIV could boast of." "I will take upon me to affirm," wrote the Irish patriot

---

35. *The Duty of a Freeman, Addressed to the Electors of Great Britain* [London, 1780], 3; Richards, *History of Lynn*, II, 959.

Edward Stratford of Britain's prospects at the war's end, that "we are, and shall continue, the greatest empire, as to riches, commerce, and manufactures, in Europe, mistress of its seas, and the ballance of its power." Although such judgments failed to capture the full complexity of the Revolution's legacy for Britain, they served as a reminder that, for all the government's perceived shortcomings, it had ultimately avoided the full brunt of the storm forecast by its critics.[36]

As important as Britain's external situation, however, was the relationship between the partisans of the two sides in England. Although the American Revolution generated exceedingly heavy domestic burdens, Lord North and his supporters were ultimately free to prosecute the war without having to worry overly about the activities of metropolitan critics and opponents. In part the result of habits bred by nearly a century of constitutional government and civil liberty, this often grudging acquiescence also reflected the fact that even a potentially unsuccessful war on behalf of Britain's empire was a conflict that patriots dared not oppose too strenuously, even when the patriots in question were as disaffected as William Jones and Lady Spencer. It is not clear exactly what sort of reply John Cartwright expected when, shortly after the outbreak of fighting in the colonies, he declined Lord Howe's offer of a naval commission by sending the admiral a copy of his pamphlet *American Independence*. For his own part, Howe chose to respond—through a letter from his secretary—by affirming, "Opinions in politics, on points of such national moment as the differences subsisting between England and America, are to be treated like opinions in religion, whereon he would leave every one at the liberty to regulate his conduct by those ideals which he had adopted upon due reflection and enquiry." The two might disagree fundamentally over the war in America, they might even find each other's positions difficult or impossible to understand, but Howe was clearly free to reply with the tolerance and grace of someone who knew he spoke from a position of moral and legal superiority.[37]

36. Josiah Tucker, *Four Letters on Important National Subjects, Addressed to the Right Honourable the Earl of Shelburne* . . . (London, 1783), 12; John Andrews, *An Essay on Republican Principles, and on the Inconveniences of a Commonwealth in a Large Country and Nation* . . . (London, 1783), 91; [Baptist Noel Turner], *The True Alarm* (London, 1783), 4, as quoted in Langford, *Polite and Commercial People*, 618; Edward Stratford, *An Essay on the True Interests and Resources of the Empire of the King of Great-Britain and Ireland* . . . (Dublin, 1783), 30. This is the way British historians have tended to present the war's end; see esp. Colley, *Britons*, 143–144.

37. Letter dated Feb. 12, 1776, in Cartwright, ed., *Life and Correspondence of Major Cartwright*, I, 77.

The Experience of Defeat

THE BRITISH LEGACY OF THE
AMERICAN REVOLUTION

Of the various publications to appear in British book shops in 1789, few lived up to their billing more fully than Olaudah Equiano's *Interesting Narrative* of his own life. A West African native and former slave residing in London, Equiano had worked at various points over the last thirty years as a field hand in Virginia, a cabin boy in the British navy, a steward on ships sailing to places as distant as Asia Minor and the Arctic Ocean, even, for a period during the American Revolution, as a servant with the Devonshire Militia while it was at Coxheath—an experience he found too "uninteresting to make a detail of." But probably the most remarkable thing about Equiano's life was the exceptional success of his autobiography, which he wrote to assist the growing movement to end the British slave trade. The *Narrative*'s subscribers ranged from radicals like Granville Sharp and Thomas Hardy to British admirals, Anglican bishops, peers of the realm, and members of the royal family. In Ireland alone, where Equiano made a promotional tour in 1791, the book sold nearly two thousand copies, and by the time of his death six years later, the story of his life had gone through eight editions in England and had been translated into Russian, French, and Dutch. Assuming, perhaps, that this success was indicative of a larger shift in attitudes, Equiano dedicated subsequent imprints to both houses of Parliament, hoping his story would "excite" in them "a sense of compassion for the miseries which the Slave-Trade has entailed on my unfortunate countrymen."[1]

Such optimism turned out to be sadly premature, for Parliament proved no more willing to embrace the cause of abolition than it did most of the other reforms mooted during the final quarter of the eighteenth century. Indeed, the broad appeal that Equiano's story held for the reading public seems hard to square with what we know about British politics following the American Revolution. For many Britons, the imperial crisis produced a growing sense that the Hanoverian regime had allowed its subjects too much "political liberty" in the years before the war, as Lord Chancellor Thurlow insisted in 1789. This authoritarian attitude was especially pronounced overseas, in places like Bengal, Upper Canada, and Ireland where the conservative response to the American Revolution helped inaugurate an "imperial revolution in government." Even in England, where the government's position appeared unassailable, the war's aftermath witnessed an abandonment by Whig apologists of all but the most perfunctory suggestions of popular sovereignty, a renewed emphasis on subordination and civil obedience, and a marked reluctance to tamper with any aspect of Britain's constitution. As Lord Sheffield observed in the opening paragraph of his influential defense of the Navigation Acts, "the independence of America [had] encouraged the wildest sallies of imagination" among radicals and would-be reformers everywhere. But Sheffield was confident—and so, as it turned out, were most of his British readers—that more than a century of "successful practice" was far preferable to untested "systems" and "rash theory."[2]

1. Robert J. Allison, ed., *The Interesting Narrative of the Life of Olaudah Equiano, Written by Himself* (1791; Boston, 1995), 15–16, 30, 185; J. R. Oldfield, *Popular Politics and British Anti-Slavery: The Mobilisation of Public Opinion against the Slave Trade, 1787–1807* (Manchester, 1995), 125–126. The 1791 edition of Equiano's autobiography contains some additional material not found in the first London imprint. For the typicality of the experiences related by Equiano, see W. Jeffrey Bolster, *Black Jacks: African-American Seamen in the Age of Sail* (Cambridge, Mass., 1997).

2. Thurlow to Grenville, Sept. 1–10, 1789, quoted in David Milobar, "Conservative Ideology, Metropolitan Government, and the Reform of Quebec, 1782–1791," *International History Review*, XII (1990), 51; C. A. Bayly, *Imperial Meridian: The British Empire and the World, 1780–1830* (London, 1989), 116–121; John [Holroyd], Lord Sheffield, *Observations on the Commerce of the American States . . .* rev. ed. (1784; New York, 1970), 1. For the conservative drift of British politics, both at home and within the empire, see also H. Butterfield, *George III, Lord North, and the People, 1779–80* (London, 1949); H. T. Dickinson, *Liberty and Property: Political Ideology in Eighteenth-Century Britain* (London, 1977), chap. 8; J. G. A. Pocock, "The Varieties of Whiggism

Nonetheless, the success of Equiano's abolitionist *Narrative* is an important reminder that, even as the British rejected all but the most modest impulses for reform, they recognized the complex, multiracial character of the empire that remained in 1783. Even Protestant settlers in Upper Canada, Nova Scotia, and the West Indies no longer seemed as unproblematically British as they once had. Indeed, given the tenuousness of British authority over colonists who claimed the rights of Englishmen, people increasingly touted the sort of humanitarian paternalism advocated by writers like Equiano to justify their support for Parliament's continuing role as an imperial sovereign. When it came to actually remedying abuses like the slave trade or the East India Company's harsh administration of Bengal, of course, these enlightened professions usually amounted to little more than talk. Still, the changing sense of empire born of the American Revolution fostered a much clearer awareness of the conditions that distinguished Britons who lived within the confines of England, Scotland, and Wales from those who did not. Although rarely stated in explicit terms, Parliament's failure to govern the Americans as so many members of a single nation meant that the British had to make at least a tacit admission that colonial administration could not be handled in the same way as matters of metropolitan governance and that the Americans who regarded the British Empire as a quasi-federal polity were not nearly as mistaken as many people had once believed.[3]

I. THE LIMITS OF GREATER BRITAIN

Insofar as it involved the thirteen colonies, recognizing the limits of their own nationality was something many Britons came to reluctantly. Throughout the war, the North ministry's apologists insisted that the government was fighting to reestablish the same sort of authority in the

---

from Exclusion to Reform: A History of Ideology and Discourse," in Pocock, *Virtue, Commerce, and History: Essays on Political Thought and History, Chiefly in the Eighteenth Century* (Cambridge, 1985), 277–279; P. J. Cain and A. G. Hopkins, *British Imperialism: Innovation and Expansion, 1688–1914* (London, 1993), 96–97.

3. Eliga H. Gould, "American Independence and Britain's Counter-Revolution," *Past and Present*, no. 154 (February 1997), 107–141. See also David Brion Davis, *The Problem of Slavery in the Age of Revolution, 1770–1823* (Ithaca, N.Y., 1975), chap. 9; P. J. Marshall, "Empire and Authority in the Later Eighteenth Century," *Journal of Imperial and Commonwealth History*, XV (1987), 115–120; Linda Colley, "Britishness and Otherness: An Argument," *Journal of British Studies*, XXXI (October 1992), 309–329; Colley, *Britons: Forging the Nation, 1707–1837* (New Haven, Conn., 1992), 144–145.

settled regions of North America that the king and Parliament enjoyed in England, Scotland, and Wales. As the Scottish literatus Sir John Dalrymple observed in 1775, the conflict over parliamentary taxation had given rise to "a singular war" because it pitted "English Subjects against English Subjects." The archdeacon of Surrey, John Butler, made the same point in a sermon at the end of 1776: "We cannot with Indifference . . . behold a large number of Fellow-creatures, in Language and Blood our Countrymen, so self-condemned, and afflicted under the mighty Hand of God." Even in Ireland, where Parliament's imperial sovereignty raised many of the same problems as in the colonies, observers like Trinity College's Thomas Leland did not hesitate to describe the American war as a national contest, which the king's ministers were fighting for the welfare of "our brethren and fellow-citizens, for that empire in whose bosom we are protected, for every member in its extended circuit; for parents, kinsmen, friends, the rising age, and every future generation."[4]

There was obviously more than a little wishful thinking in such statements. Indeed, one of the Revolution's great ironies was that Britain's authority in North America proved to be far more tenuous in those regions controlled by English settlers than it did in the lands beyond the boundary established by the Proclamation of 1763. Despite Congress's avowed wish to "liberate" the people of Quebec, for example, neither the province's Catholic habitants nor more recent Protestant immigrants showed much interest in joining their rebellious neighbors to the south. With a few notable exceptions, the British were also able to count on the allegiance of Indian leaders like the Mohawk sachem Joseph Brant, and in so doing to retain control over the vast swath of territory that stretched from the southern coasts of Florida to the strongholds of Detroit and Fort Niagara. Although they had to be careful not to offend loyalist sentiment in the Lower South and the West Indies, British officers even made effective use of escaped slaves belonging to supporters of the Revolution, several thousand of whom flocked to join the king's troops in exchange for the freedom that General Henry Clinton promised them in the Phillipsburg Proclamation of 1779. When Parliament passed Grenville's Stamp Act (1765), most Britons had assumed that the greatest

4. [Sir John Dalrymple], *Considerations upon the Different Modes of Finding Recruits for the Army* (London, 1775), 14; John Butler, *A Sermon Preached before the Honourable House of Commons, at the Church of St. Margaret's, Westminster, on Friday, December 13, 1776* . . . (London, 1777), 10; Thomas Leland, *A Sermon, Preached before the University of Dublin, on Friday the 13th of December, 1776* . . . (London, 1777), 17–18.

threat to their North American empire would come from the alien peoples that inhabited the lands outside areas of English settlement. Following the commencement of hostilities in Massachusetts, however, the British found themselves engaged in an increasingly multicultural project, where they had to draw on the services of Indians, blacks, and Catholics in order to restore Parliament's authority among the Protestant colonists on the eastern side of the Appalachian Mountains.[5]

This fact was deeply unpopular with the British public, many of whom took the willingness to use such forces as yet another indication of the war's "bloody, barbarous, and ferocious" character, as the earl of Chatham assured the House of Lords in 1777. Despite the revulsion and concern evident in such statements, though, even the government's critics continued to regard the American Revolution as a struggle with people who were still British subjects. In the months before his dramatic, fatal collapse in the House of Lords, Chatham repeatedly insisted that he could see no reason why the Americans "should not enjoy every fundamental right in their property, and every original substantial liberty, which Devonshire or Surrey, or the county I live in, or any other county in England, can claim." In a similar manner, Edmund Burke opposed the American war largely because the colonists' membership in "the communion of our country" made it impossible to separate the government's actions in America from "our legislative spirit" in England. In a possible allusion to more radical friends of America like Richard Price and John Cartwright, both Chatham and Burke even worried that the brutality of the war in the colonies would encourage people on all sides of the issue to engage in similar excesses in Britain. "Civil wars strike deepest of all into the manners of a people," Burke explained in his *Letter to the Bristol Sheriffs*. "They vitiate their politicks; they corrupt their morals; they pervert even the natural taste and relish of equity and justice. By teaching us to consider our fellow-citizens in an hostile light, the whole body of our nation becomes gradually less dear to us."[6]

5. For a perceptive analysis of the multicultural character of Britain's response to the Revolution, see Edward Countryman, "Indians, the Colonial Order, and the Social Significance of the American Revolution," *William and Mary Quarterly*, 3rd Ser., LIII (1996), 342–362. See also G. A. Rawlyk, "The American Revolution and Canada," in Jack P. Greene and J. R. Pole, eds., *The Blackwell Encyclopedia of the American Revolution* (Oxford, 1991), 500–502; Colin G. Calloway, *The American Revolution in Indian Country: Crisis and Diversity in Native American Communities* (Cambridge, 1995); Sylvia R. Frey, *Water from the Rock: Black Resistance in a Revolutionary Age* (Princeton, N.J., 1991).

6. Chatham's speech of Dec. 20, 1777, as reported by Hugh Boyd, in William

Despite these apprehensions—or perhaps because of them—both Burke and the Chathamite Whigs gradually came to accept the inevitability of recognizing American independence in one form or another.[7] For the government and its supporters, however, it proved impossible to dispense altogether with a vision of the settled regions of the North American seaboard as integral parts of the British nation. As the king's chaplain, Henry Stebbing, noted in a sermon preached during the national fast at the end of 1776, the case of the American loyalists was especially important in this respect, for "they are a part of us, a member of our political body, and *if one of our members suffer,* we feel to our sorrow that *the whole body suffers with it.*" In fact, as the British politicians who negotiated the Treaty of Paris (1783) learned to their cost, one of the final obstacles to concluding a satisfactory peace with the United States lay in finding some way to compensate those men and women who had suffered because of their allegiance to Britain. Without some such provision, warned the Philadelphia émigré Joseph Galloway in 1782, "the loyalists will *justly* think themselves finally betrayed and abandoned, and will entertain the most *horrid,* I wish I could not say at the same time, the most *just* opinion of British *treachery and inhumanity.*" "Even Lord Oxford and Lord Bolingbroke," wrote another pamphleteer in early 1783, "would not thus have abandoned their miserable fellow-citizens, who had bled and perished in their cause! They . . . only sacrificed the *Catalans.*" Although such professions made little difference to the war's final outcome, they carried enough weight for the government to make the loyalists' future safety and well-being a necessary condition for ending what was otherwise coming to seem like a pointless and ruinous contest.[8]

<hr/>

Stanhope Taylor and John Henry Pringle, eds., *Correspondence of William Pitt, Earl of Chatham,* 4 vols. (London, 1838–1840), IV, 454–455n, 474n (hereafter cited as *Chatham Papers*); *A Letter from Edmund Burke, Esq: One of the Representatives in Parliament for the City of Bristol . . .* , 2d ed. (London, 1777), 20–21.

7. See esp. Edmund Burke, "Speech on Powys's Motion on American Commission," Apr. 10, 1778, in W. M. Elofsen, ed., *Party, Parliament, and the American War, 1774–1780* (Oxford, 1996), 374–376, vol. III of Paul Langford, ed., *The Writings and Speeches of Edmund Burke;* see also Conor Cruise O'Brien, *The Great Melody: A Thematic Biography and Commented Anthology of Edmund Burke* (Chicago, Ill., 1992), 205, 220–225. For the Chathamite Whigs, who were slower to accept American independence, see Peter Brown, *The Chathamites: A Study in the Relationship between Personalities and Ideas in the Second Half of the Eighteenth Century* (New York, 1967), 79–80, 88–91.

8. Henry Stebbing, *A Sermon on the Late General Fast, Preached at Gray's Inn Chapel, on Friday the 13th Day of December, 1776 . . .* (London, 1776), 4; [Joseph Galloway],

Even as they continued to insist on the bonds of a common nationality, though, the British were gradually forced to acknowledge a
number of important distinctions between their own situation and that
of the colonists. By far the most prominent of these involved the enthusiastic spirit that seemed to infuse the proceedings of Congress and its
supporters. Although there was little consensus on just how widespread
this spirit was, ministerial apologists had no doubt that the Revolutionary leaders were conducting themselves in a manner reminiscent of
the fanaticism that had characterized England's own Presbyterians and
Congregationalists during the seventeenth century. According to the
accounts that inundated the British press, the colonists routinely engaged in all sorts of atrocities, including mistreating prisoners of war,
mutilating enemy corpses, and brutally silencing anyone who questioned
their actions. "No history will furnish us with more barbarity and savage
rage, than in the mode of the present war carried on by the Americans,"
wrote one pamphleteer in 1776. As Joseph Galloway described the situation, Congress had "suppressed the liberty of the press, disarmed every
person whom they thought disaffected to their measures, and passed a
number of laws to compel the people to abjure their allegiance to their
Sovereign"—all of which, Galloway assured his British readers, "were
carried into execution with the greatest inhumanity." In short, wrote the
English jurist John Lind, the Americans were behaving as though they
possessed "some superior sanctity, some peculiar privilege, by which
those things are lawful to them, which are unlawful to all the world
besides."[9]

Not surprisingly, apologists for the Church of England took a leading role in perpetuating these allegations. Although most Anglicans

---

Fabricius; or, Letters to the People of Great Britain . . . (London, 1782), 5; [Portius], *A
Letter to the Earl of Shelburne on the Peace* (London, 1783), 13–14. It is worth noting that
the earl of Shelburne, under whose administration the Treaty of Paris was finalized,
actually saw the question of the loyalists in the same light as his critics. See, for
example, Shelburne's letter to British peace commissioner Richard Oswald, Nov. 23,
1782, P.R.O., C.O. 5/8/3, 347. For the loyalists' problematic relationship to Britain and
the British government, see Mary Beth Norton, *The British-Americans: The Loyalist
Exiles in England, 1774–1789* (Boston, 1972); Bernard Bailyn, *The Ordeal of Thomas
Hutchinson* (Cambridge, Mass., 1974).

9. *The Duty of the King and Subject, on the Principles of Civil Liberty: Colonists Not
Intitled to Self-Government, or to the Same Privileges with Britons* . . . (London, 1776), 30;
[Joseph Galloway], *Letters to a Nobleman, on the Conduct of the War in the Middle
Colonies* (London, 1779), 19–20; [John Lind], *An Answer to the Declaration of the
American Congress* (London, 1776), 120–121.

FIGURE 26

The Bostonian's Paying the Excise-Man; or, Tarring and Feathering. *1774*.
*Based on the tarring and feathering of John Malcomb, the British customs officer
in Boston. Colonial Williamsburg Foundation*

were careful not to identify Parliament's imperial authority too closely with the church's own particular interests, the enthusiasm evident in the American Revolution provided a vivid reminder of the overwhelming superiority that Dissenters enjoyed in every colony except Maryland and Virginia. Throughout the war, one of the recurring charges in the ministerial press was the part played by the Dissenting clergy in "breathing the spirit of rebellion on the people." "Every body knows that they have an inveterate hatred to our constitution both in church and state," wrote one pamphleteer; "the principles they suck in with milk naturally lead to rebellion . . . whilst they pretend, in the canting style of the last century, to exalt the dominion of king Jesus, [but] have nothing really at heart but to erect their own." The fact that patriotic mobs frequently singled out the church's missionaries for particular retribution only enhanced this impression, leading one pastor, the Reverend Charles Inglis of New York, to suggest that the story of his fellow divines "would be no bad supplement to *Walker's sufferings of the clergy*." "Religion itself, or rather the Appearance of it, [has been] humbly ministered as an handmaid to Faction and Sedition," observed Myles Cooper, president of New York's King's College, in his controversial sermon before the University of Oxford in December 1776. "And it is well known, that solemn Prayers, public Fastings, and pathetic Sermons, were some of the most effectual means that were employed to invigorate the Rebellion."[10]

Language like this was clearly meant to serve a number of purposes, one of which was to enlist the support of those people likely to accept a Tory version of England's own experience with "teachers and *preachers* of

10. *A Letter from an Officer at New-York to a Friend in London* (London, 1777), 3; *Reflections on the Present Combination of the American Colonies against the Supreme Authority of the British Legislature, and Their Claim to Independency* . . . (London, 1777), 7; letter from the Rev. Mr. [Charles] Inglis, New York, Oct. 31, 1776, in *The Proceedings of the Society for the Propagation of the Gospel in Foreign Parts* . . . (London, 1777), 58 (hereafter cited as *SPG Proceedings*); Myles Cooper, *National Humiliation and Repentance Recommended, and the Causes of the Present Rebellion in America Assigned* . . . (Oxford, 1777), 15. The controversy surrounding Cooper's sermon was over his implication that the power of king and Parliament was "divinely ordained." The Revolution's character as a war of religion is the subject of J. C. D. Clark, *The Language of Liberty, 1660–1832: Political Discourse and Social Dynamics in the Anglo-American World, 1660–1832* (Cambridge, 1994); for more nuanced versions of the same interpretation, see Rhys Isaac, *The Transformation of Virginia, 1740–1790* (Chapel Hill, N.C., 1982), chaps. 11, 12; Patricia U. Bonomi, *Under the Cope of Heaven: Religion, Society, and Politics in Colonial America* (Oxford, 1986), chap. 7; Jon Butler, "Was There a Revolutionary Millennium?" in Butler, *Awash in a Sea of Faith: Christianizing the American People* (Cambridge, Mass., 1990), chap. 7.

the Presbyterian schism," in the words of John Shebbeare. As more than a few observers pointed out, though, such allegations carried their own dangers in terms of the church's relations with Dissenters elsewhere in Britain's empire. For this reason, the government's apologists, including many among the higher Anglican clergy in Britain, often preferred to attribute the Revolution's enthusiastic tendencies, not to any one set of beliefs, but to a generalized lawlessness born of the colonists' republican- ism—"what they call the Spirit of Liberty, but what is in Fact the spirit of Licentiousness." In his sermon denouncing the American Revolution- aries' principles, the archbishop of York, William Markham, urged that "Christianity be spared" since "it lends no aid" to either party in the current dispute. Likewise, James Yorke, bishop of St. David's and a scion of one of Britain's oldest Whig families, insisted that even those with religious "truth" on their side ought to act "with the greatest caution, in a situation where moderation and mutual forbearance ought principally to be inculcated." Indeed, Charles Inglis of New York warned that apolo- gists for the Church of England's American communicants needed to avoid making allegations that might offend "the sober and more rational among the Dissenters (for they are not all equally violent and frantic)."[11]

Even when they omitted specifically religious arguments, British ob- servers continued to insist that the Americans were prosecuting the war with a savagery unknown to all but the most barbarous nations. Follow- ing the battles of Lexington and Concord, reports circulated in the press claiming that wounded regulars had been scalped and had their ears chopped off and eyes gouged out. Elsewhere, commentators noted how usurping the king's "legal authority" had opened the way for unruly

11. John Shebbeare, *An Essay on the Origin, Progress, and Establishment of National Society* . . . , 2d ed. (London, 1776), 157; *American Resistance Indefensible: A Sermon, Preached on Friday, December 13, 1776, Being the Day Appointed for a General Fast* . . . (London, [1776–1777]), 9; William Markham, archbishop of York, *A Sermon Preached before the Incorporated Society for the Propagation of the Gospel in Foreign Parts* . . . , in *SPG Proceedings* (1777), xviii; James [Yorke], bishop of St. David's, *A Sermon Preached before the Lords Spiritual and Temporal in the Abbey Church of Westminster, on Tuesday, January 30, 1776* . . . (London, 1776), 15; letter from Inglis, Oct. 31, 1776, in *SPG Proceedings*, 67. Inglis's observation was confirmed in the report from the Rev. Dr. Behnot in Nova Scotia about the number of Dissenters among the loyalist émigrés from New England (*SPG Proceedings*, 45). For the higher clergy's reluctance to use explicitly Tory language or to turn the contest into a struggle over Anglican principles, see Gould, "American Independence and Britain's Counter-Revolution," *Past and Present*, no. 154 (February 1997), 123–128; Paul Langford, "The English Clergy and the American Revolution," in Eckhart Hellmuth, ed., *The Transformation of Political Cul- ture: England and Germany in the Late Eighteenth Century* (Oxford, 1990), 125–126.

mobs to inflict summary justice of the worst sort. "No age or sex was spared," claimed one account, "and the more respectable the character, the more obnoxious was [the crime]." Indeed, some of the most affecting stories involved the suffering that the Revolutionaries had inflicted on women, children, and the elderly. "The utmost industry of the Ministry is employd, to inflame mens minds here," observed an American resident in Britain, and another cautioned a friend in Virginia about the importance of appearing "respectable in the eyes of Europe" through a scrupulous regard for civilized customs like "the treating prisoners with humanity—the shielding age and womanhood from the horrors of war— [and] the not being too hasty in making reprisals." "This is the land of liberty" was how Hugh Finlay, Surveyor of the Posts in North America, described his own hapless situation during the spring of 1775. "A man may say and do whatever he will, if he will execrate Lord North, call the Parliament a pack of corrupted rascals, every officer of Government a pitiful tool, and speak contemptuously of all friends of Government." Apologists for the Revolution might agree with Thomas Paine that the institution of parliamentary monarchy had only served to make Britain's "kings more subtle—not more just." But many people were convinced that the Americans would soon discover—in the words of a loyal address from Exeter—"that peace, and happiness, and liberty, are only to be secured . . . by the protecting power of this country."[12]

As Britain's own history illustrated, of course, neither republican nor religious fanaticism was a peculiarly American malady. As the war dragged on, however, the government's apologists increasingly blamed such inhuman transgressions on those features of American society that differentiated the colonists from their "fellow subjects" in Britain. At times, metropolitan observers described this distinction in racial terms,

12. *Comprehending the Campaigns of 1775, 1776, and 1777* (London, 1780), 87, vol. I of *The History of the Civil War in America;* two anon. letters, second to Robert Carter Nicholas, both dated Sept. 22, 1775, P.R.O., C.O. 5/40/1, 17, 22; Hugh Finlay to his brother, May 29, 1775, enclosed in Anthony Todd to John Pownall, July 7, 1775, in Richard Arthur Roberts, ed., *Calendar of Home Office Papers of the Reign of George III, 1773–1775* (London, 1899), 366; Thomas Paine, *Common Sense* (1776), in Jack P. Greene, ed., *Colonies to Nation, 1763–1789: A Documentary History of the Revolution* (1967; New York, 1975), 273; "The Humble Address of the Mayor, Aldermen, and Common Council of the City of Exeter" (Sept. 25, 1775), P.R.O., H.O. 55/11/7. For British allegations regarding the Americans' penchant for scalping and gouging, see *An Address to the People on the Subject of the Contest between Great Britain and America* (London, 1776), 11; anon. letter from Boston, July 5, 1775, in *A View of the Evidence relative to the Conduct of the American War . . .* (London, 1779), 72.

suggesting that the colonists had adopted the same manners as the "brutal savages" who made the lands beyond the Appalachian Mountains such a lawless zone. On other occasions, commentators noted the way the vastness of the Atlantic Ocean encouraged the Americans to believe unfounded charges and allegations "about public Persons, Measures, and Events" in Britain. Echoing Samuel Johnson's famous question—"How is it that we hear the loudest yelps for liberty among the drivers of negroes?"—still other writers attributed the Americans' penchant for violence to the colonial institution of slavery and the reckless arrogance that it encouraged in planters like Washington and Jefferson. But whichever factor they chose to emphasize, the Americans' rebellion increasingly seemed to spring from its own sources. "It has been asserted," remarked the member of Parliament William Innes in November 1775, "that the colonists are the offspring of Englishmen, and as such, entitled to the privileges of Britons. [But] I am bold to deny it, for it is well known that they not only consist of English, Scots, and Irish, but also of French, Dutch, Germans innumerable, Indians, Africans, and a multitude of felons from this country. Is it possible to tell which are the most turbulent amongst such a mixture of people?"[13]

Each of these differences between metropolitan and provincial society undermined the notion of a greater British identity, an identity that had seemed so compelling only a few years before but that increasingly looked like a fiction. Of the various factors that contributed to this gradual disillusionment, however, probably the most important was the government's inability to uphold the rule of law as it existed in Britain. To be sure, the North ministry continued to maintain that Britain's ultimate goal should be to restore what the Carlisle Peace Commission of 1778 termed "the Blessings of Civil Government" under the benevolent sovereignty of "His Majesty in Parliament." In keeping with this position, polemicists like John Lind argued that the king's troops were

---

13. *Comprehending the Campaigns,* 87; Butler, *Sermon Preached before the Honourable House of Commons,* 8–9; [Samuel Johnson], *Taxation No Tyranny: An Answer to the Resolutions and Address of the American Congress* (London, 1775), in Donald J. Greene, ed., *Political Writings* (New Haven, Conn., 1977), 454, vol. X of *The Yale Edition of the Works of Samuel Johnson;* R. C. Simmons and P. D. G. Thomas, eds., *Proceedings and Debates of the British Parliaments respecting North America, 1754–1783,* 6 vols. (Millwood, White Plains, N.Y., 1982–1986), VI, 203. For the concerns of conservative Whigs regarding American slavery, see also Josiah Tucker, *A Treatise concerning Civil Government . . .* (London, 1781), 167–168; J. G. A. Pocock, "Josiah Tucker on Burke, Locke, and Price: A Study in the Varieties of Eighteenth-Century Conservatism," in Pocock, *Virtue, Commerce and History,* 174–179.

engaged in a defensive action not unlike that which they undertook when they protected "dutiful and loyal subjects" from the threat of rioters in England. To underscore the point, ministerial writers paid particular attention to the "humanity" and "good conduct" that British officers allegedly displayed, even in districts known to contain avowed supporters of the Revolutionary cause. Indeed, as long as the government continued to regard the colonists as British subjects, there were good reasons to argue that the law required the king's troops to act with such restraint. "It has happened," explained Lind, "that bodies of peasants have risen, and armed, in order to compel the farmer to sell at a lower price. It has happened, that the civil magistrate, unable to reduce the insurgents to their duty, has called the military to his aid. But did ever any man imagine, that the military were sent to punish the insurgents?" "The law is suspended only in part, even in cases of Rebellion," reported another pamphleteer in 1777. The war in America might resemble a foreign conflict in many respects; however, the government's ultimate objective was not just to defeat Washington's ragged army but to do so in ways that affirmed the protection that British law still afforded to the king's predominantly loyal subjects.[14]

The problem with this position, however, was that establishing the sort of civil authority under which even the Revolutionary leaders might be tried in an English court of law depended on achieving a complete military victory. In the absence of such an outcome, royal officials found themselves making ever more liberal concessions to Congress and the Continental army, which, taken together, introduced a creeping federalism into the rebellious colonies' formal relationship with metropolitan Britain. General John Burgoyne's surrender at the battle of Saratoga in October 1777 proved to be a watershed in this respect. Even before news of the army's humiliation reached the British public, oppositionists like

14. Memorandum from the earl of Carlisle, Sir Henry Clinton, and William Eden to Lord George Germaine, New York, Oct. 16, 1778, BL Add. MSS 34,426, 60; [Lind], *Answer to the Declaration of the American Congress*, 130 (both passages quoted); [George Chalmers], *An Answer from the Electors of Bristol, to the Letter of Edmund Burke, Esq., on [the] Affairs of America* (London, 1777), 23–24; *A Letter to the Earl of Chatham, concerning His Speech and Motion in the House of Lords . . .* (London, 1777), 17. The author of the last pamphlet happened to make the above observation in opposition to continuing the American war. The government's defenders often made the same observation but noted that restoring Parliament's unlimited sovereignty had less to do with achieving military victory than it did with bringing the American rebels to justice in a court of law. See *Letter from an Officer at New-York*, 1–2, 7; Edward Topham, *An Address to Edmund Burke, Esq., on His Late Letter relative to the Affairs of America* (London, 1777), 4.

Edmund Burke had made a point of noting the anomaly in the government's decision to conduct hostilities "upon the usual footing of other wars." "Whenever a rebellion really and truly exists," Burke explained in his *Letter to the Bristol Sheriffs,* governments were obligated to decline any "intermediate treaty" that might put the "rebels in possession of the law of nations with regard to war." In the wake of Burgoyne's capitulation, these concerns acquired considerably more weight. "Where do you find in the *British* Annals," queried one witness, "that a disciplined gallant Army ever surrendered themselves, with arms in their hands, to a Militia,—to a Rabble?" By agreeing to formal terms with General Horatio Gates, the British commander had implicitly granted both Congress and the Continental army many of the attributes of sovereignty so assiduously denied them by the government's apologists. "The history of nations affords no instance of a convention or treaty, made with Rebels," insisted one of Burgoyne's many critics. "Their words and their actions are discordant," another observer wrote of the government's conduct. "They call the *Americans,* Rebels; yet in every instance they are treated like the Subjects of an Independent State."[15]

Along with France's subsequent conclusion of a treaty with the United States, Burgoyne's defeat thus inevitably complicated the notion that the Americans ought to be treated like a set of traitors or bandits who had violated the municipal laws of England. Upon returning from New York, Burgoyne himself commended the professionalism and hospitality with which he had been treated by American officers. Furthermore, during the spring of 1778, the North ministry took the fateful step of sponsoring a new Declaratory Act renouncing forever Parliament's right to tax the colonies and sending a peace commission under the earl of Carlisle to New York with the authority to negotiate directly with Con-

15. *Letter from Edmund Burke, Esq.,* 11–12; anon. letter from New York, Dec. 16, 1777, in *Historical Anecdotes, Civil and Military: In a Series of Letters, Written from America, in the Years 1777 and 1778 . . .* (London, 1779), 34; *A Letter to Lieut. Gen. Burgoyne, on His Letter to His Constituents* (London, 1779), 19; anon. letter from New York, Feb. 7, 1778, in *Historical Anecdotes,* 65. Burke's point was that granting rebel troops rights under the customs of war would make it impossible for them to be tried subsequently as traitors: "We ought to remember, that if our present enemies be, in reality and truth, rebels, the king's generals have no right to release them upon any conditions whatsoever; and they are themselves answerable to the law, and as much in want of a pardon for doing so, as the rebels whom they release" (13). For more on the British position on observing the rules of war during the American Revolution, see Piers Mackesy, *The War for America, 1775–1783* (1964; Lincoln, Nebr., 1993), 32–37. For Saratoga, see Max M. Mintz, *The Generals of Saratoga: John Burgoyne and Horatio Gates* (New Haven, Conn., 1990).

FIGURE 27

The Congress; or, The Necessary Politicians. *1775? Two delegates of the
American Congress occupy a latrine (or "necessary"), presumably in Philadelphia.
One reads a response to Samuel Johnson's* Taxation No Tyranny; *the other has
clearly been using a sheet of congressional resolutions for less lofty purposes.
Courtesy of the John Carter Brown Library at Brown University*

gress, "as if it were a legal body." "To treat with those who denied, and
took up arms in opposition to the authority of parliament; to treat with
declared enemies, and above all, with the *unlawful* and *vagrant* assembly,
the Congress, were once considered so contrary to the dignity of government as not to be submitted to" was how one hostile pamphleteer described the commission's significance. The effects of this decision were
especially dramatic in the House of Commons, where Lord North's
announcement of his ministry's intentions left the advocates of parliamentary sovereignty at a loss for words. According to an account that
later appeared in Edmund Burke's *Annual Register*:

A dull melancholy silence for sometime succeeded to this speech. It
had been heard with profound attention, but without a single mark
of approbation to any part, from any description of men, or any

particular man in the house. Astonishment, dejection, and fear, overclouded the whole assembly. Although the minister had declared, that the sentiments he expressed that day, had been those which he had always entertained; it is certain, that few or none had understood him in that manner; and he had been represented to the nation at large, as the person in it the most tenacious of those parliamentary rights which he now proposed to resign, and the most remote from the submissions which he now proposed to make.[16]

The incomprehension that greeted North's speech is a reminder of just how long it took Britons to grasp the extent to which the course of events in America had given rise to an independent state—or confederation of states—based on a separate nationality.[17] For colonial loyalists, however, this growing independence had immediate consequences. Although British officials continued to regard the loyalists' well-being as one of their principal responsibilities, the government's willingness to conduct business with both Congress and the Continental army produced a corresponding tendency to treat even those colonists who retained their allegiance to the king as members of a separate political society. As early as the winter of 1776–1777, there had been reports from New Jersey and southern New York that Hessian troops in the government's employ were committing indiscriminate atrocities on both "friends and foes," including rape and the destruction of property. Such accounts usually originated in the opposition press. Increasingly, though, even the loyalists seconded them. Speaking about the war in the middle colonies, Joseph Galloway of Philadelphia noted the treatment that British officers had meted out to rebellious and obedient inhabitants alike. "Thousands came in wherever the army marched, and took the oath, but the Royal faith, pledged for their safety, was shamefully violated. The unhappy people, instead of receiving the protection promised, were plun-

16. *The Substance of General Burgoyne's Speeches, on Mr. Vyner's Motion, on the 26th of May* . . . (London, 1778), 8–10; William Cobbett, ed., *Parliamentary History of England from the Norman Conquest to the Year 1803*, 36 vols. (London, 1806–1820), XIX, 764; [Edmund Jenings], *Considerations on the Mode and Terms of a Treaty of Peace with America* . . . (London, 1778), 9; "The History of Europe," *Annual Register*, XXI (1778), 133–134.

17. See, for example, the response of John Morton in the House of Commons: "[He] ironically congratulated Lord North upon the cordial assistance he had received from his new allies. But said, the taxation Bill could not pass into a law, without a new constitution in America; because the subjects of Great Britain, wherever they are, are taxable by the parliament of Great Britain, whose power has no bounds" (Cobbett, ed., *Parliamentary History*, XIX, 802–803).

FIGURE 28

The Commissioners. *1778. A confident America turns away from members of
North's peace commission. Colonial Williamsburg Foundation*

dered by the soldiery. Their wives and daughters were violently polluted
by the lustful brutality of the lowest of mankind; and friends and foes
indiscriminately met with the same barbarian treatment." "Where the
Army is," concurred the Reverend Leonard Cutting, Anglican missionary at Hempstead on occupied Long Island, "Oppression, such as in
England you can have no Conception of Universally prevails." In the
terse words of another loyal New Yorker, the upshot of this harsh treatment was that "we shall all soon, I believe, be Rebels."[18]

For all the embarrassment occasioned by such unsettling reports,
though, the British increasingly acted as though the imperial connection
for which the government was contending would depend on a combination of conquest and some sort of looser union, rather than the firmer
authority of English law and Parliament's unlimited authority. From
1778 onward, it was not hard to find demands in the metropolitan press

18. *A Letter to the English Nation, on the Present War with America*... (London, 1777),
24; [Galloway], *Letters to a Nobleman*, 42; letter from Cutting, Dec. 9, 1781, as quoted in
Joseph S. Tiedemann, "Patriots by Default: Queens County, New York, and the British Army, 1776–1783," *William and Mary Quarterly*, 3rd Ser., XLIII (1986), 48; anon.
letter from New York, Feb. 7, 1778, in *Historical Anecdotes*, 71.

for the government to prosecute the war with "greater severity" and for the king's troops to conduct themselves as though they were contending with an ordinary foe. According to Adam Ferguson, the Edinburgh professor of moral philosophy who accompanied the Carlisle Commission to America, the only hope for victory lay in employing "every Species of War that is lawful against an ordinary Ennemy," including the punishment of civilian resistance in courts-martial, the destruction of any matériel with military potential, and the imposition of mandatory requisitions on occupied provinces. As the Carlisle Commission described the transformation in its North American manifesto of October 3, 1778, considerations of "policy" and "benevolence" on Britain's part had "thus far checked the extremes of war." "But when that country professes the unnatural design not only of estranging herself from us but of mortgaging herself to our enemies, the whole contest is changed." Although there was no question that the British were still fighting to preserve some sort of imperial connection in North America, it was becoming more unlikely that the basis for that connection would depend on a uniform nationality or a common system of law shared by men and women on both sides of the Atlantic. As Allan Ramsay, the Scottish painter turned pamphleteer, remarked in 1777, the American Revolution had produced "a new class of men" in the colonies, men who were neither entirely "foreign" nor fully "English." Although Ramsay hoped that the British might yet discover a solution to this problem, he was sure that the Americans would be the source of continual difficulties until "their true relation to Great Britain is accurately known, and a suitable mode of proceeding with regard to them adopted."[19]

II. "THE ISLE OF LIBERTY AND PEACE"

Because the war ended with an unambiguous recognition of American independence, the British were ultimately spared the pain of making the sorts of legal and constitutional concessions necessary to keep Ramsay's "new class of men" within the empire. Although France's intervention led Parliament to offer to surrender its fiscal sovereignty, Congress's intransigence enabled Britain to conclude the war on the same terms that had led Westminster to attempt taxing the colonists almost twenty years earlier. As Lord Sheffield noted in his defense of the Navigation

19. "Notes on House of Commons Inquiry into Sir William Howe" (n.d.), "Manifesto and Proclamation to the Members of the Congress . . ." (New York, Oct. 3, 1778), both in BL Add. MSS 34,416, 38, 329–333; [Allan Ramsay], *Letters on the Present Disturbances in Great Britain and Her American Provinces* (London, 1777), 20.

Act, the British would henceforth have to treat the Americans as citizens of a "foreign and independent nation." But when it came to administering the remaining dominions of the crown, Sheffield could see no reason for Parliament to abandon any of the abstract rights or specific policies that had made Britain the most powerful maritime nation in Europe. "England survives; and it is to be hoped will survive her American misfortunes, notwithstanding the declamations of her internal enemies, and it is to be hoped she will learn wisdom from what has happened."[20]

If the Revolution left the Whig system of government unchanged, though, metropolitan Britons began to discover that they had reasons of their own to accept the more constricted sense of nationhood that was the war's inevitable result. Although few people openly said so, the enthusiasm and chaos in America suggested that the best way to safeguard Parliament's authority at home lay in reinscribing the boundary between metropolitan and provincial politics. After all, though Britain was scarcely invulnerable to civil unrest, the king's metropolitan subjects enjoyed a measure of security unavailable to those who lived beyond the confines of the British mainland. Only the most disaffected radical would have questioned the Reverend William Vyse, rector of Lambeth, when he maintained before the House of Commons that "no nation under heaven hath greater reason to praise God than we have, for those many and invaluable blessings he hath bestowed upon us." "For my own part," wrote the Scottish humanitarian John Stevenson in 1778, "I bless *God*, that I was born in Britain, and educated a Protestant; that I first beheld the solar ray in the reign of George the second; and that, under the mild government and safe protection of his illustrious grandson, I now enjoy civil and religious privileges, surpassing the subjects of every other state."[21]

---

20. Sheffield, *Commerce of the American States,* 2, 272. It is worth noting on this point that, although the Declaratory Act of 1778 declared that Parliament would never again tax the colonists "for the Purpose of raising a Revenue," the sheer breadth of the doctrine of parliamentary sovereignty meant that Parliament could not actually "destroy its fundamental right to do so"; see the editorial remarks, along with the excerpts from the Declaratory Act, in Frederick Madden and David Fieldhouse, eds., *The Classical Period of the First British Empire, 1689–1783: The Foundations of a Colonial System of Government* (Westport, Conn., 1985), 592, 611, vol. II of *Select Documents on the Constitutional History of the British Empire and Commonwealth.*

21. William Vyse, *A Sermon Preached before the Honourable House of Commons, at the Church of St. Margaret's, Westminster, on Friday, February 27, 1778* . . . (London, 1778), 6–7; John Stevenson, *Letters in Answer to Dr. Price's Two Pamphlets on Civil Liberty* . . . (London, 1778), 20.

This tendency to focus inward was especially evident in the distinction that even conservative Whigs drew between the breadth of Parliament's domestic authority and the far more attenuated powers that it could exercise abroad. To be sure, most Britons remained committed to the general premise that every member sat in Parliament as a representative of "the commons of all the British empire," as the Methodist vicar John Fletcher put the matter in 1777. But as American independence became likelier, Whig polemicists began to acknowledge that insisting on Parliament's unlimited authority had produced nothing but so many "visionary attempts to gain the empire of America." As an anonymous writer noted during the general election of 1780, the war appeared to have persuaded even the ministry's supporters that insisting on colonial taxation had been "a very *impolitic* measure, whatever may be thought of the *justice* of it." "No miraculous illumination could ever persuade him that government should attempt impracticable things" was how the lord advocate for Scotland, Henry Dundas, justified his own decision to support the renunciation of Parliament's right to tax for revenue in 1778. Upon introducing his ministry's conciliatory measures, even Lord North appeared to abandon his commitment to Parliament's imperial authority by claiming—somewhat disingenuously—that he had never favored taxing the colonists: "He had always known that American taxation could never produce a beneficial revenue; that there were many sorts of taxes that could not at all be laid on that country, and that few of them would prove worth the charge of collection."[22]

North's critics were quick to question his sincerity on this score. Still, from 1778 onward, a growing number of observers were inclined to accept the impossibility of extending Westminster's unlimited fiscal powers beyond England, Scotland, and Wales. Indeed, people across the political spectrum worried that continuing with the unrealistic policy of colonial taxation would eventually jeopardize Parliament's authority at home. According to Henry Seymour Conway, the war threatened to weaken the metropolitan basis of the constitution because of the way in which "the Honour of Parliament was ostensibly, indeed ostentatiously, held out as the cause of quarrel." Allan Ramsay made the same point, noting how the war had contributed to "more than an ordinary disorder

22. [John William Fletcher], *American Patriotism Farther Confronted with Reason, Scripture, and the Constitution . . .* , 2d ed. (London, 1777), 66; *Free Thoughts on the Continuance of the American War, and the Necessity of Its Termination . . .* (London, 1781), 13; *An Inquiry into the Origin and Consequences of the Influence of the Crown over Parliament* (London, 1780), 10; Cobbett, ed., *Parliamentary History,* XIX, 762–763, 803.

FIGURE 29

The Sinking Fund. *1779. Ordinary men and women line up to pawn their*
possessions so they can pay the heavy taxes necessitated by the American war.
© *The British Museum*

in our political system" by encouraging Parliament to squander its domestic authority by making laws that it could not possibly hope to
enforce in the colonies. There were even conservative Whigs like Josiah
Tucker who recommended emancipating those parts of the empire that
had remained loyal during the American Revolution. According to
Tucker, none of Britain's colonists (including the English "settlers" in
Bengal) would prove any more amenable to Parliament's unlimited authority than the men and women who declared their independence in
1776. "Our distant, unwieldy Colonies, and our ruinous Wars for their
Sakes, are the real Causes of all our Complaints," wrote Tucker. "It is
these which involve us in thousands of Distresses, of which we should
have been happily ignorant, had it not been for such Connections."[23]

23. *The Speech of General Conway, Member of Parliament for Saint Edmondsbury, on*
Moving in the House of Commons (on the 5th of May, 1780) . . . (London, 1781), 24;
[Ramsay], *Letters on the Present Disturbances,* 17–18; Josiah Tucker, *Treatise concerning*

Not many Britons shared the full extent of Tucker's hostility to empire. But such ideas resonated widely enough for George III's eventual recognition of American independence to strike many Britons as a personal sacrifice worthy of Bolingbroke's patriot king. This was certainly how the earl of Stair envisioned the king's obligation at the start of 1781: "Sovereign of willing subjects, husband of a virtuous wife, father of many children of great hopes, King, husband, father, by all and each of those tender ties, public and private, I adjure you to stop on the extreme verge of the precipice where we stand." "Long after we shall have fallen asleep in the grave," wrote another pamphleteer two years later, "may the faithful historian record these changes, as happy, and have reason to inform posterity, that the Constitution was saved, and public virtue restored in the twenty-second year of the reign of George III." Those who made such claims were obviously discounting the role that the king had played in initiating the colonial crisis during the early 1760s. Although no one in Britain had greater difficulty accepting the inevitability of American independence, however, the king's willingness to withdraw from the costly and unwinnable war nonetheless suggested that even he was more in touch with the nation's welfare than his critics were prepared to concede.[24]

Somewhat unexpectedly, this generous interpretation even extended to the concurrent discussions over whether to alter the existing system of representation in the House of Commons. For the supporters of the Society for Constitutional Information and Christopher Wyvill's county associations, the doggedness with which Parliament supported the government's North American policies—even as the ruinous effects of those policies became increasingly clear—demonstrated a pressing need for electoral reforms that would ensure its members were more attentive to the welfare of the people they were supposed to represent. With the end

---

Civil Government, 248–250. For explicit proposals to grant a general emancipation, see [Thomas Pownall], *A Memorial, Most Humbly Addressed to the Sovereigns of Europe, on the Present State of Affairs, between the Old and New World*, 2d ed. (London, 1780), 106; Sir John Sinclair, *Thoughts on the Naval Strength of the British Empire*, part 2 (London, 1782), 17–18.

24. [John Dalrymple, earl of Stair], *Considerations Preliminary, to the Fixing the Supplies, the Ways and Means, and the Taxes for the Year 1781* . . . (London, Jan. 13, 1781), 36; *Thoughts on the Present War, with an Impartial Review of Lord North's Administration, in Conducting the American, French, Spanish, and Dutch War* . . . (London, 1783), 78. For the continuing appeal of Bolingbroke's famous panegyric, see David Armitage, "A Patriot for Whom? The Afterlives of Bolingbroke's Patriot King," *Journal of British Studies*, XXXVI (1997), 397–418.

of the American war, however, such arguments inevitably lost much of their force. Indeed, for all its obvious flaws, Parliament's support for recognizing the United States suggested that the lower house still "sympathized with the people." "The conduct of the House of Commons in the last session," wrote a polemicist of the peace deliberations in late 1782, "afforded the most satisfactory proof of its wisdom, its temper, and its disinterestedness." As William Paley observed three years later:

> We *have* a House of Commons composed of five hundred and fifty-eight members, in which number are found the most considerable landholders and merchants of the kingdom; the heads of the army, the navy, and the law; the occupiers of great offices in the state; together with many private individuals, eminent by their knowledge, eloquence, or activity. Now if the country be not safe in such hands, in whose may it confide its interests? If such a number of such men be liable to the influence of corrupt motives, what assembly of men will be secure from the same danger?[25]

As Paley's remarks suggested, acknowledging Parliament's limited capacity for colonial government did nothing to diminish the nearly boundless authority that Whig polemicists still claimed on its behalf at home. Indeed, as Britain's involvement in the American Revolution came to a close, the debate over the existing system of government in England, Scotland, and Wales frequently betrayed a hardened, almost reactionary determination to reaffirm Parliament's absolute metropolitan sovereignty. In a typical response to the county associators, the Scottish Whig Joseph Cawthorne drew on a universal principle of "subordination" to demonstrate that parliamentary constituencies were "mere

25. *A Dialogue on the Actual State of Parliament* (London, 1783), 53; *An Examination into the Principles, Conduct, and Designs of the Minister* (London, 1783), 58; William Paley, *The Principles of Moral and Political Philosophy* (1785), in *The Works of William Paley, D.D.* . . . (Philadelphia, 1857), 127. On learning of Parliament's ratification of the peace preliminaries, Wyvill remarked:

> It is true, the Minister of Corruption has found, that, in the hour of national calamity, his accustomed arts were of little avail. . . . But can it be forgotten that even this tardy interposition depended on a multitude of contingencies, without whose casual combination the British people might yet have been groaning, without a prospect of relief, under the complicated misery of a corrupt Administration and a War of Ambition, for the forcible subjugation of their American Brethren!

See "Account of the Debate at a General Meeting of the County of York," Dec. 19, 1782, in Christopher Wyvill, ed., *Political Papers, Chiefly respecting the Attempt of the County of York, and Other Considerable Districts* . . . , 6 vols. (York, 1794–1802), II, 46–47.

cyphers" of the state; that the vote was a privilege "of very short duration"; that popular rights were "absolutely conveyed to, and totally absorbed in the Parliament"; and that the British people might petition their representatives in the House of Commons, but had "no constitutional right to force a hearing." In a similar manner, Paley took care to differentiate his own qualified endorsement of electoral reform from "those writers who insist upon representation as a *natural* right," and he argued that, if Parliament ever did alter the franchise, it would do so for the sole purpose of enhancing the magisterial authority of government. In the words of Josiah Tucker:

> The King and both Houses of Parliament, that is, the supreme Legislature of this Country, have a general, unlimited Right to make Laws for binding the People, in *all Cases whatsoever*. They have this Right, because it is impossible to define exactly in what particular Instances they ought *not* to be entrusted with such a Right, or how far their Power ought to extend in every Case, and every Circumstance, which might occur, and where it ought to be stopped.[26]

In stating the scope of Parliament's powers in such stark terms, however, polemicists like Tucker were not abandoning their firm conviction that the British still enjoyed far broader personal freedoms than any other people in the world—including the rebellious Americans. This was particularly true in matters of religion, where apologists for the Church of England frequently contrasted the enthusiasm bred by the abolition of Established Churches in the United States with the benefits of their own confession's moderate supremacy. In his sermon before the Society for the Propagation of the Gospel in 1778, the bishop of Worcester, Brownlow North, insisted that England's religious toleration gave even Catholics and Dissenters more secure rights to worship as they chose than if they lived amidst the chaos of "an equality of sects under one government, without any established church at all." According to many observers, nothing demonstrated this truth more fully than Parliament's decision in 1778 to relax the penalties against English Catholics— and the king's willingness two years later to quell the bloody riots that resulted. One of the first things the South Carolina émigré Louisa Wells

---

26. [Joseph Cawthorne], *A Constitutional Defence of Government* (London, 1782), 13–14; *Moral and Political Philosophy*, in *Works of Paley*, 127; Tucker, *Treatise concerning Civil Government*, 109–110.

noted upon landing near Dover was her satisfaction to be "once more in a Country where we could pray for our Sovereign without endangering our Necks." "We have learned," remarked the bishop of Exeter in 1779, "to treat all who differ in opinion from us with brotherly affection and charity, and to leave them at liberty to determine for themselves, what they ought to believe as necessary to salvation."[27]

If this was true of religious liberty, it also held for the various other rights upon which the British had long prided themselves. In the words of Adam Ferguson, the genius of Britain's constitution lay in the way it afforded "every class and order" a degree of liberty "not proportioned to the power they enjoy, but to the security they have for the preservation of their rights." Indeed, Whig polemicists liked to argue that their "countrymen of the lower class" had at least as much to gain from preserving the existing system of government as those with greater wealth and status. In a pointed jab at Britain's own radical movement, Josiah Tucker even suggested that the rights of virtual representation that the present system of government conferred on all women and most men permitted a degree of equality between the sexes that would be lost if masculinity ever became the sole qualification for the vote. Likewise, Paley noted wryly that "every plan of representation that we have heard of, begins by excluding the votes of women; thus cutting off, at a single stroke, one half of the public from a right which is asserted to be inherent in all." No doubt both men were speaking partly in jest, but their remarks attest to the deep ambivalence that many Britons felt about even the slightest departure from the lessons of their own history. As Beilby Porteus, the

27. Brownlow North, bishop of Worcester, *A Sermon Preached before the Incorporated Society of the Propagation of the Gospel in Foreign Parts . . .* , in *SPG Proceedings* (London, 1778), 17; Louisa Susannah [Wells] Aikman, *The Journal of a Voyage from Charlestown, S.C., to London, Undertaken during the American Revolution . . .* , (1779; reprint, New York, 1906), 67; John [Ross], bishop of Exeter, *A Sermon Preached before the Lords Spiritual and Temporal . . .* (London, 1779), 11–12. For the official response to the Catholic Relief Act and the Gordon Riots, see esp. the king's speech and the resulting parliamentary debates in Cobbett, ed., *Parliamentary History*, XXI, 689–714, as well as Robert Pool Finch, *A Sermon Preached in the Church of St. Michael, Cornhill . . .* (London, 1779), x–xi; Jesse William, *A Remonstrance, Addressed to the Protestant Association; Containing Observations on Their Conduct, and on Their Appeal to the People of Great Britain* (London, 1780), 35–36; *Observations on "An Appeal from the Protestant Association to the People of Great Britain"* (London, 1780), 11–12; Colin Haydon, *Anti-Catholicism in Eighteenth-Century England, c. 1714–80: A Political and Social Study* (Manchester, 1993), esp. 235–238.

Virginia-born bishop of Chester, assured the House of Lords in 1778, Britain remained what it had been since the end of the last century, the freest nation on earth.

> It is here that civil liberty has fixed her throne; it is here that protestantism finds its firmest support; it is here that the divine principle of toleration is established; it is here that a provision is made by government for the poor; it is here that they are with a boundless munificence relieved both by private charity and public institutions; it is here in fine that the laws are equal, wise and good, that they are administered by men of acknowledged ability, and unimpeached integrity, and that through their hands the stream of justice flows with a purity unknown in any other age or nation.[28]

Affirmations of this sort served a variety of purposes. During the war's early years, the benevolent effects of Parliament's sovereignty at home had underscored the moderate nature of the authority that the government was seeking to restore in the colonies. In a similar manner, for a period after the intervention of France and Spain, claims to this effect helped Lord North's apologists to continue making the case that it was not the British but the Americans and their Bourbon allies who were threatening the liberties of Europe.[29] With growing frequency, though, insisting on the perfection of Britain's matchless constitution merely reinforced the perception that a yawning gulf separated those men and women who lived within the realm's metropolitan boundaries from those who did not. "How shall I describe what I felt, when I first set my foot on British ground?" wrote Louisa Wells in 1779. "I could have kissed the gravel on the salt Beach! It was my home: the Country which I had

28. [Adam Ferguson], *Remarks on a Pamphlet by Dr. Price, Intitled, Observations on the Nature of Civil Liberty* (London, 1776), 11; *An Address to the People of Great Britain on the Meeting of Parliament* (London, 1779), 20; Tucker, *Treatise concerning Civil Government*, 359–65; *Moral and Political Philosophy*, in *Works of Paley*, 127n; Beilby Porteus, bishop of Chester, *A Sermon Preached before the Lords Spiritual and Temporal . . .* (London, 1778), 18–19. The problematic status of women in British radical thought and practice is the subject of Anna Clark, *The Struggle for the Breeches: Gender and the Making of the British Working Class* (Berkeley, Calif., 1995), esp. chap. 8.

29. For more on both points, see Gould, "American Independence and Britain's Counter-Revolution," *Past and Present*, no. 154 (February 1997), 112–121. See also [David Williams], *Unanimity in All Parts of the British Commonwealth, Necessary to Its Preservation, Interest, and Happiness . . .* (London, 1778), 7–8; [Edward Gibbon], "Justifying Memorial of the King of Great Britain, in Answer to the Exposition, Etc. of the Court of France," *Annual Register*, XXII (1779), 397–406; *Remarks on the Rescript of the Court of Madrid, and on the Manifesto of the Court of Versailles . . .* (London, 1779).

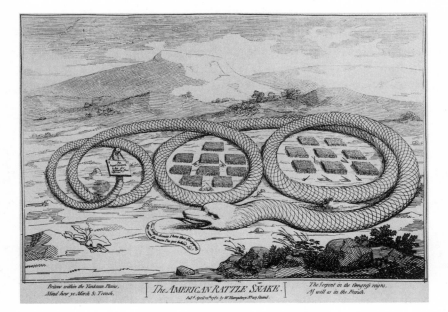

FIGURE 30
The American Rattle Snake. *1782. The armies encircled in the two coils
symbolize the British forces lost at Saratoga and Yorktown.
Colonial Williamsburg Foundation*

so long and so earnestly wished to see. The Isle of Liberty and Peace."
Although the self-evident benefits of British government extended well
beyond these limits, Whigs of all persuasions increasingly thought of
Parliament's unlimited capacity to guarantee the blessings of "liberty
and peace" chiefly in terms of its authority at the empire's center.[30]

Historians have wondered whether the British might have retained
some sort of ascendancy over the thirteen rebellious colonies. Considered from a purely military or diplomatic standpoint, the case for Britain's ability to salvage at least the semblance of victory in North America
has generally appeared to have some merits. By the time Lord North resigned in 1782, however, the British people had already made far greater
sacrifices than they had in any previous war. When faced with the military and fiscal demands that a British victory was likely to entail, even
the staunchest supporters of Parliament's imperial sovereignty decided
that maintaining the dominant features of Britain's matchless constitu-

30. [Aikman], *Journal of a Voyage from Charlestown,* 61–62.

tion at home far outweighed whatever allegiance they still felt to the transatlantic patriotism that once had seemed so unshakable. No matter how disgraceful they found the government's eventual abandonment of the loyalists, most observers concluded that the domestic political costs of refusing to do so were even less acceptable. Indeed, on the single issue of ending the American war, Whigs of all varieties found themselves in broad agreement. In recognizing American independence, of course, the ministries of Lord North and his successors did not act out of any sympathy for the Americans or their Revolutionary principles. Still, most Britons accepted peace for the simple reason that domestic considerations ultimately counted for more than the welfare of even the most loyal colonial subjects. There could be no endangering Parliament's domestic authority, no entertaining speculative proposals for reform, and certainly no sacrifice of individual liberty on behalf of their fellow subjects in North America. The greater British patriotism that undergirded the longest colonial war in Britain's modern history turned out to be every bit as self-referential as the Americans had always claimed it was.[31]

III. A MULTIRACIAL EMPIRE

Even so, Britain's history as an imperial power did not end in 1783. Not only were the West Indies and Canada still securely in British hands, but the East India Company had laid the basis for a vast new empire in southern Asia, and even broader vistas beckoned in the Pacific. Indeed, within a decade of the debacle at Yorktown, the British Empire resumed expanding at such a prodigious rate that by the early nineteenth century its subject peoples included nearly a quarter of the earth's population.

31. The fullest and most compelling argument for Britain's military ability to win the war in the colonies is in Mackesy, *War for America*, esp. 510–516. But see the problems with this position as noted in John Shy, "The Military Conflict Considered as a Revolutionary War," in Shy, *A People Numerous and Armed: Reflections on the Military Struggle for American Independence* (New York, 1976); John Brewer, *The Sinews of Power: War, Money and the English State, 1688–1783* (New York, 1989), 176–178. With considerable insight, Stephen Conway has recently argued that the level of popular mobilization in England, Scotland, and Wales made the War of American Independence "the first war of the new order" (see Conway, *The War of American Independence, 1775–1783* [London, 1995], 34–40). I largely agree with Conway's conclusions; however, I would argue that the British made every effort to prevent the war from escalating in this manner and that the government finally had to sue for peace because of this general unwillingness to depart from the pattern of earlier conflicts. In a sense, the more Britain became involved in the American Revolution, the less willing most people were to continue the struggle.

FIGURE 31

Confucius the Second; or, A New Sun Rising in the Asiatic World! *1783.*
A cartoon that satirizes the concern of politicians like Charles James Fox for
the peoples of India but also demonstrates the rising hopes for and new fears
of the East India Company's expanding jurisdiction on the subcontinent.
© *The British Museum*

Those blue water patriots who had feared that the loss of the American colonies would reduce Britain to dependence on its European neighbors turned out to be very much mistaken. "Notwithstanding our late losses and calamities," wrote John Andrews in 1783, "we are yet in a situation to cherish the fairest hopes and expectations of a happy futurity; we have honourably concluded a glorious, tho' an unprosperous war; we have stood the brunt of the most powerful confederacy that was ever formed against any State; and tho' we have not been conquerors, we yet remain unconquered."[32]

But in a number of important respects, the empire that remained at the end of the American Revolution appeared quite different from what it had once been. To an earlier generation, Britain's colonies on the

32. John Andrews, *An Essay on Republican Principles, and on the Inconveniences of a Commonwealth in a Large Country and Nation . . .* (London, 1783), 91.

North American seaboard had seemed like so many fragments of metropolitan society, Anglophone provinces that, if they did not replicate
English norms completely, nonetheless came close enough for people on
both sides of the Atlantic to conceive of them as comprising a single
nation. By contrast, the distinctions between conditions at home and
abroad seemed only too clear in the early 1780s. Where the British had
once assumed an unshakable bond based on the ties of a common nationality and Parliament's uniform sovereignty, they now thought in
terms of a looser consortium defined by cultural differences and the
paternal obligations that a civilized people owed their less enlightened
cousins. In a word, the second British Empire was at once more diverse
and more authoritarian than the one George III had inherited twenty
years before.

As historians have noted, this new awareness of the empire's diversity
had to do with the fact that the colonies still subject to British rule
appeared far less homogeneous than the thirteen that seceded to form
the United States. With their enormous wealth and strategic potential,
Bengal and the other provinces governed by the East India Company
played an especially important role in this reconfiguration of the empire's metropolitan image. Next to the war in America, no imperial issue
loomed larger in British politics during the early 1780s than the question
of how far Parliament could go in imposing the municipal law of England in India, and how much "latitude" Britain's rulers ought to allow
judges and administrators who governed "a country where the laws,
habits, religion, and manners, differ totally from those of England."
Although he claimed to favor governing Bengal according to English
norms, even Edmund Burke thought India resembled nothing so much
as the Holy Roman Empire, with its bewildering array of laws, manners,
and confessions. "It is . . . the height of absurdity," wrote the earl of Stair
in 1784, "to think the Indians are unhappy because they do not live under
the same constitution as the inhabitants of this island." There was little
agreement over exactly how the British ought to respond to this apparent fact, but few people supposed that the government owed the people
of Bengal the same measure of English liberty that even the most hardened conservatives once had been prepared to allow the Americans.[33]

33. *Considerations on the Administration of Justice in Bengal* . . . (n.p., [1780]), 4; *Mr.
Burke's Speech, on the 1st December 1783, upon the Question for the Speaker's Leaving the
Chair* . . . (London, 1784), 14 ("All this vast mass, composed of so many orders and
classes of men, is . . . infinitely diversified by manners, by religion, by hereditary
employment, through all their possible combinations"); John Dalrymple, earl of Stair,

India was obviously an extreme example of the empire's growing diversity. But even Britain's Atlantic empire seemed to have a different complexion in the Revolution's aftermath. Although both Canada and the West Indies were still firmly controlled by Anglicized elites, only Nova Scotia, New Brunswick, and the loyalist settlements that would shortly become Upper Canada (and later Ontario) could boast the sort of white, Protestant majority that had characterized all of the former mainland colonies except for South Carolina. In the years preceding the Revolution, it had been relatively easy to imagine the typical colonist as someone like the painter Benjamin West, Anglican bishop Beilby Porteus, or even Benjamin Franklin—Protestants of English or British stock whose aspirations to be accorded the same status as their fellow subjects in Britain carried enough weight for them to gain a hearing at the highest centers of social and political power. Figures like this did not disappear from the imperial stage in 1783; however, metropolitan understandings of what it meant to be a colonial increasingly included people like Olaudah Equiano and Mary Brant and her brother Joseph, Mohawk leaders that served the crown with such distinction during the Revolutionary war. Both Joseph Brant and Equiano were received at court—Brant for his role as leader of the Iroquois alliance during the war, Equiano as the author of a petition demanding an end to the slave trade—but each clearly stood outside the norms of English society. Indeed, one explanation for the extraordinary success of Equiano's *Interesting Narrative* is the demand it satisfied among British readers eager to learn more about just what sort of empire they still possessed in the western and southern reaches of the Atlantic.[34]

The Proper Limits of the Government's Interference with the Affairs of the East-India Company, Attempted to be Assigned . . . (London, 1784), 15. For scholarly treatments of the post-Revolutionary awareness of Britain's growing ethnic diversity, see esp. Marshall, "Empire and Authority," *Journal of Imperial and Commonwealth History*, XV (1987), 105–122; Colley, *Britons*, 132–145; Colley, "Britishness and Otherness: An Argument," *Journal of British Studies*, XXXI (October 1992), 309–329.

34. On the Brants, see Colin G. Calloway, *The American Revolution in Indian Country: Crisis and Diversity in Native American Communities* (Cambridge, 1995), 135, 139; for Equiano's representativeness of a much wider pattern of diversity, see Philip D. Morgan, "British Encounters with Africans and African-Americans, circa 1600–1780," in Bernard Bailyn and Philip D. Morgan, eds., *Strangers within the Realm: Cultural Margins of the First British Empire* (Chapel Hill, N.C., 1991), 157–159, 217–218. The view that the North American colonies that became the United States represented white polities obviously ignored the heavy dependence on slave-based agriculture in the Chesapeake and the Lower South. In both Maryland and Virginia, though, white

In many ways, this growing sense of the empire as a multinational polity was not all that surprising, at least insofar as it involved Britons of color. What was unforeseen was the way this sense of colonial diversity often carried over into metropolitan perceptions of the white settlers who were still a powerful, if somewhat diminished, presence in Britain's colonial population. Given the determination with which Parliament had defended its sovereignty during the American Revolution, the men and women in the remaining colonies of settlement—many of them loyal refugees who had fled persecution in the United States—could have been forgiven for expecting the government to continue with a concerted policy of imperial centralization based on the notion that Parliament enjoyed the same authority over the rest of the empire as it did at home. But, in fact, something rather different happened. Although officials on both sides of the Atlantic demonstrated little patience for the sort of radical politics that had contributed to the American Revolution, the British assiduously avoided policies that might revive the debate over the precise nature of Parliament's imperial sovereignty. As Lord Sheffield remarked in 1783, the surest way to bring stability to Canada and the West Indies was for the British government to grant its settlers there the same degree of legislative autonomy—including the exclusive right to tax themselves—that Lord North and the Carlisle Commission had held out to the Americans in 1778. Indeed, during the discussions that preceded the Canada Act of 1791, it was readily apparent that, by abandoning the right to tax "for the purposes of general defence or of internal regulation and improvement" during the American Revolution, the North ministry had placed definite limits on how far someone like Lord Chancellor Thurlow could proceed in his determination to check future colonial aspirations for political liberty in the remaining parts of British North America.[35]

---

planters and farmers represented a large enough majority to prevent the sort of creolization characteristic of the British West Indies; see, esp., Edmund S. Morgan, *American Slavery, American Freedom: The Ordeal of Colonial Virginia* (New York, 1975), esp. chap. 18. For the persistence of such selective patterns of racial identity even in India, see P. J. Marshall, "The Whites of British India, 1780–1830: A Failed Colonial Society?" *International History Review*, XII (1990), 26–44.

35. Sheffield, *Commerce of the American States*, 174–179, esp. 177. Because of his support for the Navigation Acts, Sheffield was only speaking of taxation for revenue, but his position was so firm that he even objected to such levies when they originated in a specific colony, as in an East Florida statute that created a perpetual revenue to be placed at the disposal of Parliament (177n). On the Canada Act (1791), see esp. "Memo-

This is not to deny the counterrevolutionary character of many of the policies implemented in the Revolution's aftermath. Nor is it to suggest that Parliament was not still capable of concerted, unilateral action in matters of colonial administration. After all, as the burgeoning debate over slavery and the slave trade made clear, only Parliament possessed the necessary authority to end Britain's role in perpetuating the evils of the Middle Passage. Significantly, there were quite a few Whigs who welcomed the way ameliorating the horrors of slavery promised to restore some of the imperial authority that Britain had lost during the American Revolution—in this case by affirming Westminster's supremacy over the successors to the Royal African Company and the West Indian colonies. Olaudah Equiano, for one, was certainly aware of this potential. "May Heaven make the British senators the dispersers of light, liberty, and science, to the uttermost parts of the earth" was how the former slave described the prospect of Parliament's intervention, and he insisted that, by abolishing the slave trade, the British government would adopt a measure "suitable to the nature of a free and generous government, and, connected with views of empire and dominion, suited to the benevolence and solid merit of the legislature."[36]

Although in theory Parliament retained the same abstract rights that it had claimed before the American Revolution, the fact that the defenders of those rights had to go to such lengths to justify their continued existence is a reminder of how far the actual exercise of power had devolved back onto the colonies. Because the peace concluded in 1783 spared Parliament the agony of having to write into an international treaty the terms that its members had been prepared to offer the Americans, the federal implications that the Revolution held for the British Empire remained submerged. Yet even the most devoted proponents of

randum on the Issues Relating to a Change in the Constitution [of Canada]" (1789), enclosed in William Grenville to Governor Baron Dorchester, Oct. 20, 1789, in Madden and Fieldhouse, eds., *Select Documents*, III, 442.

36. Allison, ed., *Interesting Narrative*, 192–193. In one of the more interesting plans for resolving the imperial crisis, David Hartley actually proposed repealing all parliamentary taxes in exchange for colonial acceptance of a statute guaranteeing slaves the right to a trial by jury; see G. B. to Benjamin Franklin, Nov. 14, 1775, P.R.O., C.O. 5/40/1, 69–73; Simmons and Thomas, eds., *Proceedings and Debates*, VI, 332, 336–338. On the other hand, the potential for antislavery to revive Parliament's imperial powers bothered others—including Burke—who claimed to sympathize with the general cause of abolition. For Burke's ambivalence over antislavery's implications, see his parliamentary speech of June 5, 1777, in Elofsen, ed., *Party, Parliament, and the American War*, 340–341.

Westminster's unlimited authority proved unwilling to defend those rights indefinitely. In this sense, the American Revolution cast a long shadow indeed. As the great imperial historian Sir John Seeley would write exactly a century after the war's end, the "secession" of the North American colonies had left "in the English mind a doubt, a misgiving, which affects our whole forecast of the future of England." Never again would the British think of any part of their empire as an extension of their own nation—at least not in the way they had before 1776.[37]

37. J. R. Seeley, *The Expansion of England: Two Courses of Lectures* (1883; Boston, 1900), 17. See also Eliga H. Gould, "A Virtual Nation: Greater Britain and the Imperial Legacy of the American Revolution," *American Historical Review*, CIV, no. 2 (April, 1999).

Manuscript Sources

Bancroft Library, University of California, Berkeley
  Chesterfield MSS

Bodleian Library, Oxford
  Dashwood MSS
  Shelburne MSS

British Library
  Misc. MSS   Add. MSS 20,005
  Rainsford MSS   Add. MSS 23,653–23,655
  Almon MSS   Add. MSS 20,733
  Wilkes MSS   Add. MSS 30,865–30,881, 30,895
  Newcastle MSS   Add. MSS 32,526–33,004 (used selectively)
  Auckland MSS   Add. MSS 34,415–34,417, 34,426
  Hardwicke MSS   Add. MSS 35,351–35,893 (used selectively)
  Liverpool MSS   Add. MSS 38,208–38,309 (used selectively)
  Westminster Assoc. MSS   Add. MSS 38,594–38,595
  Francis MSS   Add. MSS 40,759
  Misc. MSS   Add. MSS 42,568
  Adair MSS   Add. MSS 50,829
  Holland MSS   Add. MSS 51,375–51,385
  Bentinck MSS   Egerton 1755
  Douglass MSS   Egerton 2182
  Leeds MSS   Egerton 3500
  Misc. MSS   Stowe 249
  Althorp Papers   Boxes F8, F9 (unfoliated)

Cambridge University Library
  Cholmondley (Houghton) MSS

Huntington Library, San Marino
  Loudoun MSS
  Stowe MSS

National Register of Archives, London
  Foljambe of Osberton MSS   Report No. 20442

Public Record Office, London
  Colonial Office, Series 5
  State Papers Domestic, Series 36, 37, 41, 44

Treasury Solicitor Papers, Series II
Home Office, Series 51, 55
War Office, Series 1, 68
Amherst MSS
Chatham MSS

Scottish Record Office
Melville MSS

Suffolk County Record Office
Barrington MSS

Journals and Magazines

Craftsman
Gentleman's Magazine and Historical Chronical
Monitor
Annual Register

Short–Title Pamphlets

(arranged chronologically)

This is an extensive but necessarily selective list of pamphlets relevant to British politics in the age of the American Revolution. Unless otherwise stated, all pamphlets were published in London. Because of the nature of eighteenth-century print culture, readers may discover discrepancies elsewhere in details like authorship, editions, and punctuation. The location of each pamphlet is indicated with a shelf-mark (when known) and one of the following abbreviations:

BL	British Library, London
Bod	Bodleian Library, Oxford
HL	Huntington Library, San Marino, Calif.
Houghton	Houghton Library, Harvard University
Hutzler	Hutzler Library, The Johns Hopkins University
Folger	Folger Shakespeare Library, Washington
NLS	National Library of Scotland, Edinburgh
RPI	Research Publications Inc., Woodbridge, Connecticut (including the "Eighteenth Century" and "Goldsmith-Kress" microfilm collections)

BEFORE 1742

[Barton], Thomas. *A Sermon Preach'd before the House of Lords*. 1739. BL 4473.g.10 (8).
Bate, James. *An Assize Sermon Preach'd at Maidstone*. 1734. BL 4473.g.10(7).
The Case of the Hessian Forces. 1731. Bod. G.Pamph.854(5).
Clarke, Samuel. *Six Sermons on Several Occasions*. 1718. Houghton *EC7.C5566.B718s.
[Davenant, Charles]. *Essays upon: I. The Ballance of Power; II. The Right of Making War; III. Universal Monarchy*. 1701. Folger.

[Defoe, Daniel]. *An Argument Shewing, That a Standing Army Is Not Inconsistent with a Free Government.* 1698. NLS.

[———]. *The True-Born Englishman: A Satyr.* 1700. NLS.

An Enquiry into the Conduct of Our Domestick Affairs. 1734. Bod. G.Pamph.854(10).

[Fletcher, Andrew]. *A Discourse of Government with relation to Militia's.* Edinburgh, 1698. NLS.

[———]. *An Account of a Conversation Concerning a Right Regulation of Governments.* Edinburgh, 1704. NLS.

German Cruelty: A Fair Warning to the People of Great-Britain. 1741. BL T.1113(4).

[Hervey, John]. *Ancient and Modern Liberty.* 1734. Houghton *EC7.H4459.734a.

[———]. *Observations on the Writings of the Craftsman.* 1730. Houghton *EC7.H4459.730o.

[———]. *The Conduct of the Opposition.* 1734. Houghton *EC7.H4459.734c.

Hughes, Obadiah. *National Deliverances Thankfully Acknowledged.* 1739. Houghton *EC7.H8748.B740s(2).

[Maddox], Isaac. *A Sermon Preach'd before the House of Lords.* 1739. Houghton *EC7.M2646.739s2.

Molyneux, William. *The Case of Ireland's Being Bound.* Dublin, 1698. Folger 160390.

[Morris, Corbyn]. *A Letter from a By-Stander to a Member of Parliament.* 1741/2. BL 1103.f.15, Houghton *EC75.M8315.7421.

[Moyle, Walter]. *The Second Part of an Argument.* 1697. RPI.

Reasons Shewing the Necessity of Reducing the Army. 1728. RPI.

[Somers, John Lord]. *A Letter, Ballancing the Necessity of Keeping a Land-Force.* 1697. In *A Collection of State Tracts.* II. 1706. Hutzler.

Tindall, Mat[thew]. *An Essay concerning the Laws of Nations.* 1694. In *A Collection of State Tracts.* II. Hutzler.

———. *An Essay concerning Obedience to the Supreme Powers.* 1694. In *A Collection of State Tracts.* II. 1706. Hutzler.

[Trenchard, John]. *An Argument, Shewing, That a Standing Army is Inconsistent with a Free Government.* 1697. RPI.

[———]. *Free Thoughts concerning Officers.* [1705]. RPI.

A Vindication of the Honour and Privileges of the Commons. 1740. BL 8132.b.31.

1742

[Carte, Thomas]. *A Full Answer to the Letter from a By-Stander.* BL 1103.f.15(3).

An Enquiry into the Present State of Our Domestick Affairs. BL T.1672(10).

The H——r Heroes; or, A Song of Triumph. BL 1482.f.40.

Hughes, Obadiah. *Obedience to God the Best Security against Our Enemies.* Houghton *EC7.H8748.B740s(3).

An Important Secret Come to Light. BL T.1695(11).

A Key to the Business of the Present S——n. BL T.1695(2).

A Letter from a Member of the Last Parliament. BL T.1695(4).

A Letter to the Author of An Enquiry. BL T.1695(7).

[Lyttleton, George]. *The Affecting Case of the Queen of Hungary.* BL T.1695(3).

[Morris, Corbyn]. *A Letter from a By-Stander.* 2d ed. BL T.1813(10).

National Unanimity Recommended. BL 101.g.25.

Plain Matter of Fact; or, Whiggism the Bulwark of These Kingdoms. BL 8132.b.84.

The Present State of British Influence in Holland. BL T.1695(8).

[Pulteney, William]. *A Proper Answer to the By-Stander.* BL T.1813(5).

[Ralph, James]. *The Conduct of the Late Administration.* BL T.1813(9).

Remarks on a Pamphlet, Intitled, An Inquiry. BL 1695(5).

Terrick, Richard. *A Sermon Preached before the Honourable House of Commons.* BL 11659.cc.1 (6).

[Turner, G]. *An Inquiry into the Revenue, Credit, and Commerce of France.* BL T.1695(6).

1743

[Carte, Thomas]. *A Full and Clear Vindication of the Full Answer to a Letter from a By-Stander.* BL 9510.c.8.

[Chesterfield, Philip Dormer Stanhope, earl of]. *The Case of the Hanover Forces in the Pay of Great-Britain.* BL 1093.d.102.

[——]. *The Interest of Hanover Steadily Pursued.* BL T.1111(6).

[——]. *A Vindication of a Late Pamphlet, Intitled, The Case of the Hanover Troops Considered.* BL 1093.d.89.

An Exact Relation of the Siege of Prague. BL 1672(1).

[Hervey, John, baron]. *The Question Stated with regard to Our Army in Flanders.* BL T.1672(7).

A Key to the Present Politicks. BL T.1672(9).

Letters and Negociations of M. Van Hoey. BL T.1672(2).

A Letter to a General Officer. BL 599.k.19(9).

The Lords Protests on a Motion to Address His Majesty to Exonerate His Subjects of the Charge and Burthen of Those Foreign Troops. BL T.1672(7*).

[Morris, Corbyn]. *A Letter to the Reverend Mr. Thomas Carte.* BL 1093.d.97.

Observations on Swedish History. BL T.1599(13).

Observations on the Conduct of Great-Britain, in respect to Foreign Affairs. 2d ed. BL T.1672(4).

[Perceval, John, Lord]. *Faction Detected.* 2d ed. BL T.1111(7).

Popular Prejudice concerning Partiality to the Interests of Hanover. BL 101.g.62.

The Present Measures Proved to Be the Only Means of Securing the Balance of Power in Europe. BL 8122.aa.1(4).

Serious and Impartial Reflections on the Conduct of the Several Princes. BL T.1672(3).

Seventeen Hundred Forty-two: Being a Review of the Conduct of the New Ministry. BL T.1672(5).

The Triumphant Campaign. BL 8132.b.48.

[Walpole, Horace]. *The Interest of Great Britain Steadily Pursued.* BL 1093.d.93.

1744

The Advantages of the Hanover Succession. BL T.1813(14).

An Apology for the Conduct of the Present Administration. BL T.1112(2).

A Defence of the People. BL T.1112(1).

The English Nation Vindicated from the Calumnies of Foreigners. BL 101.g.63.

Free Thoughts on the Late Treaty of Alliance Concluded at Worms. BL T.1695(10).

German Politicks; or, The Modern System Examined. BL 1475.a.25.
The Review: A Poem. BL 1493.c.17(46).

1745

[Britannus]. *Considerations Addressed to the Publick.* [n.p.]. BL 1092.d.107.
[Britannus]. *A Letter to a Certain Foreign Minister.* BL 102.c.17.
[Cibber, Theophilus]. *The Association.* BL 1493.c.17(5).
The Conduct of Our Officers, as Well General as Inferior. BL 90708.bbb.4.
Considerations on the State of the British Fisheries in America. BL 599.k.19(13).
A Continuation of the Plain Reasoner. BL T.1813(12).
The Criterion of the Reason and Necessity of the Present War. BL 1481.b.37.
The Duty of a Soldier. BL 716.d.14.
An Earnest Address to Britons. BL 1489.w.10.
An Enquiry into the Causes of Our Late and Present National Calamities. BL 8132.de.1(1).
The Folly and Danger of the Present Associations Demonstrated. BL 8132.b.44.
Hanoverian Politicks. BL 8072.c.42.
[Harper, William]. *The Advice of a Friend to the Army and People of Scotland.* Aberdeen. BL 522.b.11.
Herring, Thomas. *A Sermon Preach'd at the Cathedral Church.* York. BL 225.f.22(2).
The Importance of Cape Breton to the British Nation. BL 599.k.19(12).
King George for England, a New Ballad to an Old Tune. BL 1493.c.17(6).
[Martin, Samuel]. *A Plan for Establishing and Disciplining a National Militia.* 2d ed. BL 716.d.14(1).
A Modest Enquiry into the Present State of Foreign Affairs. BL 103.g.52.
A Particular Account of the Taking Cape Breton from the French. BL 599.k.19(11).
A Plain Answer to the Plain Reasoner. BL 102.c.9.
The Plain Reasoner. 2d ed. BL T.1813(11).
The Present Ruinous Land-War. BL 8132.c.51.
A Proprosal for a Regular and Useful Militia. Edinburgh. BL 8132.aa.30.
Ridley, Glocester. *Constitution in Church and State.* BL 225.f.22(11).
Seasonable Considerations on the Present War. BL 599.k.19(4).
Suger, Zachary. *The Preservation of Judah . . . A Sermon Preach'd at York, on Sunday the 29th.* York. BL 225.f.22(8).
Terrick, Richard. *A Sermon Preach'd before the Rt. Honble. the Lord Mayor.* BL 11659.cc.1 (8).

1746

A Bill for the Better Regulation of the Militia. RPI.
Brekell, John. *Liberty and Loyalty.* BL 8132.c.10.
[Burgh, James]. *Britain's Remembrancer.* BL 8133.a.19.
The Disbanded Volunteers' Appeal to Their Fellow-Citizens. Exeter. BL 8814.bb.52.
An Enquiry into the Causes of the Late Rebellion. BL T.1806(1).
[Hervey, Thomas]. *A Letter to William Pitt, Esq.* BL 1093.e.13.
The Important Question Discussed. BL 102.c.21.
The Lords Protest on a Motion to Address His Majesty. BL T.1623(5).
The New System. BL T.1112(4).

[Pepperrell, Sir William]. *An Accurate Journal*. Exeter. BL T.1623(6).
Power and Patriotism. BL 1493.c.17(26).
The Present Condition of Great Britain. BL 8132.df.3(1).
A Proposal for Arming, and Disciplining the People of Great Britain. BL 102.c.24.
[Squire, Samuel]. *A Letter to a Tory Friend*. BL 102.c.36.

1747

An Enquiry into the State of Affairs. BL 8132.c.35.
An Expostulatory Letter to a Certain Right Honourable Person. BL T.1615(2).
[Fielding, Henry]. *A Proper Answer to a Late Scurrilous Libel*. BL T.1791(3).
[Fortescue, James]. *The Expedition*. BL C.145.a.15.
The Free-Born Englishman's Unmask'd Battery. BL T.1600(4).
A General View of the Present Politics and Interests of the Principal Powers of Europe. BL 8132.c.38.
[Granville, John Carteret, earl of]. *The State of the Nation for the Year 1747, and respecting 1748*. BL T.1632(6).
The Groans of B——n. BL 8132.c.9.
[Lane, Richard]. *To the Honourable, the Commons of Great-Britain in Parliament Assembled*. BL 14000.k.34(11).
[Lyttleton, George]. *A Letter to the Tories*. BL T.1750(13).
Memoirs of the Most Christian-Brute. BL 8122.aa.1(4).
Monteith, William, earl of. *The Fatal Consequences of National Discord*. Edinburgh. BL 8139.a.5(2).
[Morris, Corbyn]. *An Essay towards Deciding the Important Question*. BL T.1112(6).
The State of the Nation Consider'd, in a Letter to a Member of Parliament. BL T.1623(1).
[Walpole, Horace]. *A Letter to the Whigs*. BL T.1615(6).
[Winnington, Thomas]. *An Apology for the Conduct of a Late Celebrated Second-Rate Minister*. BL T.1791(1).

1748

An Apology for a Late Resignation. BL T.1615(3).
An Answer from a Gentleman at the Hague. BL 102.c.55.
An Authentick History of the Late Revolution at Amsterdam. BL 114.l.15
The Case Re-stated. BL T.1791(6).
The Conduct of the Government with regard to Peace and War, Stated. BL T.1632(7).
A Congratulatory Letter to Selim. BL 1093.e.23.
A Free Comment on the Late Mr. W——g——n's Apology for His Conduct. BL T.1791(2).
An Impartial Review of Two Pamphlets. BL 102.c.58.
A Letter from a Gentleman in London to His Friend in the Country. BL 101.k.58.
A Letter to a Certain Distinguished Patriot. BL 8132.c.79.
A Letter to a Noble Negotiator Abroad. BL 8133.aaa.5(2).
Manning, T. *A Review of the Late Mr. W——n's Conduct and Principles*. BL T.1791(5).
National Prejudice, Opposed to the National Interest. BL T.1600(5).
The Natural Interest of Great-Britain. BL 102.c.51.
The Patriot Analized. BL T.1791(4).

The Pr—t—st of the M—ch—ts of G—t B—n. BL 102.c.54.

Sayer, Joseph. *An Introductory to the History of the Principal Kingdoms and States of Europe.* 2 vols. Hutzler D103.P84.1748.

[Sharpe, Gregory]. *A Short Dissertation upon That Species of Misgovernment, Called an Oligarchy.* BL 521.i.10(3).

Some Thoughts on the Constitution. BL 8122.aa.1(6).

The State of the Nation. 2d ed. BL 1102.h.9(4).

Truth, but No Treason. BL 8138.df.19(4).

[Walpole, Horace]. *A Second and Third Letter to the Whigs.* BL T.1615(7).

1749

Advantages of the Difinitive Treaty. BL 1609/3678.

The Alarm Bell. BL T.13*(4).

The Conduct of the Two B—rs Vindicated. BL T.1633(2).

Conybeare, John. *True Patriotism.* BL 225.f.19(17).

A Dialogue between Thomas Jones, a Life-guard-man, and John Smith. BL T.1112(10).

Dodsley, R. *The Triumph of Peace, a Masque.* BL T.13*(10).

[Egmont, John Perceval, earl of]. *An Examination of the Principles, and an Enquiry into the Conduct, of the Two B—rs.* BL 8132.de.2(15).

[——]. *A Second Series of Facts and Arguments.* BL 102.c.64.

A Free Apology in Behalf of the Smugglers. BL 8229.c.24(2).

The Impostor Detected and Convicted. BL T.2031(28).

An Inquiry into the Rights of Free Subjects. BL 8132.a.9.

A Letter from a Friend in the Country to a Friend at Will's Coffee-House. BL 8133.a.54.

A Letter to a Member of Parliament: in relation to the Bill for Punishing Mutiny and Desertion. BL 8135.bb.29.

A Letter to the Author of an Examination of the Principles. BL 102.c.63.

Miscellaneous Reflections upon the Peace, and Its Consequences. BL 104.b.59.

A Modest and Impartial Reply to a Pamphlet. BL T.1633(4).

Observations on the Last Session of P—rl—m—nt. BL 1485.c.4.

Pasquin and Marforio on the Peace. 3d ed. BL T.1599(15).

Rolt, Richard. *An Impartial Representation of the Conduct of the Several Powers of Europe.* 4 vols. BL 302.i.8–11.

Some Considerations upon Taxes, and upon the Debts of the Nation. Eton. BL T.13*(7).

To the Good People of Great Britain and Ireland: The Humble Address of Daniel Dettingen. BL 8145.aaa.20.

[Warburton, William]. *A Letter to the Editor of the Letters on the Spirit of Patriotism.* BL 494.f.25(7).

1750

Seasonable and Affecting Observations on the Mutiny-Bill. BL 103.g.21.

1751

A Seasonable Letter to the Author of, Seasonable and Affecting Observations on the Mutiny Bill. BL 1568/1025

1752

[Middlesex, Charles Sackville, Lord]. *A Treatise concerning the Militia.* Dublin. RPI.

1753

Blackett, Edward Bridges. *A Sermon Preach'd before the Honourable House of Commons.* BL 11659.cc.1.
A Letter to a Member of Parliament, on the Registering and Numbering the People of Great Britain. BL T.1113(3).
[Thornton, William]. *The Counterpoise: Being Thoughts on a Militia and a Standing Army.* 2d ed. RPI.

1754

Kennedy, Archibald. *Serious Considerations on the Present State of the Affairs of the Northern Colonies.* BL 104.c.47.
[Townshend, Charles]. *A Letter to the Freeholders of the County of Norfolk.* BL 8138.df.19(6).

1755

An Answer to a Pamphlet, Called, A Second Letter to the People. BL 8026.bb.11.
A Constituent's Answer to the Reflexions of a Member of Parliament. BL 8133.aaa.34.
Free Thoughts, and Bold Truths. BL 8138.bb.22.
The History of Tom Dunderhead. BL 8145.e.83*(12).
[Huske, Ellis]. *The Present State of North-America, Etc.* 2d ed. HL 32487.
Hutcheson, Francis. *A System of Moral Philosophy, in Three Books.* 2 vols. Houghton *EC7.H9706.755s, 1–2.
[Jones, John]. *A Letter to a Friend in the Country.* BL 102.c.48.
A Letter from a Member of Parliament to . . . the Duke of——. BL 8133.c.43.
The Opposition. BL 8133.c.44.
Reflections upon the Present State of Affairs, at Home and Abroad. BL 8133.c.31.
Some Material and Very Important Remarks. BL 8026.c.34.
[Tucker, Josiah]. *The Important Question concerning Invasions.* BL 8133.c.49.

1756

An Address to the Electors of England. BL 8132.c.29.
An Address to the Great. HL 309998.
An Appeal to the Sense of the People. HL 87287.
Bell, William. *A Dissertation on the Following Subject.* HL 272277.
[Bever, Samuel]. *The Cadet.* HL 291926.
The Conduct of the Ministry Impartially Examined. HL 65369.
A Constituent's Answer to the Reflexions of a Member of Parliament. HL 138574.
[Cooper, John Gilbert]. *The Genius of Britain.* HL 180775.
Davies, Samuel. *Religion and Patriotism.* HL 55391.
——. *Virginia's Danger and Remedy.* 2d ed. Glasgow. HL 121676.
England's Warning. HL 312527.

An Enquiry into the Present System. HL 15049.

Evans, Lewis. *Geographical, Historical, Political, Philosophical, and Mechanical Essays.* HL 123471.

The Freeholder's Ditty. BL C113.hh.3(5).

[Hayward, Samuel]. *A Letter to the Inhabitants of Great Britain and Ireland.* HL 310825.

A Letter from a Frenchman at Paris. HL 138666.

A Modest Address to the Commons of Great Britain. 2d ed. BL T.1113(5).

A New System of Patriot Policy. RPI.

The Parallel; or, The Conduct and Fate of Great Britain. HL 138976.

[Payne, J.]. *The French Encroachments Exposed.* HL 87856.

The Progress of the French. HL 86232.

Reasons for Building of Barracks. HL 301590.

Reflections on the Welfare and Prosperity of Great Britain in the Present Crisis. HL 138738.

A Scheme for Establishing a Constitutional Militia. RPI

[Shebbeare, John]. *A Fourth Letter to the People of England.* 6th ed. BL 1608/5723(2).

[————]. *Letters on the English Nation.* 2d ed. BL 291.k.30.

[————]. *Three Letters to the People of England.* 6th ed. BL 1608/5723(1).

The Voice of the People. RPI.

1757

[Brown, John]. *An Estimate of the Manners and Principles of the Times.* 2d ed. Hutzler, HN388.B75.1757.

[Burke, William]. *An Account of the European Settlements in America.* 2 vols. HL 113576.

[Burn, Richard]. *Observations on the New Militia Bill.* HL 308736.

Christian, Joachim. *A Political Discourse upon the Different Kinds of Militia.* Trans. Thomas Whiston. RPI.

Davies, Samuel. *The Crisis.* HL 138963.

Donaldson, William. *North America, A Descriptive Poem.* HL 311024.

An Essay on the Expediency of a National Militia. RPI, HL 302764.

The Fall of Public Spirit. HL K-D 24.

Fatal Consequences of the Want of System in the Conduct of Public Affairs. HL 311559.

Further Objections to the Establishment of a Constitutional Militia. RPI.

[Henley-Ongley, Robert]. *An Essay on the Nature and Use of the Militia; with Remarks on the Bill Offered to Parliament Last Session.* HL 328714.

[Jenkinson, Charles]. *A Discourse on the Establishment of a National and Constitutional Force in England.* BL 1103.g.32.

A Lamentation for the Departure of the Hanoverians. HL 315889.

A Letter from a Merchant of the City of London. HL 65489.

A Letter from Sir William —— Deputy Lieutenant of the County of —— to His Tenants and Neighbours. HL 342705.

A Letter to a Member of Parliament, on the Importance of the American Colonies. HL 138964.

A Letter to the Gentlemen of the Army. HL 281454.

[McCulloh, Henry]. *Proposals for Uniting the English Colonies on the Continent of America.* HL 48248.

[Morgann, Maurice]. *An Enquiry concerning the Nature and End of a National Militia.* RPI.

Motives for a Peace with England. HL 138668.

New Manual Exercise as Performed by His Majesty's Dragoons.

Occasional Reflections Addressed to the People of Great Britain. HL 65429.

A Plain Address to the Farmers, Labourers, and Commonalty of the County of Norfolk. [n.p.]. RPI.

The Political Freethinker. HL 138723.

Postlethwayt, Malachy. *Britain's Commercial Interest Explained and Improved.* HL 138522.

———. *Great-Britain's True System.* HL 215924.

Scott, Thomas. *Great-Britain's Danger and Remedy.* Ipswich. HL 280507.

[Shebbeare, John]. *A Fifth Letter to the People of England.* 2d ed. BL 8135.cc.53(4).

[———]. *A Sixth Letter to the People of England.* 2d ed. BL 1568/4782.

[Shirley, William]. *Memoirs of the Principal Transactions of the Last War between the English and French in North America.* HL 86473.

1758

The Conduct of a Noble Commander in America, Impartially Reviewed. 2d ed. HL 138579.

[Egmont, John Perceval, earl of]. *Things as They Are.* 3d ed. HL 143395.

Leland, John. *Serious Reflections on the Present State of Things in These Nations.* HL 340825.

A Letter to the People of England, upon the Militia. HL 138667.

A Letter to the Right Honourable W. P., Esq. Exeter. HL 65433.

The Present Interest of the People of Great-Britain, at Home and Abroad. HL 141277.

Railton, John. *Proposals to the Public, Especially Those in Power.* HL 140578.

[Stevens, George]. *Albion Restored, or Time Turned Oculist.* HL K–D 4.

[Temple, William]. *A Vindication of Commerce and the Arts.* Bod. G.Pamph.1862(1).

Whitehead, William. *Verses to the People of England.* HL 94632.

[Williamson, Peter]. *French and Indian Cruelty.* 2d ed. York. HL 146057.

———. *Occasional Reflections on the Importance of the War in America.* HL 138578.

———. *Some Considerations on the Present State of Affairs.* York. HL 146055.

1759

[Carlyle, Alexander]. *Plain Reasons for Removing a Certain Great Man.* HL 303573.

Considerations on the Importance of Canada. HL 65371.

A Dutiful Address to the Throne. HL 138561.

The English Pericles. HL 302699.

Genuine Letters from a Volunteer, in the British Service, at Quebec. HL 32214.

Grove, [Joseph]. *A Letter to a Right Honourable Patriot.* HL 48207.

[Hanway, Jonas]. *Thoughts on the Duty of a Good Citizen.* 2d ed. HL 310911.

Hints for the Carrying into Execution the Acts, for the Better Ordering of the Militia Forces. HL 29744.

The Honest Grief of a Tory. HL 16285.

The Invasion, a Farce. HL 129020.

A Letter from the Duchess of M——r——gh, in the Shades, to the Great Man. HL 303115.

A Letter to a Late Noble Commander of the British Forces in Germany. HL 301619.

A Letter to the Right Honourable Lord Viscount Ligonier. HL 306502.

Montagu, E[dward] W[ortley]. *Reflections on the Rise and Fall of the Antient Republicks.* BL 8005.cc.39.

A Second Letter from Wiltshire to the Monitor. HL 141124.

Smith, William. *Discourses on Several Public Occasions.* HL 43532.

[Stona, Thomas]. *A Letter to the Norfolk Militia.* Bod. G.Pamph.1862(4).

[Young, Arthur]. *Reflections on the Present State of Affairs at Home and Abroad.* HL 146567.

1760

[Almon, John]. *A New Military Dictionary; or, The Field of War.* HL 22756.

An Answer to the Letter to Two Great Men. HL 224111.

[Burke, William]. *Remarks on the Letter Address'd to Two Great Men.* HL 113581.

A Candid and Fair Examination of the Remarks on the Letter to Two Great Men. 2d ed. 1760. HL 138631.

[Carlyle, Alexander]. *The Question Relating to a Scots Militia Considered.* HL 86210.

Cockings, George. *War: An Heroic Poem.* HL 138706.

The Complete Militia-Man. BL 8827.aaa.16.

[Douglas, John]. *A Letter Addressed to Two Great Men, on the Prospect of Peace.* HL 138605.

Fownes, Joseph. *The Connexion between the Honour of Princes.* Shrewsbury. HL 227620.

[Franklin, Benjamin]. *The Interest of Great Britain Considered.* HL 65509.

[Hanway, Jonas]. *An Account of the Society for the Encouragement of the British Troops, in Germany and North America.* HL 298005.

A Letter from a Militia-Man to His Colonel. BL 102.h.21.

A Letter to an Honourable Brigadier General, Commander in Chief of His Majesty's Forces in Canada. HL 146147.

A Letter to the Right Honourable William Pitt, Esq. HL 288564.

Lockman, John. *Verses on the Demise of the Late King.* HL 139825.

Massie, Joseph. *A Representation concerning the Knowledge of Commerce as a National Concern.* BL 104.g.26.

[Mauduit, Israel]. *Considerations on the Present German War.* BL 1093.e.67.

Military Maxims. HL 34384.

New Military Instructions for the Militia. BL 1398.d.23.

One Thousand Seven Hundred and Fifty Nine: A Poem. HL 181090.

Plan for Raising a Militia in That Part of Great Britain Called Scotland. Edinburgh. HL 326575.

Political Thoughts. BL 8026.bb.40.

Reasons for Extending the Militia Acts. Edinburgh. HL 316760.

Reflections without Doors on What Passes within. BL 8132.c.73.

A Refutation of the Letter to an Honourable Brigadier-General. HL 68676.

Remarks on a Pamphlet Entitled, Reasons Why the Approaching Treaty of Peace Should Be Debated in Parliament, Etc. HL 141127.

[Ruffhead, Owen]. *Reasons Why the Approaching Treaty of Peace Should Be Debated in Parliament.* HL 152955.

[Shebbeare, John]. *The History of the Excellence and Decline of the Constitution.* 2 vols. BL 713.d.38.

Thoughts on the Present War and Future Peace. HL 138611.

[Tucker, Josiah]. *The Manifold Causes of the Increase of the Poor Distinctly Set Forth.* HL 83109.

A Vindication of the Right Honourable Lord George Sackville. 2d ed. BL 518.e.16(4).

The Voice of Peace. HL 138613.

1761

An Account of the Ceremonies Observed at the Coronation of Our Most Gracious Sovereign George III. HL 319655.

An Answer to a Letter to the Right Honourable the Earl of B——. HL 138612.

Brown, John. *On the Natural Duty of a Personal Service.* BL 693.d.6(10).

The Case of the British Troops Serving in Germany. BL E.2052(1).

The Case of the Late Resignation Set in a True Light. HL 138618.

The Conciliad. HL 67032.

The Conduct of a Rt. Hon. Gentleman in Resigning the Seals of His Office. HL 138610.

Constitutional Queries, Humbly Addressed to the Admirers of a Late Minister. HL 138616.

The Country Gentleman's Advice to His Son. BL T.1113(15).

The Crisis. HL 138617.

Dalrymple, Campbell. *A Military Essay.* HL 70628.

A Detection of the False Reasons and Facts. HL 48208.

[Douglas, John]. *Seasonable Hints from an Honest Man.* HL 65458.

Essay on the Art of War. HL 351952.

An Examination into the Value of Canada and Guadaloupe. HL 16108.

[Ferguson, Adam]. *The History of the Proceedings in the Case of Margaret.* 2d ed. HL 268329.

[Francis, Philip]. *A Letter from a Right Honourable Person.* HL 66677.

[——]. *A Letter from the Anonymous Author of the Letters Versified.* HL 138622.

Henderson, Andrew. *Considerations on the Question.* HL 132256.

Impartial Reflections upon the Present State of Affairs. HL 65501.

A Letter from a British Officer Now in Germany. HL 318919.

A Letter to His Grace the Duke of N——. BL 8132.d.48, HL 65493.

A Letter to the Right Honourable the Earl of B——. BL T.1709(5), HL 138726.

[Massie, Joseph]. *Brief Observations concerning the Management of the War.* 2d ed. HL 66678.

[——]. *General Propositions relating to Colonies.* HL 138731.

[——]. *The Rotten and Tottering State of the Popular Part of the British Constitution.* 5th ed. BL 746.c.17(1).

[Mauduit, Israel]. *Considerations on the Present German War.* HL 138615, BL 1093.e.67.

[——]. *Occasional Thoughts on the Present German War.* HL 138607.

[——]. *The Plain Reasoner.* HL 138602.

Reasons for Keeping Guadaloupe at a Peace. HL 68672.

Reasons in Support of the War in Germany. HL 65524.

Seasonable Hints from an Honest Man. BL E.2052(6).
A Second Letter to the Right Honourable, the Earl of B——. BL T.1709(6), HL 138601.
A Serious Address to the Common People. 3d ed. Newcastle. BL 4477.aaa.118(2).
Thoughts on Continental Connections by Marriage. HL 318872.
[Wilkes, John]. *Considerations on the Expediency of a Spanish War.* HL 138584.

1762

[Almon, John]. *A Review of Mr. Pitt's Administration.* HL 138740.
[——]. *A Review of the Reign of George II.* 2d ed. HL 138741.
[Bollan, William]. *Coloniae Angilicanae Illustratae. Part I.* HL 138764.
[Butler, John]. *An Address to the Cocoa-tree.* BL T.1554(6), HL 138974.
The Causes of the War between Great-Britain and Spain. HL 138813.
[Cockings, George]. *War: An Heroic Poem.* HL 138853.
The Comparative Importance of Our Acquisitions from France. HL 110448.
A Consolatory Epistle. HL 138810.
[Debaufre, Peter]. *A Scheme, by which Great Advantages are Proposed for the Government as Well as for the People of Great-Britain.* HL 314949.
Directions for the More Faithful Execution of the New Militia Act. HL 215977.
An Enquiry into the Merits of the Supposed Preliminaries of Peace. HL 297653.
An Epistle to the King. HL 307971.
A Fair and Compleat Answer to the Author of the Occasional Thoughts on the Present German War. HL 138874.
[Francis, Philip]. *A Letter from the Cocoa-tree to the Country-Gentlemen.* HL 281370.
A Full and Complete Answer to the Author of the Occasional Thoughts on the Present German War. HL 138874, 138751.
A Full Vindication of the Right Honourable Wm. Pitt. HL 319687.
Letter from a Gentleman in East-Lothian. Edinburgh. HL 277651.
A Letter from Arthur's to the Cocoa-tree. HL 281631.
A Letter to a Member of the Honourable House of Commons. HL 322056.
A Letter to the Right Hon. Charles Townshend, Secretary at War. 2d ed. HL 312268.
Letters to a Young Nobleman. HL 40815.
A Letter to the Whigs. HL 309484.
[Marriott, Sir James]. *Political Considerations.* HL 65441.
[Mauduit, Israel]. *The Parallel.* HL 65430.
Otis, James. *A Vindication of the Conduct of the House of Representatives of . . . Massachusetts-Bay.* Boston. HL 146971.
A Political Analysis of the War. HL 138757.
Proceedings of a General Court-Martial. BL 518.e.15(2).
The Proper Object of the Present War with France and Spain Considered. HL 138755.
[Savile, Sir George]. *An Argument concerning the Militia.* BL T.1556(5), HL 281395.
The Sentiments of an Impartial Member of Parliament. HL 138743.
[Shebbeare, John]. *One More Letter.* 2d ed. HL 138715, BL E.2221(1).
Some Reasons for Serious Candor. HL 224112.
A Speech without Doors. HL 302844.
A Third Letter to the Right Honourable the Earl of B——. HL 138716.
Thoughts on the Times. HL 311653.

1763

An Address to Sir John Cust, Bart., Speaker of the House of Commons. HL 355707.

An Address to the People of Great-Britain and Ireland, on the Preliminaries of Peace. HL 138856.

[Almon, John]. *An Impartial History of the Late War.* BL 9006.bb.8.

[———]. *A Letter to the Right Hon. George Grenville.* 3d ed. BL T.1554(12), HL 322099.

The Annual Register of World Events. Dublin. HL 120612.

An Appeal to Knowledge. HL 27702.

The Appeal of Reason to the People of England. BL 8138.aaa.17, HL 65382.

[Baillie]. *Patriotism: A Farce.* HL 75560.

[Bath, William Pulteney, earl of]. *Reflections on the Domestic Policy Proper to be Observed on the Conclusion of a Peace.* HL 68671.

[Bayley, Anselm Yates]. *The Advantages of a Settlement upon the Ohio.* HL 373483.

[Bentley, Richard]. *Patriotism, a Mock-heroic.* HL 227817.

[Butler, John]. *An Address to the Cocoa-tree, from a Whig.* HL 65386.

[———]. *A Consultation on the Subject of a Standing Army.* HL 302835.

[———]. *Serious Considerations on the Measures of the Present Administration.* BL T.1554(7), HL 139676.

Considerations on the Present Peace. HL 65372.

The Constitution Asserted and Vindicated. HL 225988.

Dobson, John. *Chronological Annals of the War.* Oxford. HL 122770.

Egmont, John Perceval, earl of. *To the King's Most Excellent Majesty, the Memorial of John, Earl of Egmont.* HL 48045.

Entick, John. *The General History of the Late War.* 5 vols. 1763–1764. HL 89530.

[Goldsmith, Oliver]. *The Martial Review.* HL 125856.

[Henriques, Jacob]. *An Epistle to the Dictator, in His Retirement.* HL 315589.

Herring, Thomas. *Seven Sermons on Public Occasions.* Houghton *EC7.H4357.B763s.

The History of Prime Ministers and Favourites, in England. HL 143382.

An Impartial Examination of the Conduct of the Whigs and Tories. HL 225935.

Impartial Observations, to be Considered on by the King, His Ministers, and the People of Great Britain. HL 32435.

A Letter from Jonathan's to the Treasury. HL 138862.

A Letter from a Member of Parliament in London to His Friend in Edinburgh. Edinburgh. HL 317632.

A Letter from the Cocoa-tree to the Country-Gentlemen. 3d ed. BL T.1554(5).

A Letter to the Right Honourable Ch——s T——nd, Esq. HL 65496.

A Letter to the Right Honourable Earl Temple with regard to Mr. Wilkes. HL 310104.

A Letter to the Right Honourable the Earl of H——x. HL 224103.

A Letter to the Right Hon. the Earl of Temple, on the Subject of the Forty-fifth Number of the North-Briton. HL 138860.

The Military History of Great Britain. HL 138857.

The Opposition to the Late Minister Vindicated. HL 65385.

Political Disquisitions Proper for Public Consideration. HL 138828.

The Present War. HL 131512.

Reflections on the Terms of Peace. 2d ed. HL 146970.

A Review of the Arguments for an Immature Peace. HL 311294.
[Ruffhead, Owen]. *Considerations on the Present Dangerous Crisis.* 2d ed. HL 225989.
Shadwell, Charles. *The Female Officer . . . a Comedy.* Dublin. HL K–D 203.
[Tucker, Josiah]. *The Case of Going to War.* HL 16286.
[Whitworth, Sir Charles]. *A Collection of the Supplies, and Ways and Means, from the Revolution to the Present Time.* HL 225935.
The Wilkiad, a Tale. Edinburgh. HL 314476.

1764

An Answer to the Budget. HL 67038.
[Bollan, William]. *The Ancient Right of the English Nation to the American Fishery.* HL 113061.
[Boulanger, Nicolas Antoine]. *The Origin and Progress of Despotism.* HL 146953.
[Brecknock, Timothy]. *Droit le Roy.* HL 225925.
The British Coffee-house. HL 308350.
The Crisis. HL 138868.
Dickinson, John. *A Speech Delivered in the House of Assembly.* HL 122376.
[Goldsmith, Oliver]. *An History of England.* HL 145292.
[Guthrie, William]. *An Address to the Public, on the late Dismission of a General Officer.* HL 138785, BL E.2226(3).
[———]. *A Reply to the Counter-Address.* HL 138784.
[Hartley, David]. *The Budget.* HL 66679.
[Lee Arthur]. *An Essay in Vindication of the Continental Colonies of America.* HL 147018.
A Letter from Albemarle Street to the Cocoa-tree. HL 302839.
A Letter to the Proprietors of East-India Stock. BL 583.g.1(1).
A Letter to the Right Honourable Charles Townshend. HL 281562.
[Lloyd, Charles]. *An Honest Man's Reasons for Declining to Take Any Part in the New Administration.* 2d ed. HL 138808.
Newton, Thomas. *Of Moderation.* BL 694.i.18.
Pownall, Thomas. *The Administration of the Colonies.* HL 147024.
[Prime, Benjamin Young]. *The Patriot Muse.* HL 47276.
The Question of the Independency of Military Officers. BL 8138.bb.44, HL 215964.
The Question on Some Late Dismissions Fully Stated. BL 1473.c.15, HL 302894.
A Supplement to the Narrative of What Happened in Bengal, in the Year 1760. BL 583.g.1(3).
[Thompson, Edward]. *The Soldier: A Poem.* HL 227822.
[Wallace, Robert]. *A View of the Internal Policy of Great Britain.* HL 138835.
[Walpole, Horace]. *A Counter-address to the Public, on the Late Dismission of a General Officer.* HL 321911.
Whitworth, Sir Charles. *The Succession of Parliaments.* HL 436841.

1765

[Adair, James]. *Thoughts on the Dismission of Officers.* HL 283341.
An Address to Both Parties. HL 86202.
[Bollan, William]. *The Mutual Interest of Great Britain and the American Colonies Considered.* HL 113065.

A Brief State of the Services and Expences of the Province of the Massachusett's Bay. HL 384428.

[Cato]. *Thoughts on a Question of Importance.* HL 138863.

Entick, John. *The General History of the Late War.* HL 137364.

[Fothergill, John]. *Considerations relative to the North American Colonies.* HL 145109.

Griffith, John. *Some Brief Remarks upon Sundry Important Subjects.* HL 220296.

[Hartley, David]. *The State of the Nation.* HL 76336.

[Jenyns, Soame]. *The Objections to the Taxation of Our American Colonies.* HL 146562.

[Knox, William]. *The Claim of the Colonies to an Exemption from Internal Taxes.* HL 65949.

[———]. *A Letter to a Member of Parliament, Wherein the Power of the British Legislature, and the Case of the Colonists, Are . . . Considered.* HL 147006.

A Letter to the Public. HL 90735.

[Mauduit, Israel]. *An Apology for the Life and Actions of General Wolfe.* HL 87323.

[———]. *Some Thoughts on . . . Improving and Securing the Advantages Which Accrue to Great-Britain from the Northern Colonies.* HL 138759.

Oppression: A Poem. HL 147003.

[Otis, James]. *Considerations on Behalf of the Colonists.* 2d ed. HL 86100, HL 138872.

The Political Balance. HL 146975.

Pownall, Thomas. *The Administration of the Colonies.* 2d ed. BL 1061.d.20.

Rogers, Robert. *A Concise Account of North America.* HL 31205.

———. *Journals of Major Robert Rogers.* HL 146974.

A Second Letter to the Right Honourable Charles Townshend, Occasioned by His Commendations of the Budget. HL 65434.

Six Medallions Shewing the Chief National Services. HL 144963.

[Smollett, Tobias]. *A North Briton Extraordinary.* BL T.1709, HL 84157.

[Whately, Thomas]. *The Regulations Lately Made concerning the Colonies.* HL 87322.

[———]. *Remarks on the Budget.* HL 66561.

1766

An Application of Some General Political Rules, to the Present State of Great-Britain, Ireland, and America. BL 8133.bb.26, HL 111194.

[Bollan, William]. *A Succinct View of the Origin of Our Colonies.* HL 147520.

British Liberties; or, The Free-Born Subject's Inheritance. BL 8133.dd.7, HL 403297.

[Burke, William]. *An Account of the European Settlements in America.* HL 50076.

Considerations on the American Stamp Act. HL 48212.

Constitutional Considerations on the Power of Parliament to Levy Taxes on the North American Colonies. HL 120590.

The Crisis; or, A Full Defence of the Colonies. HL 128020.

[Dickinson, John]. *The Late Regulations respecting the British Colonies on the Continent of America.* HL 122567.

[Dulany, Daniel]. *Considerations on the Propriety of Imposing Taxes in the British Colonies.* HL 65875

Four Dissertations. HL 108153.

Free and Candid Remarks on a Late Celebrated Oration. HL 147609.

The General Opposition of the Colonies to the Payment of the Stamp Duty. BL T.1050(1), HL 147597.

Good Humour; or, A Way with the Colonies. HL 277646.

[Hopkins, Stephen]. *The Grievances of the American Colonies.* BL 8175.b.4, HL 147600.

The Justice and Necessity of Taxing the American Colonies. HL 144975.

The Late Occurrences in North America. BL T.766(4), HL 32496.

A List of the Minority in the House of Commons. BL T.767(4), HL 32223.

[Lloyd, Charles]. *An Examination of the Principles and Boasted Disinterestedness of a Late Right Honourable Gentleman.* BL T.1115(17), HL 139723.

[——]. *A True History of a Late Short Administration.* BL T.1115(16), HL 68657.

A Man of Abilities for the Earl of B——e; or, Scotch Politics Defeated in America. BL 8132.d.10, HL 317540.

[Maseres, Francis]. *Considerations on the Expediency of Procuring an Act of Parliament for the Settlement of the Province of Quebec.* HL 90166.

[Mauduit, Jasper]. *The Legislative Authority of the British Parliament with respect to North America.* BL 8132.d.44, HL 73747.

The Necessity of Repealing the American Stamp Act Demonstrated. BL 8154.aa.1, HL 147516.

[Otis, James]. *The Rights of the British Colonies Asserted.* HL 147001.

A Parallel; Drawn between the Administration . . . of Queen Anne, and . . . George the Third. HL 302745.

[Pitt, William]. *The Celebrated Speech of a Celebrated Commoner.* BL 1061.h.25(6), HL 147300.

Pownall, Thomas. *The Administration of the Colonies.* 3d ed. BL 1061.g.74.

Protest against the Bill to Repeal the American Stamp Act. BL 1061.h.25(7).

Reflexions on Representation in Parliament. HL 147602.

The Rights of Parliament Vindicated. HL 147519.

A Short History of the Conduct of the Present Ministry. BL T.767(1), HL 66111.

A Short View of the Political Life and Transactions of a Late Right Honourable Commoner. BL 1481.b.39, HL 17595.

The True Interest of Great Britain, with respect to Her American Colonies, Stated and Impartially Considered. BL 104.i.8, HL 147596.

[Tucker, Josiah]. *A Letter from a Merchant in London.* BL 8132.d.8, HL 66621.

[Whately, Thomas]. *Considerations on the Trade and Finances of This Kingdom.* BL 1102.h.10(4), HL 137067.

1767

An Attempt to Pay off the National Debt. BL 583.g.1(4).

[Bingham, Sir Charles]. *An Essay on the Use and Necessity of Establishing a Militia in Ireland.* Dublin. BL 1102.h.18(6), HL 371572.

[Jenyns, Soame]. *Thoughts on the Causes and Consequences of the Present High Price of Provisions.* BL 1027.b.16(2), HL 87318.

[Keith, Sir William]. *Two Papers on the Subject of Taxing the British Colonies.* BL T.766(6), HL 124133.

[Lloyd, Charles]. *The Conduct of the Late Administration Examined.* BL T.1116(3), HL 86584.

Lowth, Robert. *A Sermon Preached before the Lords Spiritual and Temporal.* BL 694.i.18.

A New and Impartial Collection of Interesting Letters. BL 291.k.12, HL 137022.

[Shebbeare, John]. *A Seventh Letter to the People.* HL 137073.

A Speech, in Behalf of the Constitution. HL 66100.

[Wilkes, John]. *A Letter to His Grace the Duke of Grafton.* BL 8133.bb.37, HL 225924.

1768

An Address to the Electors of Great-Britain, on the Choice of Members to Serve Them in Parliament. BL 8132.d.27, HL 225960.

[Canning, George]. *A Letter to the Right Honourable Wills Earl of Hillsborough.* BL T.1683(3), HL 48215.

A Cautionary Address to the Electors of England. BL 1481.c.10, HL 225959.

The Constitutional Right of the Legislature of Great Britain to Tax the British Colonies in America. BL 102.e.39, HL 15058.

[Dickinson, John]. *Letters from a Farmer in Pennsylvania.* BL T. 1612(7), HL 68575.

Dow, Alexander. *The History of Hindostan.* 3 vols. 1768–1772. BL 148.e.7–9.

The First Measures Necessary to Be Taken in the American Department. BL 8176.e.27, HL 137162.

[Hollis, Thomas, ed.]. *The True Sentiments of America.* BL1061.h.10, HL 144296.

Howard, Middleton. *The Conquest of Quebec.* Oxford. BL 11649.f.17(2), HL 372154.

[Knox, William]. *The Present State of the Nation.* BL 0231.d.45, HL 65954.

Pownall, Thomas. *The Administration of the British Colonies.* 4th ed. BL 292.k.30.

The Present State of the British Empire in Europe, America, Africa, and Asia. BL 796.h.5, HL 137111.

[Sayre, Stephen]. *The Englishman Deceived.* BL 102.e.36, HL 148032.

Windham, William and George Townshend. *A Plan of Discipline.* 2d ed. BL 1140.h.6.

Wilkes, John. *The History of England.* I. BL B.4946, HL 267287.

1769

[Bancroft, Edward]. *Remarks on the Review of the Controversy between Great Britain.* BL T.683(3), HL 65613.

Bernard, Sir Francis. *Copies of Letters.* BL 1196.i.25(1).

Bland, Richard. *An Enquiry into the Rights of the British Colonies.* BL 102.e.44, HL 106350.

[Burke, Edmund]. *Observations on a Late State of the Nation.* BL 1103.k.81, HL 67046.

The Case of Great-Britain and America. BL T.1612(4), HL 73600.

A Collection of the Letters of Atticus. BL 8006.dd.9, HL 65381.

Considerations on the Times. BL T.1117(5), HL 312647.

Dalrymple, Alexander. *A Plan for Extending the Commerce of This Kingdom, and of the East-India-Company.* BL 280.h.22(1).

The Description of a Parliament in No Instance Similar to the Present. BL T.1117(5), HL 225938.

[Erskine, John]. *Shall I Go to War with My American Brethren?* BL 696.d.16, HL 48214.

An Inquiry into the Nature and Causes of the Present Disputes between the British Colonies . . . and Their Mother-country. BL 8175.c.9, HL 48012.

Junius. *The Political Contest.* BL T.1117(8), HL 66017.

[Knox, William]. *An Appendix to the Present State of the Nation.* BL 1104.c.24(3), HL 32613.

[———]. *The Controversy between Great Britain and Her Colonies.* BL 103.h.31, HL 148421.

[Langrishe, Sir Hercules]. *Considerations on the Dependencies of Great Britain.* BL 1104.c.24(4), HL 87267.

Letters to the Ministry. BL 1196.i.25(2), HL 112297.

Letters to the Right Honourable the Earl of Hillsborough. Boston. BL 1196.i.25, HL 107808.

A Letter to the Right Honourable the Earl of T——e. BL 1481.b.12.

An Ode upon the Present Period. BL 1488.i.28(2), HL 315774.

Otis, James. *A Vindication of the British Colonies.* BL T.683(2), HL 148413.

[Phelps, Richard]. *The Rights of the Colonies.* BL 102.e.41, HL 148411.

Private Letters from an American in England. BL 12330.aaa.24, HL 137114.

[Ramsay, Allan]. *Thoughts on the Origin and Nature of Government,* HL 148412, BL T.1611(2).

A State of the Publick Revenues and Expence, from the Year 1751 to 1767. BL 8225.bb.50, HL 138441.

The True Constitutional Means for Putting an End to the Disputes between Great-Britain and the American Colonies. BL 8132.bbb.5(1), HL 277675

Wilkes, John. *English Liberty.* BL 8132.g.2, HL 180719.

[———]. *A Letter to the Right Honourable George Grenville.* BL T.1155(4)

1770

Adams, Amos. *A Concise, Historical View of the Difficulties, Hardships, and Perils Which Attended the . . . Improvements of New-England.* Boston. BL T.683(4), HL 110851.

Additional Observations to . . . the Horrid Massacre in Boston. BL T.1683(2).

An Address to Junius. BL 102.e.45, HL 316716.

An Appeal to the World. BL 1196.i.25(3), HL 86109.

An Authentic Copy of Lord Ch——m's Speech. BL 1609/512, HL 66122.

The Beginning, Progress, and Conclusion of the Late War. BL T.917(5), HL 147160.

[Bickerstaffe, Isaac]. *The Recruiting Serjeant.* BL 11777.g.77, HL K–D 189.

[Burke, Edmund]. *Thoughts on the Cause of the Present Discontents.* HL 350869.

A First Letter to the Duke of Grafton. BL 8132.d.33, HL 32472.

Guthrie, William. *A New Geographical, Historical, and Commercial Grammar.* BL 10004.ccc.8, HL 66305.

The Importance of the British Dominion in India. HL 137236.

[Johnson, Samuel]. *The False Alarm.* BL 102.f.8, HL 146265.

[Lee, Arthur]. *The Political Detection.* BL 8132.d.40, HL 143650.

Macaulay, Catharine. *Observations on a Pamphlet Entitled Thoughts on the Cause of the Present Discontents.* BL 1608/5642, HL 148426.

[MacFarlane, Robert]. *The History of the Reign of George the Third.* BL 600.e.3, HL 137048.

[Maseres, Francis]. *Considerations on the Expediency of Admitting Representatives from the American Colonies into the British House of Commons.* BL 1061.h.28(4), HL 148616.

Pittman, Philip. *The Present State of the European Settlements on the Mississippi.* BL 145.b.8, HL 31692.

Priestley, Joseph. *A Description of a New Chart of History.* 2d ed. BL 304.d.27, HL 282354.

Publicus. *A Free Address to the Author of the Essays on the Characteristics.* BL 4375.aaa.43, HL 402384.

A Seasonable Address to the People of London and Middlesex. BL 1609/3517, HL 317826.

A Short Narrative of the Horrid Massacre in Boston. BL 1061.h.11, HL 16132.

Stevenson, Roger. *Military Instructions for Officers Detached in the Field.* Glasgow. BL 54.a.22.

Toze, [Eobald]. *The Present State of Europe.* BL 582.d.10–12, HL 215911.

The True Alarm. BL 100.k.43, HL 137237.

The Twelve Letters of Canana. BL 8135.c.15, HL 310581.

Two Speeches of a Late Lord Chancellor. HL 303183.

[Wesley, John]. *Free Thoughts on the Present State of Public Affairs.* BL 8133.b.80, HL 277823.

[Wheelock, Matthew]. *Reflections Moral and Political on Great Britain and Her Colonies.* BL 1481.b.15, HL 148617.

[Wilkes, John]. *A Letter to Samuel Johnson.* BL T.1155(5), HL 230021.

[Wynne, John Huddlestone]. *A General History of the British Empire in America.* BL 1446.i.18, HL 14254.

1771

An Address to the Representatives of the People. Dublin. BL 1608/4275.

[Andrews, John]. *Reflections on the Too Prevailing Spirit of Dissipation and Gallantry.* BL 112.d.26.

The Genuine Letters of Junius. BL 8007.bbb.22.

[Gordon, John]. *The Causes and Consequences of Evil Speaking against Government.* BL 694.i.11(4)

The History of All Nations. 3d ed. BL 9004.aa.13.

Holloway, Robert. *A Letter to John Wilkes, Esq.* BL 8132.a.58.

[Johnson, Samuel]. *Thoughts on the Late Transactions respecting Falkland's Islands.* BL C.38.f.44(2).

[Johnstone, George]. *Thoughts on Our Acquisitions in the East Indies.* BL T.796(3).

Pownall, Thomas. *Two Speeches of an Honourable Gentleman.* BL 8042.d.16.

Priestley, Joseph. *An Essay on the First Principles of Government.* BL T.1116(11).

Reflections upon the Present Dispute between the House of Commons and the Magistrates of London. BL 102.e.54.

The Trial . . . for the Murder of Crispus Attucks. BL 518.e.15(1).

1772

Adye, Stephen Payne. *Considerations on the Act for Punishing Mutiny and Desertion.* BL 103.3.64.

Bolts, William. *Considerations on India Affairs.* 3 vols. 1772–1775. BL 146.d.5-7.

[Dalrymple, Alexander]. *A General View of the East-India Company.* BL 1029.c.22(1).

[———]. *Considerations on a Pamphlet, Entitled "Thoughts on Our Acquisitions in the East-Indies".* BL 1029.c.22(2).

An Enquiry into the Practice and Legality of Pressing. BL 1397.d.48(1).

An Enquiry into the Rights of the East-India Company. BL 100.m.31.

Hope, John. *Letters on Certain Proceedings.* BL T.1155(7).

[Jenyns, Soame]. *A Scheme for the Coalition of Parties.* BL 8140.e.28(1).

[MacAllester, Oliver]. *The Popular Budget.* BL 102.f.9.

Military Orders and Instructions. Chelsea. BL 58.d.4.

Nowell, Thomas. *A Sermon Preached before the Honourable House of Commons.* BL 694.i.19(17).

A Plan for the Government of the Provinces of Bengal. BL 583.h.26(1).

The Present State of the English East-India Company's Affairs. BL 100.m.23(1).

Price, Richard. *An Appeal to the Public.* BL T.1143(14).

Remarks upon Dr. Price's Appeal to the Public. BL 08230.b.24(8).

Simes, Thomas. *The Military Guide for Young Officers.* BL 63.a.1.

Verelst, Harry. *A View of . . . the English Government in Bengal.* BL 984.f.6.

[Webb, Francis]. *Thoughts on the Constitutional Power.* BL 8138.df.19(7).

[Wimpey, Joseph]. *The Challenge.* BL 104.d.63.

[———]. *An Essay on the Present High Price of Provisions.* BL 104.l.28.

Young, Arthur. *Political Essays concerning the Present State of the British Empire.* BL 189.a.22.

1773

Bonar, John. *A Discourse on the Advantages of the Insular Situation of Great-Britain.* Portsmouth. BL 91.h.9.

A Collection of Tracts. 4 vols. BL T.766-T.769.

[Hinchcliffe], John. *A Sermon Preached before the Lords Spiritual and Temporal.* BL 694.i.19(3).

The History of the British Dominions in North America. 2 vols. BL 145.d.6.

Lambart, Richard. *A New System of Military Discipline.* BL 62.c.1.

Letters to an Officer, Stationed at an Interior Post in North America. BL 10409.aa.17.

Lochee, Lewis. *An Essay on Military Education.* BL 1030.g.5(3).

The Opinions of Mr. James Eyre. BL T.796(1).

The Present State of the British Interest in India. BL 100.m.20.

The Revolution in New-England Justified. BL 8175.aa.79.

[Stuart, Andrew]. *Letters to the Right Honourable Lord Mansfield.* BL 518.l.28(1).

[Woolman, John]. *Serious Considerations on Various Subjects.* BL 4152.aa.48.

1774

Additional Preface to a Pamphlet. BL 8229.c.24(4).

Allen, William. *The American Crisis.* BL 102.3.70.

America Vindicated from the High Charge of Ingratitude and Rebellion. BL 8175.b.5.

Answer to Considerations on Certain Political Transactions of the Province of South Carolina. BL 102.e.66.

An Appeal to the Public. BL 102.f.25.

An Argument in Defence of the Exclusive Right Claimed by the Colonies to Tax Themselves. BL 102.f.20.

Baillie, Hugh. *A Letter to Dr. Shebear.* BL 102.f.43.

Bollan, William. *The Petition of Mr. Bollan.* BL 102.f.10(1).

[——]. *The Rights of the English Colonies.* BL 102.g.30.

[Boucher, Jonathan]. *A Letter from a Virginian, to the Members of the Congress to be Held at Philadelphia.* BL 102.f.13.

A Brief Review of . . . New England. BL 102.f.28.

Burgh, James. *Political Disquisitions.* 3 vols. 1774–1775. BL 288.e.18.

[Cartwright, John]. *American Independence the Interest and Glory of Great Britain.* BL 8175.b.8.

[Chandler, Thomas Bradbury]. *A Friendly Address to All Reasonable Americans.* BL 102.3.62.

Colonising; or, A Plain Investigation of That Subject. BL 102.h.29.

Continental Congress. *Extracts from the Votes and Proceedings of the American Continental Congress, Held at Philadelphia.* BL E.2239(1).

——. *A Clear Idea of the Genuine and Uncorrupted British Constitution.* BL T.229(8).

[Crowley, Thomas]. *Dissertations, on the Grand Dispute between Great Britain and America.* BL T.207(6).

[Cunninghame]. *Strictures on Military Discipline.* BL 58.c.12.

Dickinson, John. *An Essay on the Constitutional Power of Great-Britain over the Colonies in America.* BL 8176.b.28.

[——]. *Letters from a Farmer in Pennsylvania.* BL 103.h.36.

[——]. *A New Essay by the Pennsylvanian Farmer.* BL 102.e.68.

Entick, John. *The Present State of the British Empire.* 4 vols. BL 291.n.5–8.

[Franklin, Benjamin]. *The Causes of the Present Distractions.* BL 8176.a.51.

[Gray, John]. *The Right of the British Legislature to Tax the American Colonies.* BL T.691(2).

Hancock, John. *An Oration.* BL 1324.c.5.

[Jefferson, Thomas]. *A Summary View of the Rights of British America.* BL 1061.h.27(4).

[Johnson, Samuel]. *The Patriot.* BL 102.e.58.

[Knox, William]. *The Interest of the Merchants and Manufacturers of Great Britain.* BL 102.f.18.

[——]. *The Justice and Policy of the Late Act of Parliament.* BL 1061.h.25(4).

[Lee, Arthur]. *An Appeal to the Justice and Interests of the People of Great Britain.* BL T.207(1).

[——]. *A True State of the Proceedings in the Parliament of Great Britain.* BL 105.f.16.

A Letter from Thomas Lord Lyttelton, to William Pitt, Earl of Chatham, on the Quebec Bill. BL 8175.aaa.58.

A Letter Humbly Submitted. BL 102.f.12.

A Letter to Doctor Tucker. BL T.691(3).

A Letter to Sir William Meredith. BL T.683(5).

[Massie, Joseph]. *To the Principal Landholders of England.* BL Place 20(9).

[Meredith, William]. *A Letter to the Earl of Chatham, on the Quebec Bill.* BL 102.f.26.

[Morris, Matthew Robinson]. *Considerations on the Measures Carrying on with respect to the British Colonies in North America.* BL 1061.h.28(5).

Pownall, Thomas. *The Administration of the British Colonies.* 2 vols. 5th ed. BL 1061.d.28.

———. *The Administration of the British Colonies. Part the Second.* BL 292.k.30(2).

[Prescott, Robert]. *A Letter from a Veteran.* New York. BL 1061.h.29(2).

Quincy, Josiah. *Observations on the . . . Boston Port-bill.* BL 102.f.17.

A Review of the Present Administration. Bod. G.Pamph.1186(4).

[Seabury, Samuel]. *A View of the Controversy.* BL 102.f.38.

Sharp, Granville. *A Declaration of the People's Natural Right to a Share in the Legislature.* BL 959.b.3.

[Tooke, William]. *A Letter to Sir Fletcher Norton.* BL 8133.e.20, HL 215.i.4(114).

Tucker, Josiah. *Four Tracts on Political and Commercial Subjects.* Gloucester. BL 1093.e.86.

[Wilson, James]. *Considerations on the Nature and the Extent of the Legislative Authority of the British Parliament.* Philadelphia. BL 8135.b.41.

[Young, Arthur]. *Political Arithmetic.* BL 288.c.13.

[Zubly, John Joachim]. *Great Britain's Right to Tax Her Colonies.* BL 102.f.21.

1775

An Address to the Right Honourable L——d M——sf——d. BL 102.f.51.

Americanus. *The False Alarm; or, The Americans Mistaken.* BL 102.f.69.

An Answer to a Pamphlet, Entitled Taxation No Tyranny. BL 102.f.64.

[Baillie, Hugh]. *An Appendix to a Letter to Dr. Shebbeare.* BL 102.g.2.

A Brief Extract, or Summary of Important Arguments. BL 102.f.67.

Burke, Edmund. *The Speech of Edmund Burke, Esq. on American Taxation.* BL 834.i.22.

———. *The Speech of Edmund Burke, Esq. on Moving His Resolutions for Conciliation with the Colonies.* BL 1500/247.

[Cartwright, John]. *A Letter to Edmund Burke, Esq. Controverting the Principles of American Government.* BL 102.f.31.

Common Sense: in Nine Conferences. BL 8175.l.11.

Conciliatory Address to the People of Great Britain and of the Colonies, on the Present Important Crisis. BL 102.f.48.

Considerations upon the Different Modes of Finding Recruits for the Army. BL 103.g.20.

Considerations upon This Question, What Should Be an Honest Englishman's Endeavour? BL 103.i.62.

U.S. Continental Congress. *An Address of the Twelve United Colonies of North America.* Philadelphia. BL C.38.f.31(1).

———. *A Declaration by the Representatives of the United Colonies of North-America.* BL C.38.f.31(2).

———. *Journal of the Proceedings of the Congress.* BL T.207(3).

———. *To the People of Great Britain.* BL 8177.de.7.

———. *The Twelve United Colonies.* BL C.38.f.31(3).

[Dalrymple, John]. *The Address of the People of Great-Britain to the Inhabitants of America.* BL 102.g.1.

[Erskine, Thomas]. *Observations on the Prevailing Abuses in the British Army*. Bod.
  G.Pamph.1186(7), 1775, BL 103.g.10.
An Essay on the Nature of Colonies. BL 102.f.32.
[Freneau, Philip]. *The Present Situation of Affairs in North-America*. Philadelphia. BL
  11687.cc.43(1).
A Full and Circumstantial Account of the Disputes between Great Britain and America.
  Glasgow. BL 1076.l.25(8).
A Full and Impartial Examination of the Rev. Mr. John Wesley's Address to the Americans.
  BL 1487.a.21(2).
The Genius of Britain: An Ode. BL 164.h.33.
[Gray, John]. *Remarks on the New Essay of the Pennsylvanian Farmer*. BL 103.c.3.
Hanway, Jonas. *The Defects of Police the Cause of Immorality*. BL 30.f.12.
Harris, John. *An Essay on Politeness*. BL 1030.f.8(2).
Hartley, David. *Speech and Motions*. 2d ed. BL 8138.f.5(1).
Jebb, John. *A Short State of the Reasons for a Late Resignation*. BL 4225.c.32.
[Johnson, Samuel]. *Taxation No Tyranny*. BL 102.f.72.
[Lee, Arthur]. *A Second Appeal to the Justice and Interests of the People*. BL E.2240(5).
[———]. *A Speech, Intended to Have Been Delivered in the House of Commons*. BL 102.f.35.
[Lee, Charles]. *Strictures on a Pamphlet Entitled "A Friendly Address to All Reasonable
  Americans."* Philadelphia. BL 1389.a.20.
[Leonard, Daniel]. *The Origins of the American Contest*. BL 102.f.46.
A Letter, to the Rev. Mr. John Wesley; on His Calm Address. BL 8175.aa.89.
[Lind, John]. *Remarks on the Principal Acts of the Thirteenth Parliament*. BL 884.i.21.
Macaulay, Catherine. *An Address to the People of England, Scotland, and Ireland, on the
  Present Important Crisis of Affairs*. BL 102.f.36
[Mather, Moses]. *America's Appeal to the Impartial World*. Hartford, Conn. BL
  8175.aa.12.
A New System for the Establishment . . . Etc. . . . of the Army. BL 103.g.9.
Pitt, William. *Plan Offered by the Earl of Chatham, to the House of Lords*. BL T.917(8).
———. *The Speech of the Right Honourable the Earl of Chatham*. BL T.13(9**).
A Plain State of the Argument. BL 103.h.38.
*A Plan for Conciliating the Jarring Political Interests of Great Britain and Her North
  American Colonies*. BL 103.c.7.
The Present Crisis. BL 102.f.40.
*A Proposition for the Present Peace and Future Government of the British Colonies in
  North America*. BL 103.i.63.
The Reply of a Gentleman in a Select Society. BL 102.f.55.
Resistance No Rebellion.. BL 103.c.5.
[Scott, John]. *Remarks on the Patriot*. BL 102.f.33.
[Shebbeare, John]. *An Answer to the Printed Speech of Edmund Burke*. BL 8135.bb.17.
———. *An Answer to the Queries, Contained in a Letter to Dr. Shebbeare*. BL 102.e.73.
The Supremacy of the British Legislature over the Colonies. BL 1061.h.27(2).
Taxation, Tyranny. Addressed to Samuel Johnson. BL 102.f.54.
Three Letters to a Member of Parliament on the Subject of the Present Dispute. BL
  1061.h.27(5).
[Towers, Joseph]. *A Letter to Dr. Samuel Johnson*. BL 102.f.57.

Tucker, Josiah. *An Humble Address and Earnest Appeal.* BL 1196.i.24(4).
——. *A Letter to Edmund Burke, Esq. . . . in Answer to His Printed Speech.* BL T.683(7).
——. *Tract V. The Respective Pleas and Arguments of the Mother Country.* BL T.683(8).
Warren, Joseph. *An Oration.* Boston. BL 12301.h.12.
Wesley, John. *A Calm Address to Our American Colonies.* BL 1487.a.21(1).
Wilkes, John. *The Speech of the Right Hon. John Wilkes.* BL 102.h.32.
[Williamson, Hugh]. *The Plea of the Colonies.* BL 103.c.25.

1776

Additions to Common Sense. BL 1141.d.1(10).
An Address to the People of Great-Britain in General. Bristol. BL 103.c.15.
An Address to the People on the Subject of the Contest. BL 103.c.18.
America, an Ode. BL 164.n.39.
The American Military Pocket Atlas. BL G.19826.
American Resistance Indefensible. BL 694.i.8 (9).
An Appeal to the Unprejudiced. Oxford. BL 103.c.20.
Apthorp, East. *A Sermon on the General Fast.* BL 694.i.8 (6).
Britannicus. *The Political Mirror.* BL 102.g.16.
[Cartwright, John]. *Take Your Choice!* BL G.16269(2).
[Chalmers, James]. *Plain Truth.* BL 1141.d.1(9).
Civil Liberty Asserted . . . against the Anarchical Principles of the Reverend Dr. Price. BL 100.l.19.
[Dalrymple, John]. *The State of the National Debt.* 2d ed. BL 1890.b.4(26).
Darwall, John. *Political Lamentations.* BL 11659.cc.1 (9).
[Dawes, Matthew]. *A Letter to Lord Chatham, concerning the Present War.* BL 103.h.40.
[Day, Thomas]. *The Devoted Legions.* BL 163.l.59.
A Dialogue on the Principles of the Constitution. BL 102.g.8.
The Duty of the King and Subject. BL 102.g.26.
An Essay on the Rights of the East India Company. BL 100.n.11.
Estwick, Samuel. *A Letter to the Reverend Josiah Tucker.* BL 102.g.28.
Experience Preferable to Theory. BL 100.l.14.
[Ferguson, Adam]. *Remarks on a Pamphlet Lately Published by Dr. Price, Intitled, Observations on the Nature of Civil Liberty.* BL 100.l.4.
[Fletcher, John William]. *American Patriotism Farther Confronted with Reason, Scripture, and the Constitution.* BL 8133.a.52.
[——]. *A Vindication of the Rev. Mr. Wesley's "Calm Address to Our American Colonies".* BL 1487.a.21(3).
Glascott, Cradock. *The Best Method of Putting an End to the American War.* BL 4475.c.48.
[Goodenough, Richard]. *The Constitutional Advocate.* BL 102.g.5.
[Hampson, John]. *Reflections on the Present State of the American War.* BL 102.g.23.
The Honor of Parliament and the Justice of the Nation Vindicated. BL 102.g.27.
Janus. *The Critical Moment.* BL 103.c.23.
[Leonard, Daniel]. *Massachusettensis.* BL 163.m.28.
A Letter to Lord George Germain. BL 102.g.12.

A Letter to the Author of a Pamphlet Entitled Considerations upon the Different Modes of Finding Recruits for the Army. BL 103.g.19.

A Letter to the Noblemen, Gentlemen, Etc. Who Have Addressed His Majesty on the Subject of the American Rebellion. BL.103.c.19.

A Letter to the Rev. Dr. Richard Price. BL 100.1.21.

A Letter to the Right Honourable Frederick, Lord North. BL T.229(10).

[Lind, John]. *An Answer to the Declaration of the American Congress.* BL 102.g.32.

[———]. *Three Letters to Dr. Price.* BL 523.g.19(2).

[MacPherson, James]. *An Answer to the Declaration of the American Congress.* BL E.2228(6).

[———]. *The Rights of Great Britain Asserted against the Claims of America.* 2d ed. BL 8135.cc.9, HL 102.g.24.

[Maseres, Francis]. *The Canadian Freeholder.* BL G.13557(1).

[Mauduit, Israel]. *Considerations on the American War.* BL T.229(6).

[Morris, Matthew Robinson]. *A Further Examination of Our Present American Measures.* BL 102.g.36.

[Paine, Thomas]. *Common Sense.* BL 1141.d.1(8).

Price, Richard. *Observations on the Nature of Civil Liberty.* 2d ed. BL G.16309(3).

[Ramsay, Allan]. *A Plan of Reconciliation.* BL 102.g.7.

Remarks on Dr. Price's Observations. BL 100.1.3.

Shebbeare, John. *An Essay on the Origin, Progress and Establishment of National Society.* 2d ed. BL 8175.dd.1(1).

A Short Appeal to the People of Great-Britain. BL 103.c.17.

Smith, William. *An Oration in Memory of General Montgomery.* Philadelphia. BL T.229(9).

Stebbing, Henry. *A Sermon on the Late General Fast.* BL 694.i.8(4).

Stone, Francis. *A New, Easy, and Expeditious Method of Discharging the National Debt.* BL 104.e.21.

The Tears of the Foot Guards. BL 11630.d.11(5).

The Trial of the Cause on an Action Brought by Stephen Sayre. BL 516.m.12(4).

Tucker, Josiah. *Four Tracts on Political and Commercial Subjects.* 3d ed. Gloucester. BL 522.g.5(1).

———. *A Series of Answers to Certain Popular Objections.* BL 522.g.5(1).

[Yorke], James. *A Sermon Preached before the Lords Spiritual and Temporal.* BL 694.i.19(6).

Young, W. A. *The History of North and South America.* 2 vols. BL 9551.a.6.

1777

[Abingdon, Willoughby Bertie, earl of]. *Thoughts on the Letter of Edmund Burke, Esq.* Oxford. BL 523.g.19(3).

An Address to the Citizens of Edinburgh. Edinburgh. BL 1303.k.17(7).

The Advantageous Situation of Great Britain on the Reduction of America. BL 103.h.42.

[Almon, John]. *A Collection of Interesting, Authentic Papers.* BL 1061.h.9.

[Barron, William]. *History of the Colonization of the Free States of Antiquity.* BL 522.k.12.

Burke, Edmund. *A Letter from Edmund Burke.* BL 1061.h.23(3).

[Burke, William]. *The Letters of Valens.* BL 08138.dd.50(7).

Butler, John. *A Sermon Preached before the Honourable House of Commons.* BL 694.i.8 (2).

Campbell, George. *The Nature, Extent, and Importance of the Duty of Allegiance.* Aberdeen. BL 694.i.8 (8).

Carlyle, Alexander. *The Justice and Necessity of the War with Our American Colonies Examined.* Edinburgh. BL 111.f.12.

[Chalmers, George]. *An Answer from the Electors of Bristol.* BL T.1050(8).

[Clark, Samuel]. *A Letter to Richard Price.* BL 113.n.59.

Common Sense: A Letter to the Fourteen Incorporations of Edinburgh. Edinburgh. BL 1303.k.17(3).

Cooper, Myles. *National Humiliation and Repentance Recommended.* Oxford. BL 694.i.8 (3).

[Croft, Herbert]. *An Answer to the Letter of Edmund Burke.* BL T.1050(4).

[Dawes, Matthew]. *A Letter to Lord Chatham, on American Affairs.* BL 103.k.66.

[Day, Thomas]. *The Desolation of America: A Poem.* BL 163.m.24.

[Elphinston, James]. *An Essay on British Liberty.* BL 8133.a.43.

Essays Commercial and Political, on the Real and Relative Interests of Imperial and Dependent States. Newcastle. BL 8132.d.30.

Finch, Robert Pool. *The Denunciation of Christ against Jerusalem.* BL 694.i.8(5*).

[Fletcher, John William]. *American Patriotism Farther Confronted with Reason, Scripture, and the Constitution.* 2d ed. BL 3752.aa.28(3).

[Freeman, Stephen]. *England's Glory: A Poem to the King.* BL 11602.gg.25(14).

Humphreys, Francis. *A Sermon Peached at Hampstead.* BL 91.h.61.

Hurd, Richard. *A Sermon Preached before the Right Honourable the House of Lords.* BL 11659.cc.1 (4).

Leland, Thomas. *A Sermon, Preached before the University of Dublin.* BL 694.i.8 (7).

A Letter from an Officer at New-York to a Friend in London. BL 103.c.33.

A Letter to Dr. Price on His Additional Observations on the Nature and Value of Civil Liberty. BL 100.l.9.

A Letter to the Earl of Chatham, concerning His Speech and Motion in the House of Lords. BL 103.c.28.

A Letter to the English Nation. BL 1061.h.23(2).

A Letter to Us, from One of Ourselves. BL 102.g.34.

Markham, William. *A Sermon Preached before the Incorporated Society for the Propagation of the Gospel.* BL 686.f.23(4).

[Moore], John. *A Sermon Preached before the House of Lords.* BL 694.i.19(7).

[Morris, Matthew Robinson]. *Peace the Best Policy; or, Reflections upon the Appearance of a Foreign War.* BL 103.c.44.

Price, Richard. *Additional Observations on the Nature and Value of Civil Liberty.* BL 523.e.l(2).

[Ramsay, Allan]. *Letters on the Present Disturbances.* BL T.713(2).

Reflections on the Present Combination. BL 103.c.40.

A Sequel to Common Sense. 2d ed. Dublin. BL 8175.ee.4(1).

[Topham, Edward]. *An Address to Edmund Burke.* BL 102.g.43.

[Warwick, Thomas]. *The Rights of Sovereignty Asserted.* BL 11630.e.2(2).

Washington, George. *Letters from General Washington to Several of His Friends*. BL 103.c.37.

1778

Address to the Rulers of the State. BL 102.h.13.
Burgoyne, John. *The Substance of General Burgoyne's Speeches*. BL 102.g.47.
Butler, John. *A Sermon Preached before the House of Lords*. BL 694.i.8 (10).
Considerations on the Alleged Necessity of Hiring Foreign Troops. BL 102.h.24.
[Dalrymple, Alexander]. *Considerations on the Present State of Affairs*. BL 103.c.64.
[Dalrymple, John]. *Three Letters from Sir John Dalrymple*. BL 8132.e.20.
The Delusive and Dangerous Principles of the Minority. BL 103.c.49.
An Examination into the Conduct of the Present Administration. BL 103.c.61.
Four Excellent New Songs. Edinburgh. BL 11621.b.6(3).
[Galloway, Joseph]. *A Letter to the People of America*. BL 103.c.46.
Hartley, David. *Letters on the American War*. BL 8177.h.5.
[Hawes, William]. *An Address to the Public*. BL 1039.c.39(1).
The History of the Rise, Opposition to, and Establishment of the Edinburgh Regiment. Edinburgh. BL 8142.e.15.
An Impartial Sketch of the Various Indulgences Granted by Great-Britain to Her Colonies. BL 103.c.57.
[Jenings, Edmund]. *Considerations on the Mode and Terms of a Treaty of Peace with America*. BL 103.c.47.
Letters Addressed to Sir Thomas Charles Bunbury. BL 8133.e.16.
A Letter to Lord George Germaine. BL 103.c.63.
A Letter to Sir George Saville. BL 111.c.20.
A Letter to the Honourable Mr. C——s F——x. BL 103.c.55.
Lofft, Capel. *Observations on Mrs. Macaulay's History of England*. BL 1502/160.
London. Court of Common Council. *Addresses Presented from the Court of Common Council to the King*. BL 8133.b.61.
[Mauduit, Israel]. *Remarks upon Gen. Howe's Account of His Proceedings on Long Island*. BL 103.c.48.
[Meredith, William]. *Historical Remarks on the Taxation of Free States, in a Series of Letters to a Friend*. BL 816.k.1(5).
North, Brownlow. *A Sermon Preached before the Incorporated Society for the Propagation of the Gospel in Foreign Parts*. BL T.2142 (3).
Observations upon the Administration of Justice in Bengal. [n.p.]. BL 708.i.26(4).
The Patriot Minister. BL 643.k.26.
The Patriot Vision: A Poem. BL 163.m.28.
Pitt, William. *Lord Chatham's Speech in the British House of Lords*. BL 8132.bb.14(5).
Plan of Re-union between Great Britain and Her Colonies. BL 102.g.44.
Porteus, Beilby. *A Sermon Preached before the Lords Spiritual and Temporal*. BL 694.i.19 (8).
Price, Richard. *Two Tracts on Civil Liberty*. BL 100.l.15.
[Pulteney, William]. *Thoughts on the Present State of Affairs with America, and the Means of Conciliation*. BL T.713(4).
[Sharp, Granville]. *An Address to the People of England*. BL T.1819(1).

[Stevenson, John]. *Letters in Answer to Dr. Price's Two Pamphlets.* BL 100.l.5.

[Symonds, John]. *Remarks upon an Essay, Intituled, The History of the Colonization of the Free States of Antiquity.* BL T.917(9).

[Tasker, William]. *An Ode to the Warlike Genius of Great Britain.* BL 1346.k.23.

[Temple, William Johnston]. *On the Abuse of Unrestrained Power.* BL 1568/1694.

To the Honourable the Commons of Great Britain. BL 1879.c.4(70).

Vyse, William. *A Sermon Preached before the Honourable House of Commons.* BL 694.i.8 (11).

[Williams, David]. *Unanimity in All Parts of the British Commonwealth, Necessary to Its Preservation, Interest, and Happiness.* London, 1778. BL T.220(2).

1779

An Address to the Gentry of the County of Durham. Newcastle. BL 1568/8705.

An Address to the People of Great Britain. BL T.1051(3).

An Address to the People of Great Britain on the Meeting of Parliament. BL 103.f.5.

An Address to the Representatives in Parliament, upon the State of the Nation. BL 103.d.8.

Alexander, Andrew. *The Advantages of a General Knowledge of the Use of Arms.* Strabane. BL 4474.e.1.

An Appeal from the Protestant Association to the People of Great Britain. BL 8132.aaa.1(11).

At a General Meeting of the Subscribers of Monies. BL 8135.c.61.

At a Meeting of the Inhabitants of the Parish of St. George Bloomsbury. BL 1882.c.2(269).

The Attendance of the Citizens Is Requested at the Guildhall. Bristol. BL 746.f.12(4).

A Brief Examination of the Plan and Conduct of the Northern Expedition in America, in 1777. BL 8132.d.27.

Burgoyne, John. *A Letter from Lieut. Gen. Burgoyne to His Constituents.* BL T.987(7).

By an Act Passed in This Session of Parliament. BL 746.f.12(3).

Cole, John. *The American War.* Beverley. BL 11688.c.25.

Considerations on a Spanish War. BL T.1118(8).

Considerations upon the French and American War. BL 8026.c.9.

Eden, William. *Four Letters to the Earl of Carlisle.* 2d ed. Bod. G.Pamph.1187(7).

An Enquiry into the State of the Militia. BL 103.g.6.

An Epistle from Edward, an American Prisoner in England. BL T.12(7).

Erskine, John. *Prayer for Those in Civil and Military Offices Recommended.* Edinburgh. BL 4473.e.24(7).

Finch, Robert Pool. *A Sermon Preached in the Church of St. Michael.* BL 694.f.9 (4).

[Flood, Henry]. *A Letter to the People of Ireland.* Dublin. BL 8145.cc.45.

[Galloway, Joseph]. *Considerations upon the American Enquiry.* BL T.1051(2).

[———]. *Cool Thoughts on the Consequences to Great Britain of American Independence.* BL 103.d.25.

[———]. *Letters to a Nobleman.* BL T.1051(4).

[———]. *A Letter to the Right Honourable Lord Viscount H——e.* BL T.1095(8).

Great Britain. War Office. *Copy of the Secretary at War's Circular Letter to the Sheriffs.* BL 1304.m.1(32).

———. ———. *Secretary at War's Circular Letter to the Sheriffs of Newcastle upon Tyne.* BL L.R.264.b.1(98).

Historical Anecdotes, Civil and Military. BL 523.g.21(1).

The History of the War in America. Dublin. BL 9604.b.6.

The Honest Sentiments of an English Officer in the Army of Great Britain. BL 288.c.9.

[Hughes, William]. *A Sermon.* Northampton. BL 4475.aaa.107.

[Jebb, John]. *An Address to the Freeholders of Middlesex.* BL 8135.b.66.

Knight, D.M. *A Proposal for Peace between Great Britain and North-America.* Birmingham. BL 103.d.21.

A Letter to Lieut. Gen. Burgoyne, on His Letter to His Constituents. BL 103.c.70.

A Letter to the Right Honourable the Earl of Hillsborough. BL 116.g.34.

A Letter to the Whigs. BL 103.d.3.

[MacPherson, James]. *A Short History of the Opposition during the Last Session of Parliament.* BL T.1051(1).

[Miles, William Augustus]. *A Political Mirror.* BL T.1118(13).

A New Plan to Save the State. Addressed to the Ladies. BL 164.b.54.

The Patriot Divine to the Female Historian. BL 11631.g.30(15).

Patriotic Perfidy: A Satire. BL 11630.e.4(11*).

Pitt, William. *Genuine Abstracts from Two Speeches of the Late Earl of Chatham.* BL 103.d.20.

Price, Richard. *A Sermon, Delivered to a Congregation of Protestant Dissenters.* 2d ed. BL 686.f.21(6).

[Pulteney, William]. *Considerations on the Present State of Public Affairs.* BL T.1118(9).

Remarks on the Rescript of the Court of Madrid. BL 518.c.33.

A Reply to Lieutenant General Burgoyne's Letter to His Constituents. BL 103.c.69.

A Rhapsody on the Present System of French Politics. BL M.L.h.93(2).

[Ross], John. *A Sermon Preached before the Lords Spiritual and Temporal.* BL 694.i.19 (9).

A Serious Address to the Gentlemen —— Clergy ——. Pembroke. BL 1104.b.19.

A Short History of the Administration. BL 8132.df.6(1*).

Spirit and Unanimity. BL 1600/1517.

[Sullivan, Richard Joseph]. *Thoughts on Martial Law.* BL 708.g.7(2).

[Tasker, William]. *An Ode to the Warlike Genius of Great Britain.* BL 1346.k.23.

Thoughts on the Present Alarming Crisis of Affairs. BL 8138.dd.12(1).

Three Letters to the Rev. Dr. Price. BL 8175.aa.34.

[Tod, Thomas]. *Observations on American Independency.* [Edinburgh]. BL 8176.eee.23(1).

A View of the Evidence relative to the Conduct of the American War. BL 103.d.26.

[Walker, George]. *The Duty and Character of a National Soldier.* BL T.1046(8).

W[eldon], T[homas]. *A Sermon for the General Fast.* Prescot. BL 4477.aaa.121 (2).

Yorke, James. *A Sermon Preached before the Incorporated Society for the Propagation of the Gospel in Foreign Parts.* BL T.2142 (4).

Young, Arthur. *Political Arithmetick. Part II.* BL 104.a.81.

1780

[Abingdon, Willoughby Bertie, earl of]. *Dedication to the Collective Body of the People of England.* Oxford. BL 8132.e.8.

An Address to the Gentlemen, Forming the Several Committees of the Associated Counties, Cities, and Towns. BL T.220(6).

Appendix to the Comment on the Petition of the British Inhabitants of Bengal. [n.p.]. BL 708.i.26 (2).

The Associators Vindicated. BL 103.h.60.

At a Committee of the London Foot Association. BL 1850.c.10(128).

Authentic Pieces Respecting the Proceedings in both Houses of Parliament. York. BL 1509/1508.

Bird, Robert. *Propposals for Paying Great Part of the National Debt.* BL 8140.e.41(3).

Burke, Edmund. *A Speech of Edmund Burke.* BL 1027.b.24(3).

Cartwright, John. *The People's Barrier against Undue Influence.* BL 103.h.62.

———. *A Summary of a Treatise by Major Cartwright.* BL 8140.e.32(2).

Common-Place Arguments against Administration. BL T.1119(3).

Considerations on the Administration of Justice in Bengal. [n.p.]. BL 708.i.26(3).

Cooke, William. *Civil Liberty.* Cambridge. BL 4476.cc.27.

Cornwallis, James. *A Sermon Preached in the Cathedral and Metropolitan Church of Christ.* Canterbury. BL 694.i.9.

The Crisis: Now or Never. BL 102.g.49.

Day, Thomas. *Two Speeches of Thomas Day.* BL 8140.e.32(5*).

[Delaval, Thomas]. *To the Independent Free Burgesses.* Newcastle. BL L.R.264.b.1(115).

[Downing, George]. *The Volunteers.* BL 11780.c.41.

The Duty of a Freeman. BL 8140.e.32(6)

[Erskine, John]. *A Vindication of the Opposition to the Late Intended Bill for the Relief of Roman Catholics in Scotland.* Edinburgh. BL T.1032(5).

An Essay on the Interests of Britain. BL 103.d.34.

[Galloway, Joseph]. *A Candid Examination of the Mutual Claims of Great-Britain, and the Colonies.* BL 103.d.36.

[———]. *Historical and Political Reflections on the Rise and Progress of the American Rebellion.* BL T.1051(5).

General Meeting of the Nobility, Gentlemen, Clergy and Freeholders of the County of Wiltshire. Salisbury. BL 103.d.28.

The Gladiators. BL 643.m.16(27).

Hanway, Jonas. *The Citizen's Monitor.* BL 515.k.13.

The History of the Civil War in America. BL 9602.cc.29.

[Holcroft, Thomas]. *A Plain and Succinct Narrative of the Late Riots and Disturbances in the Cities of London and Westminster.* BL 1415.h.58.

[Hunter, Henry]. *A National Change in Morals.* BL 686.f.21(7).

An Impartial History of the War in America. 2d ed. BL 9602.b.5.

Jones, Sir William. *An Inquiry into the Legal Mode of Suppressing Riots.* BL 115.f.48.

A Letter to Lord North, on His Re-election into the House of Commons. BL 103.d.27.

A Letter to the New Parliament. BL 2140.e.41(1).

A Letter to the Right Honourable Viscount Cranborne. BL 8135.cc.15.

Markham, Robert. *The Wisdom of Appointing and Supporting the Civil Magistrate.* BL 694.h.2(12).

Mitchell, Archibald. *Thoughts on the Treaty Now Agitating between Government and the East India Company.* BL 102.h.40.

Mortimer, Thomas. *The Elements of Commerce, Politics and Finances.* BL 712.k.3.

[Murray, Alexander]. *A Speech Intended to Have Been Delivered at a General Meeting of Protestants.* 2d ed. Newcastle. BL 3840.h.4(1).

Murray, James. *An Impartial History of the Present War in America.* 3 vols. Newcastle. BL 9602.bbb.16.

A Narrative of the Proceedings at the Contested Election. 2d ed. Norwich. BL 10361.c.42(2).

[Neither a Bigot nor Enthusiast, but a Friend to Society]. *An Address to English Protestants.* Newcastle. BL 4411.f.22.

A New Song of Paul Jones. Newcastle. BL Rox.III(684).

[Nugent, Robert Craggs]. *An Inquiry into the Origin and Consequences of the Influence of the Crown over Parliament.* BL 8132.df.8(4).

[O'Beirne, Thomas Lewis]. *Considerations on the Late Disturbances.* BL 108.f.45.

[———]. *A Short History of the Last Session of Parliament, with Remarks.* BL T.1119(1).

Observations on "An Appeal from the Protestant Association." BL 108.f.44.

Observations on the Opinion of Mr. G. Rous. BL 8139.bbb.1(4).

O'Leary, Arthur. *Mr. O'Leary's Remarks on the Rev. Mr. Wesley's Letters.* BL 3938.aa.14.

Philonomos. *The Liberty of the Subject, and Dignity of the Crown.* T.1119(12).

[Pownall, Thomas]. *A Memorial.* 2d ed. BL 8132.e.38.

Protestant. *A Defence of the Act of Parliament Lately Passed for the Relief of Roman Catholics.* BL T.1032(4).

Remarks on the Petition of the British Inhabitants of Bengal. [n.p.]. BL 708.i.26(6).

Remonstrance of the American Officers. Exeter. BL 1876.f.27(6).

[Rous, George]. *The Power of the Crown to Establish Peace.* BL 516.m.18(84).

Savile, Sir George. *To the Gentlemen, Clergy, and Freeholders, of the County of York.* Newcastle. BL Cup.600.d.1(6).

Sawbridge, John. *To the Worthy Livery of the City of London.* BL 1850.c.10(130).

[Sharp, Granville]. *Annual Parliaments.* BL E.2099(13).

[———]. *Appendix to "The Legal Means of Political Reformation".* 3d ed. BL 522.d.11(3).

[———]. *A Circular Letter to the Several Petitioning Counties.* BL E.2099(6).

———. *A Defence of the Ancient, Legal, and Constitutional, Right of the People.* BL 8135.aa.33.

[———]. *The Legal Means of Political Reformation.* 7th ed. BL 522.d.11(1).

[Short, J]. *The Rights and Principles of an Englishman Considered.* Exeter. BL 8133.d.8.

Simes, Thomas. *The Regulator.* BL 62.b.17.

———. *A Treatise on the Military Science.* BL 61.f.12.

Smelt, Leonard. *An Account of Some Particulars relative to the Meeting Held at York.* BL 682.d.21(1).

Society for Constitutional Information. *An Address to the Public.* BL 8140.e.32(1).

———. *Copy of a Letter from the Right Honourable Lord Carysfort.* BL 8140.e.31(3*).

———. *The Gentlemen Under-mentioned.* BL 8133.i.14(9).

———. *Report of the Sub-committee of Westminster.* BL 8140.e.32(4).

The System Occasioned by the Speech of Leonard Smelt. BL 8139.bb.39(1).

Thomas, John. *A Sermon Preached before the Incorporated Society for the Propagation of the Gospel in Foreign Parts.* BL T.2142 (5).

[Tooke, John Horne]. *Facts: Addressed to the Landholders.* BL T.1119(5).

To the Free Burgesses of Newcastle. Newcastle. BL L.F.264.b.1(123).

Totton, William. *On the Important Duty of Subjection to the Civil Powers.* BL
   4475.f.52(1).
Trenchard, John. *Abridgment of That Eminent Patriot Mr. John Trenchard's History of
   Standing Armies in England.* BL 8140.e.32(3).
[Tucker, Josiah]. *Dispassionate Thoughts on the American War.* BL 103.d.33.
———. *An Earnest and Affectionate Address.* BL C.31.a.10.
A Volunteer's Queries. Dublin. BL 8145.bb.122.
[Walker, George]. *Substance of the Speech of the Rev. Mr. Walker.* BL 8135.b.12(14).
Watson, Richard. *A Sermon Preached before the University of Cambridge.* 2d ed. Cam-
   bridge. BL 694.i.9 (8).
Weales, Thomas. *National Unanimity Recommended and Enforced.* BL 694.h.2(27).
William, Jesse. *A Remonstrance, Addressed to the Protestant Association.* BL 10347.ee.7(3).
[Williams, David]. *A Plan of Association, on Constitutional Principles.* BL 8132.d.30.

1781

*An Abstract of the Charter, and of the Proceedings of the Society for the Propagation of the
   Gospel in Foreign Parts.* BL 686.f.23 (5).
An Account of an Arrest, Made at Dacca. BL 708.i.26(5).
[Almon, John]. *A Letter to the Right Honourable Charles Jenkinson.* BL 816.k.l(7).
Andrews, John. *Letters to His Excellency the Count de Welderen.* BL 103.d.48.
Burnaby, Andrew. *A Sermon Preached before the Honourable House of Commons.* BL
   694.i.9.
Cincinnatus. *The Patriotic Mirror.* BL 103.d.50.
[Cockings, George]. *The American War.* BL 992.k.26(1).
Cooke, William. *A Sermon Preached before the University of Cambridge.* Cambridge.
   BL 4475.cc.32.
[Committee of Association of the County of York]. *An Address.* York. BL 816.k.1(8).
[———]. *A Second Address.* 2d ed. York. BL Add. MSS 30,895, 31.
The Constitution; or, A Full Answer to Mr. Edmund Burke's Anti-constitutional Plan. BL
   523.f.33.
Conway, Henry Seymour. *The Speech of General Conway.* BL 103.d.47.
[Dalrymple, John]. *Considerations Preliminary.* BL T.1143(15).
A Dispassionate Enquiry into the Cause of the Late Riots in London. BL 1509/457.
A Dissertation upon the Perpetual Mutiny Bill. Dublin. BL 1509/835.
Douglas, Stuart. *A Military Dissertation.* BL 58.d.24.
[Eden, William]. *Considerations Submitted to the People of Ireland.* Dublin. BL
   601.f.17(11).
Free Thoughts on the Continuance of the American War. BL 8175.bb.2(2).
Gilbert, Thomas. *A Plan of Police.* BL B.732(8).
Grattan, Henry. *Observations on the Mutiny Bill.* BL 116.g.41.
Hartley, David. *An Address to the Committee of the County of York.* BL 8132.e.43.
Ibbetson, James. *A Dissertation on the National Assemblies under the Saxon and Norman
   Governments.* BL T.921(13).
[Jenings, Edmund]. *A Translation of the Memorial.* BL 8007.e.83(1).
Jenkins, Joseph. *The National Debt.* Shrewsbury. BL 4135.aa.101(3).
A Letter from Britannia to the King. BL 8133.d.24(2).

A Letter to the Right Honourable William Eden. BL T.1088(4).

[M'Kinnon, Charles]. *Observations on the Wealth and Force of Nations.* BL 521.a.34.

Necker, Jacques. *State of the Finances of France.* BL T.1645(4).

Northcote, Thomas. *Observations on the Natural and Civil Rights of Mankind.* BL Add. MSS 30,895, 3–30

On the Debt of the Nation, Compared with Its Revenue. BL 08139.d.107(6).

Pownall, Thomas. *The Right, Interest, and Duty, of Government.* BL 100.n.3.

Price, Richard. *A Discourse Addressed to a Congregation at Hackney.* BL 686.f.21(11).

Principles of Law and Government with An Inquiry into the Justice and Policy of the Present War. BL 521.k.22.

[Ramsay, Allan]. *Observations upon the Riot Act.* BL T.1078(5).

Raynal, Guillaume Thomas François. *The Revolution of America.* BL T.354(7).

Scott, James. *A Sermon Preached at York.* York. BL 694.i.9(12).

[Sheridan, Charles Francis]. *A Review of the Three Great National Questions.* BL 103.d.49.

Strictures on a Pamphlet Lately Published. Dublin. BL 8145.cc.47.

Tracts, concerning the Ancient and Only True Legal Means of National Defence. BL 1509/880.

The Trial of George Gordon. 3rd ed. BL 516.m.12(8)

Tucker, Josiah. *Cui Bono?* Gloucester. BL T.318(1).

——. *A Treatise concerning Civil Government.* BL 522.g.6(3).

Upton, Catherine. *The Siege of Gibraltar.* BL 115.h.40.

[Warren], John. *A Sermon Preached before the Lords Spiritual and Temporal.* BL 694.i.19 (11).

Wood, William. *The Christian Duty of Cultivating a Spirit of Universal Benevolence.* Leeds. BL T.1035(11).

1782

[Almon, John]. *An Address to the Interior Cabinet.* BL 1602/466(2).

[——]. *The Revolution in MDCCLXXXII Impartially Considered.* BL 1486.l.17(4).

Anderson, James. *The Interest of Great-Britain.* BL B.717(2).

At a Meeting of the Committee This Day for Raising a Corps of Volunteers. [Manchester]. BL 1856.c.5(28).

At a Meeting of the Principal Inhabitants of the Town and Neighbourhood. [Manchester]. BL 1856.c.5(44).

At a Meeting of the Society for Constitutional Information. BL 8135.b.12(17).

[Cawthorne, Joseph]. *A Constitutional Defence of Government.* BL 103.d.56.

A Complete and Accurate Account of the Very Important Debate. BL T.318(3).

Considerations on the Attorney-General's Proposition for a Bill for the Establishment of Peace with America. BL 103.d.70.

Cooper, William. *Reflections on the Intercourse of Nations.* Edinburgh. BL B.601(3).

Day, Thomas. *Reflexions upon the Present State of England.* BL 8176.bb.20.

[Dorset, Michael]. *An Essay on Defensive War.* BL G.1624.

Fox, Charles James. *The Speech of the Right Honourable Charles James Fox.* BL 8132.df.5(3).

Franklin, Benjamin. *Two Letters from Dr. Franklin*. Bod. G.Pamph.308(1).

[Galloway, Joseph]. *Fabricius*. BL 103.d.63.

A Hint to a Patriot Parliament. BL 110.e.53.

[Jones, William]. *An Inquiry into the Legal Mode of Suppressing Riots*. 2d ed. BL
    515.c.28(2).

[——]. *The Principles of Government*. BL 8133.e.21.

A List of Subscribers for the Purpose of Building a Ship of War. Ipswich. BL 10350.g.2(2).

[O'Bryen, Denis]. *A Defence of the Right Honorable the Earl of Shelburne*. BL 1478.b.17.

[Osborne, Francis Godolphin]. *An Address to the Independent Members of Both Houses
    of Parliament*. BL 8133.bb.39.

Paine, Thomas. *A Letter Addressed to the Abbe Raynal*. BL 1141.d.1(12).

A Plan of Reconciliation with America. BL 103.d.61.

The Recovery of America Demonstrated to be Practicable by Great-Britain. BL 103.i.58.

A Serious Address to the Electors of Great-Britain. BL 8138.bb.29.

[Sharp, Granville]. *The Claims of the People of England*. BL 8138.df.19(8).

A Short but Serious Reply to the Author of A [Mock] Defence of the Earl of Shelburne. BL
    010856.k.5.

[Sinclair, John]. *Considerations on Militias and Standing Armies*. BL 1609/1437.

——. *Thoughts on the Naval Strength of the British Empire*. BL 533.c.14(1,2).

Society for Constitutional Information. *A Second Address to the Public*. BL 8135.b.12(8).

Speculative Ideas on the Probable Consequences of an Invasion. BL 103.i.59.

[Stair, John Dalrymple, earl of]. *Facts and Their Consequences*. BL T.1645(3).

To That Class of the British Military Establishment. BL 1865.c.4(156).

[Tooke, John Horne]. *A Letter to Lord Ashburton*. BL 103.d.53.

[Towers, Joseph]. *A Letter to the Right Honourable the Earl of Shelburne*. BL 8135.c.73.

Tucker, Josiah. *Four Letters on Important National Subjects*. Gloucester. BL 8135.c.87.

Two Letters Addressed to Sir Thomas Charles Bunbury. Doncaster. BL 8132.ee.13(1).

A View of the History of Great Britain. BL 8133.d.24(4–5).

[White, Robert]. *The Anticipation of the Crisis*. BL 8132.df.5(2).

[Williams, David]. *Letters on Political Liberty*. BL 8132.e.47.

[Williams, Joseph]. *Parliamentary Reformation*. BL 793.l.40(3).

[Williamson, John]. *Advice to the Officers of the British Army*. BL 1080.I.22.

[——]. *A Treatise of Military Finanace*. BL 8826.a.50(1).

[Wilson, Charles Henry]. *A Compleat Collection of the Resolutions of the Volunteers,
    Grand Juries, Etc. of Ireland*. Dublin. BL 809.i.2.

1783

[Almon, John]. *Free Parliaments*. BL 8135.ccc.7(2).

[Anderson, James]. *The True Interest of Great Britain Considered*. BL 8247.a.4.

Andrews, John. *An Essay on Republican Principles*. BL 8138.bb.58.

[Bagot], Lewis. *A Sermon Preached before the Lords Spiritual and Temporal*. BL 694.i.19.

Ball, Tho[mas]. *A Sermon Preached at Mildenhall*. BL 694.h.9 (1).

[Basset, Francis]. *Thoughts on Equal Representation*. BL 100.l.33.

The Case and Claim of the American Loyalists. Bod. G.Pamph.308(13).

Clinton, Henry. *The Narrative of Lieutenant-General Sir Henry Clinton*. BL 1093.e.101.

———. *Observations on Some Parts of the Answer of Earl Cornwallis.* BL 1061.h.14(4).

A Collection of the Letters Which Have Been Addressed to the Volunteers of Ireland. BL 8145.c.37.

Cornwallis, Charles, earl of. *An Answer to that Part of the Narrative of Lieutenant General Sir Henry Clinton.* BL T.129(7).

An Examination into the Principles, Conduct, and Designs of the Earl of Shelburne. BL 8132.e.53.

The Inadequacy of Parliamentary Representation Fully Stated. BL 100.l.34.

[Jones, William]. *A Letter to a Patriot Senator.* BL 1483.c.25.

[King, John]. *Thoughts on the Difficulties and Distresses in Which the Peace of 1783, Has Involved the People of England.* 5th ed. BL T.1119(11).

[Kippis, Andrew]. *Considerations on the Provisional Treaty with America.* BL 103.e.7.

A Letter of His Grace the Duke of Richmond. BL 116.g.49.

A Letter on Parliamentary Representation. BL 100.l.36.

A Letter to the Author of a Pamphlet Entitled Free Parliaments. BL 8135.cc.8.

Ninth Report from the Select Committee. [n.p.]. BL 748.c.9.

O'Bryen, Dennis. *Remarks upon the Report of a Peace.* BL 103.e.3.

Observations on the Fifth Article of the Treaty with America. Bod. G.Pamph.308(10).

Paine, Thomas. *A Letter to the Earl of Shelburne.* BL 1141.d.1(13).

———. *Thoughts on the Peace.* BL 1141.d.1(14).

The Particular Case of the Georgia Loyalists. Bod. G.Pamph.308(12).

[Porteus], Beilby. *A Sermon Preached before the Incorporated Society for the Propagation of the Gospel in Foreign Parts.* BL 686.f.23 (6).

[Portius]. *A Letter to the Earl of Shelburne on the Peace.* BL 8140.ff.6.

[Powis]. *A Dialogue on the Actual State of Parliament.* Dublin. BL 100.l.32.

Pownall, Thomas. *A Memorial Addressed to the Sovereigns of America.* BL 103.d.69.

Price, Richard. *The State of the Public Debts and Finances.* BL 1102.h.11(7).

Proceedings relative to the Ulster Assembly of Volunteer Delegates. Belfast. BL 1568/1460.

A Reply to the Defence of the Earl of Shelburne. BL 103.d.68.

Sheffield, John Baker, earl of. *Observations on the Commerce of the American States.* 2d ed. BL 1102.h.18(2).

A Short Address to the Chartered Companies of England. [n.p.]. BL 08139.ccc.44(8).

[Sinclair, John]. *Hints; Addressed to the Public.* BL T.1643(8).

Stair, John Dalrymple, earl of. *An Address to the Public.* BL 1103.d.9.

———. *An Argument to Prove, That It Is the Indispensible Duty of the Creditors of the Public to Insist.* BL 8132.d.18.

———. *An Attempt to Balance the Income and Expenditure of the State.* BL T.1643(6).

[Stratford, Edward]. *An Essay on the True Interests and Resources of the Empire.* Dublin. BL 8135.aa.7.

Thoughts on the Conduct and Continuation of the Volunteers of Ireland. Dublin. BL 8145.dd.43.

Thoughts on the Present War. BL 103.e.4.

Tucker, Josiah. *Four Letters on Important National Subjects.* 2d ed. BL 522.g.6(2).

[Williams, John]. *A Constitutional Guide to the People of England.* 2d ed. BL 103.h.47.

Willoughby, Bertie. *The Celebrated Speech of the Earl of Abingdon.* BL 1880.d.1(49).

AFTER 1783

Bowdler, Thomas. *Letters Written in Holland.* 1787. BL T.164 (1).

Burke, Edmund. *Mr. Burke's Speech.* 1784. BL 08139.ccc.44 (1).

Day, Thomas. *Four Tracts.* 1785. BL 8133.d.23(1).

[Ellis, George]. *History of the Late Revolution in the Dutch Republic.* 1789. BL T.164 (2).

Hurd, Richard. *A Sermon Preached before the Right Honourable the House of Lords.* 1786. BL 694.i.20 (1).

A Short Vindication of the French Treaty. 1787. BL 8132.e.34.

Stair, John Dalrymple, earl of. *The Proper Limits of the Government's Interference.* 1784. BL 08139.ccc.44(6).

[Watson], Richard. *A Sermon Preached before the Lords Spiritual and Temporal.* 1784. BL 694.i.19 (14).

The Whole Proceedings on the Trial of the Indictment. 1784. BL 516.m.12(11).

[Wilson], Christopher. *A Sermon Preached before the Lords Spiritual and Temporal.* 1785. BL 694.i.19 (15).

Whately, Thomas, 119–120; on military policy, 111, 113, 116, 143; *The Regulations Lately Made* of, 115, 117, 119

Wheelock, Matthew, 142

Whigs

—as governing party, 48; European diplomacy of, 4, 13, 30, 50, 53; military service and, 14, 23, 24; venality of, 16; colonial policies of, 16, 153, 179; religious toleration and, 20, 22; negative liberty and, 22; English militia and, 25, 75, 79–80, 82, 88, 89; Hanoverian policy and, 37, 39, 46, 47; strategy of, during Seven Years' War, 37, 52, 58, 69–70; foreign policy of, 39, 41, 51, 69, 115; and justification for American war, 163–164, 186; on electoral system, 171; on inadvisability of colonial taxes, 200. *See also* Britain

—in opposition: British trade policies and, 11; Hanover and, 37, 44–45, 47, 51–52; Tories and, 39, 42; Peace of Utrecht and, 40–42; on need for

imperial reform, 49, 67–68; authoritarian tendencies of, 49, 79–82; libertarianism of, 49–50; as "friends of America," 162

Wilkes, John, 84, 131, 136, 137–138, 143, 173, 178

Williamson, Peter, 66

Windham, William, 101, 102n

Women, 81, 120, 205, 206; as political participants, 17, 81n, 178; in English militia riots, 85; at Coxheath and Warley Common, 157; Revolutionary atrocities and, 191

Wyvill, Christopher, 164, 167, 169, 171, 174, 177, 179, 202, 203

Yorke, Charles, 85n, 99–100

Yorke, James, 190

Yorke, Philip, Lord Royston, 24, 25n, 92

Yorkshire, 25, 26, 85–86

Yorkshire Association, 167, 169, 170, 173, 176

Yorktown, battle of, 177, 207, 208